A Spectrum of Voices

A Spectrum of Voices

Prominent American Voice Teachers Discuss the
Teaching of Singing

Second Edition

Elizabeth L. Blades

ROWMAN & LITTLEFIELD
Lanham • Boulder • New York • London

Published by Rowman & Littlefield
A wholly owned subsidiary of The Rowman & Littlefield Publishing Group, Inc.
4501 Forbes Boulevard, Suite 200, Lanham, Maryland 20706
www.rowman.com

Unit A, Whitacre Mews, 26-34 Stannary Street, London SE11 4AB

British Library Cataloguing in Publication Information Available

Library of Congress Cataloging-in-Publication Data

Names: Blades-Zeller, Elizabeth.
Title: A spectrum of voices : prominent American voice teachers discuss the teaching of singing / Elizabeth L. Blades.
Description: Second edition. | Lanham : Rowman & Littlefield, [2018] | Includes bibliographical references and index.
Identifiers: LCCN 2017034757 (print) | LCCN 2017035147 (ebook) | ISBN 9781538107010 (electronic) | ISBN 9781538106990 (cloth : alk. paper) | ISBN 9781538107003 (pbk. : alk. paper)
Subjects: LCSH: Singing—Instruction and study.
Classification: LCC MT820 (ebook) | LCC MT820 .B63 2018 (print) | DDC 783/.043071—dc23 LC record available at https://lccn.loc.gov/2017034757

∞ ™ The paper used in this publication meets the minimum requirements of American National Standard for Information Sciences Permanence of Paper for Printed Library Materials, ANSI/NISO Z39.48-1992.

Printed in the United States of America

Contents

Preface to the Second Edition

There is a small, painted shadow box in my music room, sent by my sister during a very dark time in my life. It simply states, "Don't look back . . . you're not going that way."

Generally speaking, that has proven to be sound advice, but this opportunity to revisit *A Spectrum of Voices*, chock-full of wisdom and insights collected more than twenty years ago, has been the exception. Back then, I was exceedingly fortunate to sit down with exemplary voice teachers and "pick their brains," unaware that their collective responses would become an important historical document preserving late twentieth-century practices in the field of comparative vocal performance pedagogy. It was a labor of love (and qualitative research) then as it is now in this second decade of the twenty-first century. Sadly, eleven of the original "prominent American voice teachers" have left us; this book preserves their comments, as fresh and current as they were in the early 1990s. The list includes Edward Baird, Marcia Baldwin, Oren Brown, Lindsey Christiansen, Barbara Doscher, Shirlee Emmons, Helen Hodam, Bruce Lunkley, William McIver, Richard Miller, and Dale Moore.

So, what is different about this second edition? Jack Coldiron, Cynthia Hoffmann, Marvin Keenze, and Laura Brooks Rice agreed to review and edit their remarks to reflect present-day teaching. Leslie Guinn, Helen Swank, Joan Wall, and Carol Webber have graciously permitted me to retain their first-edition responses. I am delighted to include six "new contributors": Meribeth Dayme, Robert Edwin, Stephen King, Jeannette LoVetri, Mary Saunders-Barton, and Edith Davis Tidwell. All embrace traditional "bel canto" classical training; three of them (Edwin, LoVetri, and Saunders-Barton) specialize in "contemporary commercial music" (the term created by LoVetri) and musical theater pedagogy, reflecting the booming popularity and acceptance of these "nonclassical" styles. Dayme is exploring and developing what she identifies as "a more universal approach to teaching and performing." To provide ease in locating the "new participants'" comments, I have arranged them alphabetically at the end of each topic question; the first-edition teachers remain in their original intentionally random order.

Unquestionably, profound developments have occurred over the past twenty to twenty-five years—in the world, society, and in the field of vocal performance and pedagogy. Acknowledging these changes, a new, very comprehensive question was asked of the respondents: "In the last twenty-five years, advances in technology, voice science, and medicine have had an impact on our profession. Please speak as to how these fit into your own teaching." Their answers appear in part 2. As expected, the opinions expressed are wide-ranging, varied, and most discerning.

If you care to follow any particular teacher's comments in a more comprehensive manner, the "Index of Teacher's Remarks" lists them by name with page number for each topic. I have retained the same original interview questions and general organization by area.

Those of you who are new to the book will find it helpful to read the introduction for greater detail into this book's inception. For those who own and appreciate the first edition, my wish is that you find this updated version to be a valuable addition to your personal library.

I welcome comments and can be reached via e-mail: betsy@elblades.com.

Acknowledgments

I am indebted to all the teachers—previously included in the first edition and the six who have joined the ranks for this second edition—for taking the time from their busy schedules to contribute to this book. Thank you!

A heartfelt tribute to those teachers whose passings impart a sense of legacy to their words as presented herein.

Special thanks to Mary Saunders-Barton, who carved out time from her very busy schedule at the NATS National Conference in Chicago, summer 2016, to sit down with me and offer ideas and suggestions for the second edition.

Sincere thanks to John Nix, Kristen Ruiz, Steven Paul Spears, and Elizabeth Stanley. Your positive comments and enthusiasm for the original *Spectrum of Voices* did much to ensure its second edition.

I am beholden to Rowman & Littlefield editors Natalie Mandziuk and Kathleen O'Brien for their patience, guidance, and advice throughout the revision process.

And, finally, thank you to the countless teachers, singers, students, and coaches who have expressed appreciation for the wisdom and inspiration that *A Spectrum of Voices* has provided over the span of two decades.

Introduction

In 1723, Pier Francesco Tosi wrote, "The best singer in the world is still a learner and must be his own master."

That wise counsel can certainly be extended to the present. It's equally appropriate to replace "singer" with "teacher of singing." Teaching excellence is determined not only by the erudition and experience one imparts to students; it is also reflected in the teacher's desire for continued education and self-development. Guidance from a country's best teachers can provide a particularly rich resource for such continued education.

We are most fortunate to have an abundance of excellent vocal pedagogues in this country. Overall, the field is replete with involved and caring teachers who devote themselves to thoughtful instruction. Our "gross national product" (i.e., professional singers) has attained a well-deserved international reputation for outstanding training and preparation. "How are professional American singers taught?" It was this question that led me to investigate a far more sweeping question: "How do the nation's most outstanding teachers of voice performance teach?" Finding an answer to that question required a direct approach: I talked with the most highly regarded voice teachers in the country.

I knew of several prominent voice teachers who had national reputations for pedagogical excellence, but I was determined to remove myself from the selection process. Because the project began as a qualitative research study for my doctoral dissertation, it was essential to avoid "researcher bias." I needed to identify "outstanding vocal pedagogues" without involvement in the process. The answer seemed apparent: go right to the source—other voice teachers.

I devised a survey to elicit endorsements. In order to poll a diverse and geographically broad area, the survey was sent to the entire voice faculty at each of the following universities and conservatories, all of which embrace highly regarded voice departments. I procured those names from the *College Music Society Directory of Music Faculties in Colleges and Universities, USA and Canada*. The institutions included the following:

- Cincinnati Conservatory of Music, University of Cincinnati
- Eastman School of Music, University of Rochester
- Indiana University
- The Juilliard School
- Manhattan School of Music
- The Mannes School

- New England Conservatory
- Northwestern University
- Oberlin College
- San Francisco Conservatory
- University of Illinois
- University of California, Santa Barbara
- University of Michigan, Ann Arbor

As an added measure, I also wrote to the Officers and Regional Governors of the National Association of Teachers of Singing (NATS). The letter was straightforward: I explained who I was and what I was researching, and asked for their help in identifying pedagogues who, in their opinion, were "exemplary teachers of applied voice, teaching in the United States." Attached was a sheet upon which to list their choices. They could write one name or fifty—no limits. I sent out nearly 150 surveys.

In a short time, responses began to pour in. Some chose to list only one or two names; others provided up to twenty or more. As the master list quickly grew, certain names repeatedly appeared. By the time I was finished compiling my "master list," there were 257 names representing endorsed "exemplary vocal pedagogues" (a point that demonstrates both the depth of teaching in this country and the magnitude of regard for respected teachers!).

From that master list, I created a sublist of teachers receiving three or more endorsements (a purely arbitrary but effective procedure). Upon completion, the process netted a target group of about thirty names. I wrote to each teacher, explained my project, and requested an interview. For a number of reasons, some declined, but a significant number also accepted.

In any study, whether qualitative, quantitative, scientific, sociologic, or philosophical, it's crucial to first identify the questions you hope to resolve (equivalent to, "If you don't know where you're going, how are you going to get there?"). Before I could develop questions for the interviews, I had to decide what it was I was attempting to research.

I drew upon my (then) twenty years of personal voice study and ten years of voice teaching experience for guidance in developing the interviews. I asked myself what concepts and issues were involved in teaching voice and vocal performance? What other components came into being? After much reflection, these crucial points emerged to inspire the research questions:

1. How are American singers being taught to sing and perform?
2. What concepts and how are these concepts of vocal technique being taught? (I.e., how do America's top vocal pedagogues approach teaching the fundamental concepts of breathing, breath support [appoggio], tonal "focus" or "placement," lyric diction, registration, and free production?)
3. Do America's expert vocal pedagogues agree upon how to teach these fundamental techniques, or as is widely believed, do they more often disagree?
4. How do these teachers teach the more intangible concepts (i.e., musical and emotional expression—those factors that often constitute the difference between a mediocre performance and an artistic one)?
5. Where and from whom did this country's outstanding vocal pedagogues receive their own voice training?
6. What kinds of auxiliary training do they recommend to their students?
7. How do these teachers stay current in their field?
8. How do they perceive today's young professional singer? To what factors would they attribute the professional American singer's success?

In any interview, it is important to establish a sequence that will foster a comfortable and logical "flow." For guidance, I turned to the manual *How to Use Qualitative Methods in Evaluation* by Michael Quinn Patton. The progression of questions should, according to Patton, "encourage the respondent to talk descriptively. . . . Once some experience to activity has been described, it is appropriate to ask about interpretations, opinions, and feelings about the behaviors and actions described. Opinions and feelings are likely to be more accurate at this point in the interview because the respondent has just verbally relived the experience. Thus a context is established for expressing feelings and opinions."

With this in mind, I shaped the interview to begin with a straightforward discussion of technical concepts. Questions that required the most thought and reflection were reserved to the latter part of the interview, when the respondent was "warmed up" but not "talked out." Timing is very important because the last question is devoted to the topic that represents the focal idea of the entire study.

I was careful to ask clear, open-ended questions. Supplementary questions (called "probes") were utilized only when the interviewee requested further clarification. For the most part, I restrained myself from joining in the discussion—my role was to ask the question and then stay quiet while the teacher talked. For someone who loves this field and loves to engage in conversation regarding technique, singers, music, and performance, it was a subtle form of torture. But larger goals prevailed over immediate temptation.

The original interview evolved to this final form:

1. Describe your approach to teaching the following concepts of vocal technique:

     a. Posture
     b. Breathing and breath support (appoggio)
     c. Tonal resonance (i.e., voice "placement" or "focus")
     d. Diction
     e. Registration
     f. Unification (i.e., evenness of voice throughout the range)
     g. Tension—eliminating tension problems

2. Do you make use of certain images that help your students grasp these concepts? If so, what are they? How do you explain them? When and how did you first become acquainted with these images?
3. With whom did you study? What aspects of their teaching(s) have you incorporated into your own approach?
4. What kinds of auxiliary training do you recommend to your students?
5. Whose work do you admire?
6. How do you stay current in the field?
7. What is your opinion of today's professional career-track singer? Do you feel they are in general of a high caliber in vocal performance? What are some of the attributes you feel contribute to the success of a young professional singer?
8. In your opinion, do you think there is an "American sound" or "vocal stamp," characteristic of American-trained singers? If so, how would you describe it? Is it indicative of an "American school" of singing?

I proceeded with the study, conducted the interviews, analyzed the results, and wrote the thesis (*Vocal Pedagogy in the United States: Interviews with Exemplary Teachers of Applied Voice*, available from University Microfilms, Ann Arbor, Michigan, and featured in the *Jour-*

nal of Research in Singing and Applied Vocal Pedagogy [Spring 1994]). At the conclusion of the dissertation, I presented "Recommendations for Further Study" in which was stated,

> This study represents the first phase of analysis performed on the interview data. Analysis reveals patterns, themes, and categories that emerge from the data; deeper levels of analysis are evident as one continues to study the interview transcripts. The deeper one probes, the more information is revealed; the following categories represent a wider scope beyond the limits of this current study:

- pedagogues' goals and objectives
- pedagogues' priorities in teaching
- pedagogues' teaching philosophy
- assessment of own teaching, of others' teaching, of students and different learning styles, of the field of vocal pedagogy
- approach to problem solving (i.e., cause and effect)
- pragmatism (the "whatever works" approach)
- nurturing the student's own self-analysis

The same group of teachers could be interviewed again with additional questions to provide an even more complete view of their ideas and methods. These might include the following:

1. When you hear a student audition, what do you listen for? What are your audition acceptance criteria?
2. How do you teach a first lesson?
3. What attributes do you feel are desirable in a voice teacher?
4. How do you guide a student to practice?
5. How do you structure a lesson?

It was not difficult to devise a second set of interview questions; I already knew what I wanted to ask:

1.
   a. How do you approach the first lesson with a new student?
   b. How do you structure a typical lesson?
   c. How do you guide a student's practice? What advice do you give?

2. When you hear a student audition, what do you look and listen for? What is it that for you sets that student apart?
3. What are your personal goals and objectives in your own teaching? What are your priorities?
4. How do you nurture and guide the student's "self-discovery?"
5. In his book *The Performer Prepares*, Robert Caldwell writes, "Performance work—the time spent to craft a rich inner experience to take into the performance—is essential because a correct interpretation played with correct technique is simply not enough to build a powerful performance . . . the performer must build compelling inner experiences beforehand and take them into performance." How do you strive to help the student find that complete union of music and inner experience that results in a powerful performance?
6. What attributes do you feel typify the "outstanding" or "exemplary" vocal pedagogue?

Because most of the first group of interviews was collected under the aegis of my doctoral study, I met with participants in person. The interviews were conducted one-on-one and were both audiotaped and videotaped. I talked with those teachers wherever it was most convenient: at their studios, in their homes, and at voice conferences (the 1990 NATS convention in Little Rock, Arkansas, and the International Congress of Voice Teachers Conference in Philadelphia in 1991).

I conducted the second interview through sit-down, face-to-face meetings or through taped phone conversations between February and April 1994. A number of the original "thirty names" who were not available for interviews during the first go-around were now able to participate. They kindly agreed to discuss both the first set of interview questions and those in the follow-up interview. The final group includes (with teaching affiliation at time of interview) the following:

Edward Baird, University of North Texas, Denton
Marcia Baldwin, Eastman School of Music (emerita), Rochester, New York
Oren Brown, the Juilliard School (emeritus), New York City
Lindsey Christiansen, Westminster Choir College at Rider University, Princeton, New Jersey
Jack Coldiron, then at Southwestern Baptist Theological Seminary, Fort Worth, Texas
Barbara Doscher, University of Colorado, Boulder
Shirlee Emmons, private teacher, New York City
Leslie Guinn, University of Michigan, Ann Arbor
Helen Hodam, New England Conservatory, Boston
Cynthia Hoffmann, the Julliard School, Manhattan School of Music, the Curtis Institute of Music
Barbara Honn, Cincinnati Conservatory and the Academy of Vocal Arts, Philadelphia
Marvin Keenze, Westminster Choir College of Rider University, Princeton, New Jersey
Bruce Lunkley, Southern Methodist University, Dallas
William McIver, University of North Carolina, Greensboro
Richard Miller, Oberlin College Conservatory, Oberlin, Ohio
Dale Moore, Indiana University, Bloomington (from 1996 to 2000, at the Eastman School of Music)
Laura Brooks Rice, Westminster Choir College at Rider University, Princeton, New Jersey
Helen Swank, the Ohio State University (emerita), Columbus
Joan Wall, Texas Woman's University, Dallas
Carol Webber, Eastman School of Music

(2017 note: Please see the "About the Author and Contributors" section for current status.)

Second edition new participants include the following:

Edith Davis Tidwell, professor emerita, University of Louisville, Kentucky
Meribeth Dayme, founder/director of Get in Tune and CoreSinging
Robert Edwin, Robert Edwin Studio, Cinnaminson, New Jersey
Stephen King, Shepherd School of Music, Rice University, Houston, and Houston Grand Opera
Jeannette LoVetri, the LoVetri Institute of Somatic Voicework in residence at Baldwin Wallace University, Berea, Ohio
Mary Saunders-Barton, professor emerita, Penn State University, and private studio, New York City

Upon completion, the interviews were transcribed word for word from the audiotapes. These written transcripts were sent to the respective pedagogue for review, editing, and approval. From these transcriptions I have included direct quotes that best represent the teachers' views, ideas, and insights. In some areas, a particular teacher's statements might not appear or are very brief; in those cases, the teacher did not address that area, was not asked the question, or preferred to decline.

This list of "exemplary vocal pedagogues" is not intended to be all inclusive; for every name that appears, many others could equally deserve the title "outstanding voice teacher." Inevitably, there are some important omissions. Several prominent teachers were unavailable or declined an interview. At the same time, I could conceivably conduct another survey, poll the same (or different) institutions, and arrive at a whole new list. Many of the same names would surely appear, but different ones would also surface. Regardless, the teachers quoted in this book should be considered spokespersons for all fine teachers who equally deserve the title "outstanding voice teacher."

Teaching voice and vocal performance is by nature a subjective and amorphous pursuit. Only singers and teachers of singing can really understand that. But in any area where diverse opinion coexists, healthy controversy signifies vitality. As you read through the quotes and consider the discussions, there will inevitably be statements with which you disagree. That's a given. In spite of that certainty, my greatest hope is that you close the book saying "I learned."

HOW THE BOOK IS ORGANIZED

The order of the interview questions served a specific purpose but one very different from the objectives of this book. Therefore, I have reordered the questions and responses into what will best serve the reader. I intend the book to function as a quick and handy reference to the studio teacher; it can also serve as a text for vocal pedagogy courses to supplement the many fine books available on physiology and vocal mechanics; and, finally, it provides an "insider's guide" to advise prospective young singers who anticipate a career in singing. I have organized the book to facilitate quick and easy reference by area. Each part is divided into chapters that correspond to the interview question posed. A brief discussion introduces each chapter; most important, direct quotes from the teachers contain rich, descriptive detail to support the concept or issue.

The book is divided into three parts. Part 1, "Vocal Concepts," presents the teachers' statements and strategies for teaching specific technical concepts (i.e., posture, breath, tone, etc.). Part 2, "Training Singers: Practical, Artistic, and Professional Development," includes insights and advice to define the well-rounded evolution of a singer-artist. Part 3, "Teachers' Professional Training," addresses issues that pertain to continued growth for the teacher of voice. In this section, the master teachers provide guidance, suggest strategies, and clarify goals for all vocal pedagogues.

Voice performance and pedagogy contains terminology and idioms characteristic of the profession. In the course of their conversation, the teachers often refer to techniques and conditions that might be unfamiliar to the student or teacher-in-training. With this in mind, I have compiled a glossary of definitions.

The book holds a wealth of teaching strategies to guide and inspire students, the novice teacher, and even the highly experienced teacher of singing.

For the practicing voice teacher, I hope you'll look upon this book as a valuable and handy studio reference. It offers the opportunity to refresh forgotten ideas and acquire new or different tactics designed to enhance your customary, successful method.

For the novice teacher, there might be times when you look at the trusting student before you and think, "Now what do I do?" The wisdom, experience, and suggestions contained here offer ready advice, practical strategies, exercises, and solutions, as well as all-embracing philosophies to direct you for years to come.

And finally, for the aspiring "professional young career-track singer," you can count on the advice and encouragement offered by these teachers. It's the best from some of the best.

Part 1

Vocal Concepts

The first interview began with this very comprehensive question:

Describe your approach to teaching the following concepts of vocal technique:

- posture
- breath and "breath support" (appoggio)
- tonal resonance (i.e., voice "placement" or "focus")
- diction
- registration
- unification (i.e., evenness of voice throughout the range)
- tension mediation and elimination

A related question followed:

Do you make use of certain images that help your students grasp these concepts? If so, what are they? How do you explain them?

After the entire question was read, the pedagogues answered individual concepts in turn. For sake of clarity, I have organized these sections accordingly.

Chapter One

Posture, Alignment, Body for Singing

One of the fundamental precepts of voice instruction is "posture." Nearly all vocal pedagogues agree that work on posture precedes all other areas of instruction. Only after the body is aligned and operating in a state of freedom can other areas of voice instruction proceed. Nearly every pedagogue stated that proper posture is essential to good breathing and that the first thing taught to students is a good singing stance.

WHAT CONSTITUTES GOOD POSTURE?

1. The body that is buoyant and elastic.
2. The body feels tall and elongated.
3. The body feels centered and solidly rooted.
4. The torso is not slumped or collapsed.
5. The rib cage feels open and expanded.
6. The body alignment involves the spine, neck, and shoulders, with weight distributed to the feet.
7. The stance has nobility.

TEACHERS' REMARKS

Carol Webber

Regarding posture, an analogy that is useful is to describe what it's like if the concert pianist tries to play from the stage with the lid down—they're missing the real full use of the instrument. For a singer to sing with poor posture is the same—it limits the instrument.

Many students haven't thought in terms of the whole body as the instrument. Therefore, they think and work primarily from the neck up, maybe from the waist up. Few students think of the body all the way to the floor.

Postural work can be gained from more than just the voice teacher. . . Alexander Technique, other methods; often there are people who work specifically on body balance, maybe not through any particular school of thought, but once you know that they are good and have a gift for that, they can be very helpful. A lot of teachers try to work with someone like that.

Edward Baird

We work posture, first of all, which I feel is the prerequisite to all good breath support. I ask for an expanded rib cage and a feeling of . . . often I used the term "broad shoulders," or expanded shoulders, rather than a raised rib chest, because that can sometimes result in artificially high chest position.

Helen Swank

My feeling is that perfect posture is first and foremost. By that, I mean a very tall and very relaxed kind of stance. Aikido (one of the oriental martial arts) works with this lengthened spinal relationship: relaxation and lengthening the muscles of the back so that you stand as tall as you possibly can and as well rooted as you possibly can. It's a whole body concept.

It's been a very easy way for the students to find out how it feels, and I suppose there's some slight hypnosis that goes along with it. I take them through the whole process of closing their eyes and go through some instructions that will help them get the physical sensation we're after. If the aikido is really functioning, you can press against their head or their body, but they're really in the stance and very solidly rooted, and yet that stance appears relaxed. You can look at them and know they're right, and they feel themselves that they're right. The process gets them there quickly. They find when they open their eyes that their posture is perfect and their breathing is low and relaxed. While it's not the first thing I go to, it's the one I go to if people have trouble understanding my "lengthened" spine and "straight" back. I've not ever had it [aikido] not work.

Marcia Baldwin

"Stance" is the first item to discuss with each student. A straight line beginning at the top of the head down the back to the heels. The knees should not be locked, but bent. This is particularly important if the student exhibits symptoms of swayed back or protruding buttocks. Moving the legs forward slightly usually alleviates the problem.

Cynthia Hoffmann

To achieve good posture or alignment, it is important to find an inner sense of balance and poise. For example, if one becomes rigid or fixes a position (e.g., pinning the shoulders back or trying to hold the chest too high) one can narrow or tighten the space between the scapula, making it more difficult to achieve a deep and relaxed breath. In Alexander terms, the sense of the head balanced upon the spine is the key to feeling the flow of body energy and the release of tension in the jaw, neck, shoulders, and so on down the spinal line. I try to guide and encourage a feeling of lightness and sense of space between the ears and behind the eyes. As this balance is achieved, one has a better sense of the body as a whole, and consequently, one usually experiences greater ease in breathing. This release can also help the student to "feel the floor"—the energy flowing to it and the "bounce" back up from it. There is an overall sense of up-and-down stretch and elasticity.

Of course, not everyone can study the Alexander Technique, and as with any other study, it takes a commitment of time to find out what it is all about. One can also choose to study yoga, tai chi, modern dance, and so forth. For example, a student whom I had not seen for several months came for a lesson. Her posture looked much improved, and I asked her what she had been doing. She replied, "Karate, three times a week." That was a revelation.

Dale Moore

I think the body must be in line. I have attended some Alexander [Technique] classes and find myself pretty much in agreement with how they want the body to line up: the chin isn't jutting out, nor pulled in, and the body is supported with the feet slightly apart, one foot ahead of the other—the old "tripod" idea. I think Richard Miller puts it very well—it's called the "noble posture," as opposed to any kind of slump.

Lindsey Christiansen

The whole body is the instrument. I think it's important that the posture be built from the bottom up, with knees loose, feet slightly apart, pelvis tilted slightly forward (that's a very important concept for me) so that swayback doesn't happen. Also, [there should be] a feeling of lifting the ribs up and out of the pelvis, the shoulders down and back, and the head high. The pelvic bone, the ribs and shoulders, the knees, and the feet somehow have a relationship to one another.

I talk about the nature of the body and the feeling of what I sometimes call the "environment for singing"—a feeling of openness and width in the ribs, width, and length in the vocal tract with the nose open. It's all a part of having the body ready to sing.

Helen Hodam

I start at the feet and work up. First, I talk about what the requirements of good posture are. It must be the kind of posture that you can maintain over a long period, as in an opera, and it must, most of all, be the kind of posture that will permit relaxed breathing. It must not be stiff, and it must have a feeling of elasticity or resiliency so you can get a relaxed, but adequate, inhalation onstage. It must be the kind of posture that will permit free movement of the body—and it must look good.

Leslie Guinn

I avoid suggesting special singing postures for students. I do address the elements of basic healthy posture without inducing rigidity or military bearing. We then work to find a well-coordinated breathing pattern that often assists them in tweaking their posture to what is optimal for them.

Jack Coldiron

The singer should stand with feet shoulder-width apart, one foot slightly forward of the other and the hands hanging at the sides.

The alignment is such: ears, shoulders, hips, and knees should line up as closely as possible. The head should look directly ahead, eyes at a level as if looking far into the distance. The chest remains erect but not in a "military" posture. Finally, the singer must maintain a sense of alertness and looseness of the body.

Joan Wall

In my opinion, posture is a word that can be limiting because it can infer stillness and a single correct position. I find the term *body use*—which originated with the Alexander Technique—more useful. This term enlarges the student's concepts to include the whole body, and it emphasizes ease, freedom, and flexibility of movement. I think singers should realize that they never really stand still—their body is continually moving whether the movement is small or large. Even breathing is movement!

Good body use should be one of the first steps in learning to sing. It includes a balanced, aligned, and tall posture, with poised, light flexibility in the body. The chest should be high, and the neck, shoulders, waist, hips, legs, and knees should be free from tension. The torso should move flexibly for breathing. The head should assume an easy position over the top of the body so that the neck is free. A slight forward tilt of the head is helpful to avoid a common problem of jutting the chin forward on ascending pitches.

Marvin Keenze

I'll have the students play around with positions until they find their best posture. I might ask them to do the wrong thing in order to find the best position (i.e., where is the sound best for you?).

I use a traditional language that includes the terms of alignment, balance, appoggio, and centering. The Alexander Technique works as well as other body coordination disciplines have influenced my teaching and have given to me an awareness of the body, the breath, and the sound relationships. The challenge is to encourage these ideals without the student developing rigidity or a self-consciousness that does not allow the body to adapt to a variety of musical and poetic demands. I use the "listening posture" as described by Paul Madaule in his book based on the work of Alfred Tomatis, *When Listening Comes Alive*. This concept encourages the singer to adapt a posture that allows the optimum balance between bone-conduction and air-conduction hearing. On this concept, the entire body acts as an ear and participates in the listening process. The singer soon learns when the listening is at its best and will maintain the posture that provides it. When the alignment changes, the hearing changes and therefore the voice changes. Then the ear becomes the controller of the body's response, and the alignment responds.

Edith Davis Tidwell

[Posture should be] buoyant, proud, and with a sense of expectancy.

Meribeth Dayme

First of all, I don't use the word "posture," and I've eliminated it forever from my vocabulary because of the preconceptions derived from old ideas that were taught to children and those still promoted in some fitness studios. I teach what I call "dynamic balance." That means that the energy of the body is flowing and mobile. It's not a rigid position as some people perceive posture, but it has to do with imaginary lines of energy, which stabilize and ground a person in standing and moving. This is a concept taken from the martial arts and balances a singer beautifully and enables the performer to breathe freely without restriction.

When a singer is rigid, all the muscles are being used to "hold that singer together," and not for singing. The singer then has to work to make singing happen rather than allowing it to flow. I begin with dynamic balance, as this is a way of keeping the joints "soft," the eyes alert, with the body balanced and grounded. First, it is important that the feet are pointed forward like the numeral 11 rather than turned out. The energy is weak with turned-out feet. The difference in the sound is often dramatic. We then create imaginary lines of energy and send them down to the ground from the sacrum, up to the sky from the upper back, and down to the ground from the elbows. By using downward lines from the elbows, the shoulders stay down (a big problem with many singers). Most people correct the shoulders, but singers typically hike their arms up, and the shoulders will come up with them. So now there is a lovely polarity in the body and energy field.

In today's singing, there's a lot of movement . . . whether it's musical theater or CCM [contemporary commercial music]. Fortunately, the classical people are beginning to look less like robots and move a little as well. It's a start, and for me it's the most important start because the moment you are out of balance, every muscle in your body starts to work to keep you in balance. This means the singer is under a huge burden and obstacle to try to stay balanced and sing at the same time. The body needs to be in a place where it can respond to what you want to do when you sing. It's what I call "respond-ability or response-ability." Beginning with "dynamic balance" sorts out a lot of other issues such as breath and physical tension.

Robert Edwin

My fact-based and gender-neutral approach to voice pedagogy impacts all aspects of my teaching from posture to performance. I like to call the major components of singing the "tions"—body position, respiration, audiation, registration, resonation, articulation, and emotion. For example, body position (posture) is primarily influenced by the rib cage. All my students are taught a very quick and effective check of posture. Put your arms over your head. If you feel a significant lift of the rib cage, your body position is not where it needs to be. Ideally when you lift your arms above your head, the only major movement should be your arms. Many of my new students have to spend a lot of time with their arms over their heads to correct poor body position.

Stephen King

With posture, I'm not a systematic person in terms of trying to teach everybody the same way. I teach so many different types of singers, in terms of age, experience, and Fach that I find it necessary to individualize my instruction. I work in various ways with posture: having singers warm up against the wall with the lumbar curve touching the wall. This means they have to squat a little or even a lot depending on height and then stand up from that position to try to find some sort of alignment in the hips, shoulders, and neck. Some singers profit from kneeling in a chair to stabilize the core and gaining that feeling of balance before standing again. Tilting forward from the hips is yet another way to engage while exhaling/inhaling and then carefully standing again to find the same awareness. Posturing as if picking up the piano or trying to push down the door may help those who find it especially challenging to feel some engagement. In short, one should try to find what works for each student based on what you hear and see that is missing.

I have an exercise ball in my studio and a kinesthetic primer board or "K board" that has been around for some time. In fact, I gave my board for the summer to the only undergraduate student I have. [I told her,] "Here, take this board, and every day, get on this and warm up." She's someone who's been taught "up" and not taught "down." She's completely off the floor, and so, working on that to find her legs and some sort of axial alignment . . . I'll do just about anything I can to get people to engage their body in an athletic way.

It might be somewhat controversial, but I'm not a big believer in Alexander. I've seen a number of people do that and they accumulate some awareness of their bodies, but I also see them get so relaxed that there's not enough immediacy in the body. And then, I find tension creeps in, especially above the shoulders . . . at least, that's what I've seen. Most everywhere I've worked, there have been Alexander lessons or somebody dedicated to teach that, and (of course, I've done no study on this) my observation for the singers has been that it's not been too useful, whereas for people in other disciplines—let's say, piano or violin—it might be more useful. But for singers, I've seen negative results related to the dynamic postural energy needed to facilitate expert breath coordination.

Other disciplines such as yoga are being widely practiced by singers with good results. But this is just my observation and may not be the experience of others.

I use movement when they're singing: sliding a drink coaster across the piano, marching in place, walking across the room, or walking backward across the room. Their limbic system is turned on, and they're aware of their balance. That helps a lot of people when they walk backward (from where the piano is toward the exit door); they have to maintain their balance and their sense of awareness, and almost immediately, you get a better postural result. I try different things, and it just depends on the person.

I played sports growing up, and I still play a lot of golf when I have time, so I'm a big believer in balance and people finding the ground with their legs and using the ground for support. With most of the professional singers I work with (people in their thirties and forties and older who are singing in the big theaters), one of the first things that comes out of their mouths is "grounded" or "anchored." Those are people who are doing it all the time, and that is definitely what I teach: getting people to find their feet, find the floor, and sing from the floor, sing from their toes if you will, to get the body engaged. I don't see how you can just relax everything and do what you have to do over an orchestra.

With younger singers, you go through times with them overdoing, pushing, and misappropriating what energy is, and energy ends up above the neck. Then we don't have the right balance in the posture.

Jeannette LoVetri

Head over torso, torso balanced over hips. Neck released. Pelvis parallel to the floor. Knees unlocked. Shoulders relaxed. Upper chest [sternum] comfortably lifted. Weight slightly forward over the feet. Feet hip-width apart or in "second position" [ballet].

The ribs have to be lifted and should be wide at the bottom before inhalation. The lower abs engage to help lift the ribs. The inhalation should not lift the ribs further, [straight up toward the ceiling], and the sternum should not drop during exhalation. Some people call this "appoggio." I don't use this term.

Mary Saunders-Barton

Posture is a dynamic concept. Because many of my students are proficient dancers and movers, I find it useful to incorporate what they understand about their bodies when they dance in order to bring a sense of that freedom and "lift" even when they are absolutely still. Preparing for a pirouette or preparing to dive off a high diving board can help gather them in a relaxed readiness.

STRATEGIES FOR TEACHING POSTURE

Helen Swank

I help the student find a raised rib cage; a straight, relaxed, lengthened spine; and to experience the feeling of "opening the ribs."

I have good luck with using aikido, one of the martial arts. I take them through the whole process: They close their eyes and go through the visualization that will help them experience the whole body stance. When they open their eyes, they find their posture is perfect and their breathing is low and relaxed. Aikido helps me get them there quickly.

We use the old Quaker saying "peace at the center." When they can visualize the "peace at the center" being something of a central core and all the extremities hanging from it, it tends to bring relaxation into the body and acts on the relaxation of these little muscles that relate to articulation, voice production, and all that.

Carol Webber

I recommend Mabel Todd's *Thinking Body* to students whose eyes light up with curiosity and who seem interested in further physiology. This is not a book written for singers, and I think that's one of its values; it's very general and talks about the relationship of bone and muscle and the structural balance of the whole body, the integration of thought and movement. Todd talks a lot about the concept of wanting to perform a certain task and how that fires the muscles. I think that's very helpful.

For people who aren't that curious or don't want to read the whole book, I use excerpts from several books that discuss the concept that the muscles of the pelvic region receive the weight of the torso, distribute it through the legs, into the feet, and into the floor. This actually creates an upright position.

Oren Brown

If students have a problem, or there's any question about it, I ask them to lie on the floor on their backs. This makes them aware of alignment. This can also check on how much they are arching the small of the back. Many people arch this area in the lumbar region too much and being on the floor will help them be aware of that. If there's too much arching in the small of the back, a correction would be to raise their knees and bring that part of the body down. When they get used to that, see if they can hold that position while they slowly let their feet straighten out. At the same time, they feel they are almost bringing their chin in, which will help to elongate the spinal cord. This elongation helps to bring about good alignment of the body. Within that alignment, the diaphragm has its freest motion.

So you're getting two things: you're getting the body ready for breathing and making the space possible for it. Students get the feeling of what this is and are aware that their breath is coming in easily (I don't ask them to breath any special way but to become aware of how their breath is moving in this posture). Once they realize how their breath moves in this posture, I ask them to stand and make believe that the floor is still behind them. They can sense the same elongation of the body and simply become aware of how their breathing is moving within this framework.

Laura Brooks Rice

I start each lesson with posture exercises. I'll have them stretch from side to side, find the bottom of the rib cage, and lift the rib cage. Then I have them bend over and stretch the lower back, á la Jane Fonda, coming up one vertebra at a time. I have them lift their arms and lift the rib cage, and then lower their arms but not lower the rib cage.

I have learned many things to help my students find their best posture and physical balance for singing: making sure heels, hips, and ears are aligned. Making sure that the hips are not tight and, for that, using psoas stretches. The combination of stretching the psoas and breathing into the back helps them realize that hyperextending the knees and locking the hips

prevents this interaction between muscle groups. Breathing becomes more efficient and connected to the body as a whole.

I have a bosu ball in the studio where I have them stand to find core balance, pilates bands
to open up the rib cage and expand the back, and shiatsu neck massagers to find release in the
back of the neck.

Barbara Doscher

I don't teach posture per se; as a matter of fact, I think that in many ways posture is more
connected with phonation than it is with breathing. If you don't have the correct balance of the
head on the shoulders, it's very difficult to get phonation that isn't muscular. In my book, the
chapter on posture follows the one on phonation.

William McIver

I often ask students to picture Greg Louganis on the end of a diving board. He epitomizes what
one wants for a singing posture: not totally relaxed (or they'd be lying in a heap on the end of
the diving board) but without overt tensions in the body. A diver gathers energy for a tremendous leap off the diving board. I think a singer must find the same combination of energy
ready to be released.

I don't use very many images, but those I do use often have to do with posture—for
example, the image of somebody walking on a tightrope: if they relax, they fall off; if they
tense up, they fall off. There is something in between; a singer has to find that tonicity.

[Richard] Miller talks about axial alignment, asking students to stand on one leg and swing
the other—I use that as well. I also use the idea of crossing the arms in front of one's chest to
make sure it feels nicely elevated. Try to find the center of your body [the axial alignment]
while keeping the appendages [arms and legs] free.

Helen Hodam

I talk a lot about the torso, all the activity above the hips—I address that when we talk about
relaxed breath, but it's mainly that the upper part of the body, the trunk and torso, is not
slumped. I demonstrate that you can look very good but can be just a bit caved in so the lower
ribs will not be involved and the breath suffers. We also work for balance of the neck and the
shoulders, as that's where most of the [interfering] tension centers.

Joan Wall

My goal as a teacher is to help my students improve their overall kinesthetic awareness. I want
them to be sensitive to their whole body as they walk, sit, stand, and use their body expressive-
ly in singing. I use a gentle touch to guide their standing, sitting, and walking so they can
become more aware of their bodies and find out what it means to feel tall, to lengthen and
widen the body [terms used in the Alexander Technique]. I want singers to achieve ease
freedom, and flexibility throughout their entire body as they stand to sing.

Responding to the needs of the individual singers, I may instruct from feet upward or from
head downward. I often have singers lie on the floor to do relaxation techniques and to observe
how their body is aligned. Sometimes I have students sing while standing on a balance board.
[The balance board, developed by a physical therapist, was demonstrated by Barbara Doscher
at a National Association of Teachers of Singing (NATS) master class.]

I also want to help singers be more emotionally connected to their bodies. Since body use
and posture reflect longtime habits and the emotional makeup of the person, I do dramatic and

psychological processes with students, such as theater games, rhythmical movements, and introspective exercises. I also suggest other activities that will help them become more aware of their body. Relaxation techniques, dance, Alexander classes, Feldenkrais classes, tai chi, yoga, counseling, massage therapy, and simple physical exercises.

Leslie Guinn

We talk about posture along with freedom in the neck and laryngeal area. We have access to an Alexander teacher here. I'm not of the school of the superelevated chest area. I like a nice comfortable, natural posture, which expands below without the chest heaving.

Cynthia Hoffmann

In addition to using the tools I have gained through the Alexander Technique, I use balancing a book on the top of the head, which can aid in bringing awareness of the poise and balance of the head in relation to the rest of the body (Lillian Nordica used this tool). "Panting" and the whispered "ah" can help "lengthening, widening and releasing upward." I ask students to balance their weight on the front of their heels and toes, to have easy knees (not locked), to "think" of releasing the tailbone rather than pushing it down and stand with the feet at about a forty-degree angle to help "square the hips." The distribution of weight should lean more to the inside of the foot rather than the outside, which can aid a deeper breath. I also suggest one foot slightly in front of the other (I have one leg slightly shorter than the other and have found it helpful to put the shorter leg slightly forward of the longer leg). This helps me feel more balanced and ready to move on the stage.

Chapter Two

Breath

Breath functions as a very complex but critical basic and fundamental area. It has historically been a hotly contested subject, with widely divergent approaches endorsed by reputable voice teachers. As was expected, the statements regarding breath, breath support, and the constitution of optimal function in breath management were varied and diverse. However, given the tradition of controversy and contradictory beliefs about breath and "breath support," a surprising degree of consensus was also evident among the pedagogues.

1. Good singing posture is a prerequisite to good breath.
2. Breath is airflow energy, which becomes utilized sound.
3. Through expansion of the rib cage and the contraction of the diaphragm, a partial vacuum is created in the lungs. Air will then rush in to fill the partial vacuum.
4. Breath management is a dynamic balance using airflow and a low base of "support."
5. Breath management requires pacing the breath to the demands of the phrase.
6. Breathing involves a "release"; breath renewal should be incorporated into the "release" of the sound; and the "release" is the replenishment of breath (i.e., the release is the new breath).

TEACHERS' REMARKS

Cynthia Hoffmann

A discussion of breath in singing is a subject about which there is diversity of thought and use regarding technique. Knowledge of anatomy (or lack thereof), body types, alignment, production of sound, emotion, and even repertoire can influence the kind of breath, how it is taken, and how it is maintained.

Starting with good alignment and poise of the body, ideally, breath for singing should be a response to the musical/textual phrase one is about to sing—the thought of the phrase should inspire the breath (by "thought" I mean hearing/creating the phrase one is about to sing before producing it aloud). A frequent saying in our business is "never breathe for nothing." When the thought of the phrase initiates inhalation, a better balance of air pressure is established that can help eliminate "overbreathing." As a result, the expression of the phrase (and the amount of air needed for it) is "inspired" through the thought. Elly Ameling has suggested breathing after finishing the phrase rather than breathing before the next one, which can aid in "hearing ahead" and avoid "overbreathing."

Once the air has been taken in for the phrase, there are two choices: one can exhale by using the rib cage or the lower abdominal wall. If the ribs start the exhalation, the abdomen does not do much and the ribs contract to exhale. However, if inhalation (ribs staying with the inspiratory position of the breath) is maintained for the first beat (a slight suspension of the breath that Nellie Melba also suggested), then the abdominal wall will contract to support the breath needed for the phrase, and the ribs will stay more in the position of inspiration. This is one idea behind the "appoggio."

When we want to say something, we normally breathe in for what we are about to say, suspend our breath, and then say it. In speaking for the stage, however, a different kind of breath energy is involved; declamation/elongation of the text to fill a certain space requires more energy and support than normal speech, and singing for the operatic or recital stage is akin to that. A text set to music may have a longer duration in the completion of a sentence than in normal speech. The vowel line is often extended to describe the feeling and inspiration of the words. Having the muscles of inspiration "win out" against the muscles of expiration keeps the body more open and the tone more flowing without effort. This support from below is more of a "gathering" rather than a push in from there—more like a baby's cry or "tug." This is a more efficient way to support the tone, maintaining the position of inspiration through the phrase, and it is more columnar with respect to resonance. Of course, the amount of airflow, resistance to it, and support of it are key factors that must be balanced.

Quite often, I notice that young singers confuse what they are doing with what they think they are doing in regard to taking in air. They sometimes confuse lower abdominal expansion and the fullness of a "deep breath" in that area with the presence of "air." But there is no air there. When you point this out, of course, they realize it, but somehow the "wish" for the air to "feel deep" creates this confusion and misapplication. When the breath is taken in without pushing for a result—when the air dropping into the bottom of the lungs is allowed to create the expansion—there is a natural filling out of the back (sometimes described as an anchor), front, and sides of the body, centering around the waist but also radiating out from there. It might look the same, but it isn't. The breath itself must "inspire" the fullness and expansion, and the body needs to be in an optimum position to receive it.

Richard Miller

I think you have to know exactly how breath management is accomplished. You have to know how to stay in the inspiratory position—what the Italians call appoggio—for as long as possible. There are specific exercises I use (described in my book *The Structure of Singing*) that develop both the musculature and the coordination for remaining near the inspiratory position. You don't say, it's like balloons, or it's like umbrellas; you say what it is, which is a much simpler way to teach.

Dale Moore

I try not to make a fetish of breathing. I do take it up, and we discuss it at the first lesson with any new student, regardless of how advanced he or she might be, because there's no telling what the student has been taught in the past.

I think it's very important, especially with younger students, that they look upon the breath as their friend, and not as something they are fighting or gasping to get.

I find, for instance, the type of exercise that Richard Miller has in his book (*The Structure of Singing*) of the "onset—restoring the breath—onset" very useful, and I use many exercises such as that. Even with young students, I use a staccati arpeggi that "jells" the breath. Early on, I try to wean them from the "epigastral thrust," which I'm very much against.

The most important concept is that of the so-called vocal struggle: keeping the ribs out as much as possible during the course of the phrase. I often find that even advanced students have never felt any activity in the area below the ribs and in back, so we spend time on that. I encourage the students to think about these things and try them out; from then on I keep a watchful eye as to whether or not things are falling into place.

Of course, the root of all breath coordination is posture; if the posture really is correct, then breath management is at least simpler.

Shirlee Emmons

In 1987, the Voice Foundation invited me to give a speech at one of their annual meetings in New York on the teaching of breathing for singers. As I remember, they asked me in February, and the speech was to take place in June. In March, I started worrying seriously. All these doctors were going to be listening to me!

So I started reviewing. I thought, It's been fifteen years since I actually thought about this anew, concretely and systematically. I took out all my old books and read them during my commute back and forth to Boston, in airports, trains, and buses. Then I stated rethinking the whole matter, reevaluating my methods. Being forced to reevaluate was as good for me as it was for my students. In the course of doing that, I reread Ralph Appelman. Everyone thinks of him as a "vowel" man, the person who offers mostly information about vowel shapes. But, indeed, his chapter about breathing is spectacular. Because he was a fellow member of the American Academy of Teachers of Singing, I called him up even though I had never met him. When I told him how wonderful his breathing chapter was, he said, "That's what I always thought, but nobody seems to take it seriously."

His major point is that you must have antagonism between the abdominal muscles and the rib muscles, the intercostals. According to Appelman, when one overbalances the other, you are bound to be in some kind of trouble. Allowing the abdominals to overbalance the effort to extend the ribs results in a glottal opening that is more tightly closed and excess tension in both the extrinsic and intrinsic muscles of the larynx. Singers who breathe like this usually sing forte most of the time and have difficulty singing softly. Allowing the intercostals to overbalance the abdominal effort (which is seldom the case; more likely to happen with those singers who adopt a method of hanging the stomach out without moving it) results in a glottal opening that is too wide and with the extrinsic and intrinsic laryngeal muscles too relaxed. This produces a weak and breathy tone. Singers who adopt this method usually have great difficulty producing a supported, full sound.

Most of my students are advanced singers who have already acquired abdominal strength. With a singer who is still developing, I teach the abdominals first, to be sure the singer has command of these. Then I work on not letting the ribs collapse. For this, I have the singer use exercise bands, obtainable in a sporting goods store. The singer, using the heaviest band he or she can handle (there are three sizes), holding the arms straight out so that the leverage is poor and effort must be made by the ribs, pulls the ends of the rubber bands apart. This makes the back and the ribs do what they are supposed to do. The action is overt, evident, and teaches the ribs while toning them. The singer does the exercise with and without the bands. They do, unfortunately, make the shoulders tense, so it is best to give them up after the intercostal activity has been learned.

Along with the extra strength in the intercostals, the recti abdominii must be relaxed. These muscles are properly posture muscles. Pushing them out results in abdominals that overbalance the ribs, which puts tension into the larynx. Under such circumstances, no matter how hard the singer tries to relax his or her throat, it cannot be done while the recti abdominii are pushed outward.

Some five years or so later, still adapting, I began to properly call the upper torso strength "appoggio." I limit this word, which serves many purposes for Italian singers, to one function only: keeping the sternum high so as to supply the constant compression badly needed for big skips, high notes, low range control, ease and clarity of agility, and command of pianissimo. I ruthlessly keep a watchful eye on the unwavering height of the sternum, accompanied by mandatory low, relaxed shoulders, and insist that the inhalation be taken "sideways," meaning that the singer concentrates solely on the action of the upper parts of the transverse abdominus and the low obliques. When the singer has achieved a consistently elevated sternum that is unaccompanied by undue tension, he or she will also have stability, longer air, and more command over the other vocal skills.

Helen Swank

I think it's very hard to separate breath flow from the idea of placement, because I need for them to get away from their concept of sound being made at the throat. I think it's necessary that the breath be utilized in tone and that they develop the concept of resonating tone, rather than making tone.

Joan Wall

Good breathing, the source of power for singing, supports the tone and enhances the emotional qualities of the song. It should be deep, unobtrusive, expressive, and rhythmical.

Singers should inhale deeply, around the center of the body, avoiding high chest and shoulder involvement. Air enters the body because a vacuum is created in the lungs. The singer expands the rib cage, causing a lateral expansion across the body, and lowers the diaphragm, causing an outward movement at the front of the body, particularly around the waist. These actions stretch the lungs and cause a partial vacuum. Air rushes into the lungs to fill the vacuum.

Singers inhale through the nose, the mouth, or both simultaneously. Unfortunately, some singers "suck in air" through the nose and "gasp in air" through the mouth. When they gasp, singers excessively open the mouth, stretch the throat, move the head down and back, and jut the chin up and out—all of which interferes with free, expressive singing.

Good exhalation requires precise control over the speed and pressure of the outward-flowing air. During onset of sound, singers must keep the rib cage expanded, the chest high, and control the outward-flowing air from the abdominal muscles.

To get their best tonal control, singers must learn to balance the speed and pressure of their exhaled air with minimum laryngeal effort. They must discover how much—or how little—breath pressure to use for the vowel, the pitch, the timbre, intensity, and the duration of the tone.

Marvin Keenze

I think that what I teach about breathing is fairly traditional, at least about inhalation/inspiration. I approach it from the standpoint that the natural action of the rib cage and the diaphragm allows the air to rush into the lungs to fill the partial vacuum or to equalize pressure between the inside and the outside atmosphere. If we create the space in the lungs, the air will rush in. I try to encourage that early on so the student experiences an inhalation that is based on that information. Right away, students realize that if they create the right environment, the lungs will respond.

I believe that the breath is taken with the phrase in mind. The onset becomes inevitable when it is timed with the inhalation. Again, I believe that the ear guides the inhalation process as well as the alignment. Once we have thought it, we have done it.

Lindsey Christiansen

I think there are a lot of good ways to sing. I teach one way, but I think there are a lot of ways that can work, especially with breath management. Some ways may work better than others. My own feeling is that there is "tension" required for singing but that tension should be as low in the body and as far away from the area of the throat, jaw, and tongue as possible.

For me, breath management has to do with having the body ready to accept that dynamic tension. I talk about the ribs staying full, and I talk a lot about the spin of every note vibrating. I also talk about the breath as a "release," of not being pushed out. If there's any pressure at all, it's a pressure against the body, not a pressure against the voice. The air is released. I think the onset of the tone is probably the next step—readiness for phonation. There's a sensation of being ready before one really breathes for whatever sound is going to happen. It's very important that the air not stop between notes.

I know one of the controversial areas in breath management is the issue of what happens after the inhalation—whether there's a split second of turnaround. I talk about when you take in the breath, there's a split second of readiness so that you don't get on a merry-go-round that has the ribs moving in and out.

The onset of the tone is the next step. It's important for students to understand the idea of readiness for phonation so there's not a closing of the neck and closing in of the chin. There's a sensation of being ready before one really breathes for whatever sound is going to happen. The tongue and jaw position are important: the tongue should be arched forward, touching the lower teeth. The back of the tongue must be very loose and low, the front of the tongue being the area that does most of the shaping of vowels. The jaw must be back—not just down, also back. Supporting the voice with the jaw and tongue are major problems for most students. I work toward helping them get away from that kind of wrong support, rather than allowing the breath to manage their tone.

Oren Brown

Regarding breath, "breath support" is a bad word for me. I like to think in terms of "breath pressure" or "breath compression." This is a sensation that I find students are not really aware of until their voices are pretty well developed. To have a proper resistance in the larynx, which is going to use this support, the larynx has to arrive at a good condition, a good "tonus." In other words, with young students, all the sounds have a tendency to be a bit breathy. You can't help that tone by pushing air through or anything of that sort. I like to think that one is taking a breath and releasing it.

My approach to so-called breath support is to allow the breath to activate the vocal folds. In time, these vocal folds get well tuned (this will be quite far along in the student's study); the vocal folds will have become firmer and will not allow as much air to pass through. It will not be as breathy a sound. There will be a back pressure with a smaller opening. The students will then become aware of something very firm in their body mechanism.

Through research, we've found that good singers take a breath and as the breath is going out, they keep the diaphragm a little bit activated so that the breath doesn't go out too fast. This creates a counteraction. I heard one time that a racing driver keeps one foot on the brake as well as on the throttle—there is a counterbalancing for control. Similarly in singing, we're not simply letting the air rush out. It isn't the quantity of breath but the fine stream of air that produces the efficient sound.

I like to have everything as natural as possible. Ordinarily, we breathe through our nose—that's why it's on our face, in addition for smelling! I like to have a student breathe through his or her nose when there's time because this prevents the mouth and throat from drying out so much. Of course, in catch breaths, you have to breathe through your mouth.

I encourage the students to feel that they're maintaining their posture and then allowing these muscles to automatically take the breath in, just as they would breathe in their sleep. You don't think about taking a breath in normal breathing. In singing, you have to breathe when the beat comes along; you have to take a breath at a specific time. So, it's necessary to train yourself to be aware of what the natural action is, so that you can trigger that natural action. You take the automatic action and bring it into a willed process or to a conscious process. You still breathe along natural lines, but you are getting the breath when you want it, when you need it.

Helen Hodam

For the beginners, I talk mainly about what to do with the breath once it starts, that feeling of a breath connection. The breath must never be used as weight—ever. It can be energetic; it is energy. You think of your breath as energy, but it is always something that is moving. The breath is never held, and the breath sustains the tone.

I talk about the feeling that the breath is always rhythmic. The release of the breath is used in a musical fashion because if you get the feeling of the breath constantly moving, and moving forward to the next note, and the next, you have a musical phrase, your rhythmic phrase.

Right from the start, I discuss the basic principles of correct inhalation and release or use of breath. I don't overemphasize it with freshmen or students whose bodies are still growing—you can get too physical with them—but I do talk about it a lot with graduate students.

I explain the function of the lungs, the ribs, and the intercostal muscles. I talk about the diaphragm because some of them have a very vague idea of the diaphragm (where it actually is and its function). I explain its role and those of the abdominal muscles. Then I discuss inhalation; relaxation around the throat, face, around the mouth; and that the main thing they should try for is a comfortable, all-around expansion: back, sides, front, and so forth. I explain the expansion, what the movement of the ribs is.

Edward Baird

Basically I'm an "up and in" breath-support person, as opposed to a "down and out," if you want to separate the two approaches. I work a lot initially with a beginning student on breath support because I feel that's obviously the number one thing. I begin [by teaching] proper posture; then we work at [the breath] through the lifting of the abdominal wall muscles, always explaining what's going on and how it works.

How technical one gets explaining physical things, I find, needs to be something that the teacher has to vary from student to student. This applies not only to breathing but also to all areas of teaching voice.

I want the student to feel the base of the breath support to be fairly low, from the end of the sternum down through that area that really expands—those are the voluntary muscles. I explain that one controls the abdominal muscles because the diaphragm is an involuntary muscle and will work by itself.

I don't emphasize, as some people do, a lot of expansion in the back. I find that if singers are well postured and their rib cage is expanded, plus an expansion below the tip end of the sternum as they reach the full capacity of the breath—and if all of those [elements] are working—the expansion in the back is also working. Now, if there are students who aren't expanding enough and it works to ask them to expand in the back as well, then fine. The longer the phrase, and the more demanding the phrase is from the breath-management stand-point, the more you have to pace the breath. The further into the phrase or the higher it goes toward the end, the more consciously you apply that lifting process.

Laura Brooks Rice

I describe the breath very much like a swimmer's breath in that swimmers need to get from one place to another. They have a timed amount in which to take in their air when they turn their head. They have to take a good quality breath from the bottom of their lungs. Good long-distance swimmers don't take many breaths. They turn their head and get several strokes down the pool before they turn their head again. I also describe the breath for singing and for swimming as a gulp, not a gasp—good swimmers gulp their air; they don't gasp or they'd get tired.

I have learned from colleagues about how to specifically find the best possible place for optimum expansion in the breath process. Not all bodies are the same. Along with the concept of appoggio onset, I work to coordinate abdominal and intercostal/back breathing for my students. Someone might have a long torso and a short rib cage and struggle to "breathe low." That person might need to breath in a more east/west manner to access the lower back ribs instead of breathing only through abdominal breathing. I am constantly asking my students to breathe through a silent throat, so the throat is not engaged during the inhale. The ways I try to help them feel this coordination could be by using a yoga ball up against the piano and first position it on their lower abdominals so they feel the release out and then the pull in. Also with the yoga ball, [I place it] up against the wall to [help students] find the muscles at the bottom of their back ribs and to feel expansion there and then not collapsing on the exhale. I use a toy called the Floating Ball Game that helps them sense where the pressure needs to be centered in the body in order to keep the ball elevated and then slowly descend. I use this to help them find onset, suspension of breath, messa di voce, and legato.

Jack Coldiron

My teaching of breath is rather mainline: abdominal, thoracic (the side-to-side movement of the rib cage, etc.), to keep a feeling of expansion as you sing and to avoid pulling in or lifting. Also, [I use] possible "hands-on" instruction (student places hands on teacher's ribs to feel the expansion and the maintenance of that expansion as the teacher sings) to also demonstrate the idea of "appoggio" (i.e., "leaning against"). That is something I'm very familiar with and use with students—a feeling of that sense of constant support against the cords. Feeling constant and steady airflow . . . those are basic ideas with me.

Bruce Lunkley

First, I talk about how muscles work together or against one another, how that relates to posture and to a continuing energy flow. We push-pull a while (even though I object to the idea that one pulls in the abdominal wall when one wants a sound) just so they begin to understand what is happening and what might move and where it might go and what it does and why it needs to be resisted. We gradually work to a feeling of the breath being drawn into the sound from inside—drawn to the sound rather than pushing the sound out of the body. I find that works rather well. I rarely go into the secondary musculature. I don't see any reason to do that. The postural attitude generally takes care of that.

I rarely deal with the breath immediately—probably the second or even the third lesson. That's a general statement, but that's how I feel it works.

Leslie Guinn

To maximize breathing potential in the early stages, I often have students assume a variety of seated postures designed to thwart the usual sensations associated with gravity. We then work to duplicate this breathing pattern while standing. I ask them to allow a gentle, lower-belly expansion, the "down and out" approach. Next we work on exhalation, which of course is more difficult to master. Finding the right balance of tension between controlling the inevitable upward movement of the diaphragm and resistance at the laryngeal level can be quite difficult. Maintaining the feeling of fullness in the lower abdomen when singing is puzzling to many and can take a bit of time to identify. Some might call this "breath support." My preference is to not use this term.

Carol Webber

I think it's very important to teach students the specific muscles of inhalation and the specific muscles of exhalation. A lot of talk about breathing does not explain which muscles are primarily inhalers and which muscles are primarily exhalers, so you can really confuse a student by not sorting that out. Once that is understood and you can demonstrate exhalation easily, using the hissing exercise, inhalation can be seen in the rib cage. You can use someone else's body or your own to experience what that expansion can be. I also think a nice relaxation exercise, such as lying on the floor where you accomplish the same drop in breathing that happens when you go to sleep and observe exactly where the activity in the body is, is very, very helpful. It's important for students to understand that although we might use the breathing process in a very extraordinary way, it is normal. Breath is life, literally, and I find that very inspiring.

There's a marvelous paragraph in the Mabel Todd book that presents the idea that the diaphragm is the most mysterious part of the body because it divides the conscious mind from the unconscious. To understand that the measuring of the rhythm of the breath, the timing of the breathing that goes on all the time involuntarily with the diaphragm in this way that we touch both halves of our being, is very exciting. As singers in this society, we're lucky that we work this way, because a lot of our society is about really holding back emotion, holding the breath to get through a day. We singers have a more lively way of looking at our discipline.

I think we all understand more about breath support than we used to—that it's a balancing of inhalation/exhalation that creates what we've always called "support"; people now prefer to call it "breath balance."

In teaching breathing, it is always important to go further than the physiology—through the role of emotion: in conversation, the desire to speak, the need to say something, whether it be a warning, a command, or a sympathetic comment, the muscles fire better when there's a real, sincere necessity to say something. Just knowing how the breath works is not enough; just experiencing it correctly is not enough. It has to be inspired—literally, inspiration—inspired by the need to tell something. The singer has to be completely dedicated to the text and completely textually based, so that the body works at its finest, most finished way of working, spontaneous but also commanded. It's a necessity to synthesize those two things.

Edith Davis Tidwell

[I teach] intentional inhalations through nose and mouth; natural [unforced] abdominal expansion upon intentional inhalation; and filling the lungs and an involuntary downward action of the diaphragm with a mindful expansion of the rib cage (front and back) and retaining that feeling of buoyancy.

Meribeth Dayme

Dynamic balance is an alignment that allows easy, efficient breathing. I think that over the hundreds of years of teaching singing, and continuing to today, there is more misinformation, mythology, faulty perceptions, and general psychological issues about breath, breathing, and breath control than any other subject in the world of voice. What I see in the various discussion forums are discussions of so many systems of breath control (that are almost like religions); many are based on external particulars, the "symptoms," rather than understanding the bigger picture. They're based on what is obvious when a good singer sings, or how someone they liked from the past sings. Some of the things we see are faults and small details. However, these amount to symptoms and not causes. For example, if the jaw is sticking out, it may not be a problem with the jaw; it may be a problem with balance. The same is true with the breath. I see a lot of teaching around breath that has to do with people teaching pieces of breath, instead of a unified structure.

Here are some ways I consider breath:

One, dynamic balance is critical to the breath, because if that is not in place, the breathing has to accommodate to a body that is not balanced. Anyone looking at an unbalanced singer would derive a breathing system that is distorted.

Two, the brain does not know the difference between imagination and reality. Therefore, some of the images we use are useful for triggering efficient breathing. There are a lot of helpful breath exercises used in yoga, tai chi, chi gong, and various systems. You just have to make sure they really are useful for singing. One suggestion that I use is an imaginary inspiration that starts from the bottom of the spine and moves up the back of the spine to the top of the head, and the expiration moves down in front of the spine. It is imaginary, not anatomical or physiological. However, this exercise keeps the breath low and centered, discourages people from using their shoulders, and keeps them deep inside their body. It makes a difference in the sound. When I work with breath now, I don't use the physical symptoms anymore. I use balance, and I find another way to speak with people about breath. I find that most of the information about breathing that I am reading in forums and discussion is about playing with the pieces and not the whole concept. It comes from our four-hundred-year collective consciousness of what singing is all about and myths about breathing that have been generated and regenerated over the years.

Today, we have to look at the exciting studies and research that is going on with brain studies, such as neuroplasticity, new ideas in physics and biology, and quantum mechanics. This will reframe the ways we use the mind and how we use it to teach and learn singing.

Robert Edwin

Regarding respiration (breath management), I have my students put their hands on the lower part of their rib cage. If they are taking an efficient breath, their whole hand will move outward. The fingers will feel the abdominal muscles release, the thumbs will feel the lower back expand, and the crook of the hand will feel the expansion of the rib cage. It's a 360-degree breath rather than a front-loaded breath where the abdominal area is pushed out. The exhalation phase of the breath requires the air to be released while maintaining the outward pressure of the rib cage and abs (appoggio). If a student's hands move inward, it's because the rib cage is collapsing, a sign of a poorly executed exhalation.

Stephen King

I stopped using the term "breath support" about twenty years ago. I found that it causes people to think about the way a building might be supported—beams, concrete, mortar, steel, wood, and so forth. This leads to rigidity and overmuscled singing. There are always those who seem to be able to do that, but problems so often surface as they look for "connection" to something by working harder.

What I do with everybody is go into a pretty in-depth discussion about appoggio. For the past eight to ten years, I've begun using a drinking straw. I have people breathe through the straw, first with the fingers fully closing the end, which will partially engage inhalation muscles in the torso. Then I have them pinch half of it, which will engage, much more deeply, the inhalation muscles as they breathe through a [u]. I use the straw for all kinds of things, but this exercise will help them engage the inhalation muscles in the very deepest way, so they can feel the lean (appoggia) of the muscles against the pelvis, the lower ribs, and the "floating" ribs of the spine, as well as the pelvic floor. We work a lot on that so they can get into a position where they are able to be "professional exhalers." That's the hardest thing to learn and the hardest thing to teach. Then, you have to reinforce that work in all musical exercises and repertoire so that they are constantly aware of the amount of energy required to sing a legato phrase in tune with true projection. Some people are more aware; they're better athletes, so they just "get it." I know also that this is one of those things about which people don't agree, but you have to spend some amount of time just explaining it, doing it, and applying it to music.

For me, I've found that the straw is the thing that helps them feel the right feeling, and they don't overdo it; they don't overbreathe, because they can't. Their mouth is closed around the straw, so they don't distort the coordination; it's a good bit more refined already. We know scientifically that an undue emphasis on the inhalation in an effort to support brings great imbalance to the actual act of singing. Just "speaking on the breath" requires years of careful attention to the balance of the inhale/exhale coordination.

If we continue on with the exhale of the breath, I use music, exercises. If they can go from singing through the straw to lip trills, "raspberries" (tongue between the teeth)—if they can go to that and maintain the sense of connection to the inhale and stay tethered to that, then we go back until we can get that kind of connection into the vowels and through the consonants.

It's a lifelong study to get a line of breath that actually works. I spend a lot of time on that with just about everybody, unless they're already at the point where it works for them, where it's connected and it's balanced. For me, the thing that makes the biggest difference out listening in the room is, if the beginning of the sound, the onset, the attack—whatever you want to call it—is not absolutely pristine, then we don't have the right "Goldilocks breath." It's either too hot or too cold. I listen for that beginning of the sound and then the end of the sound to make sure the breath is balanced and that they're having relaxed inhale, but then they're able to maintain that inhale position while they sing out, so they're not stacking breath at the ends of phrases, breathing too much, and then re-onsetting the sound with too heavy of a subglottic pressure.

So that ends up being the first fifteen to thirty minutes of a lesson, finding coordination and becoming more consistent. I don't teach many young people anymore, but so many of the graduate students (even the gifted ones) come with . . . I'll say, "Well, what have you been working on with breath?" and they'll say, "We don't work on that," which I find amazing. They'll be really talented, and I'll think, How did you get this far? So I spend a lot of time with that; I don't see how you get very far without it and that seems to be the common technical thread that runs through everybody's success or nonsuccess. Certainly in the life of the opera house and the professional singing industry that's the first thing that gets mentioned if something's not going right with a singer. People will say, "Oh, they can't support" or "they don't know how to breathe" . . . those kinds of statements. At least in their mind, that's the number one thing, and it certainly probably should be.

Years ago, the laryngologist Wilbur Gould studied/interviewed a large group of professional singers about breathing. He gathered a wide variety of ideas about what singers thought they were doing that, in some cases, had little to do with how the body works. And yet, these people were professional singers. So what I try to explain is that what your awareness of what the breath is, is going to be different than someone who's shaped differently, who's taller, who's wider, who weighs more, or who's more or less athletic than you are. How you feel it is not necessarily going to manifest itself the same way with every person, which explains the teacher who only sees results with similar voices related to gender, Fach, body type, and so forth. A heldentenor is probably going to feel "support" differently than a light lyric coloratura. Even though we all have a diaphragm (which we are unable to consciously control), we all have inhale muscles, and we all have the same "equipment" (more or less), the sensations may be as different as the way we look.

I spend a lot of time working through the diversity of how singing is explained and practiced, particularly with young professional singers who are out and about. They are exposed to a lot of different ways of going about the practical job of maintaining a professional singing sound. Being around Placido Domingo these past few years in Los Angeles, I've never seen anybody who can breathe like that in all my goings about. Of course, he's not singing tenor anymore, but the way he manages his body is sort of superhuman. He's very powerful. Most people don't have that body, and they're just not going to be able to manage that sort of physicality and keep everything above the neck free enough to make a sound. There's an electricity popping off of him when he sings; that's part of the magnetism. People like that are at the very highest level of pro-athletes. They are exceptions to almost everything compared to the general population. We have that in singing, too.

Some of my work really becomes anecdotal because I see so many different things that I spend a long time trying to find what that person really needs to make it work better for him or her. The idea is that you really have to acquire elite breath coordination in order to sing legato, to sing in tune, and to sing through the transitions of the "even scale." A singer must be able to manage the breath, especially in this time of increased dramatic/visual demands of the opera-going public. I try to work on these ideas with everyone to help them find the balance of doing it without overdoing it . . . and there are lots of overdoers out there right now. It's sometimes complicated.

Jeannette LoVetri

Within the posture (see chapter 1), inhalation should be to the bottom of the lungs, with expansion being slightly visible in the abdominals, allowing them to move forward as the air comes into the lungs. The movement forward or out happens because the breath pressure moves the rectus abdominus. The singer should not move the belly but allow the belly to move. That's different.

On exhalation, depending on what is happening, the management of the ribs and the abdominals (plus, eventually, the back muscles) should be measured by the activity. The job of the singer is to extend the duration of a sustained exhale first on hissing and then on a sung sound and to keep the air pressure the same by pushing harder on less and less air to keep the volume the same as the air is depleted. This is a learned behavior in everyone. The rib cage must not collapse during this process.

Inhalation depends a great deal on posture, and exhalation is a coordinated and deliberate behavior of the ribs, the abs, and the sound, developed over time, through hissing and then through vocalization on various pitches, vowels, and volume levels.

Mary Saunders-Barton

My approach to breathing (appoggio) for singing would be familiar to any of my classical colleagues. As a matter of fact, observing and interacting with classical colleagues over the years has greatly enhanced my ability to communicate this aspect of technical training. Teaching breathing for singing to dancers has been evolving to accept the notion of breathing while you move, and of allowing the breath to inform the movement. I will always want to link breathing ("inspiration") with the "need to say" because it makes a quick and effective connection to purposeful action. For inhalation, I encourage a full rib swing, making sure shoulders and arms are released. Singers can feel the abdominal expansion as the diaphragm descends. For the exhalation, I encourage them to sustain the rib swing and to notice the action of the transversus, obliques, and pelvic floor muscles as they return the diaphragm to its resting position. For ballet dancers who need to keep ribs closed in front, there is plenty of room for rib expansion in the back

STRATEGIES FOR TEACHING BREATH

Informative teaching strategies employed by the pedagogues in the quest to clarify breath principles include the following.

To Encourage Coordination for Breath Management

Edward Baird

I have students frequently do staccato exercises, primarily as breathing exercises to get the feeling and the coordination of the breath apparatus working. I work from that into sustained exercises, arpeggios, and so forth, where the breath support and sustaining power are used in different ways.

In arpeggios, the breath is used in a lifting fashion to get from the lower note to the top note. On a single note, or [i–e–a–o–u] on one pitch, the breath is used in more of a sustaining nature. I always try to explain to the student what we're after with each vocalize . . . I strive to make those goals clear to them, but always working from the breath in its various requirements, whether it's lifting to get a high note, rationing it to sustain tones or to sing a long phrase, for a staccato standpoint for articulation, or other, various requirements that we have to do with our breath.

Marvin Keenze

I usually go right to the sound itself. I've discovered this technique that seems to be helpful for students to understand breath management. I have them sustain this voiced consonant, such as [v]. I have found that the sustaining of the consonant [v] creates just the right support for a clear and resonant vowel. The singers discover that they can hold the sound for a long time without any tension or feeling that they are exhaling. The guide is the sound. If the support system collapses, it is impossible to sing on a "vvvvvvv" sound. M's and n's also work well, but "vv" produces a more vibrant sound for the ear.

They take in the air and phonate with [vvvvvv]. To do a sustained [vvvvv] takes support. Just the action of that sustained [v] instantly gives the feeling of support for that particular task. They can hold that forever, and they have no feeling that they're exhaling, but they are. Their guide is the sound. And then, in the next step—this is teaching breath management—they'll find out that if they collapse, they can't do it [demonstrates (vvvv) turning into breathy (ffff)]. So the guide is the sound—that support creates the dynamic level. In this way, they learn inhalation and then manage exhalation.

As for how they take in air, I suggest an inhalation through the neutral vocal tract [] position (as in the word "could"). Air more easily passes through the mouth and pharynx in this balanced and relaxed vowel position. This vowel is also a point of reference for the other resonant vowel positions.

Cynthia Hoffmann

I use Nellie Melba's counting exercise, Lamperti's panting exercise, the whispered "ah," hissing, the straw exercise of Carola Speads, and the following exercise: While maintaining good posture, blow out the air, letting the abdomen fall inward and the diaphragm move up. Then, without breathing, let the musculature release back out. Then wait until the urge or need to breathe is very strong and let the need to take a breath inspire you.

I also use other exercises of Speads (*Breathing: The ABC's*), Barbara Honn's "ripotika" exercise, and an idea from Kiri Te Kanawa. She speaks the phrase she is about to sing in the rhythm of the music (and I would add—with your hand on your sternum to feel resonance there as well as in the head—not just from the voice box) lengthening the vowels and releasing the consonants as you would in singing the phrase. She does this without really preparing to do it, breath-wise. Then, after she completes the phrase, she breathes back the air she used to speak that phrase and sings the phrase with that amount of air.

Slouching can be helpful if someone is "overworking" posture and breath inspiration. The descent of the breath is more easily felt, and then one can gradually return to a posture that feels more comfortable and can be maintained with greater ease.

Joan Wall

With beginning students, I usually begin with simple instructions and demonstrations so they can form a good concept about the movements of the ribs, abdomen, and diaphragm during inhalation. I point out that the largest movement occurs at the center of the body and contrasts with the stillness of the upper chest.

Some students, however, do not respond well to direct physical instruction. They try too hard to be "correct" and just get worse. For these students, I use a multitude of imaginative descriptions, such as

1. imaging the body as a balloon to be expanded;
2. breathing in through one hundred noses located on a belt around the waist;
3. breathing the warmth of the earth up through the pelvis and out the top of the head;
4. breathing in as if startled;
5. breathing as if inhaling a pleasant fragrance;
6. breathing in colors and filling the entire body with the warmth of the color;
7. breathing into the arms, legs, neck, or other parts of the body; and

8. visualizing pleasant scenes for relaxation.

Placing the body into various positions during inhalation and movement exercises is helpful for many students. These may involve

1. inhaling while leaning over in a rag doll position to feel the back widen;
2. noticing the deep, instinctive inhale that occurs after a full exhalation;
3. using arm movements to expand the ribs; and
4. doing physical warm-up exercises.

Exhalation exercises will usually involve

1. rhythmical breathing without sound over slow counts;
2. strong unvoiced consonants;
3. staccato exercises with various vowels;
4. using voiced consonants to connect breath to the tone;
5. breath renewals and onset exercises (as in *The Structure of Singing* by Miller);
6. sostenuto exercises;
7. long scales;
8. messa-di-voce exercises; and
9. many imaginative exercises, such as seeing the diaphragm as a trampoline with a small man with pointed feet bouncing up and down (see *Freeing the Natural Voice* by Linklater) or feeling the vibrations of sound in various parts of the body, and other ideas that engage the emotive and expressive elements of singing.

Whatever the exercise, I want the singer to keep the rib cage open during onset. There should not be the slightest collapse as the tone is started at the beginning of a phrase.

I feel it is important to be able to vary my responses to meet the needs of the student. I use a large variety of approaches to elicit the breath action that is needed. And I have all my students view the animated video *Singer's Voice: Breath* (Wall and Caldwell 1992–2005) so that they will understand specifically what is happening.

Once the student has established easy, deep breathing, we continue breath work that occurs in a song: working with the meaning of the song, connecting the breath in a rhythmical, expressive, natural way to the music and text. Students often comment upon the circular nature of this kind of breathing.

Oren Brown

To become aware of what the breath is doing, I ask the student to take a breath and not hold it. Of course, if you don't hold it, it goes out. Then, taking another breath to see whether this breath will do any work, I ask them to place their teeth in a hissing position. They then take a breath, and as the air goes out, it creates a hissing sound. Without any pushing or anything of the sort, they become aware that having taken a breath, there is energy there that will produce a sound. I then explain that when making a sound, the resistance is in the vocal folds, rather than in the teeth. So then they take another breath and let it out with a little "haaaaa," like a sigh, and simply let the air do the work.

Helen Hodam

When I talk about a proper inhalation, I also talk about an open throat—I do the two together—it's a process of getting everything out of the way. I emphasize that they can try too hard, they can open too much, and they can pour too much breath. When they get it really right it seems very natural and not distorted. It is a process of getting everything out of the way when they take the breath.

I do short hisses followed by a long hiss. They do a lot of this type of exercise when they are beginners, but once I see that they're getting good breaths while singing, I usually leave it to the singer to do them at the beginning of the first practice session of the day.

Marcia Baldwin

I have a series of breathing exercises that I give a young student (although not necessarily a young student—many graduate students come in with convoluted ideas of breathing where they have things backward). Even more important, many of them don't know what breathing is all about. Their previous teachers have said, "Oh, just breathe."

We don't breathe with our shoulders or our collarbone—that's clavicular breathing. When they say, "I breathe with my diaphragm," I ask them where their lungs are. A lot of them have no idea. They've never seen an X-ray. So, we talk about the importance of the rib cage and that the intercostal muscles remain out. At first, that's very hard for them to do. I start by getting them to release their diaphragm, and to let the breath fall in as naturally as possible in order to avoid upper-chest and clavicular breathing. We do panting exercises to release their diaphragm—that's terribly important, particularly when you sing Bach, who doesn't give you any time to breathe. They need to feel a total release of the solar plexus and total release of the diaphragm. In time they feel the breath go to front, sides, and back. I have them do an exercise where they sit on a stool and bend from the waist. I put my hands on the back of the waist with thumbs around to the back and fingers outstretched and have them breathe into my hands. This can also be done standing and hanging over from the waist. When they're bent over, 99 percent can do it wonderfully. The trick is to get them to do that standing up. I tell them they can do these exercises by themselves: bend over and put their outstretched fingers around the waist area (an area of about six inches) to span the waist and into the back. I also have them inhale up to (ideally) sixty seconds' count and then a fast exhale. This is preferably done with a little noise so that you know that breath is being inhaled with a sucking motion. The opposite of that breathing exercise, the inhale for sixty seconds, is the exhale for sixty seconds. Take a fast inhale and then exhale through a small hissing sound through the teeth. The student can feel the compression of the air and the smallness of the focus, which is what they're going to do when they sing. Sometimes I have them do it with their hand in front of their mouth to feel and make sure the air is going out.

The support in the lower abdominals is the same as when they yell to their classmate across the hall. That's the support action.

Diaphragmatic support is a misnomer as far as I'm concerned. When I support, I support from the lower abdominals. Support of any quantity in the diaphragm creates a very tense, tight tone. The diaphragm needs to be flexible to allow the air to continue on its path. The only real firm grounding and solid muscle action that needs to occur is in the lower abdominals. And the chest—everybody seems to sink in the chest. That has to do with the rib cage staying out during the breathing process. The rib cage needs to stay out not only for inhalation but also for exhalation. It needs to stay out, and the singer then breathes down below that. We address that first in exercises without singing. Then I put them down on the floor and have them sing an entire piece. I tell them to feel that support into the ground and then transfer that same feeling to an upright position.

Edith Davis Tidwell

I have a "WAVE" exercise board for my students to stand on occasionally while singing, to promote that core connection and the sense of buoyancy.

I often encourage students to realize the engagement of the abdominal muscles by having them slowly go into a squat position while singing a phrase.

I also have some students use exercise bands, gradually expanding them with their arms as they sing phrases.

Exercises to Encourage Proper "Onset" of Breath with Phonation

Dale Moore

I find the types of exercises that Richard Miller has in his book (*The Structure of Singing*) of the "onset-restore the breath-onset" are valuable. I use many exercises such as that.

I have them sing staccati arpeggi so that they feel the breath early on, especially if they've been taught the "diaphragmatic thrust" (which I'm very much against). I try to wean them from that.

Lindsey Christiansen

I spend a lot of time having the student understand the connection of the breath to the sound— that air "hooks" with sound right away.

I use lip trills to help students feel the air and sound hook together. For most students, it is very effective.

I do some breathing exercises, some "ss-ss-ss-ss's" and "ff-ff-ff-ff-ff's." I very much like some of the exercises for breathing that Richard Miller has in his book *The Structure of Singing*.

William McIver

I believe in an approach that utilizes both rib expansion and abdominal diaphragmatic expansion. This is drilled through such exercises as Richard Miller recommends in *The Structure of Singing*: staying in a position of inhalation as one learns to onset the voice. That's first done in small segments; the idea of using quarter notes, then eighths notes, and then triplets and sixteenths is fine. I ask students to place their fingers at the line near the navel, to see that there's not any retraction of the abdominal wall while they're singing a five-step scale. That will be new to them, but eventually they'll be able to retain the inspiration position.

Barbara Doscher

I don't teach breathing by itself, either. I agree with Bill Vennard that the first thing you teach is some kind of flowing sound. Then if the person is having a lot of problems with breathing, you can always catch up on that.

In my view, breathing is based on trying never to say "breath support" because semantically that is a very difficult concept for singers. They feel as if they are trying to hold up a building or something. I base what I do on what Gauffin and Sundberg call "flow-phonation," which is the optimum ratio of airflow to air pressure (subglottal pressure), for a given frequency and dynamic level. In other words, I don't want people to leak a lot of air, but on the other hand, I'd rather have leaky air than not enough air. If you have not enough air, either you're holding back air or you have a fluctuating air stream.

I use what is commonly seen in a lot of the fitness facilities—a kinesthetic awareness board. It's about eighteen inches square, and it has a runner about an inch and a half wide that goes across the middle of the bottom of this square of wood. There are various more advanced settings; I've had some students who have skateboarded, and so forth. Generally, they are the better breathers. Now when someone who is used to using a lot of abdominal pressure (at least using the abdominal muscles more than I think is necessary) gets on this kind of board, often they feel as if they are levitating—it's so unusual for them to be free of all of that extra pressure. I talk about breath energy, but I don't use the word "support."

Chapter Three

Tone

Describing ideal singing tone is a subjective process. Pedagogical approaches to teaching the concept are equally amorphous and subject to personal preference. However, certain areas of common ground could be inferred from the statements of the interviewees; these elements have been condensed as follows:

1. Vocal sound consists of two qualities:

   - Projection (also called "ring" or "ping")
   - Resonance (amplification, warmth, color)

2. Tone is sensation based.
3. Tonal "core" (sometimes called "focus") gives uniformity of sound and projection throughout the range.
4. Tone results from good coordination of breath management, vibration, and resonance. Breath is utilized in tone, and resonance responds to a balance of breath and phonation.
5. Beautiful tone results from the proper adjustment between the vibrators (sound source, i.e., vocal folds) and vowels (the resonance adjustment).
6. Vocal pedagogues teach to certain tonal preferences.

TEACHERS' REMARKS

Shirlee Emmons

For resonance, placement, and focus, I make use of the search for 2750 Hz, the frequency of "ring," and I adopt the materials pioneered by Berton Coffin and acoustician Pierre Delattre. (Coffin said, "This is not a method. It is a body of knowledge; use it the way you want to," and I do.) The position of the tongue, the degree of jaw opening, the use of protruding lips or not—these are the tools for achieving 2750, which is "ring," and ring is focus and resonance, for all practical purposes. Inevitably, this translates to vowel and modification. There is no disputing the fact that the modification of vowels inspires much controversy. Paraphrasing Coffin, it's true that singers can sing any note on any vowel (only limited by the physical boundaries of their range), but some vowel forms will have a constructive interaction with the vocal cords and other vowel forms will have a diminishing acoustical interaction. Or, another way to say it would be to quote Oren Brown: "Good singers, whether consciously or not, depend on finding an easy adjustment for the pitch. This will be a modification." Well, my singers are taught to do it consciously. In this way, the principle is, I believe, more efficiently and more quickly learned than by means of other solutions to the problem. In addition, singers so trained are then independent of their teacher and can pursue their careers with confidence in their own abilities. Although some singers would resist the idea, the voice is a musical instrument, responsive to the laws of acoustics like any other instrument.

Edward Baird

I always say to students that the first thing I listen for in a vocal tone is the focus. That's the core in the middle of the tone that's going to make (1) the basis of uniformity of quality throughout the range and (2) the thing that is going to make it project.

I listen for a focus and a uniform focus in the sound early on, and I work for that. If it's not there, it's one of the first things I try to develop. I often exemplify by saying that it's like an electric cord: if the cord doesn't have a copper wire in the middle of it, it's not going to carry any current, no matter what color of insulation you put around it. The wire represents the focus.

Helen Swank

There's so much talk about placement being a bad word, and I know a lot of people feel very strongly about that. However, my students are very tuned into the "it feels as if" feedback. And I have the feeling that it begins to make sense to them. We have had a very strong pedagogy. They go through the program. Most of my students are upper level and graduate level, and they've had a strong anatomy base. When I'm talking placement, they know that it relates back to what's actually happening to function, and they'll ask questions accordingly. I use the verbiage that isn't scientific, but there is science going on in their minds. It works so well that way. I'm not sure that one or the other is a satisfactory way to teach; I think it has to be a combination of both. When they're singing properly, almost every student develops certain sensations, and one is that the tone is so high and so in front of them. Sometimes, on high pitches, they'll have a sensation that the tone comes from behind them. Once they become aware of these crazy sensations that go with the resonance system, they begin to have something they can hang on to on a stage or in a hall. They begin to relate to how they feel, what their sensation is, or indeed, what they should have in their mind as a goal for sensation. They don't have to try to listen to feedback.

You need to have them feel tone as a resonated sensation. It's necessary that the breath be utilized in tone, and that they have a sense of resonance as being a projected sound, rather than making it at the throat. The little tongue can go about doing its business and the student has the concept of space and projection, without having to force the tone to do anything.

Marcia Baldwin

It's important to have students feel rather than listen to themselves. You cannot hear yourself the way you are heard by listeners. Acoustics differ with varying performance space. You can sound one way in your teacher's studio, another way in the practice room, another way at home, and another way in a hall like the Eastman Theatre, which has 3,300 seats. Everywhere is different. As singers, we're out there all by ourselves. We need to have a frame of reference to know whether we're on target or not, and that is to feel the buzzing going on in the mask area.

I like to use [i], [ü], [y], [e], which is the next front vowel. I exercise on those tons and tons and tons depending on the natural placement/resonance of the voice. Some people have it and some don't. Some are singing way back in their throats, back in their heads, so I universally use a lot of those vowels, because that gets the resonance forward. I talk about the masque. I don't see anything wrong with talking about the masque, since that's where you feel the pressure of the air when you sing. That varies according to the vowels of course—you always have more on an [i], next on [ü], next on [e], next on a [u], next on [o], and next on an [ɑ], which is our hardest vowel because it is the farthest back vowel. That's what I do with resonance.

Oren Brown

Re: tonal placement" or "focus."

I was interested to read that a famous teacher, Garcia, had four students who were excellent. One of them felt the vibrations in the front of his face, another felt them at the top of his head, another thought they were coming out of his ears, and another said they were in the back of his head—and all sang very well! It is an individual thing. To me, the things that people call "placement" are sensations of which they become aware when their voices are developed.

I doubt very much that beginning students are aware of anything—they haven't gotten to that stage. I do not like to call attention to it; I suppose because in my early training I was told to give it a lot of attention, and it gave me a lot of trouble. I was trying to "put" the voice in a particular place. If you try to do anything in singing other than "release," you're heading for trouble, because you're making something happen rather than allowing it to happen.

If a student tells me, "I felt that sort of behind my eyes," and it was a good sound, I say "fine!" But I don't tell them to try to find it behind their eyes or in front of their nose, or in their soft palate, or any other place. As students become advanced and reach a professional stage, some may become aware of sensations in the head; the sound, in going high, will possibly feel "down and back." Perhaps they will feel it going forward.

I heard a French scientist give a paper on his research. He had small microphones on the ends of very thin wires. He then placed one of these inside a singer's mouth, well at the back. Another was placed just above the larynx; another was at the front of the mouth, another just outside, and another was inside on the "floor" of the nose. He could turn any one of the microphones on or off.

He had the singer sing and compared the resonance value of each area—the least amount of sound was recorded by the microphone in the nose. We tell people to put the sound in the nose to get resonance, and yet we're getting the least result there!

As far as fullness of sound is concerned, the pharyngeal space at the back of the mouth is probably the greatest contributor to resonance. It is that sense, as they say, of beginning a yawn. Resonance is a very important factor for people to develop an awareness of, but it doesn't come until they're well advanced in their study.

Leslie Guinn

We work a good bit on developing pharyngeal space and stabilizing their comfortable vertical laryngeal position, allowing the ring in the voice to develop, rather than trying to push a sound to a particular spot. In my experience, asking the student to put a sound in a special place causes them to constrict the pharynx in an effort to be doing something. Creating a larger, ringing sound without muscular conflict in the throat is often not believed until heard on tape, so I strongly recommend these lessons be recorded. The concept of finding the "sweet spot"— that same spot everyone seeks on a tennis racket or golf club—allows the sound to pour forth as if little is being done, when in truth it involves much muscle activity. After this experience, we work to help the student identify the sensations of resonance, enabling them to duplicate the experience.

Richard Miller

With regard to so-called focus or tonal placement, the voice is an acoustic instrument. You can't "focus" tone; you can't put it someplace. It is the result of the supraglottal resonator tract. It can be simply explained to any person. A student of average intelligence can grasp that concept in five minutes' time, and then you don't have to have birds whirling around your head, funnels at the back of your neck, resonance chambers where resonance chambers do not exist, sounding boards that do not exist, and pyramids that do not exist; the student immediately feels the sensation, which is part of what he/she depends upon. They sense how it feels, they hear how it sounds, and they see what it looks like. They don't have to have mental images of eyes in the middle of the forehead, or holes or chimneys on the top of the head.

Marvin Keenze

I base my teaching on the concept that "it is the ear that sings." The voice will do only what the ear can or wants to hear. The anticipated sound is what we get; therefore, voice training is first ear training. The student should realize from the first lesson that whatever sound they are making has its source in their mind's ear. This is the ear that enables us to remember sounds, pitches, and timbres. If we can hear a sound, we can repeat it because the body coordination will respond to the thought. Students seem pleased to learn that there is this relationship between their listening and what is produced. It makes their sound a personal statement of mood, poetic content, and communication. As a teacher, if we don't like the sound or feel that it is coming from tensions or lack of coordination, we can work on that, but at least the student has some control of the situation. We must respect the student's ideas. Actually, there is *no* tension in the mind's ear. The body and respiratory system responds in a remarkable way to the singer's intent.

The nature of the voice comes out of the coordination of getting the feeling of lung pressure, spontaneous phonation, and then the full resonance of the vowel in mid-range. As students sing, they will observe that pitches will be felt in different places. I don't mind that kind of placement but after the fact.

There is a quality—there is a projection and freedom of sound that comes when the sound source (larynx and vocal tract) and the vowels are tuned together.

We talk about resonance and finding the shape of the vowel that gives us a quality that we think is musical and has projection. Early on they need to be encouraged to find that resonant shape quickly.

Cynthia Hoffmann

Something that was said by Maestro James Levine during a master class at the Juilliard School has influenced me greatly over the years. After complimenting a singer on her lovely voice, he remarked (and I paraphrase), "You have a lovely voice, but it's not about the tone, it's about the words and the meaning of the words. Bring the vowel out of the word with meaning and then you will have 'tone.'"

I was struck by words of Walter Moore, pianist and professor of lied and oratorio at the Vienna Academy of Music, during a master class at the Franz Schubert Institute. "Let the language place the voice." The tactile and meaningful sense of the language helps to move the voice forward.

Carol Webber

I believe that as a teacher it is my job to have a basic understanding of the principles of good sound production but that I must be even more keenly attuned to the individuation of each voice. I try to combine instinct and knowledge as I listen to the voice and watch the person, listening for the basic center of that voice. If there's not an obvious, usable first octave, I concentrate on whatever portion of the range displays the truest sound, the most personal sound, where the resonance is automatically the best. That's where I begin to work. I try to avoid preset vocal "positions" for each voice type. I think that evokes a mandatory product, often a sound that I call "cloned" because it emphasizes similarities in all voices instead of the subtle timbral differences that make each singer unique. We're always impressed with voices that have tremendous natural ability, voices that retain a kind of spontaneous personality in sound that I feel is too easily lost. One must teach clear technique, but not at the expense of individuation in voices.

Beginning with the first octave ("middle voice"), I identify the relationship to speech in terms of mouth opening and begin on pure vowels. When that first octave is functioning in a healthy way, it's appropriate to go on to the upper voice. If a young voice, say a freshman, seems to have an aptitude for really high facility, I won't focus exclusively on that until I hear some health and continuity in the first octave. That "health" derives from the information we just discussed—an understanding of posture, an understanding of breath, and a willingness to "speak" truthfully and simply, purifying the vowels—again, with a real ear to the individuation of each person's sound, trying not to precast each vowel in the same sound for every voice.

Bruce Lunkley

I deal with tonal resonance immediately. I listen to what sound is there and project in my mind a sound that is better resonated (i.e., "better placed" or "more focused"). It doesn't matter what terminology is used (I tend to use the terms "resonance" and "focus" more than "placement").

I build on the idea to not push the air at the voice and not grab the voice with anything but rather allow the air to become the voice. That's an idea I use a lot with my students. The air reaches the vocal cords and is transformed to a new form of energy called sound. That idea (taught to me in my work with my teacher, Roy Sheussler) has been very, very helpful.

Joan Wall

Resonance is the vocal element that gives power to the voice and lets the singer shade the color of the voice. I want my students to really understand what resonance is and what it is not. Resonance is not simply a warm, rich quality of sound made by a bass singer. Resonance occurs in all sounds—bright sounds, strident sounds, throaty sounds, and warm sounds. Resonance is the amplification and modification of a sound that occurs when a sound passes through a resonator. The sound from the larynx is amplified and modified as it passes through the vocal resonator, which is composed of the throat, the mouth, and the nose.

Good resonance for singing occurs when singers get the most amplification for the least vocal effort and when the tonal quality of their voice supports the expression of the music. Some singers say that good resonance sounds "focused" or "intense." Some say it feels as if it is vibrating in the front of the face, while others say it feels as if it is out of the body. Still others describe the sound visually, saying a resonant tone feels easy and without tension or interference in the throat.

Best resonance—or a focused tone—occurs when a frequency of the laryngeal tone matches a resonance formant of the vocal tract. In bel canto singing, a well-resonated tone has four or five overtones focused into narrow bands of energy, with a strong overtone (called the singer's formant) in the area of 2800–3200 Hz.

Resonance is adjusted by changing the size and shape of the vocal tract. Singers move their tongue, lips, jaw, soft palate, and head to make the different resonance adjustments and form vowels and timbres. They learn to maintain good resonance up and down the full range of their voice by making gradual adjustments from pitch to pitch. Therefore, singers learn good resonance by practicing pure and modified vowel exercises.

Fine singers throughout the centuries have known how their best resonance feels and sounds as they sing up and down the scale. They developed a consistent tonal quality through vowel training and careful listening.

In recent years, the phenomenon of resonance has been researched by voice scientists, such as Vennard, Sundberg, and Titze. I have all my students view the animated video *The Singer's Voice: The Vocal Tract* (Wall and Caldwell 1992–2005) that clearly illustrates the adjustments of the vocal resonator.

Singers often ask, "How do I know when I've got good resonance?" The answer is, "By noticing how the tone feels and sounds."

A well-resonated tone feels easy, free, and flexible. There is no strain or tension in the throat. Breath is easy. It can move up and down the scale, change dynamics, and change timbres easily and flexibly.

Good resonance has some identifiable traits, although a well-resonated tone can have a variety of sounds. It can be a tone of bright or dark quality, a vibrant tone appropriate for concert and opera, a brassy tone appropriate for musicals, or an airy tone appropriate for popular music. To identify good resonance in my studio, I listen for good intonation; clear vowels; a vibrant and spinning quality throughout the full range of the voice; a smooth vibrato; and an appropriate tone for style and the expression of the music.

I also look to see that the singer appears as natural as possible, without excessive tension and grimaces, and has a congruent expression for the song.

William McIver

I don't think there is a separate subject of resonance. Resonance emerges when what is being done at the larynx is matched by vowel tracking above the larynx and by appropriate breath management below. Focus comes as a result of good singing. I don't spend a lot of time asking people to place things certain ways or to feel things in certain places. If I hear problems with focus that involves nasality, I will address those problems; if I hear that the sound is deficient in upper partials, I will address that, but I really think that tonal focus is a result of other things being correctly done.

Jack Coldiron

If you don't have clear phonation, you don't have an effective tone, no matter what else you do. The first thing is to find a clear sound: an efficient, clear onset of tone. A clear phonation is absolutely necessary. "Simply speaking simply" as suggested by W. Stephen Smith in *The Naked Voice* is an effective way to achieve an easy and clear onset of vocal tone. William Vennard also recommended the "Imaginary 'H'" at the initiation of phonation will help to ensure an easy approximation of the vocal lips.

Consider the main resonators: the throat, the pharyngeal areas, and the oral cavity. Next is the feeling of "masque," the sensation of the "masque" feeling, with a good idea to balance of sound. You want clear phonation; once that is done, you can also begin to think of a comfortably low laryngeal position and a balance of the dark and the bright sounds. Bright forward vowels are always possible, even when the larynx is in a comfortably low position. They are not mutually exclusive concepts.

Helen Hodam

I talk about the direction of the breath and the idea of the forward vowel and the motion of the breath. I do talk about forward vowels, facial resonance, and frontal resonance. I tell them what it may feel like in middle voice, what it feels like when it's way above the staff. I use images—a variety, because one could help someone and mean nothing to another.

I do use the word "focus," but I explain that "placement" could be erroneous because you don't "place" anything. I do emphasize that they shouldn't worry about or think about vibrato but rather feel vibration—that's so important.

For the beginners, I mainly talk about what to do with the breath once it starts, that feeling of breath connection. It can be a simple onset exercise in middle voice.

Barbara Doscher

My ideas are based on an understanding of fixed vowel formants. Coffin, Sundberg, and Helmholtz: it's been in the physics books for a hundred years. Persuading people that this is not a method is an interesting attempt. In methodology, what you do with your understanding of fixed vowel formants is your own choice.

Lindsey Christiansen

The three major areas of work that any singer must do are breath management, resonance, and phonation.

Dale Moore

One can say in a sense that there's an ideal resonance adjustment for every pitch on every vowel, not that we want to make the student so conscious of each note that he or she cannot sing.

Phonation and registration are almost one. I can tell you what my preference is: I think people have a tonal preference. My preference is a very centered sound. I talk a lot about the center of the tone. I like the sound to be brighter at the bottom than at the top, but I do like it to be even.

Laura Brooks Rice

I like to teach a balance up and down. Very quickly, they can understand what I'm talking about when I say it's very much like the balance knob on your stereo: if you turn it too much to the top, it's too tinny; if you turn it too much to the bottom (bass) it's too woofy. You want to have a nice balance between.

Finding that balance of chiaroscuro is an important goal. I introduce them to the laryngopharynx, oropharynx, and nasopharynx of the vocal tract and [point out] that these three areas of resonance need to be coordinated as we move through the registers. I like to start with finding balance in their speaking, or modal, resonance. I may have them put one hand on their collarbone and one hand on the base of their skull and have them hum or sing whatever vowel they feel has their optimum resonance. I encourage them to try to feel vibration in both areas. When they adjust the pharynx by lifting the palate and allowing the larynx to lower, they begin to feel the balance. We may intone [i][ɛ][ɑ][o][u] to find which vowel allows for the best balance and then work to align all of the vowels. Balancing resonance and registration is the next hurdle. When they understand laryngeal tilt as they move through the primo and then secondo passaggio, the voice begins to sound even from top to bottom.

Edith Davis Tidwell

I always say "Space around the Place." I go for the place first—the tiniest dot, the pinpoint (that whiney place) and then think space around that.

Also, I encourage the student to begin with a tiny whine and intone glides up and down (the siren). And beginning with that ease at onset, I use the "messa di voce" a lot in my teaching.

Meribeth Dayme

For me, optimal resonance comes with alignment and imagination. When we have these two things, the throat will respond and the resonance will happen. One good example of imagination is Bette Midler. If you managed to see her in *Divine Madness*, she sang every possible sound, from rock to classical, and it was all at the drop of the hat. It was possible because of her response to her incredible imagination along with what was going on in the story, the text, and the way she was performing. A singer needs to be in a position to respond to their imagination. When they do that, then resonance works as a part of the whole. When a singer starts trying to manipulate the pharynx in order to feel something going on there, you can bet that it's contracting and that the sound is not optimal.

Robert Edwin

It is exciting to work on resonation (the amplification and filtering of vocal fold activity) with students because most of them come into the studio with a limited understanding of their potential for a variety of vocal sounds. We have three resonators that make up the vocal tract: the throat, the mouth, and the nose. Unlike fixed-resonator instruments such as the trumpet, piano, and clarinet, the resonators of the voice are flexible, capable of changing shape and size. My students are encouraged to explore all of the tonal qualities they possess from wicked witch nasality to cowardly lion thickness and everything in between. In my "Bach to rock" studio, all kinds of sounds may be required for performance, so those sounds need to be practiced. My opera singers belt and my belters make operatic sounds.

Stephen King

What did somebody say? "Singing—once you get singing down to just breathing and vowels, you're done."

I do a lot of work with vowels and vowel tuning. I do not have the Berton Coffin chart on my piano. I'm not going to say that may not work for somebody; I don't think that, for me, it's an effective method. I am not able to commit to a system that's going to work for everybody. Because of technology we now have so much access to acoustical information. After all, that is really what we are talking about—acoustical sounds that are often, especially in opera, beyond the realm of speech. For instance, a tenor and soprano both singing "ah" on their high

F an octave apart are not doing the same thing. Yet, their job is for us to hear a well-tuned "ah."

A vowel is a complex interplay of tongue, vocal tract, larynx, and jaw. There is a positive "tension" or "traction" when vowels are well produced. This is definitely the issue that I find pretty egregious: there's a lot of "faked masque singing" in the conservatories/schools. There is far too much time spent chasing the "ring" as if it can be made rather than allowed. Resonance results from balanced phonation through tuned vowels. Maybe it's inevitable that young singers don't have the whole thing figured out yet. They come to school, and everybody says, "Oh, well you're singing too far back in your throat—get it out." Maybe in the quest to figure out the balance, they shove the sound "forward" or are encouraged to do so and cut off the ring in the voice and greatly diminish the power of the resonance. There's so much of that, it makes one wonder what we're doing. I honestly think there's a definite sound that has emerged in the American conservatory related to this and related to the use of the IPA. Writing a symbol for a vowel and thinking that it's an absolute has very many deleterious effects on the sound of the voice. If, for instance, working on Italian, the teacher/coach says, "I need a brighter 'ah' vowel," and the male student without really realizing the consequences dutifully replies with a spread "ah" vowel and an elevated larynx, a chance for complete resonance is lost.

I spend a lot of time griping to my students at school about overclosing all the so-called closed vowels, and then getting these hideous sounds with white noise all around them and breath not moving anywhere. It's really tricky, but for me, everybody I teach who I think is a great singer, when the breath is right and we're singing the sound the right way, and letting the vocal tract vibrate and letting the whole body work as an instrument, the resonance just happens. For a lot of people, when they hear the word "resonance," they immediately think of a sound that is inherently "forward" or "bright." Those are words that do not enter my vocabulary. Maybe at some point they did, but they don't anymore, because I'm definitely working the other way and trying to avoid those kinds of terms.

The goal is to get the singer to sing the word on the breath and then align everything as much as possible. Of course, there are people with what are referred to as "darker" voices—rounder, or warmer, and they may need careful tuning to find optimal resonance that carries in a hall. I am just trying to find balance, so that the voice speaks in an honest way. There seems now to be so much manufactured resonance, because there's so much available information. Because people have been bombarded with this or are attracted to it, it is very possible to avoid the way the entirety of the voice works.

I'm just trying to get the vocal tract balanced and the mouth in a comfortable position, the tongue on the teeth, the throat relaxed and yet engaged when they breathe and go from there. There's got to be some essential engagement in the whole instrument.

Jeannette LoVetri

I rarely worry about "resonance." Rather, I talk about singing undistorted vowels in a clear tone. If you do that, resonance shows up automatically. In CCM styles, singers are always miked. They do not need "singer's formant" resonance to "project." Even [with] classical singers, however, a clear tone and an efficiently shaped vowel will generate resonance and intensity coupled with increased subglottic pressure such that the sound will fill an auditorium easily. Resonance is a by-product of singing, not a way of making sound.

Mary Saunders-Barton

The interaction between registration and resonance is central to musical theater singing technique, so it is hard to separate the "source" from the "filter." Current industry demands call for singers who are literally vocal chameleons. Versatility is a priority. Singers need to be capable of reproducing the many different sounds that tell our human story authentically and sustainably without injury. Teaching such a flexible use of the voice depends on fine-tuning the instrument top to bottom by careful process of register balancing in order to achieve a reliable access to any amalgam of chest/head dominance on any given pitch.

I very much appreciate the work of Brian Gill on the advantages of shared nasal/oral resonance. A degree of nasality enhances power without added effort. The use of partially occluded exercises, humming, straw, and "ng" exercises are invaluable in establishing an effortless tone focus.

Of course, vowels always lead us where we need to go. Women and men find their head voice on [u]. Chest on [a] and [e]. The same applies to men—it's a gender-neutral approach. The terminology I use equates the male falsetto with the female head voice.

Learning to blend registers starts with "closed" vowels [u] and [i] in speech (chest dominant) quality by bridging that first passaggio for women (E4–G4), which is the second passaggio for men.

I am always grateful for the inspiration of colleague Joan Melton who reminds us that we make *all* sounds with "one voice" and that is the only one we have. Understanding how to take advantage of audio enhancement is also vital for young performers in today's musical theater profession. Yes, they can whisper or shriek onstage.

Strategies for Teaching Tone

The teachers employ a series of teaching strategies through which they convey and encourage the production of a free, resonant tone. Some strategies include vowel modification; placement or resonance sensation feedback; use of specific vowels or consonants to clarify tonal resonance; and the use of speech to find forward resonance.

Laura Brooks Rice

I show them where their resonators are. We talk about where they resonate and where they have to feel their resonance. I introduce them to the soft palate and how that helps them to feel a lift.

Helen Hodam

I talk about the motion and direction of the breath. I tell them about what it feels like in the middle voice and what it feels like when it's way above the staff. I use images. I emphasize feeling. Some people talk about the point of a triangle and that the throat is open.

You think of your breath as energy, but it is always something that is moving, never held. Breath sustains the tone. And the release of the breath is used in a musical fashion. If you get the feeling of the breath constantly moving, and of moving forward to the next note, and to the next, you have a musical phrase and a rhythmic phrase.

Lindsey Christiansen

We talk a lot about the speaking voice. I think that in the area of resonance and phonation, the use of the speaking voice can be invaluable. I have the students use their speaking voice in a way that will not feel natural but be closer to what they need to do when they sing.

I talk about the inner smile, the feeling of "smelling a rose." I talk about a feeling of width, width on the inside of the face. I have borrowed a few Berton Coffin exercises that I use for registration kinds of things: humming things, things that get the chords together without any pressure under them. I think it's very important that the cords phonate easily, that we get that very easy connection.

Dale Moore

Choice of vowel and choice of vocalize is so important because it is by that means and your communication of that to the student that you set up what is going to be their response, good or bad.

I find that "ng," "mmmmm," and "nnn" (i.e., nasals) are very helpful in helping the student find that resonance adjustment. Exercises built on "hung"—and on that "ng"—are the only exercises that have stayed with me through all thirty-six years of teaching.

Bruce Lunkley

I use a series of "non-singing sounds," especially with the female voice. With cries—a "she" cry, a "few" cry, in any comfortable spot where they just choose to do it. I encourage them to go higher and lighter until they tell you, "Oh, I felt that." Then I'll say, "Why don't you just sustain that feeling in a singing sound and not worry how it sounds—now bring it down." It works almost all the time. I use the idea of speech with women who have trouble in their middle-low registers and help them find a sound that has some presence and is easy to do.

With men, I may use some of the same cries. Most often, I use very forward speech sounds. I work very hard on that in the first several lessons. They need to feel as if they're finding something out about their voice, that they're making a better sound, and that another sound is possible. They get excited and tend to work harder. I'm big on motivation—that seems to be very helpful. They go out of the lesson feeling, "Hey, I made not only a better sound, it was easier, maybe I went higher, maybe I went lower, maybe I found out that there was more to my voice than I thought there was!" I think that's terribly important as a "kickoff."

Edward Baird

I use the phrase "arching the vowel," although I understand the people who say, "You don't want to talk about 'forward'—you can't pick up a tone and put it 'forward.'" But these things are all sensation based, and if a person is gaining a sensation that is good or is bad, you can work away from that, or you can work toward it.

Joan Wall

First, I help the singer establish good body use (posture) and breath. If there is not a good use of breath or if there is poor body use or excessive tension, resonance will suffer.

But, ultimately, most of our resonance work will be done in vowel exercises. We often whisper vowels to find the vowel shape and transfer this into singing. We talk about the position of the tongue, lips, and jaw for vowel production. My students learn the IPA so that we can more easily communicate about vowel sounds.

We do articulation exercises to achieve free movements of the jaw, tongue, lips, and soft palate. Our goal is for the student to sing clear vowels and to realize how even the smallest movement of the vocal tract has a major effect on the resonating tone.

For those singers who do not respond well to direct physical suggestions, I talk about the sensation of resonance, such as a tall feeling when singing higher pitches or not letting the tone drop for lower pitches. We do hums (such as m, n, and ng) and work with images that relate to a free jaw and good breath management.

I want my students to feel and hear the resonance in their voice, to sing with consistent tonal quality throughout the range of their voice, and to choose the most expressive timbres for the song.

William McIver

I don't spend a lot of time asking people to place things certain ways or to feel things certain ways. If I hear problems with focus that involve nasality, I will address those problems; if I hear that the sound is deficient in upper partials, I will address that, but I really think that tonal focus is a result of other things being correctly done.

I do use nasal continuants (i.e., m, n, and ng), first by themselves and then in conjunction with vowels—usually with a high forward vowel first, to help develop a sense of the upper partials that need to be in all vowels. If students feel things in certain places, and the tone is, to my ear, freely and correctly produced, then they can tell me what they feel. That can be beneficial, but I don't try to tell them what they should feel. I try to get them to sing with freedom, and then let them tell me what they did feel.

Barbara Doscher

There are many ways you can approach this concept. There are first-formant vowels that reside in certain places in the vocal frequency—this is an actual physical law. If you don't understand that, you have left out one-third of the singing instrument because you don't understand the acoustical properties. I was a student of Coffin's, and I admire him very much. Having said that, you have to realize this is where I part from his ideas. I think each voice varies in its physiology and anatomy; there are individual concepts of what an [a] vowel is. People think about these things in different ways. You have to be resilient even though you firmly believe that there are such things as fixed vowel formants.

Edith Davis Tidwell

An exercise I use is "three sets of three"—I teach arpeggios—nine pitches—do mi sol do mi do sol mi do—on three vowels—[iii ooo uuu]—hence, three sets of three—outlining that "phrase" dot to dot, lightly. This is not to exaggerate core involvement with staccati but to merely sense that pinpoint placement. Then with that same arpeggio and vowel sequence, sing with intentional legato, connecting those dots with core engagement.

Chapter Four

Registration

It is very difficult to separate discussion of "tone" from that of registration, although both are distinct elements in vocal production. Several of the comments made about tone also involved discussion of registration as well as resonance. However, for the purposes of this study and the need to isolate each concept of vocal technique for examination, registration was considered independently. Many of the comments related to the discussion of tone also apply to registration.

1. Opinions vary regarding how many registers of the voice exist.
2. Sensations of "placement" change as the singer goes through changes of registration.
3. Teachers work for freedom through registration change.
4. Resonance and registration are linked.
5. Certain conditions can be utilized to help the singer negotiate passaggi and changes of register.
6. Vowel work is an important key to registration adjustment.
7. Smooth changes of registration involve subtle adjustments of breath, phonation, and vowel resonance. Coordination of these elements is a fundamental part of vocal training.

TEACHERS' REMARKS

Joan Wall

I define a register as a group of consecutive pitches of a certain timbre produced by a certain relationship among laryngeal, resonance, and breath adjustments.

In my studio, I speak of chest, middle, head, and whistle for women, and low, mixed, head, and falsetto for men. The registers overlap each other, which gives the singer opportunity for considerable flexibility of tonal production. I also point out that every four or five notes is an acoustical change that I call a "lift of the voice."

When thinking about registration, I always keep in mind the seemingly diverse teachings of William Vennard, who taught there are two registers produced by specific laryngeal adjustments (light and heavy mechanism), and of Berton Coffin, who taught multiple register adjustments produced by a careful selection of vowels. My premise is that registers are produced by a combination of laryngeal, resonance, and breath adjustments and that singers can develop considerable control over registers.

Edward Baird

I'm basically a three-register person. I understand all the various thinkings that go along with two registers, five registers, and so forth, but basically, I believe there are three registers because that's what I find most people have when they come in to work. They've got two adjustments, which means three registers. I think that a definition of registers needs to be able to encompass all of the various theories of registration. For a large majority of singers, I find there's a change of quality, a shifting of gears, an adjustment that's audible to the ear when they come out of the chest and into the middle, and another one when they go from the middle into the head.

Helen Swank

We're back to establishing a feel for placement because that changes, and we're establishing an understanding of airflow through passaggio. It has always seemed to me that most passaggio problems come from pushing too much air through that area at the wrong time. Many of the students profit by a sense of relaxation and of "lightening" the air mentally as well as physically through the passaggio area. As they go into the lower voice, "chest voice" (whatever you want to label it), they have to learn how to utilize airflow without it being forced or pushed. Placement sense and controlled breath energy seem to work together to smooth registration problems.

When you work with aspects of placement, a student develops awareness that they "felt" they had more space here or there; they can begin to identify some of those things, and then they can begin to utilize airflow connecting to tubal space on the inside. Those little manifestations or ideas just help them in metering. Students realize that. I would never teach a student as if that was what was actually happening, but the sensation is there and valuable to understand.

Carol Webber

I think it's important to introduce a student to the standard descriptions of different voice types. This is where you can use some of the quantified information that tends to put on a chart what each voice type will embrace in terms of range, proper tessitura, and so on, so that awareness is there; then you can discuss the passaggi of the voice, the shifts that happen in terms of opening the mouth as the pitches ascend, and there's a framework through which the student can understand it. Drawing exclusively on registration is counterproductive, and again, I avoid anything that is so preset that each student has to fit it, rather than the point of view fitting each student. The most important thing to remember with any teaching, any student, in academia or professional, each time a person comes through your door, that's a unique, special individual who cannot be treated just like all your other students. The same approach and the same information is a basis, but you have to allow for each person to be unique.

Marvin Keenze

I consider registration to be the ability to color a tone in any part of the range for the communication of emotion, for poetic atmosphere, or for vocal production ease. This comes from the singer's mental image of the poetry and the situation. The ability to register the voice is developed slowly through the vocalizes that we give and the suggestions about color and meaning. This can be developed from the first lesson and our suggesting that it is the sound that carries the meaning and that vocal freedom is encouraged by a balanced registration.

Different qualities can help the student find freedom in different areas of the voice, especially in the "calling voice." The breath responds to that. You can mention that when a voice goes off kilter, it's because one or both of those two things aren't working in equilibrium. It's a balance: the breath and the phonation, the phonation and the resonation, or the registration and the pitch.

Dale Moore

I think the most important key to even registration is vowel. I don't believe in "covering" or any sudden change. There again, it is a matter of scaling each note so that the voice is prepared for entering the upper voice—the head voice in the case of the male or the upper range in terms of the female voice. I think this is done by vowel and the narrowing of the vowel—at least this is the concept that I teach. But the important thing is that we know something has to happen and that the vowel is one of the parts of singing over which we do have control. The key lies in the vowel.

Lindsey Christiansen

I think there are three registers. I think there are two mechanisms, the "heavy mechanism" and the "light mechanism," but I think they mix together in the middle. I used to say just two mechanisms, two registers, but I've found that it's more useful for students to think in terms of a middle as well as a high and a low.

I love Vennard's image of a test tube of sand and water. You mix it up and the bottom has more sand and the top has more water. The bottom and the top have some things in common—the very bottom (i.e., very low chest voice) and the very high need to have the same kind of very wide opening—there is less in the middle. The very low bottom is something women don't have to sing very often (it's something men have to deal with more than women do). What is often referred to as the "bottom" in women's voices (especially sopranos) is the really low middle, the area of middle C to G in which a large opening is not necessary. When real chest voice is needed, a large opening and obviously brighter vowels are needed. Learning to have options [is important]. To say that "always on E-flat you have to go to chest" is absurd. There should be tons of color options, and they're obviously related to registration.

Oren Brown

Passaggios! Yes, that's a tricky word. Passaggios exist because different physical things happen in the throat and in the creation of a frequency or pitch [he describes the physiology of the larynx and the muscle antagonism that takes place between the cricothyroid and the thyroarytenoid muscles]. So the ultimate in training is to make friends out of those two and to coordinate them. The finest singers have what you can call "one register." It results from a counterbalance of these muscles and a development of adjustment. I have discovered this in working with singers with dysfunctional passaggios: they are carrying too much tension in their voices too high, rather than allowing the natural adjustments to take place.

[As to the number of registers], there's been a lot of study. [Many years ago], Harry Hollien and his research group in Florida devised "loft, flute, modal, and pulse" as registers. "Pulse" is the lowest, "modal" is the speaking voice, "loft" compares to falsetto, and "flute" is the very highest. He devised these terms because these were qualities he could measure on his scientific instruments. But a word like "modal" is too easily confused with the "modes," as in "minor mode." So now the registers are designated by numbers, with "one" as the lowest, "two" as speaking voice, "three" as falsetto, and "four" as the very highest.

There are "break points" in the voice. Soprano coloratura range starts at about B-flat or B above the treble staff (B5). . . . A French scientist by the name of Tarneau tested the voice of a famous coloratura who had a high B-flat above high C (Bb6). Her change into the fourth register came at C#6—that was a very high voice.

Most people say that the so-called passaggio is at Eb or E or F, which is a higher point in both the male and female voice. The reason they say this is because they have been building their scales from the bottom up, and they keep a pressure that does not allow the vocal folds to make their change at the natural points. They hold on to the adjustment that they have and push the voice higher, until it has to do something. They are really forcing if they do not allow the voice to make the change at the natural passaggio (for low voices, around A, Bb, or B; for higher voices, around B or C). I have found that singers tend to carry tension in their voice too high, rather than allowing the natural adjustments to take place.

Laura Brooks Rice

I talk about passaggio, and I talk about how it requires an enormous amount of additional support. I talk about "pulling back" to go forward (pulling back the arches of the soft palate). You always have to feel the sound forward in the mask as you're going, no matter where you are.

Shirlee Emmons

Registration is yet another place where the acoustical vowels will be of help. When expert singers describe their successful traversal of the passaggio, they use many different locutions to translate their feelings about it: it must be "fronter, more nasal, narrower, more mask-y, shallower," and so forth. Each of these words simply describes skillful singers' own perceptions of what they are doing in a passaggio. It is my experience that in each and every passaggio of all voice categories, the transition will be aided by going through the passaggio with a smaller mouth opening, a "fronter" and higher tongue, and often with protruding lips. Therefore, I ask that the vowel modifications used in passaggi must be those that supply that kind of mouth opening, that tongue position, and (much of the time but not always) those protruding lips.

In addition, I often allude to registers in terms of percentages of head and chest content. It appears to clarify the singers' understanding of how to accommodate this complicated issue. I encourage the male singers to regard all the notes leading to the upper passaggio as versions of chest voice. In the passaggio, they are engaged in making a transition to a fifty-fifty mix of head and chest, which they continue to use for the upper range.

Female singers have several registers to traverse. Let's start on the bottom. They will handle the low voice problems much more efficiently if they understand fully what choices are available. Much time is spent on learning to execute skillfully the bottom and middle range notes in one of these gears:

1. total chest
2. a mix of predominantly chest content with some head content
3. a mix of predominantly head content with some chest content
4. a fifty-fifty mix
5. total head

The choice of which gear to use depends upon esthetic considerations and natural vocal limitations. Moving higher, the notes that lie just before the upper passaggio (the mishandling of which results in the familiar flattening in this area) should be sung ideally and most often in a forty-sixty mix, not in fifty-fifty, which is tempting. The upper passaggio is the place wherein head content must become paramount. It could be regarded as roughly twenty-five–seventy-five. Whistle I then consider to be a rough ratio of 5 percent chest to 95 percent head; and super whistle, 100 percent head. This use of approximate percentage numbers appears to help clarify a complex subject for the singers, especially in those areas where the voice has problems caused by registration. Having quantified the ideal mix, it then remains for us to learn to execute these mixes at will.

Bruce Lunkley

I think the eventual goal is a unified voice, one that can go from high to low without an obvious change to the audience, but at the same time I think you need to tell the student that occasionally you do use a register for what it's worth. You can jump down into a chest note because you want an effect or because the composer has obviously asked you to do it (i.e., some of Verdi, where the vocal line is low and there is a full orchestra). What are you going to do?

William McIver

With regard to the young male voice, I probably spend the greatest amount of time with registration. This is what separates "good teaching" from "less than good teaching." One must help young male singers understand the area between the first and second passaggi; what happens in terms of vowels as one ascends; what happens in terms of mouth opening; and what happens in terms of what I refer to as "moving to a thinner string" while retaining resonantal balance. That takes a lot of time as work can proceed in many different ways. [See the section "Strategies for Teaching Registration" for further discussion.]

Jack Coldiron

The first task is to establish a solid middle range in the voice, and to realize that the modal voice is foundational to singing. If I were required to say what I believe, I would say I believe in modal and head registration.

I do not consider falsetto to be a usable register except in the case of falsettists (countertenors). In my experience, most falsettists are truly baritones.

Marcia Baldwin

I work with the middle voice first—that's the core of the voice with all voice types. Get that solid, get the support and the resonance lined up in the middle voice, and then go up into the top and down into the bottom. For head voice, it feels as though one goes from the masque straight up into the head.

I believe in the idea of "voix mixe" for beauty of tone when one moves down into the chest voice. Keep the mask resonance while you gradually drop down into chest openness. The chest cavity has to remain open for resonance—that's very important, although I don't dwell too much on that with younger students. They tend to beef up the sound that way. If they're locking the chest, then I will talk about the chest remaining open. It adds an incredible amount of resonance to leave the chest cavity open.

To my ear, vowel modification makes singing sound unnatural. Keep the vowel pure, keep the vowel in the place in your mouth where it belongs, and drop your jaw around it.

Barbara Doscher

I find, both with male and female voices, that as far as tonal resonance is concerned, the middle voice is the most difficult area to teach (and to make coaches understand what you're doing). It's particularly difficult for high women voices. Males also have a difficult time because people continually want to hear a rich, warm sound in the middle voice. That's fine for those voices that make nice rich, warm sounds in the middle voice while at the same time staying well focused. But I would say it is not true of 75 percent of voices. The focus (i.e., the centering of the sound) has to come first. I think it will then get fuller within that voice's capabilities. The voice is going to tell you what it's going to do—you don't have to superimpose your ideas on it.

Leslie Guinn

My experience as a singer and as a teacher has led me to identify with a "two-register" system. The earliest lessons are designed to help the student feel the textures of each, gaining access to these textures through specific vowels, dynamics, and pitches. Our goal is then to coordinate the registers. We often do exercises that will catch the student's larynx unaware in order to awaken new sensations and sounds. I have found good results with rapid, vigorous arpeggi of an octave or tenth, oscillating the upper third or fourth, and then sustaining the uppermost pitch immediately on the same breath with no discernible pause or preparation. There are many variations, of course. The new, healthier technique, or balance of registers, is then identified and repeated.

Meribeth Dayme

I think registration is a matter of balance—physical, perception of sound, imagination, and mind. The mind boggles at all the studies on registration. I am certainly not an expert on registration, and I pass that on over to people who are.

Robert Edwin

Phonation and registration, the creation of vocalized sound, occurs when the vocal folds adduct (come together). Since the voice is gender neutral, all of my students use all of their voice from the lowest to the highest notes in their respective ranges. They all vocalize in the two main modes of vocal fold activity: mode 1, commonly identified by its pre-science term "chest voice," and mode 2, more commonly known as "head voice" or "falsetto." They also use mode 0 (vocal fry) and mode 3 (whistle register). Both my boys/men and girls/women are required to execute smooth mode 1 and 2 register transitions to produce a unified voice when needed. Because they are all vocalizing continually in both major modes, those transitions become much easier to do.

Stephen King

I'm in the camp of males have modal (speech) voice (mode 1) and mode 2, which is the falsetto. This is consistent with what we know about the larynx. Terms like "head voice" are not applicable to the professional male singer and only serve to confuse the training. Since all I train are male operatic singers, I just work on mode 1, unless it is a countertenor (and I only have one at Houston Grand). I use falsetto not at all, except therapeutically. I might start them in the falsetto until it transitions. That's typically with people who have hurt themselves or are hurting themselves, or are just unable to delineate the difference in the two mechanisms.

I will religiously start every male voice in the middle of the scale and gradually go up until there has to be "adjustment" to avoid the shout. I'm not going to apologize for that. I think that's how you build strong male voices and get rid of the crooning and all the spreading, "ramming it forward," and all the other "avoidance maneuvers" that we hear and see.

With women, I'm operating with the same thing: you have mode 1 (which people used to call "chest"), mode 2 (which people used to call "head voice"), and then the "bell" register, mode 3. I work on each one with women. I think that needs to be a really big part of physical understanding for everybody: that you can't teach men and women the same way. I don't think men teachers are going to have success with women if they try to teach them the way they sing; and I don't think female teachers will have success with men if they try to teach them the way they sing. That, to me, is the essential registration difference, and then how vowel tuning works in the two different voice types. I work at it from that standpoint. All my vocal exercises are from wherever I find them—some of them have been around for three hundred years. I've had people criticize me working on chest voice with female operatic singers—well, have you ever looked at a Verdi or Wagner score?

I gave a class last year (as master teacher for the NATS Foundation teaching interns), and I talked about starting from the bottom up and what I considered the essentials for young teachers. Immediately (I knew it was going to happen) somebody threw up their hand and said, "I don't think you should introduce chest voice to females." And I said, "Well if you want to build a strong signal in vocal folds that can sing flexibly and completely in the operatic repertoire, you need to know how to do that." These little oblong, breathy, undeveloped sounds that we hear with some of the young female singers are never going to generate the sort of signal necessary to sing freely in a space without amplification. I call training it training "the bicep of the voice." It's a building block of the voice. Sure, anything can be overdone, but when you do that work and you keep that limited, if you need to, and then you integrate it with everything else, I find it very useful. Most females I teach tell me, "Wow, my high voice (above the staff) is so much better because of what we did in the lower part of my range." Maybe that's just anecdotal, but I go at it that way. It's a confusing subject. I totally respect the people who say, "I'm just trying to find the legato, and I don't point out registration of passaggio at all—we just work on singing legato," and I think, "Okay, that's great, too." If you can unify a voice from a low G to high C, two and a half octaves, go for it.

Jeannette LoVetri

In CCM [contemporary commercial music] styles, you sing primarily in chest register (modal voice), TA [thyroarytenoid] dominant, or speaking voice quality 98 percent of the time. The upper register (head/falsetto) functions as an extension in most voices for expressive purposes and is necessary in the voice studio as a means to keep the voice from becoming too "stuck," "heavy," or pressured. All singers should have a developed head (loft) register even if they do not use it in their material when performing.

If you cannot hear and feel the difference between chest and head registers, it is very difficult to do anything else efficiently since the register changes are primarily vocal fold changes. This has an effect upon the vertical laryngeal position, the shape of the vocal tract, and the trans-glottal airflow (or breath flow) in any given pitch range, male or female. It is difficult to change vowel sound shaping if the larynx is not in an optimal position to make the necessary sounds for any given musical style. The vocal folds are the source of the sound, and the quality of tone they make, based upon the vocal fold response in each register, produces the sound. If you do not deal directly with registration, you will end up with a voice that is less than it could be.

Mary Saunders-Barton

Learning to blend registers starts with "closed" vowels [u] and [i] in speech (chest dominant) quality by bridging that first passaggio for women (E4–G4), which is the second passaggio for men.

STRATEGIES FOR TEACHING REGISTRATION

Marcia Baldwin

It begins with vowel purity. Once the middle voice has been warmed up, I use exercises up and down the scale and arpeggios, so the student feels how the voice goes from the front of the masque up into the head and then down into the lower voice. It's particularly important to bring the head down into the chest with descending exercises from top to bottom so that you don't have a yodel effect going into chest.

Helen Hodam

You warm up the middle voice first. You don't start suddenly sustaining a lot of high notes. First, I find out where the problems are; then I do exercises that are "long" (i.e., that take in the whole range). I do long thirds, long arpeggios. As far as "breaks," I explain to them that it has to be strengthened, that it's a general process. I do certain, short exercises where I build around the triad, where you go back and forth, back and forth on certain vowels. First you find the "best vowel" and then sometimes I work from the top and bring it down. I may only do four notes, such as 4–3, 4–3, 4–3, 2–1, changing vowels. I usually work with closed vowels—sometimes the [i] vowel works like a charm; sometimes it will be [u]. The outer fringes of the range—the very low, the very high—demand a special approach. I do talk about width opening a lot, the "inner smile," the beginning of a yawn with a smile, particularly for the high notes above the staff for the sopranos.

Edward Baird

Basically (and this will fall into another one of your subparts in working through the passaggio, in working into the various registers), I find that the most efficient and the quickest way to get at these things is through a system of vowel modification—you diagnose how they're singing a given vowel. If it's too far forward, too far back, or whatever, then ask them to modify it in the direction of some other vowel, in the direction that the tone needs to be adjusted. I work a lot through that, not only for balancing resonance, but also for finding registration. This matter of vowel modification: there's a greater tendency in the male voice to push the middle register up too high, like females tend to push the chest voice up too high. In young singers, it may be because they've just never found it; they just don't know there's another world up there. To get them to experience it, you first have to get them in the right ballpark. You might have to go to somewhat of an extreme. In using a more closed vowel, you can usually get them up there. Usually, the more closed vowels are the easiest ones to get into the upper register.

One of the exercises I use for developing uniformity of sound is [i–e–a–o–u] on a single pitch. We start in the middle register, somewhere in the middle of the range, and use closed vowels to help the adjustment as pitch goes higher. Rather than just go up to a pitch and then suddenly changing, I try to get them to go through a little mixture. You maybe go halfway in with this and then the next semitone up you go all the way through, or maybe a third, two-thirds, then all the way over. That makes the registers mesh better; you don't have a sudden shift.

Marvin Keenze

I always listen for what I consider to be the best qualities in a voice, and I work from there. I vocalize the singer through a large range on a variety of vowels and combinations of vowels from the beginning. I use the first-formant tuning chart to find the optimum vowel for particular pitches. If there are vocal freedom problems with the vowel, I go through the optimum vowel to the problem one. I use a scale that changes the vowel at the appropriate places to aid in bridging the register transition areas. The proper vowel and registration makes the pitches possible. A foolproof way of finding the right timbre for a pitch is to have the singer put a finger in each ear to cut out air conduction hearing as he or she sings. When you tune the voice to the bone-conduction hearing and then take your fingers out of your ears, the rest of the sound drops into place in a balanced registration. There is less effort put into the fundamental frequency, and the projection comes through the harmonics. The quality that is produced is just right for the individual singer. This simple act is a point of reference for the singer and a way to find an ease of production on higher pitches.

I also use the spontaneous little onset vowel [ʌ] and then go to speech. I use speech in my teaching, but a rather more dramatic, colorful speech or speech in different registers. Experiment through speech and different pitches, but not by raising anything. Therefore, you are raising the pitch of your voice by changing the registration, not by reaching for it. The student will find that he or she can sing higher with right quality; you're teaching registration with pitch. I do that early on with dramatic speech intensified. So they're finding out that different qualities can help them find freedom in different areas of their voice.

I don't find passaggio problems. If they learn to adjust the breath pressure and it is right, there is only one vowel they can sing. The vowel will modify itself because they don't have any choice. I do exercises above the passaggio on different vowels, particularly [i] and [u].

Richard Miller

Sometimes you have to go half step by half step in building the range, particularly with young males. There are many ways to do range extension, and of course, there are all sorts of arpeggiated figures that help. I'm very much given to agility factor in building the upper range first, rather than sostenuto things. I think it's a mistake to try and build the upper range (I mean, you do have to explore it)—but people who start in the extremes of the voice make a mistake because, I repeat: whatever the problems are in the middle voice will be exacerbated as you go up the scale by the very muscular activity of the vocal folds.

Lindsey Christiansen

I think the [e] vowel is a marvelous vowel for tenors in that higher passaggio area. The [i] vowel is also good for men in that so-called first passaggio area. For women, when they're dealing with the upper passaggio, I think it's very important again that it stay "lean" so that the depth that's needed for the high doesn't get "used up" in the passaggio. There's again that feeling of dark and bright at the same time. The center of the tone is very bright and very concentrated.

William McIver

With the men I try to gather the voice with the front vowels such as [i] and [e]. To that you can add mouth opening. However, should you open the mouth too much before you have some sort of feeling of head in the sound, you're generally going to get a throaty sound. I've found success on either side of the vowel spectrum with [i] and [u]. Often, the last one they learn to do in top voice correctly is [ɑ] in that it must connect with both the fronted [i] and rounded [u]. My approach is to start with [i] or [u] and then apply it to an exercise like 5–8–8–8–5–3–1, for instance, [i–i–ɑ–u–i–i–i] or [u–u–ɑ–u–u–u–u] (on those pitches). Then insert the [ɑ] in place of the [i] or [u] if they have the feeling of head voice on the [i] or [u] and can retain it without spreading in the [ɑ], then you gain something.

Bruce Lunkley

We discuss registration when it rears its ugly head. Some students have very little problem with it; others seemingly have a new register every three or four notes.

I help them find correct resonance in the pitch area above the problem and then carry it down; that tends to solve the problem.

It's also helpful to get the student to approach it without fear. When they are tentative, they simply fall back from it, and the result is a sound that also falls back. Sometimes you have to urge them to lighten as they come down because they'll carry too much of their big sound in the top down through it—it'll sort of plop over into another register, and you don't want that.

Students need to be aware that the voice sounds differently in different sections of the pitch range.

Tape recordings are very helpful. It's helpful to go by feel, rather than by how it sounds in their ear. I stress that a lot.

Joan Wall

I want singers to smooth out all register transition for an even quality throughout their voice and to develop the flexibility to use each register to its maximum for expression. We use exercises that teach the students the certain relationships of breath, pitch, and vowel that control different registers.

They learn that breath pressure changes for different registrations. A greater lift or flow in breath—and less pressure—is used for a higher register. When vowels close and round (as from [a] to [ɑ], or [ɛ] to [e], etc.) it helps the singer to make the transition from a lower to a higher registration. A relaxed neck and a slightly tilted head position help to avoid a jutting chin and unnecessary tension on the throat-neck area. This in turn helps the singer to negotiate a passage with ascending pitches that move from a lower to a higher registration.

I show singers how to use registration adjustments to sing with tonal variety and enhance the emotional and stylistic needs of the music. Working with "messa di voce" exercises, the singer learns to make register adjustments on the crescendo-diminuendo by changing the vowel (resonance adjustment) and breath pressure. They learn that a single pitch can be sung in more than one register. Our vowel exercises are structured to illustrate how vowel production relates to pitch and how this knowledge can be helpful in a song.

With women, I work to smooth out their major passaggio (around Eb4) and their secondary passaggio (around F5). I have them practice singing with a smooth tonal quality down from head voice into the middle range and then into chest—usually using a more closed to more open vowel (such as [u] to [o]). Later, we turn around and sing from their chest register up through the middle range.

I spend considerable time with the female register. Too many women carry the heavier middle register adjustments up into the high range and fail to find their pure head register. I agree with Marchesi that the head "voice" is the youth of the voice that permits a long career. Women find their head voice by using rounded or closed vowels as they go up through the secondary passaggio around F5.

I also have women sing in the whistle register and then descend in pitch to get greater ease and freedom of tone in the head register. With a good use of head and whistle registers, sopranos eliminate a common problem around the Bb5–C6 pitches.

I feel that men must develop their mixed register (just above the speaking range) before they attempt to sing in head register, which occurs above the major passaggio (around Eb4–G4, depending on voice classification). The mixed register must be sung with an easy, smooth, ringing tone, and with a feeling of "up and over." Otherwise, the man will push his voice and sing in a "shout" voice and will have difficulties developing his upper range. Men find mixed voice and head voice by rounding or closing the vowel. We do many exercises on 5–8–5–3–1 using the vowels [a–o–o–o–a] or [ɛ–e–e–e–ɛ], starting the exercise in an easy falsetto and descend the scale, moving as easily as possible through the transition into the lower register.

I recommend the vowel chart and exercises in *Overtones of Bel Canto* by Coffin. The vowel chart reveals the subtlety of vowel changes needed to achieve flexible registration and resonance throughout the voice. The vowel exercises are fun to do and guide the singers into easy, smooth resonance and register adjustments.

Jack Coldiron

You establish this solid middle voice and then maintain a constant relationship to this voice. As you ascend, you never forget that there is a connection to the modal voice (although there certainly is a lightening of weight). William Vennard used to call it "singing on a thin string" in the upper voice. [There is] the use of the "voix mixe" (the head voice or mixed voice) in men especially, and perhaps also the use of the falsetto as a possible way to introduce the head voice in the male as a way of convincing the student that a lighter mechanism can assist in achieving an acceptable tone and an easier technique necessary in the higher range. I have found it helps in combating the "macho" attitude in many male singers.

Barbara Doscher

I think blending of registers is best handled with descending vocalizes, particularly for young voices (voices under thirty years of age). As I said, if you can find a way for the middle voice to operate in a functionally efficient way, then the other areas of the scale are going to be much easier to deal with. I'm talking about not just the top voice but the chest registers as well. I believe in training females with the whistle register, and males with the falsetto (although they're entirely different registers) for the same reason. I think it promotes more ease in the top part of the mixed voice. By that, I mean it's easier for the singer to add what Vennard calls "top mechanism."

Leslie Guinn

We often do exercises that will catch the student's larynx unaware in order to awaken new sensations and sounds. I have found good results with rapid, vigorous arpeggi of an octave or tenth, oscillating the upper third or fourth, and then sustaining the uppermost pitch immediately on the same breath with no discernible pause or preparation (i.e., 1–3–5–8–10–8–10–8–10[fermata]–8–5–3–1).

Chapter Five

Evenness through the Range

The concept of evenness through the range is interconnected with tonal resonance and registration adjustment and so is very hard to define separately from those elements. Much of the discussion of resonance included a consideration of evenness; discussion of registers naturally included thoughts regarding achieving an evenness through "shift" areas (passaggios) between registers.

General observations that address the attainment of evenness through the voice embrace the following:

1. Unification of sound results from equilibrium among such factors as the balance of breath pressure with intensity, laryngeal stability, and resonance adjustment.
2. A unified vocal sound seeks a blend or even "mix" throughout the range of the voice.
3. Voice teachers use a variety of methods to help students achieve such evenness through the vocal range.

TEACHERS' REMARKS

Edward Baird

The vocal sound is basically made up of two qualities: the focus ("ping," "ring," and projection) and the resonance (amplification, warmth, depth, and color). We're always trying to get the right mix of those two things (focus and resonance), and that mix is going to vary as you go up and down through the range in various parts of the range. That's where using vowel modification can help you make the adjustment and find just the right balance.

Helen Swank

I think I try to choose to find other ways from a lot of vowel modification. I relate it to space, to how they're feeling in the back of the throat, how that uvular area is. Usually if all that settles right, I can help a student find pure vowels at any pitch without thinking too much about vowel modification.

[On achieving evenness,] we're back to establishing a feel for placement, because that changes. We establish an understanding of airflow through passaggio.

An even, healthy sound is free, bubbling, and without tension; has a vibrato that is an asset rather than a noticeable liability; and results in perfect intonation and a well-placed, even scale.

Richard Miller

You must have established freedom. Whatever the problem is, it will be exacerbated in the ascending range and ascending scale. So get rid of the problem in the lower and middle voice; you do that by the same principles I've mentioned. First of all, as you know, the voice is a tripartite instrument; it involves breath management, vibration, and resonation. If you have the freedom of the vibrator, proper coordination between the breath control and that vibrator, and the acoustical background we have talked about, you're going to have freedom in every part of the voice.

Marvin Keenze

A lot of freedom of resonance comes through the posture: the way they stand. Of course, laryngeal position relates to that—whether the chin is squashed in or not. The attitude of the larynx and the position makes a difference in sound.

I believe that a note in a range is only as good as it relates to another note in the rest of our voice. There is an acoustical connection between all of the pitches that we sing.

Laura Brooks Rice

[Evenness] involves breath support and opening the resonators as you move up.

Lindsey Christiansen

Dealing with the resonance and evenness of sound, I like to deal with top to bottom. . . . The soft palate is a hot issue, and I've gone back and forth on it, on how much I deal directly with the soft palate. I talk about the inner smile; I talk about the skin behind the back of the upper teeth, the feeling that that goes a little bit wide—and there's still a feeling of height as well. I talk a lot about height in the tone and about it not falling into the mouth. The position of the tongue is vital in this. I have students give a lot of thought to what the tongue needs to do, ensuring there's no pressure right around and underneath the neck, and that the tongue is not being sucked back.

Joan Wall

Unification of the voice is accomplished when singers have a consistent quality of voice as they sing from forward to back vowels, from high to low pitches, and from loud to soft dynamics. In a unified voice trained for bel canto singing, I hear a solid, warm, secure tonal quality with a vibrant, sparkling, high singer's formant consistently throughout the range. The singer with a unified voice usually feels that tonal production is the same through the range. No big readjustments are needed. In their mind's eye, it will look as if the sounds are connected.

Dale Moore

I think the most important key to this is the vowel. We know that certain things need to be set up by a slight modification of the vowel so that by the time we get to the second passaggio, we're already safely into the gear. The key lies in the vowel.

Shirlee Emmons

In actuality, perhaps surprisingly, evenness of voice throughout the range is actually achieved more easily when the ideal ratios of head and chest content are strictly observed. The listener perceives evenness when the singer is executing what the voice is comfortable doing. Is that too esoteric a thought? It is my observation that it is extremely practical working this way because the singers become confident of their ability to control the registration events.

Barbara Doscher

You have to understand that quality always comes before quantity when you're vocalizing or doing voice building. Equally important is the fact that the same size pipe or resonance tract throughout will not result in an even scale. There are a lot of people who seem to think that it will, but differences produce evenness, as long as you know what you're doing with the differences.

William McIver

Every vowel must connect to every other vowel without a loss of complete timbre. I think the important place for woman (especially sopranos) is the upper-middle voice. You spend time with both mezzos and sopranos working in the lower passaggio as well. I think any soprano who can't sing with some chest mixture is deficient. Even the lighter soprano roles will call for it on occasion. It is helpful to teach them to sing in chest mixture at the bottom in order to develop the full potential of the sound in the top part of the voice. I think they are related.

Carol Webber

This is an area where in singing, as in life, paradox exists: in order to make the voice sound even throughout, you can't neutralize it and ask it to behave the same way. . . . You have to really observe the differences in each register, understand how to make each register as accurate as possible so the singer actually feels the differences kinesthetically (the differences being opening the mouth more as pitches ascend). Then, as you allow these differences to predominate, you will get evenness through the range. It can easily be misunderstood. For example, the vowels in middle voice are very much like speech and don't need alteration. Investigate them, find them "delicious," and complete them, but don't alter, cover, color, or manipulate them.

I don't like to start by changing the vowel itself, by predetermining a vowel modification. I like to notice how the vowel is perceived differently by the singer as the mouth opening increases. There are certain principles that we can read and apply toward any voice: [i] tend to go toward [I], [e] toward [ɛ] . . . the higher you get, the more all the vowels seem to fit in the [ɑ] position . . . but for each person, that degree of change is different, and in each language there are subtle differences, rather than just prescribed (i.e., handing someone a sheet of paper and saying "these are how you modify your vowels: on this particular note you sing this particular vowel," and so on). I prefer to go at it more by observation and then structure that list, if needed, for each student. This is slower, longer, and harder but ultimately more valuable. I resist "cloning" sounds, even if they're not all healthy sounds!

Every singer's skull shape, jaw shape, tongue length, width of neck, and so forth, varies, so kinesthetic feeling varies. I believe this accounts in some measure for the differences in technical approaches teachers use if they teach what they each have felt while they sang.

Marcia Baldwin

You have to keep the vowel pure and not distort vowels for any vocal purpose. It's also essential to not stop the breath—keep the breath flowing throughout. Breath management is really what singing is all about. We can stop our breath in all sorts of places. A tight diaphragm, constricted larynx, and a closed chest are the three main places where the breath flow stops.

Meribeth Dayme

I think the only people involved in that are classical singers, and I'm not sure all of them are anymore. One of the joys of contemporary commercial music and musical theater is the imagination and the color with which people use their voices now. They are not so concerned about having pearl-shaped tones from top to bottom and back again. I think that the mythology of perfect sound actually can hinder spontaneity and the freedom of the voice. When I hear people working at that now—and there are some lovely sounds—there is something not quite human about it. Those very even sounds can get boring today. One of the buzz words today is "authentic," and people want authenticity. I don't care whether it's classical or pop—what genre of music it is—I believe they want to hear the real person in there. Always trying to make this perfect sound means that you've lost the message.

Stephen King

This is where I talk about the second-tuning formant for men. Once males get to this certain place in the voice, the larynx comes up and they're going to shout. They must try to find a different strategy. What I'm trying to get them to understand is that everything about the male voice is about lengthening your vocal tract from top to bottom, to get an overtone. If you don't have an overtone, no one's going to hear your speaking voice over an orchestra. I'm quite positive that no one told Pavarotti that he needed to use second-formant tuning, but somehow he figured out how to find the third, fourth, and even fifth overtone.

A few months ago, Jim Doing (who was also a master teacher at the NATS Foundation Intern Program) was in Houston. He spent a week in my studio demonstrating the uses of VoceVista. I found it very helpful to confirm or deny things with tuning, especially the male top, and keeping the "back space" all the time as they went up in pitch. I found it less useful with the women. It was good for them to see that and understand a little bit about it. Singers, if they want to, should be able to see a spectrographic analysis of their voice. I would not use that on a regular basis and none of my colleagues do, but it's nice to use that with somebody if you might be struggling to diagnose and look at what's really happening. The simple idea of looking at the period and excursion of the vibrato can be very useful for singer and teacher. When you hear somebody every week, it is easy to become comfortable with them . . . "oh, this is just how they sound." I'm not wired that way—I want everybody to find a truly professional sound with his or her voice. I'm happy to bring in some new research or try to look at it from another angle.

I spend a lot of time trying to help people understand the difference in male and female vocal production. For women, I find it's generally far easier to get to the top of the voice, open the mouth toward "ah," shorten the vocal tract, and raise the pitch. If the voice is set up right, it just takes a lot less work. The tenors—it just takes so much constant work in the top. First of all, to find the top and to maintain it and sing in a way that's not going to be fatiguing when you're taking speaking voice up that far. I don't know any other way to do it without vowel modification or adjustment to continually lengthen the vocal tract. I'm sure there are different ways to describe it, but that's the journey for the men, especially for the tenors.

I think of the professional singers that I teach—I spend far less time working on registration with women than with men. Usually, with women, it's to find the extension—the "whistle" or work on the low transition between mode 1 and mode 2. That's where most of the work is. And then, sometimes in the upper area between C#–F#, C–F, B–G, "upper passagio" people would call it, setting that up properly so they can open their mouth without going out of tune . . . just trying to get everything balanced.

Jeannette LoVetri

From a purely functional standpoint, all voices should have at least two octaves of evenly produced sound as a "home base." This implies balanced registration in mid-range, undistorted vowels (unless you are a classical singer and must modify or adjust the vowel for aesthetic purposes in the high range), and control over the volume from at least mp to mf throughout that range, without strain or forcing, as a "default" in which to vocalize regardless of what style or styles are performed.

Singers who belt or use a specific alternate vocal quality in music should also be able to vocalize in those qualities of sound easily throughout whatever pitch range they would typically cover in a song.

Mary Saunders-Barton

The balancing of registers results in the well-documented "mixed voice" of musical theater singers. It allows sopranos to be mezzos and baritones to be tenors.

Wendy LeBorgne and Marci Rosenberg use the term "vocal athletes" to describe contemporary commercial singers (which includes musical theater). In fact, we are training these singers in the same way we would train a runner or a football player. Endurance and healthy technique are paramount. The question "Can you do that eight shows a week?" hangs over all we do. The approach I have taken at Penn State is to train "both sides of the voice." Over the years, I have come to recognize the value of balancing classical vocal technique with the techniques specific to musical theater singing (bel canto and can belto).

The voice pedagogy required to meet the demands placed on today's young performers eliminates the concept of Fach completely. The goal is to bridge all transitions seamlessly by balancing the action of the thyroarytenoid and cricothyroid muscles so the voice has equivalent power in all ranges.

The technological advances in acoustic enhancement allow performers more dynamic latitude, and protects them from blowing out their voices when singing over rock bands, and so forth.

STRATEGIES FOR ESTABLISHING EVENNESS THROUGH THE RANGE

Teachers employ a variety of procedures and tactics to assist their students in acquiring evenness throughout the voice. These include addressing issues of breath consistency, using a whole system of vowel modification, using certain vowels to aid the process, and range-extension exercises.

Marvin Keenze

I use vocalizes that have large intervals, especially octaves that can relate notes harmonically. I use the piano to demonstrate this. I might play all the notes in a student's range and hold down the pedal. Then I ask them to vocalize while I continue to play these notes rather loudly. This seems to reinforce the idea that the pitches we sing are already in our head or our mind's ear and we need only to access them, not "create" them. Once we have thought it, we have sung it. I also do this with all the notes of a particular song. If a singer can sing a song as I play an accompaniment that includes all of the sustained pitches in that song, then they really know it. I have found this develops the ability to keep a consistency of quality throughout all of the range and through all vowels and consonants. There is something of every note that we can sing in every other note. If there is a weak middle register, I do use the blending of the lower, heavier mechanism into this area. I also believe that the middle voice development comes first and the "supernatural" notes above and below relate to the middle register.

Laura Brooks Rice

I talk a lot about "releasing" as you sing, not relaxing. I talk a lot about releasing, sending the air up and over and feeling that the air releases the sound that way, keeping the breath support constant as you move up the scale and feeling the release as you move up. When I talk about the larynx, I make it clear that we need to move out of the way to aid the adjustment it naturally needs to go up the scale.

Richard Miller

Depending on who the person is (it varies greatly), sometimes you have to go half step by half step in building the range, particularly with young males. There are many ways to do range extension, and of course, there are all sorts of arpeggiated figures that help. I'm very much given to the agility factor in building the upper range first, rather than by using sostenuto. But I think it's a mistake to try to immediately build the upper range; yes, you have to explore it, but people who start in the range extremes of the voice make a mistake. I think you have to get the middle voice straightened out: whatever the problems are in the middle voice, they will be exacerbated as you go up the scale, partly because of muscular activity of the vocal folds.

Helen Hodam

I find out what the problem is, and I do exercises that are long, that take in the whole range. I do long thirds, long arpeggios.

As far as breaks, I explain to them that it has to be strengthened, but it's a general process.

I do certain exercises—short exercises, where I build around the triad, where you go back and forth, back and forth, on certain vowels.

First you have to find the best vowel, and then sometimes I work from the top and bring it down—nearly always from the top. I do work the technical attacks to strengthen that. If it's an upper one, like an E, F, F#, that's where the vowel modification comes in. It depends on which vowel is best. I find the best vowel to work from there, and I work some from the top but nearly always around the triad or seconds. I might only do four notes, but I will do 4–3, 4–3–2–1, changing the vowel.

Carol Webber

You can't walk away from a certain ground level of physiological information. I think, however, that in each voice it's good to identify a "home base" vowel. "What is your favorite vowel to sing?" I ask a student. I usually begin working the brighter vowels, but when someone's "home base" vowel is darker, I begin there, starting with the best sound and then attaching the less-refined sounds in patterns with the best vowel to progress through all the vowels.

Joan Wall

I help singers develop unification through persistent vowel study. We smooth out the registration adjustments by using a good breath, phonation, and resonance throughout their range, by practicing messa-di-voce exercises, and by repeating short and long scales while listening for a consistent tonal quality.

Jack Coldiron

Avoiding negative psychological terms such as "break" or "lift" is advisable. I prefer to refer to them as "adjustment places." Explain the passaggio as an area of adjustment to the upper range and use of vowel modification to create space for the higher pitches as a way to approach the problem. I use quick-moving arpeggios to avoid the habit of slowing to adjust or taking time in approaching the passaggio. The student often sings through that area with unexpected ease and finds encouragement in having done so, thus finding encouragement and willingness to believe in the process.

Barbara Doscher

I pay a great deal of attention to what the vibrato sounds like; whenever it goes out of whack, I figure there is a fight going on between the air and the resonance track.

Marcia Baldwin

It's way up there on my list to keep the breath flowing freely without any impediment. In fact, that's what determines good singing: not just a good line but plain, old good singing.

Edith Davis Tidwell

I instruct the student to think over and down in ascending passages, and to think up, as if greeting the upper pitches, in descending passages.

I often encourage the use of [ʌ], no matter the written vowel, on the uppermost pitch in a high-lying phrase (it lifts the soft palate). If the pitch is sustained, the pure written vowel can then follow right through that feeling. The tone is free and more beautiful. I remind the student that the symbol [ʌ] itself has a point at the top and then opens.

Chapter Six

Diction

A central component of good vocal technique is diction in all its ramifications; consequently, discussion of diction generates great interest and has a significant part in vocal training. Like posture, diction is a much more tangible factor and is therefore easier to describe and discuss than the more intangible concepts of tonal resonance, registration, and unification.

GENERAL STATEMENTS REGARDING DICTION

1. Good diction should not compromise the voice but is the result of freedom within the instrument.
2. Good diction results from the balance of certain critical factors, including distinguishable vowels; clear initial and ending consonants; firm, flexible articulation; and relaxed tongue muscles.
3. Poor diction can be a diagnostic tool: it often indicates problems elsewhere in the instrument.
4. Diction and articulation result from acoustical factors that rely on proper shaping in the resonator tract.
5. Diction encompasses flow of language and the idiomatic precision of each language as it is sung.

TEACHERS' REMARKS

Marvin Keenze

When the word is beautifully shaped, the vowel is beautifully shaped and phonation is better because the tuned-in, resonant vowel frees up the vibrator. When the vibrator is right, the breath works better.

We must articulate in such a way that it doesn't disturb our instrument. Whatever vowel we are singing has to be hooked on to our whole instrument. But articulation can cause our instrument to become cheap, expensive, or small, as we change for color, quality, or whatever. When that inner mouth is quiet and calm, the base of the tongue is calm and quiet. I encourage a quiet, calm, low larynx and then lots of action in this area (the lips, teeth, and tip of the tongue), a freedom here, without disturbing the front wall of the pharynx, which is the bottom of the tongue. That's diction: freedom of articulation with minimum interference of the instrument.

Helen Swank

If you have the breath right and the body right, the body in a state of relaxation and a sense of this resonance as being how the tone is projected rather than a sense of making it at the throat, you will probably end up with a clarity of diction because you will have relaxed tongue muscles. You will have a certain freedom and separation of articulation from the resonance, so the little tongue can go about doing its business and the student has the concept of space and projection, without having to force the tone to do anything.

I look upon diction as a diagnostic tool with students. If diction is not clear, there's something wrong. Singers who are singing well will have clear diction. When there is tension in any part of the system above the larynx, there will be problems with the diction, and that can be anything from the articulatory aspects to how well that breath/tone is working to produce consonants, to the quality and accuracy of the vowel sound. If everything is mushed, something is wrong.

Jack Coldiron

Achieve clear diction without stilted affectation. Diction should be immediately acceptable to the listener. It should be speech-like in the lower range and have broader vowels in the ascending vocal line. Avoid overuse of the lips. Since most vowels are formed in the mouth and throat, a relaxed and flexible tongue is important.

Diction should be speech-like in the lower range and have broader vowels in the ascending vocal line. Give attention to the possibility for vowel migration or vowel modification as you ascend.

In English, I am looking for a general "American" (i.e., a nonregional) sound. My several years as a radio announcer have been especially valuable to my clear and accurate diction. "Simply spoken simply."

Edward Baird

If you modify things in the right direction with just the right amount, you won't distort your diction. Your vowels stay distinguishable enough, and then, of course, by always insisting on good consonants, initial and after, your vowels can modify a little without destroying the clarity of what you're saying.

Dale Moore

I'm very interested in diction. We're going through the age of the mush-mouth. I feel a lot of this has to do with, and so many diction problems stem from, a lazy tongue. I believe in keeping the jaw as quiet as possible and keeping the tongue as active as possible.

Cynthia Hoffmann

I like the idea of "tasting the words," which brings the feeling of many consonants behind the upper teeth using the tip of the tongue. The spoken adage "the lips, the teeth, the tip of the tongue"—repeat this again and again for the sense of this articulation. Middle consonants—for example, the semiconsonant "y" and also "k," "g," and "ng"—are helpful in moving the tongue forward out of the back of the throat during their articulation.

In addition, the consonants need to be surrounded by the vowel space, and vowel legato should clearly define their release and clear articulation. If the tessitura is high, consonants can be more softly applied, and in the middle voice and lower range, their crispness helps to keep the line moving forward—"release the consonant to 'get' to the vowel."

Lindsey Christiansen

Consonants should be as late as possible, as quick as possible, and as clean as possible. Another thing I like to say is that "we sing vowels, we articulate consonants, and we express text."

Oren Brown

What is diction but breaking up and slicing in various forms the stream of tone that we have coming from the larynx? The areas that actually do this are the lips, the teeth, the tongue, the jaw, and the pharyngeal spaces in the mouth. By varying these, we get various sounds. For diction, I like to have the student be aware that there must be freedom of the motion for these muscles of articulation above the source of the sound. It's two separate things done simultaneously.

For example, you can have diction with no sound; one can read lips and understand what is being said. That's because diction is shape and takes place above the larynx, where the mechanisms for pitch occur. Then the sound created in the larynx comes through the shapes; our ability to make these shapes more and more clear means we are getting better diction all the time.

We depend more on consonants for intelligibility than we do on vowels (although one without the other is meaningless). Together, it's the flow that we call language. When it's well done, we say we have clear diction. Beyond that is the inflection of the language.

Shirlee Emmons

I have found that vowel definition (and therefore diction) is a direct result of the tone being one with the 2750 Hz overtone. To make this happen, vowel modification is a must. Vowel sounds are modified in relation to pitch. If the singers play the harmonics of their pronunciation well, they will get in return better tone, better resonation, better vowel differentiation, and better consonant articulation. Coffin once said that an unknowledgeable diction teacher can undo everything about a singer's tone, and a knowledgeable one can work miracles. He also said that teachers should forget about the Italian pure vowel concept and replace it with the Italian pure tone concept. The word "pure" is tossed about irresponsibly, in my opinion. The pure singing vowel is not necessarily the same as the speech vowel; it is one that is clear on the particular pitch being sung. A pure vowel is not even the same one at different spots in the range. The vowel that works well is the one we clearly understand. The vowel that does not work well will not be understood because there is too much acoustical interference in the tone.

I'll give you an example: I once had a French gentleman visiting my studio. A friend of his was preparing one of those Poulenc songs for baritone that sit unremittingly very high. The Frenchman was sitting in the doorway of my studio, and the student was standing at the end of the piano. For a full forty-five minutes, the baritone and I worked to change the vowels of those myriad high notes into acoustically workable modifications. During this process, in my peripheral vision, I could see the visitor shaking his head woefully. I assumed he was, like a true Frenchman, hating every change we made in his beloved language. After we had finished the modifications, the baritone sang the song all the way through. At the end, the Frenchman leaped to his feet and said, "Ah, but now I understand the words!" He had not understood the diction when the baritone sang the real French words, but he did understand the words when the acoustical vowels were sung. This story and many other such occurrences are my proof when I argue this point!

With regard to consonants, I have several solutions. First of all, in order for the tongue to strike the hard palate in front of the alveolar ridge, I insist that the tongue tip sit on the cutting edge of the bottom teeth. This places the tongue a quarter inch higher and "fronter" than it would otherwise be. If nothing else, it enables the consonants T, D, N, and R (the most often used in singing languages) to sit higher and "fronter."

Second, sometimes the diction is clarified by "fudging" the consonant. This is often the most useful thing to do just before a difficult ascent or attack on a high note. But sometimes the diction is clarified by prolonging the consonant. I have been assured by a prominent voice rehabilitation medical doctor that some consonants (notably M and N) elicit head content in the tone, and some (notably the plosives P, B, G, K, T, and D) elicit chest content if they are prolonged. I adopt the one that is most useful for the particular musical spot.

Third, many European voice teachers get very good results by making sure that the consonant placed before the second note of a large skip is uttered on the bottom note, not on the top. I belong to this school, categorically, but I am circumspect about where to use it. Without a doubt, it allows a much more gentle arrival on the upper note and is, in general, less disturbing to the line.

Helen Hodam

Most of the singers (in school) are "dictioned" too much and the tone suffers. I talk about vowels a lot, the pure vowels, and about frontal consonants, which are right in line with the vowel and the breath. A frontal, initial consonant can launch you into the vowel. I like to have them feel that it's more or less one thing. If they start worrying about "this consonant has to be farther back, then this consonant goes here," they have to be awfully good singers to get involved with that (kind of activity). I know you might run into that in some of the more difficult Slavic languages, but I don't deal with it too much at this stage.

Joan Wall

To become a fully developed performing artist and a master text-painter in music, a singer must give attention to singing diction. Good singing diction can be defined as that which is understandable, is appropriate for the music, and does not call attention to itself. It has precise articulation of consonants and vowels, correct pronunciations, the natural flow of the language (patterns of rhythm, stress, inflection, and linking of words), and most of all, expressive interpretations of text. Poor diction is characterized by problems of muffledness of consonants (incomplete closure, incomplete friction, or incomplete nasality); unclear vowels; overarticulation; substitution, omission, and addition of sounds; poor duration of sounds; poor linking; and poor stressing.

So much vocal training centers upon vowels and resonance; many singers neglect learning the clear, energized consonants that are absolutely necessary for understandable, good singing diction. Without good consonants, words are indistinct and lack expressiveness.

Too many singers feel that consonants get in the way of good vocalization! In truth, it is quite the opposite! Precise consonants are supportive of good vocal technique. Most consonants—except for g, k, and ng—are formed in the forward part of the mouth (and even g and k are relatively forward when followed by a forward vowel). Vocalization becomes easier and better resonated when consonants are precisely produced.

In good singing diction, singers use both pure vowels and appropriate vowel modifications. After learning clear and precise vowel sounds, they discover how subtle vowel modifications can be used for best resonance and for clear diction as they sing up and down the scale.

Barbara Doscher

I think good diction primarily depends on the fluidity of the vowel. The consonants add the drama, but you can't compensate for muddy or strident vowels by doing diction that is mostly consonants. That just doesn't work.

Helen Swank

I look upon diction as a diagnostic tool with students. If diction is not clear, there's something wrong. Singers who are singing well will have clear diction. When there is tension in any part of the system above the larynx, there will be problems with the diction, and that can be anything from the articulatory aspects to how well that breath/tone is working to produce consonants, to the quality and accuracy of the vowel sound. If everything is mushed, something is wrong.

Richard Miller

[Regarding diction and vowel definition], that again is an acoustic matter. The voice is a phonetic instrument, even more so in singing than in speech, because you have the duration factor in singing, where if you say an [e], it's going to be an [e] for a period of longer duration. In speech, we have lots of transition sounds that are not present in the singing voice, again because of the duration factor; you generally use more time to sing than to say the same thing. Therefore, articulation and diction is an acoustic matter based on the appropriate shapes of the resonator tract for each vowel. Every vowel has its own particular acoustic formation. Each vowel has a laryngeal configuration and a corresponding vowel tract configuration that matches it. So, to have good diction, you need to track the vowel—that means have a correspondence between the laryngeally generated sound and the resonator system—and so the proper handling of the consonants and the diction will be perfect.

Laura Brooks Rice

I work quite a bit through every language. I first go to the openness of the Italian language. I teach my students to understand the different qualities that are involved in each language, and I explain the differences in the flow of language.

Finding the correct vowel positions in Italian that help find optimum resonance is crucial. I have learned from my colleagues that the frequency where Italian lives is much higher than most American accents. Ask to hear the difference especially in [ɑ], which is generally produced with a flat tongue in most American accents, and [u], which tends to sit low in the mouth. Have them hear beyond IPA, which is a wonderful tool. The closed [o] vowel in Italian, French, and German has different flavors that need to first be heard before they are duplicated. Working on the different ways to treat consonants with knowing when to voice a consonant (á la Vaccai 1) in Italian, using consonant clusters and glottals in German, and accent assistance in French helps them differentiate those three languages.

Carol Webber

People who have an aptitude for languages can become fluent in many "tongues" because lingual and labial function is so neurologically responsive. I feel singing is not a good professional choice for students who don't have strong language aptitude. I stress the meaning of the words that, when truly felt, brings the subconscious and conscious forces of the mind and body together to produce better diction than can be achieved by just having the rules all memorized. I use the word "diction" in this sense to mean "correct."

In terms of projection of diction, we all agree that we sing on vowels; consonants then delineate the vowels in describing what they are used to mean in each particular case. Without consonants, vowels won't really have enough meaning. I think that a lot of people tend to overemphasize consonants in the effort to get "good diction." It's an excessive use of consonant function that can destroy not only the musical line but also the long line of a person's voice staying evenly on the breath. We have to be attentive to a good balance.

Knowledge of the behavior of the tongue, the "picture" of the vowel, as illustrated in the IPA symbols—these things can help create a more consistent accuracy factor, but to me that is not enough for diction. Good diction cannot exist in a vacuum; it must come from the meaning and the context of the words. Each language should be intellectually and emotionally embraced; then the adjustments in each language for classical singing (lyric diction) will be part of a healthy technique.

Leslie Guinn

Most of my students come to me to address issues of vocal technique. I readily address the occasional or unusual diction problems as they arise. However, if there is considerable diction work to be done by the student, I recommend they work with one of many affordable diction coaches in the area.

Edith Davis Tidwell

No matter the language, be mindful of experiencing the feel of the phonetic process as the sounds pass through the mouth and lips.

Meribeth Dayme

In terms of diction, I think less is more—and one of the things you see with classical singing is overdiction, which then distorts the whole vocal tract and, with it, the sound. So for me, "less" means flexibility of the palate, lips, tongue, and jaw and a free neck. One exercise that I use is to very gently turn the head while breathing and singing. It stops people from locking the neck at the onset of a sound instead of beginning a breath or phrase in frozen mode. And it also stops the breath from locking; it keeps breath flow and encourages good diction. When singers hesitate or overthink, they tend to lock the neck and jaw and tense the lips. This has a huge effect on the flexibility of the tongue and palate, and the result is forced or sluggish diction. Some of the warm-ups I use to free articulation are taken from a combination of child's play, speech therapy, and sound. I use "humming and chewing," which involves chewing while making sound with the mouth closed and humming—vigorous chewing like a baby playing with its tongue and mouth. That seems to get the articulatory structures loose enough to work without overthinking.

The physical habits and speech patterns of the singer influence how a teacher works with diction. Cultural speech patterns, dialects, style of music, and many other factors are of great importance. Every teacher needs to be equipped with knowledge of how sound and articulation work. For instance, I had a Korean student many years ago, and I had to teach her how to make an [n]. Her tongue didn't move that way. Had I not studied diction and how everything moves I would have been lost when working with her.

Robert Edwin

Articulation (diction) in singing can range from casual and conversational to formal and crisp depending upon the genre, so my singers are trained to exercise their articulators (jaw, lips, teeth, tongue, and soft palate) in multiple ways. We explore the spectrum of articulation from unintelligible to overly pronounced through vocalizes and then apply the appropriate diction based on style and genre requirements.

Jeannette LoVetri

In music theater, classical, country, folk, and gospel, clear diction is necessary. Articulatory drills can be helpful in these singers, and they can be learned without pitch. I use them with CCM singers in vocal exercises that are pitch based, however, remembering that if the jaw and the tongue are not freed first through exercises, it is hard to get the tongue to do what it needs to do and the jaw and lip muscles to move enough to make clear articulation easy to do. They must all be worked on over time in order to improve.

In jazz, sometimes there are no words, and sometimes words are deliberately distorted for expressive purposes. In rock, often the sound is distorted electronically and no one really cares if every word is clearly articulated. I don't know of anyone who sings metal rock who cares about "the rain in Spain stays mainly in the plain."

Stephen King

I think we should change the name of our classes that we teach at the conservatory-university from Diction for Italian to Articulation for Italian.

To me, diction is phrasing, and the goal should be to use words with the music to create the phrase that the composer intended, rather than "here's a double consonant, and I'm going to stop my breath, because that's what we're doing in Italian Diction." If the words are not created in service of a legato singing line, there seems to be little point in singing.

This is certainly not easy! I think the rules and the sort of mandates to "do this, do that" that occur in school are often leading people to believe they are becoming great singers when they can't connect the breath through the consonants. Or they're trying to hit a target symbol, and they're not really singing an "eee" [i] vowel or an "ah" [ɑ] vowel with the resonance in their voice. Students learn grammar, and they learn a lot of rules for how to pronounce a language, but then the time to actually do that with their singing technique is somehow left to the side. There were many great singing artists prior to the advent of the IPA. The teacher must use the ear and eye to train the singer to understand and have the awareness of true lyric diction.

This seems to be less of a problem with people who sing professionally, because they routinely experience the necessity of the continuity of the voice in a hall through an orchestra. They will do what is necessary to make that work.

Of course, there are obviously some differences in a soprano singing above the staff when it comes to the diction and a baritone singing a Schubert song. It's much easier to understand a man, and it should be, because he's singing primarily in his unadjusted speaking range. Kudos for good diction (if we want to call it that) or good articulation—but I'd much rather hear Joan Sutherland sing the way she sang in the top than some of the screaming that you hear now based on "saying the right word," or being criticized for not being understood in the top. I don't think that's the point of singing a high Bb.

Mary Saunders-Barton

Diction for musical theater singers is again character-driven and dependent on the style of a piece.

My goal is to help students align their actor's voice with their singer's voice. It is an aesthetic priority to maintain a "speaking quality" without modifying vowels to the point of obliterating intelligibility, regardless of range. The diction should not "call attention to itself" or to any technical effort on the part of the singer. It should seem organic and truthful. Of course, there are pop and rock genres where vowel modifications are an essential ingredient of authentic style

STRATEGIES FOR TEACHING DICTION

Helen Swank

If it's a matter of articulation, if the tongue is tight and the consonants are not proper, I put them through some forward tongue actions: L's, D's and T's, or "tuttaka-tuttaka" as a trumpeter does, so they use both the back and the front of the tongue. If it's a combination of things not working, if the vowels are not right either, I will work on the resonance system first. Then the consonants will come and all things will fall into place.

Marvin Keenze

We must articulate in such a way that the instrument is not disturbed. I encourage a low and quiet laryngeal position and a flexible tongue that has minimum effect on the sound-production mechanism. Yet there is a definite relationship between the organs of articulation and the sound of the vocal folds. Energized articulation aids in an energetic sound. I relate all vowel shapes to the neutral [ə], as in "could" (or a southerner saying "bird"). This prevents the singers from overpronouncing and gives them a point of reference for the optimum resonant vowel position. The tongue's journey from the consonant position to the vowel is greater than in ordinary speech. I use a variety of combinations of vowels and consonants to demonstrate this and to teach that there is a resonant vowel position. Another thing I've discovered: we talk about resonance and try to find a shape for the vowel that gives us a quality that we think is musical and has projection. There is a projection and a freedom of sound that comes when the sound source and the vowels are tuned together: that's acoustics. Whatever vowel we are singing has to hook onto our whole instrument. In singing speech, the vowels are really very close together. I tell students we have a "singer's mouth." There's an inner mouth that helps to shape the vowels and it helps keep the vowels close.

I'll have them just speak [a–e–i–o–u] and then tell them "now put a consonant in front of it, but don't let the consonant make you do a harsher, more distorted and shortened vowel chain." It's cause and effect—when that "inner mouth" is quiet and calm, the base of the tongue is quiet and calm. You're going to get a brighter sound because a ring is going to be in the voice. If there's a lot of movement in this area, you're going to lose the singer's ring. So I encourage a quiet, calm, low larynx and then lots of action in the lips, teeth, and the tip of the tongue.

Dale Moore

I use exercises in vocalizes with all kinds of crazy consonants. Many American tongues are very lazy. They want to ride a little too far back and are not involved enough in the diction process.

With virtually every student, I use vocalizes built on "ga." This helps to work the base of the tongue, especially if the tongue tends to want to lie down there in the throat.

Then I use syllables related to "ga" with a "k" sound: [ka, ki, ke]. I use [da, ka]. There again, two related vowels. Of course, [ja], because that's really a semi-vowel. Any consonants that can be said without jaw involvement because I believe in keeping the jaw as quiet as possible and the tongue as active as possible.

Lindsey Christiansen

I have students sing on just the vowels of the text, or on a single vowel. Then we put in random consonants, not necessarily the consonants as dictated by the text. I think certain consonants are very helpful for vocal function. "Vvv" is one of my favorites. "Mmm" I use, too, but I usually try to use that with a chewing sensation, a humming and a chewing. I've had students come to study with me who have had vocal nodules, and so forth, and I find work with [v] and [m] is enormously therapeutic for them.

Joan Wall

The International Phonetic Alphabet is most helpful for the study of diction—it specifies how language sounds are physically produced and clarifies speech sounds and pronunciations in various languages.

I spend considerable time giving exercises and instructions to free the jaw, tongue, and lips for articulation. A loose jaw and flexible tongue are absolutely essential for fine singing. I have singers practice all vowels and many consonants. The voiced consonants v, th, m, n, mg, b, and d and their unvoiced cognates are particularly helpful.

We then turn to songs, where the singers bring this precise articulation into the natural flow of the language (i.e., the patterns of rhythm, stress, inflection, and linking of words) and, most of all, expressive interpretation of text.

Diction can be efficiently taught in class situations, where the singers can hear the spoken and sung diction of others and can get feedback from the group as well as the teacher. This work can be reinforced in the private studio, where greater emphasis can be put on expressiveness and interpretation of the words.

Laura Brooks Rice

I have students do phonetic transcriptions on their songs using the IPA (International Phonetic Alphabet). Then they read the text and intone the rhythm on one pitch to understand where they need to feel the double consonants and feel where they need to feel the sounds.

Cynthia Hoffmann

I like the Idea of "tasting the words," which brings the feeling of many consonants behind the upper teeth using the tip of the tongue (the spoken adage "the lips, the teeth, the tip of the tongue"—repeat this again and again for the sense of this articulation). Middle consonants— for example, the semi consonant "y" and also "k," "g," and "ng"—are helpful in moving the tongue forward out of the back of the throat during their articulation.

In addition, the consonants need to be surrounded by the vowel space, and vowel legato should clearly define their release and clear articulation. If the tessitura is high, consonants can be more softly applied, and in the middle voice and lower range, their crispness helps to keep the line moving forward—"release the consonant to 'get' to the vowel."

I have noticed that some students can sing in a foreign language correctly, but often, if you ask them to speak the same words they have been singing correctly, errors appear! There are differences between the hearing of a language and speaking it. This is an example of how important it is that both be used and exercised, not to mention the meaning of the language as it is spoken or sung.

Carol Webber

I concentrate on the use of the tip, not the entire tongue, for clarity of diction. I remind the student that the root of the tongue is connected to the larynx and can interfere with laryngeal freedom and stability. The entire tongue is a muscle for eating and swallowing, and the tip of the tongue is what relates to speaking. The tongue should rest in the mouth gently along the base of the lower teeth—not against but in subtle contact so that the tongue is neither pulled back nor thrust forward. This leaves the tip of the tongue alert and available for its role in speech.

Bruce Lunkley

Diction first comes in the use of consonants with exercises: placing them at the beginning of short notes, then at the beginning of runs, and so forth. For instance, I find the "y" sound before vowels ([ja, jo], etc.) extremely helpful in throwing the voice forward. I use it consistently with all voices, female and male. I use a lot of "d's" with the men, particularly in the lower register to keep them from getting gruff. It really depends on the individual. I don't find myself using any kind of a system at all. I wasn't taught that way, and I just don't tend to work that way. I try to deal with every student individually.

Chapter Seven

Vowels

As any voice teacher and singer will avow, vowels constitute a critically important part of fine vocal production. Although the pedagogues were not questioned directly concerning vowels and their role in singing, discussion about tone, resonance, vocal uniformity, and clarity of diction involved a great deal of focus on vowels. From these remarks, I have derived some observations that point to the use and importance of vowels:

1. Finding ideal vowel formation gives projection and freedom to the instrument.
2. Because of acoustical considerations, vowels must adjust to increases in pitch. There is an ideal resonance adjustment for every pitch and every vowel; tonal sensations respond to these changes.
3. Sung vowels require treatment different than spoken vowels.
4. Beautiful vowels depend on a number of factors and will have certain characteristics.
5. Vowels are available to expressive impulses and expressive choices.

TEACHERS' REMARKS

Helen Hodam

Singing is really a balance of three things: space, breath, and the forward vowel.

Marvin Keenze

The IPA is only a guide. We sing IPA plus. The plus factor is the color of the voice that is in some ways independent of the vowel. It is the part of the language that brings meaning and emotional content.

Paolo Zedda, of the Association des Professeurs de Chant, has written on this topic after making a study of singers in France and Italy. He discovered how differently they sang their native language and how little they observed the standard speech vowels of each country. They adapted the language to their individual voices and to the acoustical ideal and expressive elements.

Each language has its own frequency of speech pitch, harmonics, and consonant frequencies. When we are in the frequencies of a language, it enables us to sing or speak with the distinctive flavor of that language, and we then have less of an accent. That means our ear has to be tuned to these frequencies to speak, sing, and understand. I have my students read the text with an ear for each language's frequency areas and then put it to the song pitches. This adds that certain quality that makes a language come alive to the singer and listener. Because we must train our students in at least four major languages, including our own North American, we must guard against having all of them sound alike.

Dale Moore

One can say in a sense that there's an ideal resonance adjustment for every pitch on every vowel. I think the most important key to evenness of range is vowel. We know that something has to happen and that vowel is one of the parts of singing over which we do have control.

The choice of vowel and the choice of exercise (vocalize) are so important because it is by that means, and your communication of that to the student, that you set up what is going to be their response, good or bad. In this register or at that point of register change, you know something has to happen to the vowel—then you will get the resonance adjustment that you want.

Edward Baird

The higher you go, the closer the vowels go together—you don't make as much distinction in the higher ranges between vowels. It's really a modification. This is what allows you to build an even sound as you ascend through the various registers.

Marcia Baldwin

It has directly to do with the focus of the voice—the frontal resonance. I talk about vowel placement. I think that's highly important. I'll ask, "Where does that feel in your mouth when you sing?" [i] is right here between your front teeth—lips rounded, pursed; [e] is a little wider across the teeth between the eyeteeth; [u] feels like it's between your teeth and your lips; [o] feels like it's toward the front of the middle of your mouth (you feel it behind the alveolar ridge); and [ɑ] goes all the way from back to front. You need a lot of space for an [ɑ] because it tends to get socked in back there. Space in the soft palate area and a very big opening in the pharynx and the resonance ideally go from that space all the way forward. We need to have the consonants in the front and get rid of them as quickly as possible. No lingering on them. And vowel purity—that's why vowel placement is so important. [a, e, i, o, u], with slight variations of same. But in any and every language it has to be some form of those pure vowels, not a distortion. Because we singers have text, that's what good singing is all about.

Helen Swank

[On resonance space and vowel modification:] I choose to find other ways than a lot of vowel modification. For some students, it relates a lot to how they feel in the back of the throat, in the area of the uvula. Usually, if I can get all that to settle right, my students can find pure vowels at any pitch without thinking too much about vowel modification. Almost every student has a good vowel, and if you can find it and use it as a base to go from, then whatever modification that involves is in a sense modifying the "bad" toward the "good."

Oren Brown

I use the five primary Italian vowels: [i], [e], [ɑ], [o], and [u]. I work from one end of the vowel triangle to the other, with the open sound [ɑ] in the middle and then fill in the spaces.

I feel that vowels are like the colors in a rainbow, for example, red, orange, yellow, and blue—what is orange? When does it become orange instead of red or yellow? You can have a vowel that has a shade [demonstrates with (o)]. It takes on different colors and different meanings, whether you're very happy or very sad. You use those shadings for conveying the emotional meaning of the words.

Richard Miller

In speech, we have a lot of transition sounds that are not present in the singing voice, again because of the duration factor; you use more time to say the same thing. Therefore, articulation and diction is an acoustical matter based upon appropriate shapes of the resonator tract for the various vowels. Each vowel has its own particular acoustic formation. Each vowel has a laryngeal configuration and a corresponding vowel tract configuration that matches it. All you have to do to have good diction is to track the vowel (have a correspondence between the originally generated sound and the resonation system) and do the proper handling of the consonants.

Lindsey Christiansen

I like to say that we sing vowels, we articulate consonants, and we express text. We do not sing text; we sing vowels.

Shirlee Emmons

I have found vowel definition (therefore, diction) is a direct result of the tone being one with the 2750 Hz overtone; to make this happen, vowel modification is a must. Vowel sounds are modified in relation to pitch. If singers play the harmonics of their pronunciation well, they will get in return better tone, better resonation, better vowel differentiation, and better consonant articulation. . . . The pure singing vowel is not necessarily the same as the speech vowel; it is one that is clear on the particular pitch being sung. A pure vowel is not even the same one at different spots in the range. The vowel that works well is the one we clearly understand. The vowel that does not work well will not be understood because there is too much acoustical interference in the tone.

William McIver

I spend a great deal of time on vowel differentiation. For me, it works best to first start with a high-fronted vowel such as [i]. From that, move through [e] to [ɑ] to [o] to [u]. I try to maintain the same resonantal balance with this strategy. Most people go too far in moving from [i] to [e]; in doing so, they drop the top out of the sound. So, we work to get those two vowels to line up. When that's successful, we move on to [ɑ]. Once the [ɑ] vowels feel fairly well lined up, go on to the back vowels. Logically, if the tongue is fronted for the front vowels such as [i] or [e], then the back of the tongue is down a little bit. But all are done with the tip of the tongue at the back of the lower front teeth.

Oftentimes, I preface vowels with consonants because of the effect of the consonant on the vocal tract. I choose two particular consonants dependent upon what the student is missing in any given vowel. If it's a pressed vowel that needs more airflow, it's important to choose a consonant with a slightly higher breath flow than the succeeding vowel. If it's one where breathiness is a problem, then you might want to pick one that has slightly less airflow than the vowel that follows it. You can influence what they do in a way that will be helpful to them without burdening them with lengthy explanation.

Jack Coldiron

Use of IPA is an effective tool in gaining vowel accuracy and consistency in clear and understandable singing diction. Bright forward vowels are always possible, even when the larynx is in a comfortably low position. They are not mutually exclusive of each other.

Don't overform vowels with the lips. I want to hear the vowels; I don't want to see them.

Give attention to the possibility for vowel migration or vowel modification as you ascend.

Barbara Doscher

I think a pure vowel is one whose vibrato is even and can hook up with other vowels.

It's very easy to overthink as a singer, to the point where you become more like an automaton than having any spontaneity. You can use vowels. For instance, you might have someone whose back vowels are pretty muddy in the middle voice, yet you ask them to do an [e] vowel, they get very lateral and tight in the corners of the mouth and it sounds terrible. If you use a *ü*, which is a puckered front vowel, sometimes you can get that back vowel to have more ring in it. They begin to feel something that's a little different. Telling them what is different doesn't accomplish a whole lot.

Carol Webber

I like the traditional use of the Italian language in establishing clear vowels, but I'm concerned that if we teach native-speaking Americans only through a foreign language, we could blur their uniqueness. I like to relate the Italian vowels to words in our own language that already have conversational meaning. For example, when working to an Italian pure [i], I ask the student to speak several words in English based on [i] (tree, see, free, me, etc.). With [ɑ], I say, "What words do you use in your language in which you feel really a familiar and comfortable [ɑ]?" (father, top, stop, plot, etc.). Rather than holding all other languages "captive" to an American idiom, this simply invites the students to feel at home with vowels that have meaning in their own words, as they learn to achieve meaning (as well as correct sounds) in a new language.

Edith Davis Tidwell

"Keep vowels aligned" is one of my teaching phrases. I like to think of every vowel going through the same needle's eye and then finding its freedom (space) immediately on the other side. I also encourage students to practice, singing a phrase in the written rhythm, but on a repeated pitch, usually the median pitch in the phrase, to align vowels and reinforce a sense of legato.

Chapter Eight

Tension

Tension has a detrimental effect on the vocal instrument. Therefore, tension considerations occupy a major part of the vocal pedagogue's time and attention. Queried about tension, most of the teachers responded with answers that addressed the area of common tension and how tension can be surmounted.

Certain regions of the body are prone to inappropriate tension, which compromises vocal production. As listed by the interviewees, the area most often mentioned include the "articulators" (tongue, lips, throat, and jaw), the neck, shoulders, hands, the lower back, and the solar plexus. Because inappropriate tension impedes vocal activity, great interest is given to finding ways to isolate the areas that are tense and to then combat that tension.

STATEMENTS REGARDING TENSION AND STRATEGIES TO COMBAT TENSION

William McIver

I do address tension, but I don't tell my students to relax probably as much as a lot of teachers do. I think the places you are most likely to encounter tension are in the neck, the tongue, and the jaw, as well as an occasional perturbation in the area of breath management. When the appoggio is correct, that won't happen. It's not a feeling of relaxation; it's a feeling of balanced energization. However, many local tension issues result from the lack of a stabilized laryngeal posture achieved without tongue tension.

Marcia Baldwin

In many parts of the body, tension creates vocal problems: tension in the chest and the diaphragm, and muscle tension around the neck. First of all, you address the posture. Does the student have a straight line between the back of the top of the head and the heel? How is the neck position? Is the head too far forward? Is the jaw too forward? That's very often the case, and it's most important to correct such things. You use the muscles in the back of your neck for singing, especially when you get up into the high voice. How can you use them correctly if they're all out of alignment? A too-forward jaw totally distorts the tone. You need to get the jaw back into a normal position behind the cheekbones. A lot of singers seem to have some TMJ; you send them to a dentist or specialist. Arm and hand tension—there is tension with some singers in the armpit (underarm area), which results in arm stiffness and a hand that is shaped like a claw. First, I address the posture and then, as an exercise, I will have them move their arms as they sing, walk around the room, and so forth. We need to get rid of all possible tension points, most particularly in the head position. Tension and good energetic bodywork should not be confused, however!

Edward Baird

I think the big thing is diagnosis: you've got to figure out where the tension is. A lot of times, it's not where it seems most obvious. You have to diagnose it properly and then go after whatever you decide is really causing it, whether it's rigidity from position or posture, or from the tongue, the jaw, whatever. Once you've figured out where the tension is, you work to loosen it. A lot of times, it helps to conscientiously move or wiggle that place because a muscle in motion can't cramp to the point that it's rigid.

Bruce Lunkley

I'm not afraid to call attention to tension. I don't pursue it vehemently; I just put them in front of a mirror or give them a way of checking it themselves. If their jaw is tight, I have them massage their face and move their jaw while they're singing. They pay attention to their tongue while singing a vowel or while singing a line.

Joan Wall

Interfering tension in singing can be physical, emotional, or mental. Physical relaxation, emotional focus, and mental attitudes can support easy, free, flexible singing, as well as expressive performance.

Physical tension stems from rigidity of thought and movement. Our goal is to develop the ease, freedom, and flexibility of movement and of thought that supports fine singing. I use a multitude of sensory explorations, performance games, distractions, imagery, different expectation levels, and self-awareness processes to develop emotional and mental relaxation. We also use breath exercises to release tensions.

In addition, I suggest a variety of movement and body-use methods (Alexander, Feldenkrais exercises, tai chi, Pilates exercises, meditation, and yoga) to help students become aware of the existence of any interfering tension and to gain flexibility of the body and mind.

Helen Swank

I look upon diction as a diagnostic tool with students. If it's not clear, there's something wrong. When there is tension in any part of the system above the larynx, there will be problems with diction.

My daughter is a physical therapist. She tells me that any muscle constriction can be relieved to some extent by touch. Through touch, you can break and disturb the impulses that create the tension.

You often find that the students who have trouble with tongue tension have muscles so tight and constricted that you can feel them. When they sing, the constricted muscles bulge. Students can be their own monitors. I have them check it by asking them to put their finger beneath the jaw, feel what's happening, and develop the ability to sing without that happening. They need that kind of modification (i.e., biofeedback).

With general physical tensions, I go back to aikido. I go into the purely physical, such as bending over, stretching the back, and getting rid of whatever is creating tension in the back and shoulders by utilizing motion.

Most of all, I rely on words. With a student who's very tense, I usually can get them to relax if we have one "cue": "peace at the center" the old Quaker phrase. They tend to take that in, and they'll relax.

I tell them it's as if there's a central core to which all our extremities attach. They'll adapt to that, and I find their shoulders relaxing. That relaxation, then, tends to work inward, puts them into a more relaxed mental state, and acts on the little muscles of articulation and voice production.

Carol Webber

Continued postural work will reveal where tension points are located in each student. It's important to remember, however, that when you first present structural postural information to someone, the changes they make may feel "tense." Change is never comfortable. So it's important to have some courage in passing through the discomfort of change on the way to better habits. A fear of tension of any kind could eliminate change and progress. At the same time, the right information a bit misunderstood, misplaced, or applied wrongly can be disastrous. That's why I think the ear and the eye must be so good together. The teacher and student need frequent contact. Tension points in singing can be felt and identified by the singer more effectively than by someone else, yet the eyes and ears of an expert are needed to create solutions. Improper muscle use creates compensatory tension. Other muscles will compensate. These patterns need interruption and correction. I use the analogy of getting knots out of the shoulders.

Here is an example of common mistakes: In teaching the upright chest, it is easy to overdo. One creates a tremendous tension, thrusting the chest too high, and pulling the whole rib cage too far up. Another common tension point is created when the feet try to pull away from the ground. You get, instead of weight distribution through the pelvis to the floor, the body trying to isometrically exist somewhere between the floor and the ceiling.

Tongue tension is very common. Jaw tension is often a tongue problem. There are lots of misunderstandings; I think singers who try to "hold" vowel posture by arbitrarily shaping the vowel physically in the mouth develop a lot of tension in the tongue/jaw unit. Language (vowels) is mentally requested and neurally delivered. When you get singers to mean what they say, to "need" to tell, then the neural process completes itself. I believe this is why people sing so much better in performance when they literally know the meaning of every word and are engaged in generous communication.

Marvin Keenze

There is no tension in thought. The mind's ear can hear the desired sound. Vocal tension seems to begin between the thought and the sound, often between inhalation and phonation. When neck and articulation tension is evident, then it means that vocal control has gone from the ear to the organs that produce and modify sound. To work at the level of the tension is seldom successful. It is the causation that needs to be addressed. I appreciate the value of disciplines (such as Alexander Technique, Feldenkrais, yoga, Dalcroze, Tomatis, and others) to bring the kinesthetic and the breath and the sound into coordination.

Helen Hodam

Some students are very tense—for them, the Alexander Technique helps.

I certainly learned from one teacher that you never hold your rib cage in a tense position.

Shirlee Emmons

I am of the opinion that asking for a relaxed face or body before the singer has learned to command a vocal skill is useless. Working this way, you might get, at best, a very relaxed singer who can't do much vocally. I spend my efforts first teaching the singer to execute the particular skill correctly and efficiently (high notes, pianissimo, agility, etc.). After that has been accomplished reasonably well, then I begin the work of doing the skill with least tension surrounding it. "What tension can we remove from this particular effort without losing the skill?" "Now that you know exactly how to do this, what extraneous muscle action have you included that could be cut out?" Dividing the work into two parts like this actually improves the singer's command of the skill. They must know the skill from two sides, as it were. The skill is honed even further by knowing what excess muscle activity is not necessary.

Dale Moore

I find that as the student grows accustomed to the "noble posture," that in itself helps eliminate a lot of the tensions a student might have.

I feel that sometimes we have to go right to the heart of the matter and try to find exercises that are not only simple enough but also enough different from what the student might have done in the past. What we're fighting constantly is conditioning. If the student thinks "sing," and immediately thinks tense, or setting the jaw, or tightening of this area between the sternum and the belt or tension of any kind, then we must do everything we can to break those down. We must give the student something with which to replace the tension so there is no longer the association of "sing = tension." We have to give the student new and different patterns so those associations are broken down.

Cynthia Hoffmann

There is good and bad tension. What is interesting about unwanted or excessive tension is how to go about changing the response that produces it. Habitual use, even when it is wrong, feels right because it is familiar. This is even more complicated in singing because singers often identify with their "sound." Because it is produced within the body, students might feel uncomfortable changing their responses that also change their aural and kinesthetic sense of how they sound. I have found that the students who care more about how things feel—who want to produce their voice with greater ease and flexibility in order to better express the music—usually progress more quickly in eliminating unwanted effort.

The idea of "inhibition" (replacing an unwanted action with another more helpful action) is one of the principles of the Alexander Technique. One inhibits the old, familiar response and redirects one's energy into a new, more helpful one. I try to find out the best way students can sense what they are doing and then use that sense to help them change the habit. Alexander observed himself in a three-way mirror in order to "see" what he was doing that caused his hoarseness. He then gave himself new commands, new directions. The sense of touch coupled with the kinesthetic sense is also very important in guiding change, as is the aural sense in that it pertains to resonance.

Another important area relating to tension is emotion. One cannot perform well without it, and sometimes one cannot sing well with it! It is important to observe how and where emotional energy is channeled and physicalized when singing. I try to be sure that after working on technique the student sings a piece for me as he or she would in performance. This helps both of us to appreciate where the emotion "lives" in the body, whether the emotion is creating unwanted tension or is being channeled effectively, and so forth.

I have a sweet anecdote from one of my performance classes. A foreign student, a young tenor, was singing a song with a good deal of feeling and also a good deal of tension. I asked him where he felt the emotion when he sang. He replied, "I feel it in my heart, Ms. Hoffmann, but very quickly it goes to my neck!"

Lindsey Christiansen

I like to say, "Let the articulators articulate and not support." That's a hot issue. One of the major problems for both diction and fine singing is that the articulators often try to be the supporters. That is inappropriate. The tongue is the biggest offender; actually the tongue and the jaw are "cohorts in sin." One of my favorite quotes is what St. Paul called the tongue: the "offending member." The tongue is the offending member. I'm not sure if it offends in the same way that St. Paul thought it did. In any event, the tongue and jaw are the real issues. I can't think of a single singer I've talked to who didn't at one point have a problem with inappropriately using the tongue and the jaw to support the voice.

I spend probably 80 percent of the voice lesson dealing with tension. I try not to talk about tension negatively, but I must say that when I reflect on my own teaching, I need to figure out ways to deal positively with eliminating tension.

The sternum needs to be high with a feeling of openness. I like to talk about an "open book" in the sternum, with the shoulders down. There is a feeling of rootedness in the sternum, which, in a way, is a "good" tension. There's "good tension" in the ribs when they don't collapse inward. There's even "good tension" sometimes in the buttock muscles; I don't think you use that kind of tension very often, but it's there for you if you need it.

There should not be tension in the knees—those need to be loose. Tension in the neck muscles is just catastrophic. Tension in the back of the neck is a real problem area for a lot of students as is tension in the hands. Hands and jaw are similar; they give some kind of indication of what's going on with the air. The air is not doing its job, the hands are.

I spend a lot of time moving student's shoulders around, moving the head, and so forth. I have several things I do for jaw tension: I make students sing with their thumb on the alveolar ridge and the back of that thumb pushing the jaw back; or I have them put the tip of a finger on the nose and the knuckle on the jaw while making sure the tongue is touching the lower teeth and then have them sing a scale that way. The jaw is back as well as down.

With the tongue, it's not so much front tension as back tension that is the culprit. For that, I have students feel under their chin. Lots of times they get intensity in the sound from the tongue (tension), so I ask the student to give up some of the intensity in the sound for a period of time; just accept the fact that the sound is going to sound airier until there is more sensation of the released air being the generator of the sound rather than pressure in the tongue.

Oren Brown

I have a term that I call "noninterference." William Vennard (author of *Singing: The Mechanism and the Technique*) used to call this "freedom for action." "Relaxation" is really not a true description because if a person is truly relaxed, he or she is not going to do much of anything, except maybe die! There is activity of certain muscles, and then we remove any activity that we do not want. I use the term "noninterference." There are many physical exercises—people have worked at studies of these for years. One of the oldest studies in getting control of muscles of the body is yoga. You find out you can activate what you want and get the rest out of the way. Today, there is a lot of interest and use of the Alexander Technique and the Feldenkrais Method.

Anything that a person can do to arrive at a state of what I call a "natural poise of balance" is desirable. This is the state that a diver arrives at just before he is ready to step into his activity. He stands on the board and everything seems to line up. Then he's all ready to "press the computer," the reflexes he has trained begin to take over, and he goes through his actions. This is what we do in our training of singing: we train reflexes so they can respond to our mental impulse.

I sometimes compare singing to an act of juggling. You can't start juggling with several things at a time. You're darn lucky if you can get an object going from one hand to the other and not drop it on the floor. You find out what those muscles have to do to get that one object going and finally get to the point where the muscles are doing it by themselves. Then you can try experimenting with two. It's this way that we learn in singing—get one action so that it will respond to what we're thinking. We set up kinesthetic responses. A singer is an athlete and has to condition things one at a time. As one seems to be established, another can be added. This is the point where I start my teaching—establishing as much as possible a sense of noninterference.

Laura Brooks Rice

The two biggies are jaw and tongue tension. I find that it helps to point it out and make them aware of it. The jaw and tongue are related. I've found that if you can't get it with one, go to the other, and it usually corrects itself. I have them work a lot with the back of the jaw because very often they only work with their chin and then they press down. They need to find the sensation of the back point of the jaw releasing and pulling back into an expanded neck.

I deal a lot with the muscles in the back of the neck and the muscles at the base of the skull, and with feeling a release as you're going up and over through the scale. I've done a teeny little bit with Alexander Technique in that area. I don't do it a lot because I think it relaxes you a little bit too much to sing, but it's wonderful for this area and for feeling the release through the upper chest and the back of the neck. That usually helps them eliminate the jaw tension and the neck tension.

Jack Coldiron

I start with body posture and alignment, and loose jaw, lips, and tongue. It's important to find ways to avoid any sort of set position of the jaw or the head; instead, find a looseness about it all. Don't overform vowels with the lips. I want to hear the vowels; I don't want to see them. Find the proper position of the tongue, the tip of the tongue forward but always loose and ready to move in order to articulate. Proper breathing and support are fundamental for ease of singing and feeling less tension. We use the mirror (often) and tape the sessions on audio/video.

Practice in the intended venues of performance to adjust to the acoustics and physical "feel" of the place. This will help to negate possible surprises and possible tense situations. One of the great things for relieving tension is preparation. If you know what you're going to do (through thought and through practice), you tend to be less tense. I assign reading and the video of *The Inner Game of Music* and also *The Performer Prepares*. I have found those helpful. Singing really ought to be easy. If it's not easy, find something else to do.

Barbara Doscher

I talked about the K board already. I like yoga, Alexander, Feldenkrais—all of those things. If you have someone with extreme abdominal tension and they're so single-minded about supporting that even the K board doesn't help, then you need to get their feet off the floor. I sit them in one chair and put their feet on another so they simply can't grip the floor.

Leslie Guinn

I tell the students we are going to use distractions; then I ask them to do various physical tasks while singing that seem unrelated to singing, such as waving their arms in opposite directions, or slowly lifting one foot, and so forth. The student is distracted from the pattern that created the conflicting tensions, allowing a freer way of phonating. This easier pattern is always kinesthetically preferred and repeated until it replaces the earlier habit.

Edith Davis Tidwell

Reducing tongue tension: Be mindful of allowing the tongue to rest lightly on the bottom teeth while singing the phrase a few times.

Reducing jaw tension: sing the phrase on [bla bla bla]. Also, one can place the little fingers lightly into the outside of the cheeks at the molars while singing.

If the body (or sound) is rigid, I often have the student do an outward motion of gentle sway and/or fluid movement with the arms to inform a release and freedom from within.

Meribeth Dayme

The first problem that causes tension is *A*-ttention to the voice and the effort to "get it right" and, with it, fear of performance.

These things are not built into the way we work with the voice. For me, it's really important that when you set up a way of working with the voice, not only do you set up your *intention*, but also you have exercises that are part of your routine that are freeing, that don't have to be "right," that can be fun, and that can be played with, moved to, and improvised with and without the music. The songs we sing, whether the text is serious or not, can be done in a spirit of play and fun. Ultimately no songs are so sacred that we cannot have fun with them. When we play, we use many parts of the brain and body that facilitate learning and performance and we alleviate tension. When a singer comes in a room and starts with a scale, very seriously trying to get it "right," practice begins with analyzing and criticizing. That will ensure that I begin my rehearsal with tension.

The inner talk and the vocabulary that we use with ourselves can be a major cause of tension and negativity. Is it a vocabulary that is kind, or are the singers beating themselves up? There are so many factors that create tension in us that we have to look at the way we address these, in the way we approach music, the way we practice, the way we approach performance, the way we approach lessons, and in the way that teachers approach their pupils.

Stephen King

I don't talk about it. If I can get somebody aligned and energized and they're singing on their breath, we don't have those issues.

Jaw tension, tongue tension—I really try to avoid pointing that out. I'd rather work from the other side and not spend my limited time doing that. It gets back to finding balance, because there's got to be some sort of essential, immediate, positive tension in the body, like any athletic event, to make it work. After that, eliminating anything excessive is usually when they get better.

Jeannette LoVetri

Tension is relative. A dramatic tenor has to have a lot of "tension" within the system to sing well. Ditto a high belter. If the mechanism is predisposed to make a lot of sound, and if the singer develops a level of comfort and freedom while singing, the sound can be quite "tense" in that the mechanism is standing up to hard use, typically without repeated vocal fatigue or health issues. Tenseness, which is undue effort or strain caused primarily by unwanted constriction or use of the swallowing muscles during singing, should be eliminated through vocal exercises and breathing coordination. It takes a lot of strength to sing well at a high professional level. Most singers don't know that that means without training.

Mary Saunders-Barton

Physical tensions interrupt the flow of communication and endanger vocal health. I have a number of strategies to work on release in the studio. Engaging in familiar actions such as shooting baskets, bowling, or tennis, which require follow-through, can be useful. Many of the movement disciplines are helpful in this regard. I rely on the expertise of colleagues who specialize in the work of Moshe Feldenkrais, Catherine Fitzmaurice, and Frederick Alexander, for example, to help me with my students. I use balance boards and inflatable rings to focus attention on the abdominal core muscles and to encourage a released, energized stance. Any kind of torqued stance as in yoga-based positions is useful in accessing core muscles. Problems with tongue retraction or jaw and neck tension can be tricky and sometimes require minute-to-minute monitoring to identify and correct. If singers are not aware of the holding, there is no possibility of change.

Chapter Nine

Imagery

Imagery and the use of images to develop vocal technique is an area in which there is as much controversy as there is interest. Voice teachers use imagery to teach technical issues; others avoid imagery in teaching technique, feeling that it only has a place in the interpretive aspect of singing. With this division in mind, the pedagogues were asked if imagery played a part in their teaching or not. The purpose for asking this question was twofold: (1) to determine if the pedagogue felt imagery had a place in teaching the basics of vocal technique or to assist in training the body responses necessary to good singing; and (2) to collect representative examples of analogistic images that might capture the essence of this more intangible, yet integral, part of teaching voice.

PLACE OF IMAGERY IN THE PEDAGOGUE'S TEACHING

Do you make use of certain images that help your students grasp the vocal concepts? If so, what are they?

Cynthia Hoffmann

Imagery can be helpful vocally when it supports the physicality of the instrument. Curves, squares, and triangles can be structural reminders of physical shapes within the body. For example, "square your hips," a "square jaw," a "round shape," a "smile under or behind the eyes," the "point of a crescendo," and the "inverted megaphone" are all commonly used expressions that relate to a structural image. The image of these shapes can help the student project what is internal into an outer construct, which can be helpful as well. Artistically, images related to the text and music support the creative process in music making, and can be evocative and very powerful.

Edward Baird

I don't think that using imagination and images is bad at all; I really think it's quite useful. You might hear of some that are terribly gimmicky or so "far out" that they lack any practical connection. Anything like that has to be used with moderation, and the limits of the moderation are based upon how successful it is.

Marcia Baldwin

I will use imagery if I haven't been able to get the tone quality I'm looking for any other way. I have been known to ask a student to find a shape for that particular vowel and a color for it. I use imagery most when the vocalism on a piece is in place and it's time to get to musical interpretation and textural colors.

The images come out of my own creativity and experience in teaching. People are so individualistic in their learning styles and their ability to comprehend and conceptualize that we have to be very, very creative as teachers. So I will pull all kinds of things out of the hat if need be.

Richard Miller

The voice is an acoustic and physical instrument; it is not correct, in my viewpoint, to make up imagery about physical and acoustic processes because those factors are factual. Where imagery in singing comes is in its artistic aspects. In other words, if I am singing an aria or a song, I am absolutely visualizing everything I'm singing and, in fact, I do it in color. I'm not thinking about tones coming out of my forehead or the top of my head, or whatever, because imagery does not belong in the area of physiology.

Because the body functions a certain way and the voice functions a certain way acoustically, it's not necessary for people to make up new physiology. To tell someone that a sound is purple, green, or orange has no validity because one person's imagery, even with regard to concepts of sound, is not like another's. I think it's incorrect to try to put one's own imagery on someone else. What you need to do is give them factual information; then they can do their own imagery based upon their own sensations.

I don't believe you should use imagery for managing the physical aspects of singing; I think you should use the imagery for the interpretive aspects of singing.

Helen Hodam

I use images. I use a variety, since one may help someone and mean nothing to another. Some of the images that voice teachers use are hilarious and really not much help. But I try—as with breathing—to work from something that is a natural physical thing that they do.

Helen Swank

Yes I use images, but they must have an acoustic/physiological truth. If the image has a scientific base, if the student actually knows what is going on, [then] it can be helpful in the singing process.

When I was an undergraduate student, I seemed to get along fine without knowing about the science. But when I started to teach privately, I realized there was so much that I didn't know . . . and I'm one who has to know! I felt like I was walking on Jell-O while teaching. So I went back to graduate school, but I didn't have any of the courses (in pedagogy) like there are now.

When I began to teach at the university (Ohio State University), I was responsible for establishing some of the courses in pedagogy. I had to go to the medical school and the Speech and Hearing Science Department to get the information I wanted. To me, that information was like night and day. It gave me an understanding of the things that had been like Jell-O!

Dale Moore

I use very little imagery because I find that unless the students can hook into what you mean by that image, it doesn't mean much. Sure, we know we want the sound to be free, we know we want the sound to be beautiful, we know we want it ultimately to have resonance, but the employment of terms that really do not reflect what is actually happening, I think, are more hurtful than helpful. I think the answer is I use little, if any, imagery.

Shirlee Emmons

I try to be extremely structured and clear about technical matters because that is my primary function, but one can't avoid images. They are very useful because they are shortcuts to achieving the technical skills. I want the singers to be able to go home and practice well. If you give an instruction like "Pretend you're in a perfumed New Orleans night," they may go home, sing, and ask, "Is this what she meant? Is this what I did that she liked?" A command like "You must love this note" is well and good and probably useful, but if they cannot be executed satisfactorily a second time, then the command is virtually useless. The images I use are the ones that support the physiological evidence I have given the singers. Once I give that evidence, once I have explained why it is true, and labeled it clearly as to whether it is my opinion or proven fact, I then may use my images to help teach the singer to learn the skill. That is, my images lead the work while the singer is in the process of learning the skill, after which the singer's images remain the operative force.

This is an area in which I have changed radically since my relationship with the performance psychologist Alma Thomas, with whom I have written the new book for Oxford: *Power Performance for Singers*. She has taught me the efficacy of allowing students to choose the image that describes the skill for them. Once singers have experienced accomplishing the skill, and know they can execute the maneuver, then together we proceed to construct an image for the singers' "feeling" of doing the skill well. This image must accurately reflect both the physiological tasks and the feedback when doing the tasks well.

For example, attempting to lessen laryngeal tension during high notes by trusting the air, I follow the excellent advice of the late James McKinney. Between inhalation and singing, singers pause and suspend the air for five beats, during which time they pretend to be still inhaling (thus keeping the cords open) and searching out any tiny amounts of tension in the neck, followed by a gentle onset into tone. After singers can do this with ease, I say, "Give me three adjectives for how the throat feels during the suspension." Adjectives that were forthcoming from singers during this exercise included "buoyant," "empty," and "loose." After several more tries, the singers choose the adjective that best sums up their feelings during a successful exercise. Incidentally, most singers choose the word "empty."

Keeping the thought of "empty" during the onset and throughout the singing helps immensely. The only drawback is that I must remember each singer's adjective in future lessons! A small price to pay.

Another example is in relation to legato. I like to say there are no high notes and no low notes. On the piano, high notes are to the east, sort of. On the clarinet, they are to the north. As for vocal high notes, we have the habit of saying "up" for them because they are north on the musical page and because the resonance feels higher in the body. Because singers' bodies are their instrument, the thought of the high note being up will hinder the high note in many ways. I ask my singers to sing straight ahead. To facilitate their thoughts of straight ahead, I encourage them to make a gesture of straight ahead with the arm as the musical line goes on. At one time I also used a red velour cover draped on my piano and had the singers push against the nap while singing. Now I use a coaster lined with felt that slides easily on the wood on the piano. The singer keeps the coaster moving during the phrase and then begins again with the next phrase. Inevitably, the hand starts to move after the phrase has begun. Inevitably, the hand stops for every consonant. Inevitably, the hand stops at every pitch change, especially when going to a high note. When the singer has learned to keep the hand moving regardless of the problems, then the air is also moving and the legato has improved dramatically. The improvement comes when the singer has equated internally the movement of the coaster with the movement of the breath. Most importantly, the movement can be seen.

Alma Thomas is also convinced that voice teachers do not sufficiently use the word cues that embody images for technical skills. For example, when working the high sternum of the appoggio, I introduce the two salient word commands. While the students are singing, I can remind them of the falling sternum with the single word "up!" When the next inhalation comes along, I can remind the singer of the correct maneuver with the single admonition "sideways!" What the voice teacher must do is to construct an image that portrays the least common denominator of what the skill is all about. Images, not limited to visualization but including all the senses, play a large part in the learning and retaining of a motor skill.

As to how I became acquainted with these images, I do believe that I made them all up myself, usually at the witching hour of 3:30 a.m. when I always wake up. While getting back to sleep, I contemplate the vocal problems I have yet to solve. A lot of wonderful ideas come to me then. I am not averse to stealing other teachers' good ideas, but I always give credit to the originator. No guilt that way! I found many of the late Barbara Doscher's inventions to be extremely useful, but I told her that I was going to use them, and I gave her credit each and every time.

Bruce Lunkley

I use imagery constantly. I'm constantly saying "as if . . ." or, "like . . ." or, "imagine that . . ." For instance, I told a student that her sound was really stuck in her mouth and she really ought to try and let that sound go out over her glasses. She stood there and did it. All of a sudden, there was a high Ab down to a low Ab. She'd had about a six-note range before that. It usually doesn't work that easily—it's not magic.

I think it's important to use imagery. I've used it more and more in recent years, and I feel my teaching has become much better as a result.

Lindsey Christiansen

Yes, I use images, for some students more than others. I use images not in a technical way but in a way that combines thinking about text and technique. I find images more useful when it's necessary to use the voice in a certain way because of the demands of the text; to come up with the right image to get the kind of sound needed, I mostly use images that combine thinking about text and technique.

Oren Brown

I'll do anything I can to help them find themselves. Images? Sure, if an image is a reality to them. Sometimes I'll ask them to tell me what the image is because I'm not inside their heads.

Laura Brooks Rice

Yes, I use imagery but balanced with the facts and the sensations of singing. I talk a lot with my students. This is what I was used to in my own lessons. How does that feel? Describe it—

this was my own training. You understand the sensations of your own voice and can verbalize them.

Jack Coldiron

I don't have a set system of images, but I certainly do use images—anything that comes to my mind on the spot. I like to try to manufacture ideas that come out of the situation. I'm willing to try whatever works. I encourage imagination by the student; anything that may bring about freedom of thought and/or action to the singing expression. Imagery should not supplant the reality of necessary technique. However, I am reminded of a conversation between two world-known and respected singers as reported in *Time* magazine some years ago. Joan Sutherland and Marilyn Horne were discussing vocal technique. Sutherland suggested that it was helpful to imagine the tone opening like a blossom with ease and fullness, to which Horne is reported to have replied, "But Joan, darling, something is going on in the throat!"

Barbara Doscher

For technical matters, I speak in general to the muscles, not to the brain. Sometimes you have to speak to the brain if the students are intellectually oriented (because they simply can't tolerate not knowing about what they're doing).

As far as images, I think any idea that is based on buoyancy is fruitful. I also like to ask students questions (i.e., what they think it feels like).

Carol Webber

I use imagery; I believe that getting students to have their own imagery is important. My imagery works for me, but it might not work for you. At the same time, a good imagination and a sense of analogy that's appropriate is very helpful. These are areas in which you can introduce a little humor into the lesson. I have come to believe that we should not, as a rule, use analogies that we cannot then explain physiologically why that image works. And if you can't draw a specific relationship to the proper physiology in the body, then that image is ultimately not going to do any good and could do harm.

Leslie Guinn

I don't use imagery very often, preferring instead to help the students understand as much as possible the mechanics of achieving the desired sound. Understanding enables them to work effectively toward duplicating the sound, even on bad days. In a crisis situation, images can be unreliable as a method of correcting temporary vocal problems. I will use imagery occasionally to assist in breathing, speaking of hollow legs, balloons in the belly, and other similar illustrations. Those I use most often came from colleagues at the Aspen Music Festival, one the principal clarinetist of the Cincinnati Symphony and the other an excellent Alexander Technique practitioner from Israel.

Joan Wall

All learning is sensory based! We learn by what we feel, hear, and see.

Students use their internal sensory representations to build all aspects of their singing: vocal technique, memorization, musicianship, interpretations, characterizations, and artistic performance. Obviously, then, how we use our visual, auditory, and kinesthetic senses in teaching becomes a high-level decision—one that is seldom strongly addressed in pedagogy classes. I try to stay sensitive to what is going on inside my students.

Each of us is a unique person, and we each have our own unique set of sensory representations that are meaningful to us. The way we use our senses is highly refined: my own set of sensory representations may be quite meaningful to me but not meaningful at all to you. You and I probably view the world quite differently through our internal senses!

For example, when I was an undergraduate voice student, my first voice teacher used visual imagery for communicating ideas about vocal technique (each tone looks like a shimmery pearl on a necklace), but his images didn't seem meaningful to me and I improved slowly. My second teacher spoke in quite different terms—describing what I should feel (feel buoyant as you sing the high note) and how I should physically move (move the tip of your tongue forward for an [i] vowel), and I improved rapidly.

Only later did I understand why I responded as I did. We were experiencing the world in very different ways.

I continually remind myself that when I as a teacher give each of my students my own kinesthetic imagery, it will reach some, but it will also miss others, just as my first voice teacher's restricted visual imagery missed me. What I must do as a teacher is to respond to my student's internal world, not try to bring him or her into my world. I must step into the student's world and use his or her manner of representation—not mine. I must use the student's imagination!

This means that I must listen and look at a student to discover how he or she processes information and uses internal sensory representation. I must ask questions, using carefully designed language, to elicit the information I need to teach. I can use specific tones of voice when I talk to a specific student, or move my body in specific ways.

After I have gotten some understanding of the student, I teach a new idea by painting mental pictures and conjuring up sounds, smells, tastes, and emotions, giving physical instructions, through stories, metaphors, similes, and simple descriptions—all of which will be specific for the particular student.

The manner in which we use the senses and guide the internal representations of our students can be efficient or inefficient. As an educator, I am trying to develop a greater sophistication and specificity in the use of sensory representation for learning. I want to more quickly, enjoyably, and precisely use sensory representation in the studio—for teaching technique, musicianship, interpretation, personal confidence, and artistic performance.

Edith Davis Tidwell

I often use imagery in my teaching. I find new imagery to use every day. Things that I see in nature translate immediately into the process of singing for me (e.g., a spiderweb seems so delicate, yet is so strong! It's like a beautifully sung pianissimo phrase—it is not careful, timid, or fragile but continuously spun with intricate strength).

Meribeth Dayme

I love it!

There are obvious images that are silly. There is a history of poor and misleading imagery in the history of vocal pedagogy where people have argued for imagery or for mechanical approaches. Today, I think those two go hand in hand. You can get the body to work by having a useful image, or you can get your image to inspire the physical aspects to function better. It is a matter of understanding that it is a whole unit and not separate, that mind-body-spirit are one and they are not necessarily separate. Obviously, you have to work with what the student brings to you. There are some people who just will not do anything without an intellectual explanation first. That's the way they are and you have to meet them halfway. For me, I like to get the imagination working, because when it does, we have a different singer. The imagination feeds the voice and adds sparkle, meaning, and joy to the performance. It is particularly useful to play with the text, making sure that the text is a whole dramatic entity on its own without the music. When the drama and imagination are part of the text, that song will truly communicate with the audience.

Robert Edwin

The use of imagery in my studio is usually restricted to emotional contexts and character development. My students become very comfortable with fact-based voice technique. They learn that much of the imagery used in traditional voice pedagogy is inaccurate and misleading. Phrases like "relax the throat," "make the tone go out of the hole in the top of your head," "bounce the sound off the hard palate," "imagine a string pulling your body up," and the ubiquitous "sing from the diaphragm," are factually impossible to do and can often cause more problems than solutions. Simply explaining and obeying the laws of nature gets better results.

Stephen King

I use almost none. I'm not against them. I do use analogies, and some I get kidded about (and they're somewhat memorable), but they have more to do with images that relate to singing.

Most of what I do is hands-on, and then taking and using music to relate what we're trying to do with the technical work.

Jeannette LoVetri

I try to stick to images that have to do with the body. I ask singers to bring awareness to the face, the jaw, the lips, the neck, and the shoulders. I ask them to listen and teach them what to listen for, both subjectively and objectively. I rarely ask for subjective images unless I am working in repertoire, and only rarely then.

If a singer comes up with an image on her own, I try to incorporate that in conjunction with a functional behavior so the artist can mentally associate them. Every singer has his or her own "inner landscape" and that is more important than any image I might suggest. I found subjective imagery very frustrating when I was a student as I never understood what the teacher was seeking. Often it made things worse. Considering that I was a child performer who sang well in the first place, having a teacher give me subjective images that were meaningful to her but not to me made me self-conscious and nervous, and that absolutely worked against me for a long time. Years.

Mary Saunders-Barton

My initial response to this question was, I soon realized, completely untrue. I followed myself around for a few days, from lesson to lesson and class to class, and realized that my teaching is loaded with images, some new, some so old I can't remember where I first heard them or if I made them up myself. I told my grad students to point out every time I reached for an image and hilarity ensued. I even found myself stealing some of theirs! Although I always want to be sure I am not creating confusion about what is actually happening in the body, an image can often clarify physical actions when other approaches fail.

Here are a few that recurred again and again:

1. I use the image of a tree trunk with roots, leaves, and branches to accentuate the importance of building a strong "core" voice that supports extended range, high and low.
2. I describe mixed registration as a "train track" that can carry the voice wherever it needs to go. This embraces the concept of a continuum for seamless registration. I have heard myself say, "the mix is the red carpet to a belt."
3. For vowel "tuning," I have long used the term "shepherd vowel" in working on classical vowel production and resonance sharing. One vowel leads the others "into the corral" so to speak. In any style, finding the "lead" vowel can help negotiate tricky areas and unify resonance. For classical vowels, "hang pictures side by side on the wall" or "line up jars on a shelf." For long vowels, musical theater singers can have great success with a "Home Alone" face.
4. For tonal consistency throughout range: keep the lights on all the way up and down.
5. Images for balancing registration, which I am sure many of my colleagues use:

   > To take weight off high notes: a trampoline, a pole vault
   > To take weight off low notes: a toddler on a mattress, not a sumo wrestler; lower the bucket but hang on to the ropes

6. To reduce subglottal pressure: lift a feather, not a Steinway.
7. I use the notion of a "reset button" or "etch a sketch" to regain balance between phrases.
8. For classical versus musical theater resonance: move a mansion to a studio apartment.
9. To help with gasping releases between phrases: keep the tires inflated when you park the car (this I heard from a grad student).

It's a far from exhaustive list, but you get the idea.

EXAMPLES OF IMAGES EMPLOYED

Laura Brooks Rice

Release—that's a big buzz word for me: to release emotion, to release sound, and to release yourselves.

"Up and over"—releasing as you sing. Sending the air up and over and feeling that the air releases the sound that way.

One thing that I say a lot is, if they don't feel the support from way down low and they feel it only with their diaphragm, they'll give themselves the Heimlich maneuver. They're pushing air through instead of sending it through with the abdominal muscles.

I describe the breath very much like a swimmer's breath in that the swimmer needs to get from one place to another. They have a timed amount [in which] to take in their air when they turn their head. They have to take a good quality breath from the bottom of their lungs. Good long-distance swimmers don't take many breaths. They turn their head and get several strokes down the pool before they turn their head again. I also describe the breath for singing and for swimming as a gulp, not a gasp—good swimmers gulp their air, they don't gasp, or they'd get tired.

[Regarding tone,] I like to teach a balance up and down. Very quickly, they can understand what I'm talking about when I say it's very much like the balance knob on your stereo: If you turn it too much to the bottom (bass), it's too woofy. You want to have a nice balance between.

Marcia Baldwin

I was working with a young woman in a master class who was having trouble singing a pure [ɑ], so I had her picture the [ɑ]. First she had to decide whether it was in capital letters or script. Then we put a color to it. She decided she wanted this to be a deep blue, like below the surface of the ocean. This sort of thing works quite well. Picture an unbroken stream of air—for the air to continue to flow.

Picture the neck area (where the instrument is housed) just as wide as the shoulders so it's part of a whole breath column.

I have used the image of a steel tube (like on the top of factories, a big smokestack that has an opening) as their body and then have them visualize the breath column moving up through the tube with the tone coming out of the top.

Lindsey Christiansen

I like to talk about the nature of the body, the feeling of the "environment for singing." A feeling of openness and width in the ribs, width in the nose, and openness in the head.

I like to talk about an "open book" in the sternum with the shoulders down.

I spend a lot of time having students understand the connection of breath to sound and that air hooks with sound right away.

I talk about when you take in the breath, have a split second of readiness so that you don't get on a merry-go-round that goes all the time.

I talk about spin, every note vibrating. I think it's very important that the air not stop between notes—the impetus for making a sound is mental, really.

I talk about the breath being a release, not being pushed out. If there's any pressure at all, it's not a pressure against the voice. The air is being released out.

We talk about the feeling of just before a yawn—the smelling of a rose, or that kind of sensation of expectation, of a very inviting feeling. I like to talk about a feeling of width, width on the inside—the inner smile—a lot of openness in the nose and a smiling wideness in the eyes. I talk about height in the tone and about it not falling into the mouth.

I talk about the hollow head, feeling the nose open—it feels like you've got another set of nostrils in back that are open.

. . . the jaw almost feels as if the room was full of water and your jaw is floating in it.

. . . the constant connection of the voice as a piece of velvet. I have them push their hand along the velvet, and then imagine the velvet.

When I work with coloraturas, I tell them it's like doing an arcade game: The voice goes very quickly, but it can't touch the sides. The tone flies through, but it can't touch the sides.

When dealing with upper passaggio, it's very important that it stay "lean" so that the depth that's needed for the high doesn't get "used up" in the passaggio. There's again a feeling of dark and bright at the same time.

An image that is helpful in keeping the soft palate up is to have student imagine they are eating a hot pizza and don't want the cheese to stick to the roof of the mouth.

Oren Brown

I like to think of vowels as colors of the rainbow and to use those shadings for conveying the emotional meaning of the words.

If you know that the pitch is starting high, and you have a scale that comes down, then you want to retrace your steps. It's like a roller coaster that comes down with a zoom and then goes back up through its own momentum without any push behind it.

I sometimes compare singing to an act of juggling: we train the reflexes so they can respond to the actions that we want. You can't start juggling with several things at a time. You're darn lucky if you can get one going from one hand to another and not drop it on the floor. Then you find out what those muscles have to do to get that one object going, and finally you get to the point where the muscles are doing it by themselves. Then they can try experimenting with two. It's in this way that we learn to coordinate one thing so that it will respond to what we're thinking.

Sometimes the sound is like a waterfall going backward in your throat, not something going out. In other words, projecting is not something that you get behind and push out. Sound is something that starts right here in your larynx. From that point it is going down, back, inside, and every direction like light from a lightbulb.

Bruce Lunkley

I refer to things that are visual, physical, or aural in their experience. For example, I say, "Even when we talk about focus or registration, we talk about the fact that the voice is an acoustic instrument. When we are first learning to sing, there are times that we have to divorce it from our humanity and emotional life and just be the whistle that we really are. When we can whistle, we can whistle nicely, and we can whistle with meaning and feeling." With many, that's helpful. That's certainly not an image, but it very often finds its way into those discussions and those efforts.

Helen Hodam

As far as images for focus, placement, or resonance, I have a couple, but I emphasize that it's the feeling they will get. Some people talk about the point of a triangle and that the throat is open. One teacher I knew very well talked about big circle, small circle—the idea of a concentrated vowel but [with] room inside. I like that.

Richard Miller

I use the imagery that's there in the song. If I'm singing "By a lonely forest pathway," I see that pathway, I see the color of the trees, I see how the pathway goes down to the water, I see the reeds. If there's a moon, I know whether it's a full moon or a half moon. If I say to you "moon," you see something. That's the power of imagination; that's the artistic imagination that permits communication.

Shirlee Emmons

[On vocal high notes:] We have a habit of saying "up" for them because they are north on the musical page and because the resonance feels higher in the body. Because a singer's body is his or her instrument, the thought of the high note being up will hinder the high note in many ways. I ask my singers to sing "straight ahead."

After a period of learning what a high sternum feels like and how to inhale without disturbing the appoggio, I introduce the two salient word commands. While the student is singing, I can remind him or her of the falling sternum with the single word, "up!" When the next inhalation comes along, I can remind the singer of the correct maneuver with the single admonition "sideways!"

Marvin Keenze

When students negotiate large intervals, I sometimes find it helpful to say, "Why are you moving your throat so much? You're just moving the wrong thing. Don't move your throat—move your breath, move your sensation, but don't move your throat." They'll want to pull something up out of the bottom, rather than think of each note as a planet of its own but in the same solar system.

If they go to a high note and they've lost the [з], it means they've gone to their throat. They've lost their attachment to their little spontaneous place.

In singing speech, the vowels are really close together. I say we have a "singer's mouth." The singer's mouth is different than the chewing mouth—here's an inner mouth that helps to shape the vowels, and it helps to keep the vowels close. I tell them, "It will bring your voice closer to your soul"—in other words, closer to your emotions.

[On faulty singing:] Their tongues will pull up their larynxes—their tongues will sit so high and the hyoid bone will just pull right up. The action of articulation will disturb the inner poise of the larynx and the instrument's inner posture. So, we must articulate in such a way that it doesn't disturb our instrument. Whatever vowel we are singing must be hooked to our whole instrument.

I usually work through physical actions; I might say, "Breathe as if you are pleasantly surprised about something" or, "Stand in a dignified, noble posture."

Helen Swank

[On posture:] We use the old Quaker saying "peace at the center"—when they can visualize the "peace at the center" being something of a central core that all the extremities hang from, it tends to bring relaxation into the body.

[On breath:] As they go down into the lower voice ("chest voice," "heavy adjustment," whatever you want to label it), they need to learn how to utilize airflow. It's keeping it in a resonant tube, instead of blowing. As long as they can keep a resonant tube going, they'll have a little easier time getting across either passaggio.

Edward Baird

[The core of the sound] is like an electric cord: if the cord doesn't have a copper wire in the middle of it, it's not going to carry any current, no matter what color of insulation you put around it. The wire represents the focus.

A term I find useful is what I call "arching the vowel." When you approach that upper register, it's a matter of feeling like you're bouncing it off of your hard palate.

William McIver

I don't use very many images in technical work. My influence in this regard is Herbert Witherspoon. Witherspoon was a fine singer at the Met who was also briefly its general manager for about six weeks before he died. He firmly believed that the teacher's job is to get a student to experience what is right. He maintained that is best done by asking them to do something. We must bring the student to the correct experience. We choose exercises initially that are relatively simple and where the possibility for success is high. Then we add layers of complexity until all aspects of technical study have been covered.

Jack Coldiron

I ask for flowing kinds of sounds, unpressured kinds of sounds . . . the idea of closing your eyes and imagining how you want your voice to sound. Imagine the most beautiful sound you think you're capable of making, and then try it. Use the sense of imagination and concentration and shut out things by closing your eyes for a spell. I don't have set patterns, but I certainly think images are excellent. If I can find something that applies, I use it.

Leslie Guinn

I will say crazy things like "imagine you're singing out the back of your head" if I want them to find more space (but only after I've shown them where the soft palate is, how it raises and lowers, etc.).

I might tell them to "imagine" that the sound is coming out between their eyes, or I might ask them to imagine it coming anywhere. I always make it clear that's not really where it's coming from, that those are illusions. I really want that clear.

Edith Davis Tidwell

For large intervallic leaps upward, I visualize casting a fishing line over, into the middle of the pond—the source of energy into that release is "still standing on the bank." There becomes an ease in "dropping" that pitch over there.

I speak of a cantilever object to help the student understand the depth of abdominal support.

Inez Silberg, my first collegiate voice teacher, spoke of "extending Cheerios at the end of my nose for each vowel." That made (and still does make) sense to me—regarding vowel alignment—and "space around the place."

Another teacher, Gary Horton, spoke of seeing a small, shiny silver ball rolling on into the distance as I sustained a pitch at the end of a phrase. That kept the constant engagement of the breath and released any sense of tension or "holding" that pitch, and allowed the tone to "spin freely." I still use that exact imagery today in my own singing and teaching.

Fletcher Smith, the teacher with whom I studied the longest, used the phrase "make the mold and pour the gold." That sense of "pouring" and "allowing," with the focus or placement then being the funneling through the spout, just created freedom in the process of singing for me.

I talk of "coloring (or washing) the entire staff" downward from the pitch with the sound. This warms the sound and also promotes constant engagement of energy.

I like to think of releasing the vowel or consonant into the rest as opposed to the sense of "cut off."

I encourage the student to sense the feeling and not listen for the result. One cannot help but hear the sound, but should not listen for it.

I speak of keeping motion in the vowel and of viewing the consonants as connectors between the vowels.

Part 2

Training Singers: Practical, Artistic, and Professional Development

This section includes responses to the following questions:

- When you hear a student audition, what do you look and listen for?
- What is it that for you sets that student apart?
- How do you approach the first lesson with a new student?
- How do you structure a "typical" lesson?
- How do you guide a student's practice?
- How do you nurture and guide the student's "self-discovery?"
- How do you strive to help the student find that complete union of music and inner experiences that results in a powerful performance?
- What attributes do you feel contribute to the success of the young professional singer?
- What is your opinion of today's professional American "career-track" singer?
- Do you think there is what could be called an "American school of singing"?

An important part of the voice teacher's role is to help the singer build a sufficient and secure technique. Having established the foundation of a firm technique, the next level of training is concerned with the central goal of the singer-performer: to become an effective communicating artist. With this in mind, the teacher seeks to guide and shape the student's raw talent, to make the student aware of possibilities beyond the page.

Educating the young career-track singer transcends the immediate goals of technical proficiency. It recognizes the need to develop personal and artistic mettle that will allow the young singer to effectively compete in an increasingly complex, competitive, and demanding role— that of the professional singer. Given this concern, the pedagogues were asked to share their ideas and opinions on several issues.

Their answers contribute to an understanding of the artistic and professional development of the young singer. We gain insight and can be advised through their accumulated experience. This information, therefore, provides a valuable resource not only to the singers but also to the legions of voice teachers currently training young singers for a healthy, profitable, and successfully long career.

The association between teacher and pupil begins with the audition process and continues through the first and all subsequent lessons. The teachers were asked to share their thoughts regarding these preliminary stages of singer-teacher affiliation.

Chapter Ten

The Student Audition

When you hear a student audition, what do you look and listen for? What is it that for you sets that student apart?

Briefly, the qualities that figure most prominently in the teachers' assessment during auditions are as follows:

1. Vocal potential
2. Quality and core of the sound
3. Musical sensitivity
4. Expressiveness (also called "the need to communicate/desire to express")
5. Technical proficiency
6. Performance personality and poise
7. Vocal and performance strengths and weaknesses

TEACHERS' REMARKS

Carol Webber

The very first thing is how a person approaches a stage. You can often tell just by the way a singer gets from the edge of the stage to the curve of the piano if they want to be on the stage, if they need to be on the stage, and if they really love what they're doing. It's wonderful to be surprised when someone stumbles on and then sounds great. It's less interesting to be surprised when someone is "Johnny-on-the-spot," looks absolutely fabulous and then does not sound very good. But that need or desire to be on the stage is crucial.

Then, of course, the native sound of the instrument, whether it has real potential as a solo instrument; these are judgments we have to make whether we want to or not.

In higher levels of competition (after the junior year of college, if not before) and certainly for the young professional, the audition must show musical intention, musical integrity, and compelling communication, along with vocally healthy, vocally beautiful, projected singing.

William McIver

It very much depends on the type of audition. If you're hearing an eighteen-year-old freshman, you'll look for different things than you would in someone who is auditioning for the DMA [doctor of musical arts]. In a freshman, you're looking for potential. Oftentimes, young singers (especially men) have not sung for more than a year or two (if that) when they enter college. You might hear a little bit more polish from the women at that stage than you will from men because many of them have had more study and are vocally and physically more mature.

So, I look for potential. If I've changed any way in the last thirty years, it's that I used to look almost exclusively at the vocal potential; experience has taught me that there are concerns with musicianship and intelligence that need to be a part of the decision as well. So, I look at those areas. I look at SAT scores, and I look at class rank for incoming freshman (because we have had more success with students who have not had academic deficiencies). You might have a great voice, but it tends to be self-defeating if you're struggling with theory, history, and all the other aspects of being a music major. That doesn't mean that somebody who is very unskilled can't develop in those areas. I have certain people in my studio right now that I wouldn't trade for anything and their musical skills as juniors are just beginning to come along. Generally, nobody possesses the entire package at the beginning—so you see where they are and bring them to where they need to be.

You are still going to be involved in some remedial work at the master's level. Remediation should be minimal for doctoral students. By that time you should hear linguistic sophistication and commitment to textual immediacy and communication. If you're still having to cover those things at that level, it's difficult.

[On competition auditions:] This is a very interesting area. I find that good people, who are good teachers, still disagree on certain things in these auditions. I've thought about that a great deal. I think the reason for this is that you assess the package in front of you (i.e., a singer), and nobody's perfect. The question becomes how highly do you value their strengths or how important do you regard their deficiencies. That, more than anything, leads people (who otherwise might agree on a lot of things) to hold widely divergent opinions when judging competitions. I explain to my students, "This is the way it works, so you can't be discouraged by this. You just have to realize that what the judge may prize may not be the same things that you prize. However, if you consistently get that response from every audition that you enter, you better look at the things you value." At any level, one should expect an accurate performance. On the other hand, no matter how note perfect it is, if somebody lacks vocal talent or cannot communicate or lacks linguistic skills, it doesn't mean much to me either. I think it's a question of balancing those. You can say, "Okay, this is a terrific vocal talent, but the musical skills are lacking; or this is a very polished performance, but this singer will probably never be able to progress much beyond where he is right now because of his native vocal endowment. It depends upon the purpose of the audition: is it to uncover vocal potential that could lead to a professional operatic career, or is it to judge people who are giving the most polished performance at this particular stage of their development? I think that influences how one makes selections.

Richard Miller

For an incoming student, [I look for] potential, above all. This includes basic quality of the instrument, musicality, and communicative ability. At a competition, I look for an ability to accurately handle the chosen literature skillfully, and for an understanding of the text and the drama so that I, the listener, am drawn into the performance experience. The more important the competition, the higher the degree of finesse—both technical and communicative—required.

Helen Swank

I listen first for freedom and vitality in the singing voice. If these conditions are present, all manner of vocal technique insufficiencies can be overcome. Freedom and vitality show an undamaged instrument, and that is very basic. Of course, we always listen for beauty of quality and for expressiveness. If I hear these four things in a voice, I have great hope, and if the audition is for entrance into some vocal program, that's an exciting prospect for a teacher.

If the audition is for a role or an award, and so forth, one listens for the degree of coordination, freedom, vitality, ability to express, tonal beauty, and technical flexibility and capability. All of these things combine to give a presentation that can be adjudicated.

Jack Coldiron

I first listen for the basic quality of the voice. I also listen for what I hear as, in my estimation, the "right" sounds. If there is one note that sounds right, that gives me the basis for a starting place. I listen for ease of production. I listen for vibrato: is the vibrato constant, or is there a lot of straight tone singing? I pay attention to diction. Does it sound "natural"? Is it a diction I can accept, or is it manufactured—the stilted diction we often associate with singing (which I don't like). Also, simply, the use of language. Does the student seem to know how to sing in his or her own tongue? Does the singing interest me? Does it communicate?

I listen for personality in the voice and the whole presentation. Priorities, I would have to say, are freedom of sound, attitude and personality, and basic quality of the voice.

Marcia Baldwin

I assess the appropriateness of their dress for the stage, their poise, and an attitude of sincerity and commitment to the music. Energy in the performance and communication of text—rather than vocally showing off.

Shirlee Emmons

I would like to see the level at which the technical skills are put into the service of the singer's clear vision about the meaning of that piece. In other words, I want to see that singers have a strong sense of what that piece means to them and that they have also the technical skills with which to realize their vision. Performance supersedes technique in the real world of performance.

Cynthia Hoffmann

I listen for something that is personal and alive—what has been called a "life-affirming" quality. This goes along with a connection to the meaning of the text and the musical way in which it is expressed. Of course, if the instrument is beautiful, that is important too, but it is not the most important factor. The key thing is the way the student uses the voice to say something personal about the words and music. How this is accomplished gives me an idea of the student's awareness, balance, intelligence, and artistry.

Bruce Lunkley

I listen for what might be there, not necessarily what is there, but what might be there. I listen for musical intuitiveness because sometimes their vocal problems are getting in the way of that, but you can usually tell if they're trying to be musical or if they sense things musically. I listen for accuracy, rhythm, pitch, and language. I watch them physically to see if there are major tensions or minor tensions—are they breathing correctly, and do they know what they're doing as far as their body is concerned. Then I usually talk with them afterward, and occasionally I will even ask them to repeat the song in another key. We always use a professional accompanist for auditions.

Recently, we had a student audition with "Danza, Danza Fanciulla" in the low key. I asked the accompanist to put it up a third and asked the boy to try it there. It was much better. He said he liked that key better, but it was the only book he could find! Another girl learned the song with tape and couldn't sing it with piano. You just don't know what you're getting into.

I also look for poise and personality because that's all part of the game.

Joan Wall

When auditioning a prospective student, I look for alertness and vibrancy of personality, emotional involvement in the singing, general beauty of voice, and sensitivity to the music and the words. I notice the degree of naturalness in the singing and whether the singer displays excessive physical, vocal, and emotional tension. When interviewing singers, I will ask questions that help me evaluate their attitudes toward learning, openness to new ideas, and personal flexibility.

I work with a wide range of students—beginning and advanced, teachers, and performers. But the students I enjoy teaching the most are those who want to learn and grow, who are open to developing their emotional involvement, and who have a reasonable chance, in my opinion, to reach their goals.

Helen Hodam

I listen for how much natural voice is there. Sometimes you're not sure at first. We hear two numbers, and I look to see if they're musical and if they're involved. We give a sight-singing and tone-matching test to assess the practical side of the ear. That's always interesting; some of them don't have much voice, but they're good at those skills. It depends on their instrumental or theory background. But you want to see if there's a voice and musicality. Once in a while it's a pretty good voice, but you know they're not performers. If there is some vocal potential, you hope you can awaken and develop the musical involvement.

Oren Brown

When I hear an audition, I assess the student's technical status. Then, of course, I note his feeling for the music. I get a general impression of the voice's category, but I don't like to talk about what classification the student might be. When they start, they're a voice.

Later on, we find out where they belong, be it a coloratura, lyric, or what have you. I also listen for such technical things as diction, and so on, but most especially, I listen for technical status and musicianship.

Edward Baird

Of course, much depends upon the kind of audition it is. Generally, you first determine what is the state of their vocal and technical development. Personally, I first listen for the focus in the tone. If a singer has a well-focused tone throughout the range, that gives the core of the sound around which you can build colors and resonance. If the center of the tone isn't there, if it's not focused, that's one of the things you just have to do. I tell students that having good tonal focus throughout the range is like having an electric wire with the focus as the copper wire in the middle. You can put any color binding around it you want to, but if that core isn't there, it's not going to carry any electricity. That's one of the first things I listen for. Of course, if it's a person coming into the school or into the studio, I assess their general musicality and sensitivity from that standpoint.

Barbara Doscher

I listen to the basic instrument, no matter what the previous training has been. I listen for size and for the instrument's color. Just this afternoon, I was talking with one of my colleagues about one of his students. He said she didn't sound like much when she came in; "I heard five notes and they were gangbusters. The rest was terrible." I understand what he means.

It's those five notes that provide the building blocks for the rest of the voice.

I pay attention to the singer's appearance, stature, posture, and demeanor; what kind of self-confidence does that person have? They might talk to you and tell you one thing, but body language tells you a lot more.

I'm interested in people who, regardless of their technical level, have the desire to communicate something about the human condition, even if it's pretty crude and just the beginning of being creative. A number of times I'll ask people, "Why are you going through this agonizing training when you don't seem to have anything to say?"

Presence or charisma. I think that is what sets one student apart from another one.

Laura Brooks Rice

Things that stand out to me and what sets somebody apart from somebody else, initially, are the vocal color or natural vocal resonance; the size of the voice; a natural placement; intrinsic musical ability; phrasing and diction; and their interpretive skills at that point. Sometimes one hears a beautiful instrument that hasn't yet been influenced—I'm always willing to take a chance on those. There is what my colleagues and I call the "shiny penny" that sticks out. Sometimes those are easier to work with—those at a young age who haven't been adversely influenced—it's clearly a raw talent. On the graduate level, all of these things significantly improve and have begun to be defined and worked on.

Leslie Guinn

Experience and age, of course, will determine to a great extent the qualities I listen for at an audition. However, whatever the age, the primary attribute for me is musicality. Voices can almost always be improved, but I believe basic musical instincts are hard to come by as add-ons. Assuming musicality is present, I listen for potential in the instrument in the young voices, and intelligence and imagination in the older.

Marvin Keenze

I listen to see if there is an instrument of some character. I want to know something about the singers from the sound of their voice and from their communication of the music and poetry. I listen for the unique qualities of a voice. I look for a certain assurance in the presentation that shows me that this singer has confidence and joy in singing.

Graduate students should be able to sing convincingly in at least four languages. They should have a sense of the nature of their instrument. They should have poise and skill at the basic vocal technique areas of legato, pitch, and agility throughout their range by this time.

In order to work well with a student in my studio, there are certain attitudes that must be present. There has to be an open mind, an ability to listen, a flexibility to make changes, and a questioning mind. I like my student to ask me why I do what I do, and to let me know when they don't comprehend my remarks. I like a student who enjoys producing vocal sounds and needs to do it. I like expressive students who have a sense of humor. I like them to be passionate about the word and the poetry and to love literature and history.

Lindsey Christiansen

There are several kinds of student auditions. If it's a student auditioning for admission into the school, it's something we think about a lot because we hear so many auditions (especially in the spring).

There are really four or five things that I look for, any one of which, when absent, makes it very difficult to come to an affirmative evaluation.

First of all, I look for the quality of the voice, whether there is a beautiful instrument or a full instrument or whether the instrument is distinctive. In the voice performance degree program, we are highly selective. We only take in students we feel really have a crack at a career.

But who do I think is a person who really has a crack at it? I think it's somebody whose voice has something distinctive about it, either particularly pretty or particularly loud—even if it's ugly as all get-out. Loud can be a good predictor of vocal potential. It might not be beautiful at first, but it can certainly end up being very good. I look for a voice that I think will allow itself to release eventually. Most of all, I listen for a singer whose singing speaks to me.

I look for musicality: a joy in making music, understanding what a phrase is, and being sympathetic to changes in dynamics—musicality and a performing instinct. [There must be] a need to communicate. That is so vital. That is something that, in a way, one can sometimes learn to do, but there are people who are temperamentally just not singers. They're given wonderful voices but don't have that "biting in the stomach" that makes them need to communicate.

I also look for a real intelligence, what we call a "bright penny"—in the sense of having a sparkle and connection to text and a need to say the text. What sets a student apart?—one that moves me, one that speaks and has, for whatever reason, something to say. Even if the voice is not great, there is something that says something, that comes out of that need to communicate. Those are the ones I like the most. I find it's very rare that a student has a wonderful voice without that need. It happens occasionally, and it's sad when it happens, but for whatever reason, usually those two things go together. Musicality doesn't necessarily go with it, and intelligence doesn't necessarily go with it, nor does musical talent. Musical talent and vocal talent are two separate things; they don't always come together. It's always a sad twist of fate when they don't. By musical talent, I mean the ability to learn music quickly, accurately, and independently. By musicality, I mean the ability to bring the music alive by beautiful phrasing and insightful interpretation.

Dale Moore

For most of us, the voice, at least where it is now, is the first thing we listen for, especially if there is an intention of majoring in voice or trying for a career. We try to hear if there is real professional-caliber potential there or if this is an "avocational voice"—a person who might enjoy singing but should not be encouraged to pursue singing as a profession (at least not without a lot of work).

Here at the university level, we see where they are in terms of musicality: Do they sing musically? Do they know what a phrase is? If they are an entering graduate student, we listen to their languages.

The final factor is the most indefinable of all: Do they have the "singer's personality"—that flare that makes you want to listen to them, in spite of faults or things that might need to be solved. Does this person have that arresting quality in his or her singing that captures your attention and the audience's attention?

Edith Davis Tidwell

I listen for a free, ample, and confident sound with dimension and color, good intonation, musicality and sense of style and phrasing, clean diction, and an honest commitment to texts. I want the singer to be musically accurate but not sound academic. I want to hear music being created in an honest, authentic presentation.

Meribeth Dayme

I'm listening for a compelling performance. I want them to entice me; obviously that includes a number of things. To me it doesn't mean that "compelling" is more than technique. It's all part of a whole. That technique and communication are one thing; they are not separate. I want to be drawn in as part of the audience and really demanded to listen. That's what I listen for.

Robert Edwin

As in the audition lesson for my independent studio, I look and listen for good voice technique, the appropriateness of the repertoire, and the artistry of the performance. However, the context of the audition determines how I evaluate singers. For example, when I am at a NATS student audition chapter or regional event and my assigned judging category is lower high school women, I will tune my eyes, ears, and senses to a relatively low level of expectation so that my feedback can reflect that general level of performance. On the other hand, when I am judging a NATSAA [National Association of Teachers of Singing Artist Award] final or a music theater final at a NATS national conference, my expectations will be raised to a professional level and my critiques will reflect that. Of course, elite singers will emerge on all levels, including high school.

Jeannette LoVetri

Students do not audition for my studio. If they want to work with me, they are welcome. If I listen to an audition for some other purpose, I always listen to how comfortable the voice sounds, whether or not there is any connection to the song emotionally and through the meaning of the lyrics. I listen for vocal health within the context of style, age, and if I have the information, training. Listening to a rock song isn't going to be the same as listening to something from *The Sound of Music* or by Schubert.

What sets the students apart is their uniqueness. It could be vocal, as in having a great voice; it could be musical, as in making unexpected choices in the vocal line; it could be emotional, as in conveying compelling intention and communication. If the singers are being true to themselves and the music, it makes an impression. That's enough.

Stephen King

Where I am now, because we're very concentrated; our studios are twelve. At this level, I'm only listening for people who have the potential for singing as a career: a strong musical/expressive gift, a potentially high-level instrument, and then, a lot of intestinal fortitude. Do they have the personality to run the race? If they're a "shrinking violet" and they're going to back away at the least hint of difficulty, often that's not going to work out anyway. If they can learn through failure, through mistakes, how to get better, there is often great potential. I try to figure that out before I hear them sing. I'm looking for people who are determined enough to do it, regardless of their voice or musical talent. But for me, the musical talent is as important as the voice, and so if I don't hear this innate awareness of the music, then I'm much less interested. I know that's a cliché, but if they're musical, the voice can be deeply flawed, but a year later—and I've done this many times with people—we really have something. They just weren't singing well, but it was obvious the instrument was really good. They were out of tune, or they didn't know how to get through a passaggio, whatever the case may be . . . they just needed some help. You knew that the musical gift was big, and you knew the voice was good; it just took some time to work through that. As one of the pianists told me last year, "I'm always puzzled by some of the people you take, but then, by the time they graduate, I understand it."

Well, that's our job—that's what we're supposed to do: listen, like a mechanic who can listen to the car and know there's something wrong with it without even raising the hood. Of course, especially with the current culture, you can't help looking for people who look like they have the potential to walk onto the professional stage and inhabit a certain space. That sounds quasi-discriminatory, but I think that's just the fact of the business we're in. So, looking for people who are not necessarily like the average population, but who have certain personality onstage, who carry themselves a certain way . . . that's part of it for me, looking for people who look like operatic singers.

When we get to the next level, the stakes go up quite a bit. If I'm listening for Houston Grand, Los Angeles, or my professional studio, I'm listening for a different level of accomplishment. Of course, not all of them are going to make it. The listening "thing" is really hard to describe, because after a while, you develop some instincts where you just know that they have what they need and there's no way to learn that, no way to write it down or to teach it to anybody. It just happens over time based on your own experience as a singer and teaching lots of people. You start to see different personalities and have a pretty good idea if they can be successful. It gets easier when you get to the young artist level, because so many people have already been screened out, if you will. It's certainly much harder at the higher education level. Then it's really hard at the higher education level if everyone has nineteen people in their studio; there are four choirs and six voice studios (or more), and everybody's got eighteen. There's no way to find that many liable professional singers. But who says that everybody has to do that? Some will become teachers—some will become us! Teachers, writers, choral directors, and church musicians . . . that's all great too. I definitely did that in previous incarnations, but it's not what I'm doing anymore. So I have to listen to suit the environment that I'm in.

Mary Saunders-Barton

Auditions for our musical theater program last the better part of a day and include dancing, singing, acting, and music theory. These young people have already passed through an initial online prescreening. Our entire musical theater faculty watches all the auditions. The process requires a lot of give and take among singing, acting, and dance faculty as everyone carries their own set of priorities. Trying to decide whether a young person with extraordinary dance ability and good acting but very limited vocal training is worth the risk . . . or whether a very promising singer with no dance background can be taught enough to get by. Significant ability in all areas is rare at such a young age. So it's a balancing act. As voice teachers, we are always listening for that "special voice," something beyond technical ability, pitch accuracy, and tone. It's an ineffable quality, an inspiration to sing as if their life depended on it. You certainly know it when you hear it.

Chapter Eleven

The First Lesson and a Typical Lesson

How do you approach the first lesson with a new student? How do you structure a "typical" lesson?

The first meeting and lesson with a new student is very significant. It initiates the relationship between student and teacher, establishes the learning climate, and serves as a catalyst for ensuing work.

For the novice voice teacher, a first lesson can be intimidating; how does one begin? What strategies and procedure will be most beneficial to both the new student and to the instructor? Exactly how should one proceed?

Drawing from the teachers' responses, I have constructed a composite profile of a "first lesson."

A brief "get-acquainted" session begins the lesson. The teacher asks the student a range of questions designed to

1. learn about the student's musical and vocal background;
2. put the student at ease;
3. ascertain the student's goals, needs, and desires; and
4. get a sense of the student's personality.

Typical questions include the following:

1. What singing have you done?
2. Do you read music?
3. Do you play an instrument? If so, how long?
4. What kind of music have you studied?
5. What is your favorite kind of music to sing?
6. Who are your favorite performing artists?
7. If you've had previous voice study, with whom did you study?
8. What are your goals, aspirations, dreams, and so forth?
9. What would you like to gain from voice study? What would you like to work on and improve?

Next, the teacher vocalizes the student or has them sing a song, or both. This provides the opportunity to hear the voice and become familiar with the student's sound, range, characteristics, strengths, and weaknesses. By watching and listening carefully, the teacher can begin to assess the student's most immediate needs and where training should start.

The lesson usually concludes with some preliminary instruction. If the student is a beginner, the teacher presents some basic ideas regarding posture and breath and may assign exercises and vocalizes. The teacher may also inform the student on practice procedure; together, they may establish short- and long-term goals.

"Typical" lessons are more variable and case by case. One can, however, still draw some generalizations.

Teacher and student use the first few minutes of the lesson to discuss the week's work, problems, concerns, and successes. The teacher spends fifteen to twenty minutes on vocalizes and technical work. Some teachers asked students to come warmed up and ready to sing; others ask students (especially beginners) to refrain from warming up in advance. In that case, the teacher conducts the warm-up through vocalizes until the student has acquired a safe, healthy routine.

Repertoire and performance work occupies the remainder of the lesson.

With a half-hour lesson, the time divides differently. Some teachers spend fifteen minutes on vocalizes and fifteen minutes on repertoire work; others divide the time into thirds: ten minutes for pre- and postlesson questions and comments, ten minutes on vocalizes, and ten minutes on repertoire/performance work.

If the student is fairly advanced and has an impending performance, the teacher may ask the student to warm up in advance and come prepared to spend the entire lesson working on the performance repertoire.

TEACHERS' REMARKS

Shirlee Emmons

I ask new students to bring with them to the first lesson one piece that they believe they sing extremely well and one piece that represents their worst problems. After hearing both pieces of music, I tell them what my conclusions are about their vocalism at this time. I outline a course of study that will either bring the problems under control or solve them. We attack several spots of the defective piece to show the singer how I work. It is their right to know what it is I do, and it is necessary in order to make a decision whether to continue or not. This will either inspire confidence in me, in which case we begin a course of lessons, or it will show them that they do not wish to work my way, and a lot of time is saved for both of us.

On a typical lesson, I begin with a technical checkup, making sure the skills we are working on are proceeding apace, correcting misunderstandings from the previous lessons, and putting the singer back on the track that leads to achievement of the skill. Then I work on whatever new skill I want to introduce. Then I choose a simple piece of music on which to practice these skills. Some time is spent on Coffin exercises, choosing at random or with the specific purpose of enhancing the technical skill we are concentrating on at the moment. Some time is spent on the assigned agility exercises, Marchesi or Garcia. We finish with a half hour of working on the pieces that are being perfected for performance.

Barbara Doscher

I give two or three simple vocalizes, even if it appears to be an advanced student (certainly with a beginning student or a younger student). It's also important to spend part of the time getting to know each other—not the life history but trying to find out what kind of personality one is dealing with before leaping into technical matters.

[On a typical lesson:] Because I mostly teach advanced students, I teach one-hour lessons. I vocalize them for twenty to thirty minutes; then we work on repertoire for about thirty minutes using various pieces in various states of preparation.

William McIver

In a first lesson, I generally talk for a few minutes to get some background information on the student and to ascertain that student's goals; [I see] if it's a student enrolled in the School of Music in music education or performance studies, and so forth. I find out a little bit about their former work in voice (if any). After a few minutes of that, I like to hear them sing something, preferably a song and then some vocalizing as well, to get a feel for the strengths and weaknesses of the voice. From then on, I begin in the old traditional way (i.e., with posture and breath management). I spend as much or as little time on these concepts as seems necessary. Although I think posture and breath management are the foundation of all singing, the coordination may suffer if they are overemphasized. So I do start there, but I try not to overemphasize that to the detriment of the whole coordination. Some teachers say, "Okay, you ought to start all over." I'd never do that with a student because I think it's defeating. But if somebody is breathing clavicularly or "pouting" the belly and dropping the sternum, then you're going to have to make some fundamental changes. I try to find something that is positive in a voice. It might be a particular pitch or vowel, and we work from that to incorporate necessary changes.

From then on, it really depends on what I find. There are the various areas of vocal technique: posture and alignment, onset, agility, resonantal balance, and registration. I begin with those areas of technique.

I assign exercises that I think can be easily handled at first and then expanded upon. You can't expect to sing a nine-note scale if you can't sing a three-note agility pattern; you're not going to handle an agility pattern well if you can't first manage the onset of the voice.

I begin in the middle and work from there. I begin with the simple and move to the more complex.

[On structuring a typical lesson:] It varies from student to student. I see some of the university students for one hour a week, and others I see for two half hours. I prefer two half hours for younger students. I'd rather see them twice in the course of a week, separated by a couple of days, if possible. This seems too short when they get older, so we'll go to an hour lesson.

In the case of half-hour lessons, sometimes we're forced (by scheduling problems) to divide the work. We'll work on technique in one lesson and repertoire in the other. I'd prefer to do a little bit of technical work in each lesson and little bit of singing in each lesson, but sometimes we're forced into working the other way. Even with more advanced students in an hour lesson, I still like to reserve at least fifteen or twenty minutes for technical development. To me, it's not as much a question of warming up the voice as it is working on certain skills that are then transferred to the literature.

Cynthia Hoffmann

One thing I try to do before the first lesson is to obtain some background information from the student, preferably in writing. Besides a résumé and repertoire list, I ask them to write an autobiography, which can be as long or short, as personal or impersonal, as they wish. I am seeking information not normally included in a résumé, such as their musical and linguistic background, their vocal study/how they began, what Fach and if that has changed, with whom they have worked, if they play another instrument, and so forth. I ask male voices what they sang before the change of voice. I would like to know about relevant health issues and any medications they might be taking—also any information about their past health that might be relevant. I ask them to tell me what they consider to be their strengths (vocal and personal) and those areas that need work. What are their long- and short-term goals, and who do they like and not like to listen to and why? Lastly, I ask for a list of their "top ten" vocalizes and the new repertoire on which they want to work.

Having this autobiography usually provides information that I might not ordinarily discover initially and gives a broader perspective on their needs and goals. Also, communication through the written word can be quite insightful.

In the first lesson, the level of experience determines where I begin, but I often have students sing a song or an aria that they performed in their audition so I can get a clearer picture of how they express themselves technically and artistically. I will then point out what they are doing well and what areas need improvement. From there, I move to body alignment and some breathing exercises. Next, I try to find the vowels in the middle voice that have clarity and resonance, and also the consonants that aid this clarity and movement of the vocal line. Starting in the middle register, we usually work down and then back up again through a comfortable range. I look for the lift points of the voice and where there might be register-adjustment difficulties. I find three to five exercises that they can confidently use and develop. Finally, I try to help the student apply a few of the technical principles learned in the lesson to the music.

In a typical lesson, we do body warm-ups, starting with facial exercises (the yoga "Lion," and chewing, for example), panting, lip and tongue trills, perhaps some humming, "twisting," the whispered "ah," and the "ripotika" of [Barbara] Honn's, which I like very much. In vocalizing, I start from the middle voice and work down and then up through the range and try to cover the following: sliding or portamento, staccato and legato, registration, leaps, passaggio, messa di voce, and trill. I am listening for a slender, vertical column of sound. I include scales (Rossini's chromatic scale exercises and modal ones) and arpeggios of varying lengths, consonant articulation, and the five vowels (a–e–i–o–u), ending with all of them on a one-note legato exercise (to find a similar resonating space for all of the vowels). The student and I then review the lesson to see what has been understood and helpful.

I encourage my students to work with "an order of events"—I want to develop their ability and impulse to hear in advance the pitch, vowel, phrase, and color they are going to produce before breathing and singing aloud. Beniamino Gigli described this in the preface to *The Voice of the Mind* by E. Herbert-Caesari. When the vowel or phrase is heard in advance, an easier and more natural coordination of all the parts involved in singing occurs. I often say, "Hear it, breathe it, and say (or sing) it."

We work on pronunciation of the vowels in speech to find a clear, projected tone and discover how and where these vowels resonate. In speech, there are no "dark" vowels—just different vowel shapes. I also distinguish between what I call resonance "zones" and voice placement. I prefer the former—when the voice is freely produced, certain notes resonate in certain areas of the head and chest, but you are not "putting" the tones there. It is especially helpful for young students to have an idea of where these "zones" are located.

I will sometimes ask my students to vocalize themselves without any input from me. This can be quite helpful—even though, at first, they might not want to do it.

Ideally a sixty-minute lesson can be equally divided between technique and music, but as the student gains experience, this division can become fifteen/forty-five. Fifteen or twenty minutes still provides enough time to check on some technical aspects, and technique can be facilitated through work on the text and music. Every so often, we will devote one complete lesson to technique, one to music, and so forth.

Carol Webber

For a younger student, I ask them to bring something to the first lesson that they really love to sing in order to "charge the atmosphere with music" right away. For older, more experienced singers, I begin by interviewing them to find out their years of study, goals, perceived problems, and why they have come to me. I then begin with vocal work, vocalizing the student throughout the entire range of the voice. This gives my ear a chance to get to know the voice. The biggest job of the teacher is to listen and watch, and this initial session is crucial to begin to get to know the instrument in its as yet "unadvised" state. I then move on to that portion of the voice (usually a fifth to an octave) that I describe as the student's "comfort zone"—the place where the voice works most smoothly and easily. In this small range, technical ideas can start to be addressed.

I close the lesson by talking about repertoire wishes; there is also some discussion about breathing techniques. I will often ask the student to write out his or her understanding of breathing to bring to the next lesson. Finally, and perhaps most importantly, I reassure the student so there will be a feeling of safety and discovery within the studio at each successive lesson.

[On a typical lesson:] I try to establish two goals for each student per lesson. Those chosen goals are a result of previous observation and are at first worked on directly through vocalization. The same goals are then carried forward into the repertoire at hand. I also address any additional problems that might arise. Physiological goals (posture, breathing, etc.) always come first in any period of study.

I find it is crucial to keep good notes in order to establish upcoming goals with and for the student.

Edward Baird

First, I use a variety of vocalizes to get acquainted with the individual student's voice and to discover its strengths and weaknesses. I try to choose some area to work on in that first lesson in order for them to experience some improvement, so they feel they've accomplished something. Maybe it's one of the easier things to correct. I choose to do that rather than point out all the things that are wrong.

I use a variety of vocalizes in order to explore their voices and to pick things out. Then, if it's at an appropriate level, I try to assign at least one song. It gives them music to get started on, so they have something to work on for the next lesson. As for a typical lesson, my work is probably fairly traditional. I use the first few minutes of the lesson to vocalize. I make the students understand that in vocalizing I'm not just "warming them up." As a matter of fact, I ask students to come to lessons warmed up so that the vocalizing we do can actually be remedial work on vocal problems. I designate good warm-up exercises, but I encourage them to come ready to sing so we don't have to spend time just "warming up." What vocalizing we do works on their various weaknesses. Of course, in a university situation, you're required to cover a certain amount of repertoire each semester. The percentage of time for vocalization will change as we progress through the semester and more and more repertoire accumulates. By the end of the semester, we'll do less vocalizing (or in the last few lessons, none at all).

Helen Hodam

Before I even have a first lesson with any new student, I gather all of the new students together and have a meeting. It's really an orientation session, a review of basic vocal principles, and the order in which they are taught: posture, principles of good posture—"the proper singing position"—and exercises to help achieve it. I go on from that to breathing—what the physical process is. I don't go into great physiological detail, but I show diagrams and photographs of both the breathing process and the vocal "apparatus." I also talk about things to watch for that might interfere with a relaxed, but adequate, inhalation or a proper open throat, and what not to do. The next step is the onset of sound.

I also discuss vocal health; good physical condition and how to maintain it; warning signs of vocal fatigue or stress, and sinus and throat infection; when not to sing; vocal rest; and the important role of a good ear, nose, and throat specialist who understands singing—almost a specialty within a specialty.

When I finish talking, I hand out a detailed outline of vocal principles based on what we have discussed. This is several pages long, ending with a summary. I also ask each student to bring a list of repertoire studied (and whether it was performed) to his or her first lesson. This gives me a very good idea, together with the technical level, of which languages they know and what repertoire to choose for each individual.

I talk about the requirements for a voice major at the school. They like this meeting because they feel they've already started. I find it much easier to do this than to say it all over again at each first lesson.

When I do teach the first lesson, I'll ask if there was anything at the orientation that they found confusing or didn't understand. And I always ask how long they have studied and with whom.

If not previously distributed at the orientation, I give each student several sheets of vocalizes and remind all to be sure to bring them to every lesson.

Next, I talk about the proper order of warm-up when they practice and what we do in the lesson. I make it very clear what they should do when they practice. I tell them it's important not only to warm up properly but also to know what their most prominent need is at that moment. For some people, it's breath; for some, it's posture; and for others, it's resonance. I'm very consistent and persistent about how to warm up properly.

In a typical lesson, I first give breathing exercises and then simple exercises to warm up the middle voice first, especially with the beginning students. If they're more advanced, they do their own preliminaries and then I take them through more extended ones for certain technical problems. I have them sing more sustained exercises for legato and exercises for stretching the range or for the passaggio.

I choose repertoire for the beginners—not too much at a time. Once a semester, I have the students give themselves a lesson. I want to see what they are doing in their practice sessions, if they really understand what they are trying to accomplish. Some do very well, some are distressingly inadequate (and that includes some graduate students!). I have found giving this "exam" very effective in making them think and analyze and listen in their practice sessions.

Bruce Lunkley

The first lesson is exploratory. I think that's the best term. I want to hear what they think is their best sound. I'm willing to hear that in a song, I'm willing to hear that just in scales or arpeggios, and so forth. We talk a little bit, and I immediately try to see if that sound has other possibilities. Can it be more focused (or, if you wish, more resonant); can they go a little higher than they thought they could get (i.e., the alto who thinks she can't get above A)? [Is this] the rough, overly ripe baritone from high school who is trying to impress you, and so forth? I clean some of that out and show them how much more easily things can work.

[On a typical lesson:] During the first semester, I ask the student not to come in warmed up so that I conduct the warm-up. Depending on the state of the voice, we use between fifteen and twenty minutes for exercises and talk. I have them look in the mirror and see what the problems are, explore the sound, and get the voice ready to sing. The balance of the lesson is repertoire work with accompanist.

Joan Wall

During the first lesson with new students, I usually ask about their goals in studying voice and visit briefly to get better acquainted. Then I ask them to perform a song—or sing some vocalizes—so I can evaluate their voice and performing abilities and make a decision about where our work needs to begin.

If the student is a beginning singer, I will introduce a few basic exercises, assign a song, and describe how to practice. I feel it is particularly important that a singer have a positive experience in the first lesson, so I will ask them to do something that can be easily accomplished. This could be a suggestion for vocalization, interpretation, performance, or personal growth (such as confidence).

If the student is more advanced, I will evaluate the singing and present specific material in the area of vocalization, repertoire, or performance skills. Together, we will establish some short- and long-term goals. A typical lesson lasts one hour. It usually includes about twenty minutes of vocal technique exercises. Because students warm up their voice before the lesson, I choose vocal exercises that will improve their vocal technique. The remainder of the lesson is used to study songs.

If the songs are new, I will check musical accuracy and work on diction and foreign-language translations. We will work on any vocal challenges in the songs, study musical style, and develop interpretation.

If the songs are memorized, we will rehearse to strengthen interpretation and vocalization. During this stage of learning, we spend considerable time intensifying the sensory life of the singer and building the final performance artistry.

Throughout the entire lesson, I stay attentive to the immediate needs of the student and do those things that I feel will help and inspire the student.

Laura Brooks Rice

A first lesson varies a bit from age to age because my students include everybody from high school students to beginning freshman in college to professionals. Even so, I make a great effort not to approach the first lesson with the attitude that "they don't know anything about singing."

First, before I discuss anything, I have them sing for me. Then I talk to them and find out just where they are in their own vocal knowledge and study—what they know about singing and how well they express themselves in terms of technical facility. I address any specific problem areas that they may want to rethink. Then we get started.

It's very important to set an atmosphere right from the start that I'm not the one who has all the knowledge and that you have none. Right from the very beginning of the first lesson, I let them know we will be talking about singing a lot, discussing vocal sensations—verbalizing what things feel like and the physical sensations they have when they sing. Eventually, it helps them in their practice and in teaching themselves. If they can verbalize it, then they can teach it.

When I teach a typical lesson, we begin with a discussion of how their work progressed during the week. What sort of things did they discover? What things frustrated them? What did they accomplish this week (always with the assumption that they did practice)? I try not to assume that every week they need to be retaught. Some do, but hopefully most don't.

Although I start with a series of vocalizes, the student knows it is not meant to be just a warm-up. I tell my students to come to a lesson ready to sing an aria if we wanted to start the lesson that way. Usually we start with a series of vocalizes that deal with very specific physical vocal issues. We might need to work on getting the jaw released, on vocal placement, or on any of the variety of vocal issues that need to be addressed. The vocalizes are a means to an end. We work and then carry those vocal things into the music they're working on. I apply twenty to thirty minutes to the technical issues and then the other half hour we deal with repertoire. In the college situation, where we are required to cover lots of repertoire, a lot of the lesson is devoted to the pieces. Depending on how the semester is going, we sometimes use the whole hour to deal with technical issues through the repertoire. At other times, a student might elect (or I might elect) to have nothing but an hour of just technical issues—no working on any music; let's just dig into it.

Leslie Guinn

First, lessons will vary depending upon the age and experience of the student. At first lessons, especially with young singers, chatting a bit gives them a moment to relax and get comfortable with me, and allows me to learn a great deal about them from their speaking voice. I vocalize them a bit in ways designed to expose the basic problems, explain what I'm hearing, and how we might bring about change. I am not a paternal type of teacher but rather demanding, preferring to dig right in if I feel the student can handle the pace.

A typical lesson begins with vocalizes that are very revealing: simple scales and intervals at modest tempi. Invariably, a particular problem will surface with which we begin our work. I explain my perception of the problem and the purpose for the specific exercises. It is important not to exhaust the student's patience on one issue, so we move on after a while with instructions as to how the student should work. This also diminishes the potential for compensatory muscle involvement when the student feels fatigue. At the university level, the first half hour is usually vocalizing. The second half is working with an accompanist on repertoire, as determined by the degree in which the student is enrolled.

Helen Swank

It is important that a student be made to feel comfortable and safe with an instructor and to get the feeling that the instructor cares about the student as a whole person. Therefore, in a first lesson, some time should be allowed to get to know each other, to understand the goals and dreams of the student, and to find out where the student is coming from at the moment.

This can be accomplished while proceeding with the active part of the voice lesson in which the teacher allows the student to sing something for him or her in its entirety and also does some vocalizing with the intent of diagnosing strengths and weaknesses of the vocal performance. So much is learned through listening, both to the spoken word and to the sung tone. The performance of the song should show the teacher the level of coordination and perception of the student, and the vocalize should pinpoint range, tessitura, registration strengths and weaknesses, and quality monitoring. Breath management and the many probable concepts that the student has regarding the singing process [should be explored]. The more skilled the teacher is in diagnosis, the more comfortable this is for both student and teacher.

I think it is important that in a first lesson the students learn something new and helpful to them. This is always possible when diagnosis has been thorough. The students can leave the lesson feeling their new teacher can be of help.

[On the typical lesson:] I assume that students come to a lesson ready to sing and ready to learn, so pleasantries, although warm and sincere, are not lengthy. I begin almost all lessons with warm-up exercises and am able to make a quick analysis of voice condition on this particular day. When I am satisfied that the voice is functioning well, we move on. I usually want the student to first sing for me something that has been worked on throughout the week or in previous lessons. I like for the first song to be something with which the student is fairly comfortable. There might be some corrections and assists in this song, and having solved any problems there, we move to a song that I anticipate might need some major work, probably something new for this week.

The major part of the lesson period is dedicated to this particular work. At the conclusion of this part of the lesson, the student should be able to practice the necessary techniques for making the work of the coming week very fulfilling from a functional and a musical point of view. The student should know what to do to have success!

I conclude the lesson with music that is rather well polished so the students leave feeling that at least at the end, they did something really right.

Marvin Keenze

The first meeting is a mutual audition lesson. I tell them they will get a real lesson. They will hear my teaching language and then they can make a decision. People seem more relaxed at this first contact when they hear this.

Then I really teach them. I explain what I hear in their voice, and what I think the priorities are for improvement. I want to know if they are respecting their instrument and using it in the best possible way. To me, this means the best coordination for the demands of the music. I believe the basic sound should represent the nature of their instrument rather than a sound imposed upon it. I usually have the students sing a song that represents their best singing.

I ask them how they feel about their voice. What do they like, and what do they not like about it? What are their goals? What kinds of music do they like to sing? At the end of this audition lesson, I will tell them if I can help them and ask if they want to return.

I always have a variety of types of students. I have those who are in very good shape technically and who want maintenance work. I have students who need a rebuilding of technique and want specific information about how the voice works. And I have students who are young and in the process of growing vocally. I do not take students who need major therapy, but I have taken students recommended by laryngologists after the treatment has been successful.

[On the typical lesson:] A typical lesson begins with vocalizes that help coordinate the voice with the brain. I use vocalizes that will coordinate the breath, the sound, and the resonance as quickly as possible. I don't spend a lot of time vocalizing in a lesson, but I want the singer to know the reason for each thing we do. I use sustained tones that enable the vocal folds to produce a definite quality of registration and to give the students time to hear and to feel the tone. I especially like octaves or large intervals that develop a sense of the whole voice as a unit. I want them to think of their voice as a musical instrument and relate the pitches harmonically.

Oren Brown

I like to get acquainted with the student's background during the first lesson. Does he or she read music? Play an instrument? Has he sung in choirs? What are her goals for study? What is his age? I like to ask if the student feels she has any special problems. Then I have the student sing something to find out just where he or she is now.

I usually approach a typical lesson with a warm-up of ten to fifteen minutes; it might be longer, depending on where the student is. We might spend our whole lesson on technique. I like to have the student understand the patterns that we're using and why we use them in our lessons. Behind all of this, of course, is a fundamental understanding of posture and breathing. When you do exercises and try singing, you should be thinking a pitch and allowing the airflow to activate the vocal folds; you should not try to get in there and make things happen.

Jack Coldiron

I conduct a first lesson in the manner of a very friendly "get acquainted" session. I interview the student personally, just to get as many impressions as I can of the personality of the student—through things such as a handshake, general body language, speech, and color of the speaking voice and speech habits. We continue into their interests in life in general, and specifically their interest in music: Why does this person want to study singing? We talk about past musical experiences and previous study. We discuss long-range plans: What do they see as their future, and why do they want to do this?

[On the typical lesson:] That is quite an individual matter. It depends on the student, where that student is in his or her studies, and progress. We might begin on a very personal and relaxed note—with a chat or a bit of relaxation. Then, I generally start with some vocalizes (especially if the student has not done any warming up) just to check on the health of the voice at the time. I give attention to individual needs and the things that this particular student has been working for, ideas that I have determined he or she needs. We then turn our attention to possible literature or immediate needs that have been realized up to that point. I inform the student of my basic early expectations and perhaps my grading procedures, which can help avoid misunderstanding of what is expected in future lessons.

Marcia Baldwin

The lesson begins with information gathering (i.e., previous vocal training, musical background, etc.). I proceed with discussion of posture, breathing technique, primary sensation of support, and importance of frontal resonance.

[On the typical lesson:] I start with a short review of the week's events, including the practice sessions. This is followed by approximately twenty minutes of vocalizing, using exercises to help the student with his or her vocal development. The rest of the session is devoted to repertoire work.

Lindsey Christiansen

At the first lesson, I'm mainly interested in getting to know the student, the student's voice, and the student's sense of himself or herself as a musician. I usually ask the student to sing something (I always ask them ahead to bring something to sing for me). I listen to that, and then I do some vocalizing to see how long the voice is, what is the range (i.e., see what kind of natural things a student does). Perhaps the most important of all is to experience the musical spark that drives them. Right off the bat, I'm interested in what the student's relationship is to his or her body: what kinds of things they show about their breath management, the places they support the voice, and places where there might be tension, especially in the area of the tongue and jaw.

I chat with the students to get a sense of how much music they have studied, and if they're young students, first-year students, what kind of experience they've had. I don't have a lot of students who have never studied before, but usually I want to know how long they've studied, how much piano they've studied, how much choral experience they've had, what music they like, what has been especially fun about singing, what are their dreams, and what they hope for themselves.

Sometimes the first lesson is an audition lesson, and that can be a different kind of thing (although not necessarily very different) because at both I'll tell what I hear in the voice and in what direction I think we'll be going. I think it's always important for them to know what I'm hearing and where I think we need to be going. I'm not one who keeps that a secret, and obviously my ideas about it could change as we move along. I try to get feedback from students about what they think of themselves and their singing. If I think what they do is terrifically different from what I teach, I try not to say so, of course, but wait until we've moved on to a situation where the students can see for themselves.

If they're college students, I use the first lesson to talk about certain procedures I have in my studio: about the amount of time I expect them to practice and about the way they should learn a new song. I have a handout that I give new students. It explains how much time they should be practicing each day. I request that every student practice six days a week. If they're younger, I advise them to practice for short periods more than once a day; in fact, I encourage almost all my students to practice more than once a day for various reasons. Not every practice session has the same purpose. I often write out the exercises.

In a first lesson, I usually talk about repertoire. Again, I ask for a repertoire list from a student and make new suggestions about where we're going to go. That's probably about it.

When a student comes in for a lesson, I always say, "Tell me about this week. Tell me about your practicing this week. How has it been?" I have some students keep a practice journal, those who have trouble staying consistent with their work, or who feel they don't know what they're doing at each practice session. Right now, there are four students in my studio who have a practice journal. Their assignment is to have a goal for each practice session. At the end of the practice session, they are to write a sentence or two about what happened.

I begin by asking them about how their practicing is going. I ask them about what's coming up. What's happening in the next week or two? What do we need to be thinking about? (I have a lot of students who are at the beginning of a professional career and who are doing auditions. In that case, I try to gear the lesson toward the needs of the repertoire they will be singing.)

After that brief conversation, I begin by working on technique. I usually spend twenty minutes or so, sometimes longer. If they're in trouble, I spend lots longer than that. But if I have students preparing a recital, they come in warmed up and we do very little or nothing on technique. They come in warmed up and we just work their repertoire.

In a regular lesson, I work twenty to thirty minutes addressing technical things. I don't like to call it a warming up; I like to think they do that before they come in. We often begin the technical part of the lesson with a short, systematic warm-up until they develop a good routine for their own warm-up. I do it in a systematic way so they get into the habit of what a systematic warm-up is. Usually, I spend about ten minutes doing that kind of thing, just to make sure the voice is connected to the breath and make sure we've said hello to both ends of the voice, that we've used some coloratura as well as some legato.

I do exercises to teach them new things, new technical skills, and then we go into repertoire. Usually an accompanist comes to the last half hour of the lesson. If there isn't one, I play piano and we work repertoire. We continue the technical work into the work on repertoire but using it to release artistic performance of the music.

I have my students tape their lessons. Some of them also keep a journal. At the end of lesson time, I always write in the journal what I'd like for them to think about while they're practicing. That's the way a lesson goes. At the end, we summarize what we've done, and I tell them what I expect. I must say I really believe in very student-directed lessons, although it sounds as if maybe I don't. I like them to tell me what we're going to do. Although it really doesn't happen very often, I sometimes have a sense that the student is not keeping things going enough to get ready for the exam or the next recital. In that case, I will say, "Next time I'd like to hear so-and-so." Or, if we've been working hard on things, I might say, "I'd like to hear that coloratura section again next time."

Dale Moore

If I haven't met the student before, I find out a little bit about his or her background. If they have not had previous training, I briefly give my thoughts on breathing, vocal freedom, and so forth. They're encouraged to ask questions, which I answer.

We work through a set of vocalizes that allows me to see where they are at that moment. Depending upon their musical background (and countless other factors), I may assign them literature to begin work on. Typical lessons are fifty minutes, although they generally run a bit longer than that because we schedule in hour segments. We may spend the first fifteen to twenty minutes of the lesson vocalizing and talking about where things are technically at this moment in time. When the accompanist arrives, we spend the remaining thirty-five or forty minutes of the lesson working on repertoire. That involves technical work as well as musical and interpretive work. If the student has a big recital or performance coming up—especially a more advanced student—I tell them to come to the lesson warmed up in order to spend our time on the literature that has to be prepared.

Richard Miller

Rather than begin with abstract discussions on breath management, resonance balancing, and so forth, the teacher should first hear the student sing. (Incomprehensibly, that is not always the case!) This should consist of a song (or, with an advanced student, an aria) and a series of vocalizes specifically tailored to determine the level of accomplishment. The teacher should explore such aspects as onset, timbre balance, vibrancy, vowel definition, and range extension. We cannot teach someone without having an overall picture of performance achievement. Something is always better than something else, and whatever is more positive should serve as the starting point. Then teacher and student have a clear picture of where and how to begin.

Most subsequent lessons (excepting a few early ones with beginners) should be divided equally between technique and literature. Technique does not exist in a vacuum. It can be applied immediately to problems encountered in literature. It is a false assumption that technique and artistry are separate entities. The only reason for acquiring a technique is to permit artistic communication, and that goal should be present in the earliest instruction.

Edith Davis Tidwell

Well, it certainly depends on the level of student, but assuming this is collegiate level, I first hear some prepared pieces and then use simple vocal exercises to further assess range and technical facility. I encourage the singer to express his or her strengths and weaknesses and goals. I then express my first thoughts as to strengths and needs.

Meribeth Dayme

First of all, I want to know what they want. I want to know what they'd like for their voice. This is not a question that is asked a lot. I like to find out from them. Sometimes they are looking to try to please me, or give me a right answer. I have to really convince them that there is not a "right" answer; it's what they truly want for their voice. If someone heard them sing, what would they say about hearing them, or, *in an ideal world*, what would they say about hearing them? So I'm going to spend some time talking with the student and guiding them to some kind of intent with their voice. Why do they want to sing; what's their purpose in singing? Without that knowledge, I'm not going to have the same guidance to help them. I want to help them help themselves.

After their "intent," I would work with their balance. Obviously, I would get them to sing something for me because I would want to hear how they sounded and what they did.

I structure a typical lesson in the way I would want them to practice. We set up intent; we do some light warm-up, which includes some chi gong movements, some breathing, and some play; we play with sound; and then we go for it!

Robert Edwin

The first lesson in my studio is an evaluative one, an audition lesson. It determines whether or not I will accept a student for instruction. I begin by walking the singer through the "tions." The "tions" serve as a checklist. For example, my checklist for a certain student might read, poor audiation, shallow inspiration, strong phonation in mode 1 but weak in mode 2, nasalized resonation, clear articulation, and so on. I then have the student perform a piece of repertoire of his or her choosing. I look and listen for the talent level (innate musicality); the shaping of a phrase according to the parameters of the genre, be it classical, music theater, or CCM; the quality of the instrument (also genre specific) since a rock singer doesn't need a beautiful chiaroscuro voice but a classical opera singer does; the ability to emotionally connect with a song and an audience; a strong physical presence; and "teachability"—how open is the student to instruction? A high level in all the aforementioned is rare. I don't expect it in most students, but when one like that comes along, I thank them profusely for coming to my studio!

Once students are accepted into my studio, they learn two words that sum up everything we will do in the studio: repertoire (what you sing) and technique (how you sing it). Technique is addressed through the aforementioned "tions" and includes warm-up and cool-down exercises. Repertoire development involves finding the right songs and monologs for each individual student taking into account voice, age, personality, gender, ethnicity, body type, genre preferences, and experience.

Stephen King

Hopefully they're warmed up, and I'll have them sing something for me so I can get a baseline reading on what we hear and what we will work on. Then I'll give them one or maybe two concrete things to focus on. I don't go into a huge amount of detail on the first two or three lessons, just "let's focus on this . . . ," whatever the issue may be, and we start there with something upon which we can agree: "Okay, that's a problem and let's fix it" . . . and go slowly. It's tempting to jump on everything you see and hear the first time. I don't think you can do that, as it will just overwhelm people.

I have two "typical" lessons:

In the university/conservatory, they come in and we spend fifteen to thirty minutes vocalizing, not to warm up, because I insist that they're warmed up when the get there, but focusing on whatever the issues are that we think are needed. With men, it's often, How do we go through passaggio? How do we get into the top? Are you phonating on the breath cleanly? With the women, it's finding a lot of "oomph" or release in the sound, using the siren and getting the voice moving and getting a lot of velocity in the breath in those first fifteen to twenty minutes. Usually, after ten or fifteen minutes, I'll take something that they're doing in their music and we'll work on the music before the pianist gets there. It could be a passage; it could be one note. I do give people musical assignments that are not part of their repertoire, and we use those as exercises because so many things in music I find are better than a bunch of rote exercises. They're actually singing an excerpt from something that's applicable to what they're working on. I like finding excerpts like that and using them before they sing their repertoire.

With professional singers, I only vocalize them if we have a specific issue, because they're almost always working on roles. If I hear something, I'll say, "Try this and work on this before I see you again and see if this helps whatever that problem is, whether it's vowel alignment, a registration issue, a breath issue, or what have you. I'll introduce that mid-lesson, whenever I hear it, and say, "Work on this and then let's talk about it next time." Most of them, I spend almost no time vocalizing, going through exercises, because they've done that for quite a few years already. I'm not a systematic person, so I don't have a systematic set of exercises. I just do what I hear and see in front of me at the time.

Jeannette LoVetri

A first lesson with me is an opportunity for the student to get used to me, my studio, and what I am doing in the lesson. I go slowly and carefully and explain as I go. I have a protocol for most lessons and I stick loosely to that. I also use it as a tool for students when they practice but not right away.

It can take several lessons before I get a clear picture of what a singer can and cannot do and what the instrument is like. I do not ever tell a singer what he or she is or should be. I think of my ideas about the singer as being possibilities, not facts. The voice is something that is revealed over time and comes from the singer's throat and body. The heart of the artist will eventually guide her to the music and the sound that satisfies her desires. Voices emerge. It is not appropriate for me to tell a beginner who they are or will become as a vocal artist.

Mary Saunders-Barton

In a first meeting with a professional performer in my NYC studio, I need to get a feel for their background and previous training. There is usually some vocal issue that has brought them to me. I will want to get to that as soon as I can. The first lesson is exploratory. If it is a woman, I will listen to the range and expressiveness of her speaking voice, which already tells me a lot. I will listen to the coordination of her middle voice, the freedom of her lofty soprano, and the strength and range of the lower chest voice. Usually by now I have a bead on the problem and she will be open about confirming it. Professional students have no time to waste, and lessons are expensive. I ask her to sing a few of her go-to audition songs. If there is a significant problem we will need to address, we have an open conversation about it and take things from there. Whatever the issue, these lessons target specific technical issues arising from certain fears or misconceptions in their developmental training.

If the student is a man, I will have a similar encounter, discussing background and training. I will listen for the core modal sound, coordination of register transitions, and falsetto, and listen to audition material. Current musicals require men and women to sing higher and higher in a chest dominant mix. Learning to balance treble and bass qualities is critical for vocal longevity.

Eighteen-year-olds entering a four-year musical theater training program are a different matter. We have auditioned them, given them trial lessons, learned about their previous experience, and already identified areas of strength and weaknesses.

Chapter Twelve

Guiding Practice

How do you guide a student's practice? What advice do you give?

Student practice is an area of great concern to these pedagogues. Nearly all provide specific guidelines and practice formats for their students.

In general, students are encouraged to do the following:

1. Practice daily.
2. Divide their practice into several short sessions dispersed throughout the day.
3. Practice for no more than twenty to thirty minutes at a time if they are a beginner and no more than forty-five to sixty minutes if advanced.
4. Break the practice time up between actual vocal work and silent music study.
5. Use the voice lesson as a model for how and what to practice.

TEACHERS' REMARKS

Helen Hodam

I make it very clear how they're supposed to practice. I tell them to begin with simple warm-up exercises, particularly in the middle voice. Go on to wider (range) exercises that have moving notes; reserve the more sustained for the end. The best way to guide students' practice is to tell them to repeat the practice that is done in the lesson. I think that's most important.

With beginners, I'll have an advanced student supervise their practice, perhaps once a week, especially during the first year. It is most helpful to both. It gives a feeling of security to the beginning student in having an extra lesson. The older student begins to teach; he or she must be able to explain and to listen.

Carol Webber

I'm very specific. I've learned the hard way that you can assume students know you mean for them to apply in the practice room what you've done in the lesson. Actually, what most students do is go to the practice room and do what they've always done. They start singing and "routining" the same exercises they have done since the very first lesson they ever had anywhere. I believe you have to interrupt that and have the student start with what is new. Then ask them to show you what they are doing. Agree with the exercises that are still valid, and ask them to "put on the shelf" the exercises that are no longer really productive or are, in fact, reinforcing bad habits (with permission that those exercises may come back later and be looked at again).

I ask students to practice for no longer than twenty minutes without either taking a break or stopping and going back. The younger the student, the shorter the time, and the more frequent the application. For a freshman, I advise two sets of twenty minutes at different parts of the day (i.e., one twenty-minute session in the a.m., another in the p.m.). Older students, of course, are going to be able to pace their work. Singers can work at their craft for six hours a day, just like pianists; they just can't sing for that length of time.

So, at each stage of development, I'm very specific; even with the young professionals, I advise them what to do. Most people's attention span is relatively short. It's good to take a watch or a timer into the practice room. If, for instance, you're working on tongue issues with a specific exercise that requires a mirror and intense concentration, set the timer for three minutes and then stop and ask yourself, "Am I still looking? Am I still accomplishing my goal?"

I will do a demonstration practice session. In an academic setting, I pair older students with younger ones, so they're not responsible for teaching them but they're in the room once a week with a practicing student to make sure they're getting something done—not as a judge and jury but as a partner. I think we all work better when someone is helping us.

Marcia Baldwin

I advise a short ten-minute warm-up in the morning. A second session of fifteen to twenty minutes occurs later on, using our exercises (i.e., ascending and descending scales, slow and sustained, and then finishing the session with fast patterns extending registers in both directions).

Bruce Lunkley

I explain at the first lesson that I'm their teacher only one day a week. I prescribe for each individual student an appropriate short vocalizing routine and time that I want them to do two or three times a day. They are not assigned repertoire right away, so they are limited to the prescribed exercises (it will be a couple of weeks before they receive song literature). They are told to note problems and write them down to discuss at the next lesson. Should something spectacular happen during a practice, I give them permission to come right away, knock on my door, and tell me about it. I want to hear about it right away, not next week when they can't do it anymore! Over the years, that has proven to be a good policy—it might not happen often, but when it does, it can be crucially important.

I ask them to report how many hours they've spent singing each week (although it's usually obvious!). I find that if they are working with any kind of intelligence and dedication, there is usually a major plateau step upward by the seventh or eighth week of school. What form that takes varies from individual to individual. It could be resonance, it could be consistency, range, or total sound—it could be anything. But it will be noticeable to him or her as well as to the accompanist.

Laura Brooks Rice

The only thing that I assume from the first lesson (or any lesson) is that people don't necessarily know how to practice. Practicing needs to be taught; it's very important, especially with the young ones. I like to have them practice just technical issues; I ask them to take some of the things we did in the lesson and practice those three times a day for fifteen or twenty minutes, spread out over the day. For example, they practice at nine o'clock for fifteen minutes on a vocalize and work, for instance, on releasing their jaw, on breath energy, or whatever; I advise them to stop after the fifteen minutes (even if it's a fabulous practice), come back three hours later, and re-create that sensation. By doing this, they begin to build muscle memory. With practice, frustration diminishes.

That's just their technical work. I have very specific methods for younger college kids to learn new songs. I give them a regimen. When they are first given a new song, they deal with the text first. They recite the text and then intone the words on one pitch, using the rhythms of the piece. This helps them take care of any diction issues by forming the words on the one pitch.

Then they learn the melody. After that, they put it all together so they have a very systemized approach to learning a song. It lessens having me later correct them so much on diction or rhythms, and so forth. I give them those very specific things to do in the practice room, so they'll have tools to use, tools they understand how to use when they're by themselves.

I also have two books that I recommend to all my students: *The Practicing Mind: Developing Focus and Discipline in Your Life—Master Any Skill or Challenge by Learning to Love the Process* and *The Talent Code: Greatness Isn't Born. It's Grown. Here's How* by Daniel Coyle.

Richard Miller

Each student has a technique book in which specific exercises (and they vary from student to student) are recorded. To save time, I write scale numbers and key designations, not music notation. This book includes repertoire choices, with an indication as to when they might be completed. Depending on the need of the student, I suggest how many minutes are best spent of the designated technical areas.

Cynthia Hoffmann

I discuss time allotment. This is where the age of the student comes into play. It's apparent in the lesson if a young person is unable to concentrate for more that fifteen or twenty minutes. That might be the limit in terms of getting a coordination going—then they're tired. I have many young students who can only work intensively for about forty-five minutes—after that, you can see that's enough. If I see that happening, I try to break up an hour lesson with talking.

I advise them to practice vocal work in twenty- to thirty-minute segments, take a break, and come back later for another twenty or thirty minutes of work on the music. I also talk to them a lot about silent work in order to develop that aspect. I want them to learn how to sing from the page into their mind. I think this is very helpful when it comes to sight-reading. Many people approach sight-reading with the tendency to listen with their ear (outer ear) to the sounds that they're making while they're sight-reading. If you can learn to listen from the page directly into your thoughts, the "thought" of the pitch gives you an ability to sight-read that is far less taxing on the instrument. I talk to them about working this way so they can hear inside before they produce it on the outside. I deal a lot with pronouncing the vowel clearly (i.e., "placing" the vowel). Very often someone can have a very forward sound and yet not really be articulating the vowel in a forward way. They might not feel much resonance in their facial cavity at all, but the vowel is as bright as it could possibly be. There is a real difference between pronouncing the vowel and placing the vowel. I tend to go for the former, pronouncing. I try to advise them to feel their sensations inside but to move their thought out into the room. Rather than become overly aware of the inner, they should be aware of moving from within to the outside. That's an important aspect. You don't want them to become too self-conscious of what they're hearing inside. You want them to move that out.

To elaborate on that a little bit, I'll often see differences in my repertoire class between students who are sending their voice out there, while they themselves and their thoughts stay inside. I advise them to take that one step further: get the thought out there, ahead of the music, and then allow the voice to come through to meet that. That creates a much better performance. It can even apply to vocalization.

Another aspect of practicing is what I call "the fly on the wall." This is something some of my colleagues do that I've adopted. I'll ask a student to vocalize for me as if I weren't there. You find interesting things. For example, the students will vocalize while sitting at the piano or they're not doing the same vocalizes that you gave them. You can give feedback to this—I think it's a nice way of working. First of all, they're in charge, but you're also helping them facilitate what they're doing. At the same time, you're giving them feedback. It's nice for the student to take control of the lesson with the teacher right there to help them.

Jack Coldiron

Although I don't have much opportunity to monitor the situation, I do advise the student to practice for short periods of time (or at least reasonably short), instead of engaging in marathon practice sessions of two to three hours. They are told to "practice for thirty to forty-five minutes at one time of the day, and do that over several periods in the day." This is for several reasons: first, for vocal health and, second, because you learn through repetition. If it is done several times a day (as opposed to one), you increase your chances of doing things in a better way and also of building a sense of continuity. I always say "warm up, don't just go in and start singing high Cs"—warm up easily with light, easy warm-ups; then work on sustained single vowels, work on text memorization, or speak through the text before you do any heavy singing. I often advise my students, "If something is going well in a practice session, please come to my studio immediately. I will stop whatever I am doing to listen to you and give immediate feedback as to whether it's right or wrong." If they're having a problem and nothing's working, I tell them to please come and find me—with a quick listen, I may be able to give them help.

Edward Baird

I indicate to them that vocalizing is not just for warming up the voice (although it does need to play that role). Vocalizes ought to be chosen in some sort of order to accomplish that so they don't walk into a practice room to sing for the first time that day and launch into the most difficult singing.

One of the important things a teacher can do is to explain the purpose of each vocalize or each exercise. I find a lot of students go through a routine of vocalizes; you ask them what they're trying to accomplish, and they'll say, "Well, I don't know, Miss so-and-so has me do that." It's very important for them to understand the purpose of each exercise, what they're trying to accomplish, so that every time they do it, they can attempt to improve on it. I often explain that it's like an athlete doing calisthenics, with each one designed to strengthen some particular muscle.

As far as their practice is concerned, I ask them what they think their problems are and what they have difficulty with; then I ask them what their practice procedure is. I'll say, "How do you practice? What do you do? What is the first thing you do when you go into the practice room?" I monitor it in that way.

Barbara Doscher

If it's an undergraduate, it's best to specifically indicate what vocalizes you want them to do and in what order. Confine yourself to only two or three at least for quite a while, or they're going to practice all of their bad habits and all of their mistakes. If it's a more advanced student, I ask them how they begin their warm-up period and in what order do they do the vocalizes? I talk to them about the importance of alternating frequency areas and muscular tasks, so they don't do a staccato vocalize and follow it immediately with a pianissimo vocalize. I explain to them why that is not such a great idea.

In the beginning of the semester I sometimes devote time in my weekly performance class to mini-lectures on practicing. The problem with that is only about half are listening. It's advantageous to ask someone in a lesson, "If you were in a practice room, what would you do first?" That's really pinning them down. I think you need to do that.

Leslie Guinn

I give suggestions for practice as the lesson progresses and problems are identified. I also advise them to work in short, rather than long, sessions. The amount of practice is predicated on the student's age, how many rehearsals, upcoming performances or auditions they must attend, and general vocal health. I believe that poorly directed or uninformed practice is worse than useless. Therefore, I recommend that beginning students expend only modest time in practicing technique. The remainder of practice time is used to explore appropriate styles, depending on the student's abilities.

Marvin Keenze

My practice instruction depends on the student. Many of my students tape their lessons for reference. The vocalizations that we do in the lesson are the ones to practice. There is a sequence of exercises that I use that usually begin in the middle range and work out from there.

I do not encourage long sessions of vocalization, but I do like them to do two fifteen-minute technical workouts twice a day. I believe in setting small goals and working toward that end. I offer suggestions on how to learn a song that is efficient and hopefully enjoyable. I suggest that they read the text as a poem and with the correct inflection of the language. Next, speak the words in the rhythm of the music and speak it close to the pitch level that the composer set. This is to make them think of pitch as an emotional expression.

I ask them to work slowly and carefully, to make decisions about what vowel pronunciation works best on a particular note of the music. Finding a compatible vowel for required pitch and dynamics is an important part of my teaching style. I encourage the student to take time to really hear and feel each sound and think of it as an emotional expression. I call this "slow-motion practice." This is when each note value is held longer than its actual value so that when they sing in tempo, they are thinking in slow motion in order to experience the timbre, the vowel, and the feeling of each sound. I call this "reconciling pitch and vowel." I also encourage "a cappella" practicing.

Helen Swank

In the course of the work of the lesson, the teacher needs to ensure that the students can do the things that will make their practice a true growing experience and also that the students follow somewhat the same structure we do in a lesson: warm-up, comfortable singing, hard work, and "cool-down" experience. The students should know that if they have questions or get in trouble (pain, loss of control, etc.) they should contact me (the teacher) and feel free to do so.

William McIver

I try to make them aware of the various areas of vocal technique that I think are important and ask them then to spend some time on each of those areas every day. Then I give them appropriate exercises either by writing them out or, in most cases, by working that way in the lesson. All my lessons are recorded on video. Students take the tape home and view it before practicing. I've only done that in the last several years—I find it very helpful. You save so much time.

Regarding diction, I will read through the text with the younger students and ask them to read while I correct them. It's all on the video, so they can go back and work from that.

Oren Brown

I like to give the students the idea that they're essentially going to be their own teacher because they may work six days and I see them but one. I have them tape their lesson if they wish. I like to impress upon the student that it's better to go too slow than too fast. If something is not easy in their lesson, it's better not to fight it. I advise them to skip it until they can find something that is easy, and then in the next lesson, we'll talk about what was going on (so they don't keep working at something that doesn't seem to respond).

Dale Moore

I suggest, especially for the younger students, two twenty-five-minute practice sessions, as opposed to trying to do it all at once. I discuss the importance of being ready to practice. If they've been sitting crouched over taking notes in a class, they should loosen up the body a little bit. Next, they should decide what they're going to try to accomplish at that practice session, whether it's cleaning up certain musical spots in a piece of repertoire or working with some new (or familiar) exercise I've given them that needs some real woodshedding on their part. I try to find out from them what their practice methods are.

Joan Wall

I encourage students to practice daily, and I suggest they use their voice lesson as a model for their practice sessions.

There are several basic problems that students have about practicing. Some students consider "practicing" an onerous word. To them, practice is just effort and boredom. To those students, I often point out that practicing is "rehearsing"—a time for problem solving and playful creativity. Sometimes, just changing the terminology seems to help students have a more positive attitude toward their practicing.

I also try to make practicing more relevant to their personal goals. After I find out what they really want in their singing, I ask them to decide what they can do during the forthcoming week (or weeks) to reach their goals. As they begin to realize that the practice is relevant to their goals, they find themselves looking at practicing in a different light and they often practice more frequently.

Other students enjoy practicing once they get started but lack self-discipline. To encourage these students to practice more frequently, I set up as many performances as possible—small and large—so that it becomes immediately important for them to practice regularly to prepare for the performance.

Sometimes I ask students to keep records of the time they spend practicing, and simply keeping this record improves the length and frequency of practicing.

Finally, there are students who practice regularly but do not do it very effectively. I help these students restructure their practice time so that it specifically serves their needs. I show them how to practice to improve vocalization, learn songs, develop interpretations, and build final performance skills.

I must keep reminding myself, however, that people are unique. All people do not learn in the same way, and each person's own particular way of learning must be woven into their practicing. With each student, I find out what attracts him or her to sing and to practice. When we "anchor" this quality into their internal pictures of practicing by using a process called "future pacing," the student finds the thought of practicing more appealing.

Lindsey Christiansen

I think that's almost my entire job. Truly! I am not a teacher who believes that miracles happen in a voice studio. It's exciting when discoveries happen, but if they are not reinforced by consistent, thoughtful practice between lessons, they disappear. I really believe my job is to teach a student to practice, so I've practically spent my entire life telling them how to practice. As I told you, at the beginning of their study with me I give them a long computer printout with suggestions on learning a song, on how to structure practice time, on how to know where to go to listen to music—one of the things I request of students is that they spend some time every day listening to some music . . . and they don't! But it's important, especially when they have laryngitis or something. I have this whole section on my printout that says, "Just because you have laryngitis doesn't mean you are no longer a singer." So, I list things they need to be doing. I do think that hearing good singing, or even bad singing, just hearing singing and hearing the literature is just so very important.

So, as for their practice, I tell them what I think is a good warm-up. I feel an important aspect of my job is to teach them to practice, but even more so, my job is to make them independent singers. I give them an outline of what might be a good warm-up, but I really encourage them to come up with exercises of their own. When there are particular problems in a piece, or a part of a piece, we'll change the vowel or something, or change the way one has to take a breath. That often makes such a difference in the way a difficult passage may or may not be negotiated. I say, "Remember, when you are working this week, you're going to sing an [ɑ] vowel on that F# and you're going to remember at the end of that phrase, no matter how completely out of breath you are, you're going to take a real breath." That kind of very specific instruction is essential.

How do I teach them to practice? Almost my entire lesson is telling them how they ought to be practicing. That is really my job. I'm a firm believer in very regular practicing. I don't think one or two long ones will do it. If I have a sense a student has not put in a systematic practice (and I can usually tell!), I just don't teach them. We just don't have a lesson because it's not the point; it makes them lose perspective of what the lesson is for.

Shirlee Emmons

During the lesson, I identify the exercises that should be done every day, those that should be reviewed at least twice a week, and those new ones to be conquered. I spend some time explaining where I think we stand in the process of achieving our skill and where I would like the singer to arrive. Then we set the goals and make a plan for how to get there. I explain which pieces must be routined during practice, which must be done with a coach, and which new ones should be learned as to pitch and rhythm. I insist that each lesson must be evaluated by the singer, and conclusions drawn as to future activity. Then a plan must be drawn up for the practice session, after which that is evaluated, and a plan for the next practice session figured out by the singer. The mental skills of goal setting and planning are very important for progress.

Meribeth Dayme

I like to send them home with an action plan they've created, not me. So at the end of the lesson I'll ask them (a) what are you taking away from this lesson? and (b) what is your action plan between now and your next lesson? Obviously, if they say something that I think needs clarifying, then we'll talk about it and I may say, "If you don't do anything else this week, then I would like you to do this." But I set out a plan for the lesson, which I call "tune in, tune up, and tune out," which [means] (1) [discover] your intent for that practice period and then tune into yourself, tune into your music—use a breath, or use an exercise—anything that would ground you first; (2) then play—play with text, play with the music, do crazy things with it, and use different styles with it; and (3) lastly, sing—perform.

One thing I always advise students is that you must not leave your practice until you have fully performed something *as if* you are performing in front of a crowd of thousands. So I insist that they practice performance. This is one thing we don't get people to do enough and when they do this, the performance nerves in a real performance seem to go away.

Robert Edwin

Every student receives prerecorded voice exercises that they are encourage to upload to all the electronic devices they possess. Based on work in the studio, students use those exercises to reinforce strengths and address weaknesses on the "tions" checklist. If I am asked, How long should I practice? my answer is, How good do you want to be?

Sometimes students take that to the extreme and overpractice. If they do, it's addressed immediately with advice to seek balance and listen to their bodies. Hoarseness or pain while singing is the body saying *stop!*

Stephen King

I don't have a practice guide, but with the young singers, I will try to direct their practice. I try to convince them of the efficacy and efficiency of using a straw to warm-up. My Rice students carry them around in their pockets; they look like engineers with pencils in their pockets. People will ask, "Why are they carrying those straws around?" and I'll say, "Well, they've got six hours of singing today. They have a lesson, two coachings, and three hours of opera rehearsal." I want them to warm up and warm down, and anytime they're feeling a little fatigued, I want them to take the straw out and sing through it and sort of reset instead of going up to the overcrowded practice rooms and singing through a few scales, oversinging in a ten-by-ten room, and then going to opera rehearsal with a tired voice.

I try to brainwash them to find lowest-impact ways of working: teach them how to mark, work with the straws, anything but actual full-out singing, and to get them to conserve that for when they actually need to do it. Especially with young singers, there are only so many notes in their throat every day. That's a real issue . . . and it's always an issue in the opera house. They have an AGMA [American Guild of Musical Artists] maximum of six hours a day, and they must use that time wisely so there's not an accumulation of fatigue.

The kids in school and the kids in the young artist programs are singing typically far more than most professional singers. Then they get out in the world and they realize, "Oh! This is what professional singers are doing—wow, okay, that's pretty good, because I'm singing about half the amount I was singing when I was in the young artist program!"

Jeannette LoVetri

At the beginning, I just ask them to work with the recording of the session and practice what we did on their own. I ask them to listen and observe any singers they encounter during the time between lessons and to think of the practice as they start as exploration.

Chapter Thirteen

Technology, Voice Science, and Medicine

Impact on the Profession

In the last twenty-five years, advances in technology, voice science, and medicine have had an impact on our profession. Please speak as to how these fit into your own teaching.

Without a doubt, technological advances over the past twenty-plus years have profoundly affected vocal performance and pedagogy. As a way of "priming the pump," the teachers were offered the following list: the Internet, including e-mail, YouTube, and search engines; social media; smartphones and tablets; recording devices and development; voice science and medicine; spectrographic analysis (VoceVista, etc.); and any other topic they wished to include.

TEACHERS' REMARKS

Jack Coldiron

Regarding recording devices, the ability to record and play back the sound of the voice is an incredible help in assuring the student that what the teacher is desiring is really working. Of course, singers must eventually trust their own personal hearing and recognition of the results of the efforts of their practice. But the opportunity to hear back what the teacher is hearing offers great encouragement to the students and helps them to more quickly believe in themselves. Eventually, independence from the teacher is the absolute goal of good teaching.

Regarding smartphones and tablets, information through these devices is so easily obtained. Are we so blessed with the ease of gaining information that we have forgotten the time-honored methods of searching and possibly coming up with exciting areas that could expand our minds and spirit? I know this will sound "old school" to the younger students. But the ability to locate necessary information will also help us grow and expand our minds and perhaps give us a strong sense of accomplishment.

Regarding voice science and medicine, growth in these areas is to be admired. We are learning so much about the physical and mental human activities and actions, which for so many years was unavailable to us. We have been able to learn that some of our teachings and requests of students were actually impossible or, certainly, inadvisable. We have learned how to better care for the body and the human voice. We are now learning how to use available medicines for the good of our health and how to avoid those medicines that can be harmful to the singer. We are indebted to people like William Vennard, Richard Miller, Scott McCoy, and many others for their years of study and results in the area of voice science.

Regarding YouTube, for many years I have included in my studio lists of prominent singers whose singing I approved as well as appropriate repertoire I felt was advisable to my students. These lists were of the accepted vocal types and professional recordings with which I was acquainted. I required the students to listen to these recordings and respond with written comments as to the voice type and the repertoire that was performed. The recordings were all available in the school's music library as well as listening equipment that produced the best aural results. This requirement was often replaced by the student with results obtained through YouTube. I disapproved, to some extent, to their substitution of YouTube for my approved recordings that were obtained by the ease of hearing the singers on their computers. One of my particular reasons was the professional quality of these recordings. Another reason was that the singers were approved for their vocal technique and their professional vocal repertoire. YouTube offers a wide scope of opportunity to hear much vocal repertoire. The quality of the performances, however, is often poor to downright musically inferior as well as aurally lacking. I stuck to my guns in accepting only the best possible listening available to the student. What a person hears is often exactly imitated by the listener, leading to poor results vocally and musically.

Regarding social media, I confine my participation in social media to *e-mail*. I simply do not wish to involve my time beyond e-mail at the computer. In spite of the many advantages to the wider scope of social media, I expect that the time required for constant Facebook, Twitter, texting, and the many other possibilities often results in lack of time for personal, face-to-face contact with another human being.

I receive correspondence from many of my students over the sixty years of my efforts as a teacher of singing. One of the often-repeated phrases that gives me courage and reflects on my teaching is, "You not only taught me to sing, but you made me a better person." How did this happen? Did I preach to the students? I think not! Was I a father figure? Perhaps, but that was not my intention. I challenged them to be honest students who were involved in learning and participating in one of the finest musical arts. I insisted on preparation and serious involvement in lessons. I tried to show them by my own life and performances what I expected of them. This came about best through face-to-face contact and my investment in them personally and professionally. The personal contact is of paramount importance in the teaching process.

Cynthia Hoffmann

Our new, advanced world of recording, social media, voice science, and so forth, has changed considerably since I was originally interviewed for this book.

For example, when the newly created fiber-optic scope was demonstrated during the early years of *The Voice Foundation* by David Brewer, I was one of the singers who was asked to have (the flexible laryngoscope) inserted through my nose and down the throat to take a TV view of my vocal cords. I was asked to only think a pitch while watching on the monitor. As I thought the pitch, the vocal cords moved into place for the pitch I heard mentally and we noticed the poise of the vocal folds—slightly open, waiting for the air to set them in motion. Beautiful! This demonstration showed that [Beniamino] Gigli gave good advice in asking singers to hear the pitch mentally before producing it aloud (for a more harmonious coordination of the parts involved).

Since then, singers on vocal rest are now often advised not to practice silently, as the cords may track the pitch and not be completely at rest.

Incidentally, today's scope is *much* narrower in diameter, and more comfortable for the singer.

Edith Davis Tidwell

I have been teaching since 1976, so I'm still not "over the hump" about copied music and the accessibility for students to get music from sources and not owning scores, not owning books, because they find it (perhaps perfectly legally) online.

My mantra to my students is "Buy the book—buy the music!" There's such a vast learning opportunity when one has a volume of songs from a composer or a compilation book that quickly provides access to discover other songs. And then—and this is a big one—there are those composers who are not in the public domain whose livelihood and that of their heirs is threatened and robbed by this act of copying. So it is illegal, and I cannot condone that. I understand scanning and copying for ease of carry. That doesn't bother me if you own the music. It is just the mind-set that it is quicker to copy—it's that whole sense of being in a rush again—I don't like it!

Though I've never used it, I've been introduced to VoceVista and spectrographic analysis (per Don Miller at a NATS conference). I have also observed Ken Bozeman (at Lawrence University in Appleton, Wisconsin) and his use of acoustic pedagogy. I found it interesting but never pursued it in my teaching.

I don't Skype lessons. I'm not comfortable not being present to see and hear what's going on. Sometimes someone will send me something they are working on and I'll react to it, but I'm not comfortable teaching long distance.

I find Spotify to be helpful, because one can easily access several different singers to hear various styles and sounds on the same piece. I like the ability to find the old recordings of singers on YouTube. I yearn for students to hear tradition and style by listening—I encourage that!—but I dislike it when they tell me they heard it on YouTube, and they have no idea who they were listening to! The quality of performances can be so variable. I still encourage the students to just go to our library and listen to a recording there.

I love the ability to access the Met channel on Sirius XM radio and hear those offerings, especially the older performances from the thirties and forties; I do have the Met channel subscription on my television, as well. I've really enjoyed that. I believe these venues of recording, in addition to being enjoyable entertainment, inform me better for my teaching. And of course, for those of us without regular access to live performances at the Metropolitan Opera, the radio broadcasts and HD presentation in local theaters provide a wonderful source of education and entertainment.

I worry about students posting on social media (although it is a good way to advertise an upcoming recital or a performance) as sometimes judgment is askew.

As for recording lessons, my teaching studio was once equipped with video and audio recording devices and also a television for playback. Now the students simply set their phones to record. Recording each lesson so the student can recall what has been said and hear the difference/improvement when things have been corrected or worked through is a useful tool.

The University of Louisville voice department maintains an ongoing relationship with the Louisville Center for Voice Care. That facility, led by an otolaryngologist and a speech therapist, is affiliated with the university and offers our voice students baseline scope examinations. When indicated, follow-up treatments and therapy are also made available. I have spent time there in observation and consultation.

Meribeth Dayme

I am in touch with social media, love to discover by searching the Internet, and stay in touch with singers and teachers. My teaching today mainly is with teachers. I scour the Internet so I can be an excellent resource for the teachers with whom I work. YouTube is great fun, because you can get lost in it. You can be there forever; for instance, I found some videos of Eileen Farrell, who was my favorite singer. It was great to see her singing! People are wonderful in finding old videos—who knows how they find them, but I really appreciate what they've done for us. You can stay incredibly current with YouTube.

What I do with Facebook is find out where teachers are at—the comments they make and the things they need. It is easy to see what they need and how badly they need it. It also tells me that they must not be getting it in the pedagogy classes—otherwise, why would they have issues that they're bringing up on these forums? Most of them are not science questions; they are repertoire questions, "how do I correct this?" or "I have a young student who's doing this—what do I do with her or him?" There is a huge opportunity here to further teacher education via the Internet.

With technology, there is a lot of work in the studio with various digital sound analyses. I think that's great for information. I'm not sure it makes an excellent performer. I'm sure I would get lots of argument with that. It's wonderful, it's great fun, it satisfies curiosity, and you can say, "Oh my, I thought I was making that sound"—but it doesn't tell you how to correct it. Ideally, that is why the teacher is there. I feel the analysis is more of an intellectual pursuit rather than a practical performance tool.

I believe we are in an exciting time for voice. We are able to hear singing from any part of the world. We have global sounds in our ears, and that's fun. It is changing singing because students are exposed to such a wide variety of sounds and styles that their ears have changed. They hear a whole different kind of singing. This is causing our old-fashioned ways of teaching to expand and develop. Even classical singing has changed enormously and needs to change in order to match the contemporary ear. It doesn't mean that we water down what we are doing; it means we have so many more options, approaches, and new sounds from other cultures included in the new music we like.

Robert Edwin

I have lived long enough to have experienced and used almost all of the music technology developed in the twentieth century: 78, 45, and 33 (and a third) records; reel to reel; tapes; cassettes; CDs, and the devices to play them, all inhabit my studio. Now in this, the twenty-first century, most of the aforementioned gather dust as the Internet knows all and tells all. I even wrote a column about my tech journey ("Guiding a Voice Teacher and His Studio into the 21st Century" 62, no. 1 [September 2005]) in the NATS *Journal of Singing*. Since half of my students are under the age of eighteen, I have plenty of help available as I navigate cyberspace. Frankly, I think the supposed "good old days" before smartphones is a myth. I like having the music world at my fingertips instead of having to dig through racks of CDs and such!

Stephen King

Regarding VoceVista: That would be an auxiliary thing for me. If I had that in the school, I might take a student down to the lab and say, "Hey, look at this . . . you know what we were talking about with your vibrato . . . here it is in real time."

I have a doctoral student who teaches our physiology class. He's really good at technology, so he's setting up some things before he leaves, but I wouldn't use it in my studio.

I do have professional recording equipment with studio-quality mics; the students can burn their CD, but of course, nobody does that now. They all use their Zooms or their phones, or they'll bring a Zoom mic and then they'll have a phone recording as a backup. I can't understand why anybody would not record their lesson for whatever reason. All my students record their lessons.

I keep a list of people to whom I refer singers. At the opera house, we have an in-house physician who is a laryngologist. If I suspect that anyone has an issue, I send them for a stroboscopy. You must have a relationship with physicians who are voice specialists.

I don't like Skype teaching. I don't think that's something I'm ever going to engage in. Skype and FaceTime don't appeal to me in any way. I understand why people do it. I'd rather just listen to somebody over the phone if they've got an issue. An actual lesson? I've got to be in the room with them, and look at the body language, see the inflection and the inference of what they're doing. Maybe I'm just old-fashioned.

YouTube: One of my professional singers sent me a YouTube video of Leo Nucci giving a master class. He was demonstrating some things, and I thought, "Now, that's really useful," because Leo Nucci does not know what we call this, but he can really do it! He really gets the things that we talk about, and he can demonstrate it. He's still singing at age seventy-five, and it's pretty darn good.

I'll share something like that, but I'm not too big on telling my students to go watch so-and-so sing this on YouTube. I think there's way too much of that as a substitute for actually working on your own. I try to discourage that. Sure, you need to know how people did certain things, especially with the traditions of opera: Pavarotti did it this way, and Gedda did it that way, but that's not going to reach you how to sing. If I find something really useful, I'll send somebody to look at it, but I don't do much of that. The students all know so much more than I do about the technology that's out there. For people whose twig is bent that way, they can get a little overly carried away with that at the expense of the old-fashioned "let's get into the studio and work this out." Then you take it and work it into your own understanding so you're not channeling Pavarotti every time you go up to the high Bb. You're actually doing your thing and making your sound.

Jeannette LoVetri

I think the greatest resource for singers is YouTube. It's a wonder and a very useful tool. I also think it has expanded the way young people listen to music from all over the world. The Internet is generally a great resource for research, as so much information is now found there. We save time and energy by having these resources.

I think Internet lessons on the Web are also good, although they are still problematic in that they distort, break up, get cut off, and have technical problems unless you have very high-end connections on both ends. It isn't ideal, but it can serve decently, especially if someone is consistent in having lessons.

Social media helps young artists develop a following and allows them to cultivate a professional image. It is a means to put oneself out into the marketplace, but these days it is easy to get lost in the millions of others who are doing the same thing. Once in a while it can be magical (as it was with Adele and Justin Bieber) and produce a significant career.

As we continue to develop voice analysis software, it will be an important ingredient in both teaching and singing in decades to come. It will never substitute for a personal, live singing lesson, but it can give another tool for people to understand what happens while they use the voice.

What isn't good about the Internet are the thousands upon thousands of people selling courses and tapes that teach you "how to sing." You cannot learn to sing properly without having someone listen and watch you while you make sound. Internet tapes (like the old cassette tapes) sold by people online do only one thing—they make money for the people who sell them. Even a famous singer who has excellent skills, such as Christina Aguilera, has no idea whatsoever what she does while she sings, but she, like many others, is now "teaching singing" through Internet courses. Oh dear.

We really do not know what will be discovered in years to come both in voice medicine and in voice science, but each will continue to be an exciting field that will help us all to know more about voiced sound.

One thing is certain: rock and roll and world music will continue to exert a more dominant influence over all CCM styles. Sooner or later electronic music will come to the great opera houses of the world, and when it does (and it could be tomorrow), opera as we know it will change the world over in an eye-blink. Hybrid styles of all kinds will continue to expand, and vocalists will need to be trained to sing all kinds of music in a healthful and honest manner. Training that focuses upon vocal function but does not discount the human factor of being a vulnerable, sensitive artist will be the way of the future for singers. It will be an exciting time.

Mary Saunders-Barton

I teach acoustically in my studio. Students record their own lessons. I am working on conditioning voices primarily, and that is best achieved in an acoustic environment. The training does not include microphone technique, although I foresee it will be a required skill for musical theater performers whose vocal health depends on the sensitivity of their sound technicians. Our spring show for spring 2017 was Green Day's *American Idiot*. The voice teachers, director, music director, and sound design technicians devised strategies to prevent students from overblowing their voices in the loud rock environment. The lessons our young performers learned from this experience will be a considerable benefit to them as they enter the profession.

I do teach Skype lessons to international students and anticipate we will see more online teaching as technology advances to support it. There is no substitute for being in the room with singers, but I am mindful of the power and potential of online teaching resources.

I do not use programs like VoceVista in my own studio teaching but have seen the value of auditory feedback for voice training.

Chapter Fourteen

Artistry, Expression, Communication, and Self-Discovery

Training the successful singer incorporates much more than mere vocal and technical proficiency; the complete singer is also an effective communicator and a consummate musician. The teacher seeks to guide the students and to help them consolidate the essence of artistry and expression as a singing musician.

The teacher assists the student to understand the following observations regarding artistry, expression, and communication.

1. Singers need the ability to merge composer and poet, to reconcile the poetry with the music.
2. The purpose of good singing technique is to free the imagination in order to bring out the musical, textual, and dramatic elements in an aria or song.
3. Singers need the ability to bring a tremendous dedication and love to the art of singing and music.
4. Fantasy is essential, and a strong, specific musical imagination is connected to the excitement of singing.
5. The singer must have something to say—one has to communicate or it becomes nothing more than empty notes.

TEACHERS' REMARKS

Oren Brown

You have to really think, and contrary to what most people feel about a singer's brain being just full of sound, a head full of resonance, there has to be some intelligence there, especially if one is to communicate. One has to have something to say—one has to really communicate.

Lindsey Christiansen

Be connected to the experience. Go to the imagination, hook into strong, musical, specific things you can say musically.

Dale Moore

I find students who bring to their art and their singing a tremendous dedication and love of the art and, of course, to an extent, of music—I find that this tells on an audience, tells on managers, tells on anyone.

Richard Miller

Usually people who start talking about the emotion, the style, and the communicative aspects are putting the cart before the horse. Even if you have the world's greatest imagination, nobody's going to know it if the instrument is in bad shape. If you have a good technical foundation, which is based upon very simple principles of physiology and acoustics, then your mind is free to be imaginative during singing, and to be interpretive and communicative. It's not the other way around. People seldom learn to sing technically well, for example, by singing emotional arias. It's not the way to do it.

I'm absolutely convinced that the whole purpose of technique is to free the imagination for musical, textual, and dramatic imaginative things. I don't believe that great singers stand up and think that they're placing the tone out of the top of their heads. They're not thinking about that. That's all behind them.

Marvin Keenze

Because of the poetry and the desire to communicate all of the text, we often don't hear any music. We're trying to reconcile poetry and music all the time. Some students are great at singing but not great with words. Some are really word conscious, and there's no music. So we're trying to show how they can work together and help each other.

Shirlee Emmons

There are a lot of coaches floating around, and a lot of voice teachers who masquerade as voice teachers who are really coaches. Therefore, I feel that my first function is to get technical things in order. When those things are in order, then and only then do I attack (issues of musical and emotional interpretation).

So how do I do it? First of all, I do what it says to do in my book, *The Art of the Song Recital*. I make the students give the answer to all forty-three questions. Then I make them tell me what they thought the music showed them. Sometimes it's ambivalent. In order to delve further into this significant area, I included two specific questions in the second interview.

SELF-DISCOVERY

How do you nurture and guide the student's "self-discovery"?

Lindsey Christiansen

I think "self-discovery" is exactly the word. My job is to help students learn who they are as people, who they are as singers, and who they are as musicians. It is not a matter of my telling them; it's really a matter of their slowly unfolding their own sense of themselves. I can help them build a good technique that will help release that.

I also encourage students to go to lots of concerts and to other things besides concerts; they need to go to fine buildings, plays, and art museums; they must think in aesthetic terms. I spend a lot of time talking with students, addressing what is their "package," what is the combination of gifts they were given. We talk about how they're put together, about what are their gifts and what are the ways they can best be used. I really do believe students are combinations of gifts. Sometimes the voice is the biggest gift, but not always. I think it's helpful for them to realize that their other gifts can be used as well. The voice is not the Self—it's very close, but it's not the Self. And self-discovery is just that. The voice is just a piece of that.

As far as other "nurturing," I do feel it's important for me to attend my student's concerts whenever possible; obviously the ones at school, but also when I have a student singing in New York, I try to get up there. And I go to rehearsals. When they have orchestral rehearsals, I try to go. I want them to feel they can call me when they need me to be there.

Joan Wall

As a teacher, I try to nurture and guide the student's self-discovery in the following ways:

- respecting each student, just as he or she is;
- being a "supportive coach," rather than a "demanding teacher";
- creating a positive environment for learning, always trying to find ways to give instructive comments as feedback and problem solving, not as personal judgment and evaluation;
- inspiring students to use their own inner sensory processes and their creative processes in singing;
- setting up situations where students can interact in mutually supportive ways; and
- providing movement and body-use classes in which the students release their interfering tensions and learn how this permits a deeper flow of emotions, an improved feeling of acceptance, and a more open willingness to change without viewing the change as fixing a "problem" but simply moving to a higher level.

Dale Moore

It's as in medicine—you're teaching the whole person here. I think the holistic approach can be carried too far, but still you are teaching the whole person, and every personality is going to be different; every response from every student is going to be different than the response from any other student. A teacher has to realize this and know that each student needs different handling. One might need a lot of encouragement and a lot of loving prodding; others you might need to rein in if they tend to be all over the place in terms of what they want to sing and how they want to sing it. We have to encourage the student to dare, at least in the learning process: do it this way—if it misfires, let's fix it—but you've got to have the nerve to really try it, or we can't move from where you are now.

Helen Swank

I think that helping students maintain a healthy attitude about performances is important to allowing the freedom to feel, to emote, and to share—the wholeness of spirit that I mentioned earlier. Vocal performance is highly personal, and some students let that stop the ability to share the center of their expressive beings. Students can learn that it is normal to fail once in a while; it is not unusual to miss a high note, and the world doesn't stop if you (horrors!) breathe in the middle of a phrase.

Jack Coldiron

In order to really assist or be of help to the student, you must develop a close association with that student, marked by friendship and respect. That goes both ways: the student respects you, and you respect the student. I want to be a friend to the student. By that, I don't mean I want to pry into their lives, but I do want them to have trust in me and know that I care about them. I have great personal concern for their good and welfare. In other words, I'm on their side. I tell them that a wide background of knowledge is very important. If they are going to sing, they are going to sing about every emotion and every experience of life. If they can experience those things themselves—if they will read, listen, go to the theater, see the ballet, go to the opera, and go to the symphony, then they will see and understand a lot of these things. Obviously, they are not going to know some things for a long time because they have to learn through personal experience. But if they will simply be observant of life, it will help them to interpret things they must try to interpret, whether it is a simple hymn, a German lied, or an opera aria. Personal experience will help them in that.

They must develop a strong sense of ego. Students must think well of themselves. If you don't have a healthy sense of ego, the performance suffers. The students should have a sense of individual and personal worth. I don't mean [a huge] ego, but it is important to think, "I like my voice, I like what I'm doing. I have something to offer somebody, and I am willing to make myself vulnerable in order to communicate my wishes."

Carol Webber

Again, this has to be seen through age-appropriate eyes. The older each of us gets, the more experience each of us has, the more we're going to be able to see and perceive at the very beginning, with any student. It's important not to leap in with these observations and preset students' view of themselves.

For example, if a student is a classic overachiever, where there's been extreme parental pressure, there's a kind of tension or nervousness in the body often reflected in the voice (or it will be). In this case, it isn't helpful to say that to your student, but it's important to know it, to trust your own instincts but not to project it.

In a lesson/study environment, I think students need to feel that they don't have to come in "perfect." They need to be in an environment where it's okay to make mistakes. It's not encouraged, but the world is not going to fall apart if they make mistakes (assuming they're making every effort to prepare). If no mistakes are made, then the teacher has no avenue to really aid in the student's development. I think this is crucial to the self-discovery process in students: to be in an environment where they feel safe—not exclusively protected—but where they are welcome, faults, warts, and all.

If a student (of any age) is progressing through self-discovery that's particularly painful or difficult, rather than take that onto ourselves, I believe we need be informed about counseling or therapy options and make referrals. As a person who's had a lot of counseling and therapy, I am not afraid to say that so the student can observe that this is normal and not unusual. Our references need to be cross-checked; we can't just say, "Oh, you need to go to therapy"—in fact, if you say that, you're not going to help the student. You could say, "Is this something that you feel you can do by yourself, or is this something you feel you could use a little help with?" Basically, find a sympathetic, nurturing zone that does not cross into personal friendship or personal psychological instruction.

Edward Baird

Technical discoveries and interpretive discoveries lead to self-assurance and self-confidence in singers. These two things together develop the singer as a total artist. For example, you're teaching a lesson and the student has a breakthrough of some kind—whether breath support, tonal placement, or register blending—and something new suddenly works. That's a new discovery for that particular person on that particular day. This leads to a confidence and self-assurance that, in the long run, leads to their development as artists. Artistic singers have confidence in whatever they do (and that's not limited to singing).

Oren Brown

I like to call the students' attention to an awareness of their own inner sense of what is happening: to build a sense of proprioception, rather than students trying to listen to themselves. I encourage exercises that will give automatic release of pitches. You have to be aware that to the singers, it is going to seem a lot lighter as they get up into their top notes. It's a sense of letting the voice lighten up and loosen up as it goes up, not to carry any weight from the bottom.

Barbara Doscher

Number one, you do a lot of gentle nudging. Number two, you have endless patience. You don't expect every student to do it by the time they're twenty-one. Fortunately, I was well along before I ever discovered how to sing. I realize that it's not a lost cause.

I do insist on word-for-word translations of foreign-language text, and I want the words put above the foreign-language words. It isn't enough for them to just have a general idea. We discuss what a poem says.

Another thing I've tried is contour maps of the melody. I would like to know where the climax of the poem is and where the climax of the melody is. Do they come together? You can also explore the harmonic progressions; where do they fit into this whole thing? If the student just works by guess or by golly, without using musical things, then it's not music; it's voo-doo or something.

Helen Hodam

[On improving acting ability:] I think they do better in a class situation—I tell them to get into a beginning acting class or an opera workshop. That helps because they do basic exercises. If they are very shy or self-conscious, they feel much more comfortable portraying a character. Exposing their own personality bothers them the most.

[On communicating an art song:] I don't approach it in a personal way. We talk about the poetry, and I give them all that background. I'm very careful not to upset them by probing too deeply into personal issues. In the art song, they can be very expressive with the poetry. I've seen them blossom because they don't have to worry about where their left foot goes. They can do some wonderful singing just by experiencing the mood of the poem in an art song.

Laura Brooks Rice

I try not to demonstrate too much in a lesson. I do talk about transferring my vocal sensations to the student—we talk about that a lot. But I have a studio of twenty-one very individual voices, not twenty-one people who sound like me. We go inside and find that person's true voice. Through the therapeutic idea of release, it helps people to look inward if they have any particular problems. Self-discovery comes with vocal discovery. Voice teaching often becomes a matter of convincing people that, yes, this is your voice. It's no smaller than this, it's no bigger than this, and it's no more beautiful than this—this is your voice. The teacher becomes their mirror or their tape recorder. Teaching voice deals with the whole person and a student brings all of his or her own strengths and weaknesses to a lesson; very often the teacher is there to point those out. I know I went through that with my own learning. Half of voice teaching is psychotherapy. A lesson can be a time of self-discovery through exploration of one's own vocal obstacles. You deal with reasons you can't release your breath or reasons you can't release your jaw. Your own personality traits are reflected in your voice.

William McIver

That's one of the most rewarding things about teaching, especially with undergraduates. The time between ages eighteen and twenty-two/twenty-three is a period of great change for young people. It can happen with older students, but you don't have them as long. You might only have a master's student for two years instead of four or five, but a lot of undergraduates are taking five years to finish instead of four. It's very rewarding to see their growth. Some come in as big fish from their high school and then learn they don't know it all. Others are very insecure when they enter; for those, it's a question of building their confidence to the point where they can perform at their best. I'm not a mother hen or a father figure, but I am accessible. I think students feel they can talk to me. But when they come in for lessons, it's work. This is what I appreciated as a student. I had teachers who would talk about anything and everything in lessons, but valuable time was wasted. I keep what we do in the lessons businesslike. If students need to talk to me about other matters, then I set up times outside of a lesson. I want them to know they come into the studio to sing, and unless they're either sick or really emotionally down in the dumps to the point where they can't work, that's what they're going to do. I let them know that is part of their responsibility as students. When they walk through that door, whatever the problem, it's their job to put that aside and get to work. Between eighteen and twenty-two, one faces many problems ranging from one's love life to theory grades. One must overcome those negatives with hard work. Hearing and feeling vocal progress on a daily basis can give one confidence to face other problems.

As mentioned earlier, I attempt to eliminate the word "don't" from my teaching. I think that can be helpful. It's very tempting to say "don't do this"; it's much more difficult to phrase everything positively, but I think it bears results. It gets students thinking about something positive that they can do, rather than something they are trying to avoid. I don't think there are any secrets in that regard.

There's something very personal about the student-teacher relationship that develops in its own way. I try to teach students ethical behavior including not criticizing other students or other approaches. I encourage them to act in a way that they would want others to act toward them.

Leslie Guinn

Students must believe themselves to be in a secure environment in order to profitably explore perceptions of past experiences. I encourage them to draw on real or imagined experiences in order to relate to poetic images found in vocal repertoire. The ideal for which one strives is to be limited, if at all, only by one's imagination, not by technical shortcomings. I especially encourage younger students to develop catholic tastes in music, urging them to explore offerings of disciplines other than their own, whether musically or through other avenues. I also ask them to read on subjects outside music, and to explore their spiritual side. I do not delve into a student's personal life. Since I have had no training in counseling, I limit myself to working on the student's voice.

Cynthia Hoffmann

I try to be supportive of what they are doing and let them know when they improve vocally and artistically—it is hard for some students to hear the positive. I tell them what Patricia Brooks told me: "The compliments you receive should be deposited inside like coins into a pot of gold."

I encourage them to combine the development of their instrument with the development of their art. They should endeavor to learn to sing as well as they can, but singing does not exist in a vacuum—you should not make tonal perfection your only goal and then "later" put that into a recital or opera performance without having the meaning and emotional feeling of the text as a part of those "tones." Emotion/expression changes the voice and the body, and that is why it needs to develop in tandem with technical development. The young professionals I know who are out there doing it are certainly not perfect. They are working on their technique while they are performing. They have a commitment to the text and its expression through the music, and they are trying to sing as healthily as possible at the same time.

[A concern:] With today's absence or less choral activity in many grade and high schools, plus the lack of required physical education in some schools, students who may find they have "a voice" may not have the opportunity to develop their ear for singing in school and also identification with their bodies and that mind-body connection and coordination that these activities can help provide. This lack of physical and musical training in our schools puts those who may not have resources to study privately behind, or worse, their talent may not ever be discovered or encouraged.

Richard Miller

All fine singing is "self-discovery." But one cannot discover one's inner self if one's body is in the way. It is the job of the teacher to diagnose and prescribe what will free the singer, physically, acoustically, and psychologically, so that the mind and the spirit can discover its own resources. Although no one has ever taught anyone else to sing, almost no singing artist has excelled without having another person supply the means for discovering how the individual singing voice best emerges. Four factors are always present at every level of instruction:

1. the commonality of phonatory function;
2. the individuality of voice timbre and physical structure;
3. the uniqueness of each personality in incorporating; and
4. commonality and individuality into a communicative whole.

Shirlee Emmons

I spend a great deal of time teaching my students to view their self-concept as a set of attitudes toward the cognized self (the self within you, known only to you), the other self (the self that you believe other people perceive), and the ideal self (the self you would like to be). I help them to become self-disciplined, self-aware, and self-confident by means of their mental skills. When they have a real sense of self, all their work proceeds more swiftly and to greater recognition.

Marvin Keenze

I try to give the singers time to fix things themselves. I don't want to rush them so much that they are just following orders but rather give them time to find a way to do things themselves. I teach them to "tune" a sound until they say, "I like that." Most of them will find an acceptable way of doing something if we just give them time. This will also encourage effective practicing. Perhaps my way of teaching is slower than some, but it takes time to build a kinesthetic sense of what it takes to make music from our bodies. That is self-discovery.

I ask them questions such as, How does that feel? How did you do that? Did you like that sound? and Did you like the feeling? I want the students to be able to articulate their experiences. It is easy in my assembly-line studio teaching to forget to let the students talk. Of course, a student can take advantage of this and talk too much. Every student is so different that I can't generalize about everything. I often have to change my style for the needs of the student.

Marcia Baldwin

I seek to guide the student on a personal level. As teachers, we have the advantage of maturity and life experience. We can only help a student—when asked—with his or her personal choices.

Meribeth Dayme

We work together on that. The exercises that we use are joint; in other words, if I ask the student to do something crazy, I do it with them or we do it one after the other. I don't demand that I look at them and analyze while they're doing something strange and new—that's one thing.

The other is that I use a video camera—I want them to see how well they are doing. It's not used as a critical tool—it's used as a self-assessment tool. Did it look like you wanted; did it sound like you wanted? Very often these people find that how they think they look and sound are not the way they look and sound. It's very, very helpful, and they take home the information in a much more profound manner.

Robert Edwin

Most singers initially learn to sing by the "sing-along technique." That is to say, they copy artists in their genre of choice. They often don't realize that they are "vocal parasites" feeding off of the artist they are copying. My job is to help them discover their own voices, their own emotions, so they can tell their own stories and those of the characters they create in song.

To aid in their self-discovery, I ask a lot of questions, probing questions that force students to examine their mind, body, and soul. I ask how they feel both physically and mentally, and I expect honest, substantive answers; "How are you?" "Fine" doesn't further the process. "What makes you fine? Details, please." I ask for what is causing that to happen. If they are professionals or preprofessionals and they tell me something bad has happened in their lives, I will be sympathetic, but I might still demand a focused performance knowing that casting directors, agents, and producers will probably not care if their personal lives are interfering with the business at hand. I will ask them about their angels and their demons, their loves and their hates, and their hopes and dreams.

In addition, I will ask them to do emotionally challenging exercises in the studio to prepare for the pressure that comes with auditioning and performing. I will accompany their songs with wrong chords and inappropriate tempos. I will ask for a radical change of character in a song: "It's a serious song; now make it funny." When students ask me why I'm doing this to them, I say, "Because your accompanist may mess up and your auditioners may do similar things to test your ability to stay in character and take direction. They want flexible singers and actors, not divas and divos who feel there is only one way to do it, and it's my way." My students realize that it's much safer to be sabotaged and fail in the privacy of the studio, learn from the experience, and then be better prepared when something like that happens at an audition. Simply put, my students learn to play and even enjoy the "game" of auditioning.

Stephen King

With all of the economic issues related to the arts in general and all that's going on with regard to media and the way singers are marketed, I think there are a lot of unrealistic expectations.

There is a steady stream of inquiries from all over the country by parents and young musicians. The conversation begins with, "Johnny wants to be a professional singer." If Johnny is sixteen years old, there's no way to know if Johnny can be a professional singer. That's the sort of mind-set that is all too prevalent. If I do take an undergraduate at Rice, invariably I will be asked, "My child is coming to Rice, and it costs $50,000 a year—what can I expect him or her to be able to do when they graduate?" My first response is, "You cannot expect him or her to be a career professional singer. They're here to learn singing, but also to learn a lot about music and language. They're going to get a great education at a school like this, because it's one of the premiere schools, and all I can promise you is that you're going to have a great degree from a great university. If that leads to a career in singing, you would be in the minority of all the people who do this, but it could lead to a career in the music field." My boss at Houston Grand was one of my first students at Rice! He's a very smart guy, but he wasn't going to be a career singer. He's a terrific administrator. He is making a great contribution because he was a good student who studied singing, knows about the voice, has empathy for what a career takes, and knows how to listen.

There are all types of paths. I was just talking about this with a young professional singer, early thirties, who sings Verdi. We were talking about all the people who are dropping out of the industry because, even though they've been acknowledged to have talent, there's just not enough work for them. You have a few "stars"—if there is such a thing as a "star" anymore—and then a middle tier of singers who are really vanishing. The singers coming out of the young artist programs and coming from other countries are much cheaper, younger, and really gifted. So they're taking the roles from people who normally would have been singing them deep into their thirties. It's a real conundrum—a very real problem for beginning and sustaining a career.

Helping people find their path is a big part of teaching young professionals until they're ready to sing the roles that they're going to sing. I teach a lot of people in Europe who are doing fests, and of course, they get to sing a lot more over there. So when possible, if the management agrees to it, if I think that's the right thing for them, I encourage it. I certainly don't discourage it, because they're going to sing that many more times than they're going to sing it in the States. We definitely have gotten away from what "career-track singing" used to look like. I think that's because of all the compression in the singing business. There are so many, many less jobs; fees have gone down and not up. People who normally could make a living in the business are having a harder time doing that. You can't sing in the regional circuit forever. If you can't graduate (to the bigger houses), they're not going to hire you ten years later to sing the same role, because there's somebody who's cheaper and younger. It's a real issue, which goes back to, why are we taking so many students? Let's not take as many students, because the business just won't support it. That's where schools have got to decide what kind of mission they have, and be realistic, so we're not encouraging them to go into this when there's no work for them at the end of it. There's way, way too much of that. Maybe people who are doing that are not clued into what's happening, or they themselves didn't go through it, or they don't live in proximity to a professional opera house. I think there are a lot of unrealistic expectations. We'll hear 300–350 auditions for Houston Grand Opera over the course of a couple of months, and even though those have been prescreened, you're shocked at how somebody got this far singing this music. You might be looking for two or three people in any given year; there are really just a small number of people who can actually do it.

It's not that we're being elitist, but we're not in a position that every kid is going to get a blue ribbon! When we go down that path, we set up these expectations and then so many people are disappointed who are not going to be supported by the industry going forward because of the way they were mishandled going through the system. They could be great supporters if they're advised properly early on and people are honest with them, saying, "You're very smart and you're musically talented, but you don't have the instrument and in my opinion, I don't think you can make a living at this . . . so why don't you look at these things."

Jeannette LoVetri

The process of taking lessons and practicing puts the students in touch with their voice and their body. It teaches them to be more open to sound and to responses within the throat and body. It allows them to develop courage and discipline in surpassing their own vocal boundaries, as this is always challenging and often frightening. It develops patience, persistence, and determination and keeps them in touch with their own intuition. It is, after all, the singer's voice and body, not mine. They need to know what they both want to do comfortably and what can be an activity that is slightly beyond their capacities but not so hard as to be discouraging or tiring. In looking at songs, it is important to do material that is not beyond technical or functional ability, so choosing repertoire that is "singable" is important.

All these things, over time (years), allow an artist to emerge. It gives them permission to "try things" and see what happens. It allows them to try new sounds and go outside previous limitations. It guides them to take themselves and their voice into uncharted territory and, perhaps, find that they like singing things they never imagined they would like. It makes learning to develop control over the voice both interesting and fun but challenging and dynamic. It also provides guidelines about appropriate vocal and physical boundaries while their instrument and artistry is developing.

With a mature artist who is studying to stay in shape, it is the singers who decide what they want to express. Sometimes they aren't getting the result they want and come to me so I can facilitate getting their voice to do what they need it to do as efficiently as possible. Artists are always growing, and sometimes, in doing new things, they want outside feedback to help them decide which choice they like the best. That's different than working with a beginner or intermediate singer.

Chapter Fifteen

Performance Work

In his book *The Performer Prepares*, Robert Caldwell writes, "Performance work—the time spent to craft a rich inner experience to take into the performance—is essential because a correct interpretation played with correct technique is simply not enough to build a powerful performance . . . the performer must build compelling inner experiences beforehand and take them into performance."

How do you strive to help the student find that complete union of music and inner experience that results in a powerful performance?

TEACHERS' REMARKS

Lindsey Christiansen

I do believe that. I think finding compelling inner experience is one's life work. There are two levels on which I'd like to answer this question. I do think one has to bring an emotional connection of some sort to every piece. Ideally, one has it immediately, and then builds on it. If one doesn't, one has to find the emotional impetus for singing the song. There has to be a reason to sing. One has to go back to one's own experience, or the experience of one's friends. For example, in love songs (and this might sound just absurd!), I've gotten students to sing with more expression just by having them sing it to a beloved pet.

So, hooking in somehow—if it's a song about incredible loneliness and it's a very upbeat kid who's never really felt that, I have them think about a friend they may have known, somebody at school they know, or have seen on television or read about in the newspaper. What might that be like? Then I have them talk about what that might feel like. How would that person respond to his mother? [I] just to try to find that emotional place that will release the artist in them.

Deeper than that has to do with the way one looks at life. One must be very aware of one's inner life, and one must nurture it to connect to an inner experience. I'm going to sound a little bit sanctimonious—I don't mean it quite like this, but I do believe it's true. I do think singing is a very narcissistic profession—unfortunately, it has to be. But one has to work to mitigate that tendency all the time. I think singers need to have some sort of spiritual life, whether it's something that has theological roots or philosophical roots.

Singers need to go to concerts often. One of the biggest problems with singers is that they don't hear orchestral music; they don't hear chamber music. They get caught up in just their singing, which becomes very narrowing and limiting. It's essential for singers to go to art galleries, go look at beautiful buildings, and go to lovely places. I never will forget a speech Elly Ameling gave one time in which she said, "We have to tank up on beauty," and I really do believe that.

"Compelling inner experience" comes from having a rich inner life; again, some people have more propensity toward that than others. I don't tell people to go to church or think about Sartre or whatever, but when I talk about text, I do bring up examples of things that are important to me. I'm not afraid to say what's important to me.

I see students as complete beings; I don't just deal with their voice. That doesn't mean I meddle in their lives, either. If they want to tell me something, okay, but I really don't talk a lot about their private lives. I haven't found that to be useful. But we do talk a lot about life, about things that matter to us and to them. Sometimes that brings up other things. When there's something really awful going on, I usually find out. I do believe it's incumbent upon me to help them realize that although singing is terribly important, is it the most important thing in the world? They are learning how to connect to the human family. That's part of what makes them a better person and, as a nice byproduct, also what will make them a better singer.

The union of music and inner experience is just vital. You have to have something to sing about. Singing is not outside-in, it's completely inside-out. Sometimes you have to do outside-in, just because one doesn't always feel very spiritual or very connected to oneself. But I think as a teacher, one who has helped students hook into their very selves in order to be the best singers they can be.

Ways to do that are, first of all, just reinforcing them. I feel it's really important for me to let them know about the wonderful things they do (when they do wonderful things), praising them when they allow themselves to be vulnerable. I'm sounding like their parent—I don't think I do too much parenting, but I do think their whole life matters to me. I try to help them find a sense of their priorities; otherwise, singing is just too risky. It's not only risky, it's just lonely; essentially, nobody cares if you sing. Maybe your teacher and your husband do, but ultimately, they want you to be happy, and if you decided to be happy not singing, they wouldn't care whether you sang! I think they have to build a human being, like everybody else.

Richard Miller

The Robert Caldwell quote is well taken. Indeed, much of the problem in "coaching" at all levels is the fact that a singer is offered "correct interpretation played (sung) with correct technique," rather than being provided with an understanding of how to arrive at an individual realization of the performance at hand. However, if the performer is unable technically to cut the material, no amount of "compelling inner experiences beforehand" will serve adequately. A union of performance prowess and artistic expression begins with lesson number one! The main fault in much of voice pedagogy is adherence to a false dichotomy: technique versus interpretation. On the contrary, free the instrument technically, and you will free the artistic spirit to present compelling inner experiences.

Joan Wall

I teach a weekly performance class where the students explore multifaceted processes of "building compelling inner experiences that are taken into performance." In class, the students identify their "performance state" and then learn how to sing the song (or just to sing in general), how to focus on the meaning of the music and text, how to integrate a full sensory life into the performances, and how to resolve their inner conflicts. In fact, we use the book *The Performer Prepares* by Robert Caldwell as our text! I am fortunate that Caldwell, a personal friend, lives in this geographical area. He often visits our classes and works with some of my students.

In class, we do group activities: theater games, psychological processes, and exploratory exercises to build sensory acuity, self-confidence, self-expression, and artistic integrity. These are processes that I have developed in more than thirty years of voice teaching.

In addition to the group activities, students will sing songs in class and are given feedback about their performance by the students and me. The environment is conducive to creative experimentation—one where there is healthy feedback, and not personal judgment and evaluation.

I also spend time to "craft a rich inner experience" in voice lessons. In the luxury of an hour's lesson, we explore the individual singer's unique inner landscape and find new and exciting ways to stimulate his or her creativity.

Marcia Baldwin

Searching together, with the student, to find imagery appropriate to the melding of vocalism and musical expression—that is how I strive to help the student. A successful, mature performance takes many years of experience to develop fully.

Helen Hodam

I talk a lot in general terms. For example, in a Debussy song, I discuss Debussy's approach to music and text in general, and then in that particular poem. It's possible to overanalyze. Some students get so analytical. Once in a while I'll say, "Why don't you just sing it?"

I talk a lot about going someplace in a phrase because they begin to nitpick and completely overlook the musical phrasing. Often, as in Debussy, it's complex simplicity.

Some people just don't have the drive or emotionalism to project. Then it's very difficult to get them to express something. They either don't want to or think they are being expressive—that's the hardest of all—when nothing happens. When they're naturally musical, there's no problem.

Dale Moore

Sometimes a student has an inborn performing flare. I include in that the will to give as a performer and the will to communicate as a performer. If students have those things, they are going to bring that inner experience to it once they can perform a piece technically and interpretively. If they do not have those qualities to start with, you have to discuss it with them: yes, you're hitting all the notes and you're hitting them very beautifully, but you aren't saying anything to me. I find ways for them to make this speak and reach an audience, whether it's through the text or through the whole background of the piece itself and through themselves. Naturally, some students just don't have it; [they] are always going to be singing machines. I think the teacher should make a real game effort to try to develop it in a student if it's not there to start with. Some students you can only take so far, but you have to try and take them as far as they can possibly go.

Shirlee Emmons

We begin by discussing what the music tells the singer about the poem and what the composer thought it meant. We continue with what images (from all five senses) are called forth by the music and the words. We ask what personal connections the singer has to these images. Then we concentrate on the positive aspects: what the singer does well, not what he or she still does rather poorly. Performance mandates that this singer concentrate on the things he or she excels in, that the singer learn not to think during performance about the work still to be done. No powerful performance can go on, regardless of how well prepared it is technically, if the brain is preoccupied with skills as yet not reliable. Powerful performance exploits the things that are good now, as [my book] *Power Performance for Singers* keeps repeating.

Edward Baird

To have a powerful, complete, or total performance, one must reach a point where one is free from technical preoccupation with the voice. In other words, the technique works well enough that one is not preoccupied thinking about it. That allows immersion into interpretation of the role as much as possible. That's another thing that I tell students: develop a good technique so it works as automatically as possible. It's never going to reach the point where you don't ever have to think about technique at some point or another, on a high note or a register crossing. The more the technique becomes automatic and you don't have to think about it, the more it frees you up to think about other things—interpretation or immersing yourself in a character or role. These extra things make a good and sparkling performance.

Helen Swank

We all try to do the best we can, and if students can realize that is all we have to do, that better than we can do doesn't exist in any healthy way, then perhaps students can get to a balance in their lives and not be overcome by negatives. Then, and only then, can students be free to give that truly powerful performance. Sharing must be a joy.

Jack Coldiron

This is difficult. After cogitating for a while, what comes to my mind is the idea that I would try to overcome the students' sense of inhibition. If they can release themselves from being afraid of what people are going to think of them or say about them, then perhaps they can involve themselves in such a way that will bring forth a really good performance. Reflecting on actual experiences and allowing those feelings to be incorporated in the performance will imbue the tone and diction required to present an honest and rewarding presentation.

Carol Webber

This is interesting and it relates back to the previous question regarding knowing yourself. There's a marvelous quote from Anne Lamott, who's a wonderful writer.

She's written a book called *Bird by Bird*, which is about the basics of writing. You can substitute "singing" for writing in any case. I'll paraphrase what she says: If you don't know yourself, it's pretty hard to bring truth to any other character. Self-knowledge opens the potential for knowing someone else.

Students are going to need to be emotionally vulnerable. I must say that I agree completely with what Robert Caldwell wrote, but I think we've all had students who really aren't capable of the kind of vulnerability, self-exploration, and real instinctual perception. One of my goals in continuing to teach is to find ways to spark that in people who seem incapable of it. I believe that no one would be in music had they not had some experience—what I call an original epiphany—where music took hold of them in some way and never let them go. It's important to recover that first experience, no matter how silly it might seem or how long ago. Then flush it out with real memory: When the music hit you that way, where were you? How old were you? What were you wearing? All the things you would do if you were creating a character; rekindle and nurture that flame. Ultimately, without it, the music made by that person is not going to mean a whole lot.

If people are in singing simply because they've been told they have a good voice, and they haven't really fallen in love with music, then I don't think much is going to come from those efforts. Also, of course, if the student is singing merely for the attention it gains them as an individual, without the real love of music (definitely part of what Caldwell calls the "rich inner experience"), then there's not going to be much point. Anne Lamott says, "Why gather an audience together if you have nothing to say?"

I believe the imagination is incredibly important in this: to go to movies, to read books, to look at paintings in museums, and to try to sink into those, using your own imagination. A lot of the most imaginative artists come from artistically deprived backgrounds, where they had to imagine their own works of art. Some of the people I worked with on the West Coast and in the Midwest grew up on farms. A composer I met grew up without a piano or even a radio. These things have to be nurtured through the imagination, not just through experience. The experience, more than just being inner, has to be bigger than the inside of any one of us.

Oren Brown

Number one, I like to have the student read the words and then read them again. If it's in a foreign language, one must know the diction and know what the words mean. When that is done, I have them read the words in the rhythm of the music and then feel how the melodic flow makes music in and of itself without any words—just as a piece of music. It could be played on a violin and still be very meaningful. There is that intrinsic value of the melody itself and the harmony. Then I let the students feel their way into a union of the words and music together—to be especially aware of the rhythmic flow and dynamic stress, both of the music and of the text, and how they are interwoven.

For deeper meaning, I like to have the students relate the text to their own personal experience.

William McIver

I think the background for the performer has to be built up, honestly, brick by brick. Some performers strike me as false; they are very musical and will always be able to do something with a phrase, but after a while, you realize it's not based on knowing a whole lot about what is being said or communicated in that song. It takes time to do the background work necessary to construct vivid, accurate, plausible images and pictures, as opposed to shortcuts that lead students to quickly imagine certain kinds of things for the sake of the moment. Honest interpretive skills have to be developed.

Although I am not image oriented, I do believe there is a coordination aspect to singing that eventually transcends the technical. You're not really a performer until you've gotten to that point. I teach undergraduate and graduate students. A lot of my time is spent with their technical development. In support of my colleagues in the theory and history department, and so forth, I've taken more time in the studio to talk about form, meaning, and relating the text to musical materials. But a teacher's time is limited, and there are so many things that one needs to do. It's important to help students understand the role of history and theory in developing richer performances. The studio teacher has an obligation to reinforce the work of the academic teachers in this regard.

Here are the steps that I want them to go through: with a new piece of music, first do a word-for-word translation; find out what you can about the text and develop for yourself what the poet is saying; and discover how the composer either agrees or disagrees with you about that. Sometimes you feel a composer didn't really understand what the poet was trying to say. But if you're singing that piece, you must find a way to reconcile your choices with those of the composer.

Next come several things that one must be able to assume are correct. Use the IPA as a start toward correct pronunciation. Clap the rhythm. Pronounce the text in rhythm; sing the melody on one vowel and then on two or more. Only when one can do all of the above should the song be attempted as written. Technical progress is erratic—it will be a little bit more "iffy," it will accelerate at certain points, and it will reach plateaus and remain there for a little bit but not these musical issues. Other things can be learned and perfected by diligent, disciplined work.

Cynthia Hoffmann

Two quotes from my acting study have remained with me: "You cannot get anyone else's attention unless you can get your own first" (Paul Gleason) and "If it isn't personal, it's no good" (Sanford Meisner).

A powerful performance happens when the singer makes the personal connection to the meaning of the words as they are expressed through the music (and has the technique to make that possible). Students must go beyond a word-for-word understanding of the text; they need to understand what is behind the words. When the text is spoken or sung with meaning, it has a sense or flavor, which is the musicality of the language.

Sometimes students will have a feeling for a piece, even though they might not be familiar with the ideas expressed in the text. The music moves them. They want to experience it, personalize it, and convey it. Choosing pieces that mean something to the students is one of the ways to help them develop this inner experience, and encouraging them not to be afraid to go to those places where they feel vulnerable is another. Students need to get to know themselves emotionally and psychologically—to understand what makes them "tick" as a performer and person. This is an ongoing process of growth and awareness.

In addition, students should explore the composer's intention—the "how" and "why" the text is set in a particular way. If they can do exactly what is written on the printed page, they can gain insight into the piece from the composer's point of view. At the heart of all this work, however, is the desire and willingness to communicate in a personal way. This has to be encouraged and nurtured.

Marvin Keenze

Right from the beginning, I try to connect whatever sound they are making to an emotional response. I don't want them to make a sound that is not preceded by a sense of energy. I show that by the way I sit at the piano or stand and by the way I look at them. I want the student to know that I am living with each vibration that they make. Now, this style of teaching takes a lot of energy and is tiring. I try not to be passive about any sound they produce. I'm hoping to teach that the sound carries a symbol of something they are feeling. This dimension of sound is more important than the syllable they are singing. There isn't a moment of vibration that is not part of the total communication. This is something we teach from the very beginning. We just don't make sounds; we make them for a reason.

When I introduce a song to a student, I always begin with the poetry. I want to know how they feel about singing this poem. There are some subjects they don't feel connected to at certain stages of their lives. I again refer to my graduate student who relates to Thomas Hardy poetry. The settings that he sang changed his voice. He became a whole new performer. Suddenly, he was charming and subtle and his voice had many new colors. There are key pieces in all of our lives that become a milestone in our development as a performing artist. A certain song can lift singers into a new realm of expression. I encourage them at every singing moment to hook into some aspect of emotion. If something isn't working right, I work on technique in an isolated way. I work on the breathing, the phonation, or the resonance, but only to show that the coordinated sound is a real emotional utterance. I say that if the vibrations you make don't go out and do something or change something, it is a waste of time. Either it's going to rattle my lamp shade or it's going to rattle my heart. Recently in Nova Scotia, I adjudicated a music festival where children under twelve sang. They sang beautifully, and it was hard for me to write as I wept. These children sang with perfect tone, beautiful phrasing, and wonderful poetic expression. These little larynxes were making vibrations that were doing something to me. If you are building the voice as an instrument, it must always be attached to the spirit of the singer.

Our students should be encouraged to create an atmosphere with each song. They should have an image of the setting, the age of the person in the poem, the dress, what went on before, and what created this outburst of emotion. But as they sing, they should not forget that their voice is a musical instrument and that the drama must not interfere with the free function of it.

Leslie Guinn

Exciting and powerful performers are tremendous risk takers. Their willingness to be publicly vulnerable allows us to experience their musical and emotional ideas. I try to help the students eliminate as many vocal crutches as possible so they might feel safe while expressing strong musical impulses. Vocal freedom itself can release intense emotions in the musical student. However, feeling these same emotions while singing can and usually does have a negative effect on the singers' control over their own phonation (i.e., the constriction of the throat while crying, etc.). The students must acquire the discipline to lead an audience to experience these same intense emotions while not letting them have an effect on their vocal function.

Bruce Lunkley

I've taught primarily undergraduates all my life. My recent years at SMU [Southern Methodist University] have given me graduate students. There really hasn't been a whole lot of time to get that far into singing, and maybe I'm missing something. When you get undergraduates and you're trying to make them use their voice well, you can't use enormously difficult or deep repertoire. I think Caldwell's right, absolutely, and I do call upon them to think into their own experience if there's something they can relate the text to. Or sometimes I'll even ask them to semi-stage a song to get a feel for the physical aspect of it. But I can't say that I've gone into this with the same kind of enthusiasm and depth that I have with the rest of my approach to the teaching of singing. I'm not sure whether even my present graduate students could be accused of having a complete union of music and inner experience. But some of them will knock you off your seat, and I don't know if that is from that union or just their ability to communicate. I think it would be hard to draw the line between those two things.

Barbara Doscher

I would assign music well below the technical level of frustration of students so they aren't continually worrying, Can I make this sound? You have to do that if you expect someone to use different colors.

Second, I would be sure it was in a language that the student knows intimately. For most Americans, that means English; there are people who know Spanish almost equally well, and for them there is some wonderful Spanish music.

I encourage an extensive subtext. There are some very good questions (regarding finding subtext) in Shirley Emmons's *Art of the Song Recital*.

Last, I remind students that the way they do a song has nothing to do with the way somebody else does a song. Just because they're singing the same song as "Mary" doesn't mean that hearing the same song becomes tiresome. Each of them has their own way to say it.

I think competitions have homogenized people. I have a lot of students who have won competitions and continue to win competitions, but I have very mixed feelings about competitions. First of all, singers try to outguess the judges, which is impossible. Second of all, they think that if they don't sound like Tebaldi or Milanov, they are not competitive. Do you know anyone out there, any big-name singer, who sounds like anyone else? But it's hard to persuade them.

Laura Brooks Rice

The biggest thing I talk about is honesty in performance. I work on it myself, and I talk to my students about it from very early on. A dishonest performance really makes me angry. If someone stands up to sing merely to impress someone or to draw attention to one's self other than to communicate or share, then it's all pointless. First and foremost, I tell them to first do what the composer dictates. The composer obviously knew what the poet wanted, and knows how the music is reflecting the text, so you do what the composer dictates.

Then I have a list of things: in order to find honesty in performance, explore the text. Do research on historical influences, musical issues, and performance practice; be sure all of that is in place. Be sure the diction is correct. We need to create a palette of vocal colors so we can effectively reflect the text. That's part of learning how to sing. We can then draw on that palette of colors as we're learning how to be honest, how to express and discover "how" to perform a given song or aria. Is there a character? What's the scene in the opera? Is it a descriptive or a narrative song? What is the relationship between the singer and the accompanist?

I have some acting exercises that I've done with my students and I've done in opera workshops. One works really well in terms of song recital or standing up in front of a piano to sing. I talk about projecting a thought. I imagine that my mind or my eyes are like a movie projector, and I project a scene that I am singing about. I can project an adjective, or I can project a color or an emotion. To make an honest performance, it's important to not act but react. You see what it is that you are singing about and you react to it. It's the reaction that touches the audience; the reaction gets the point across.

To find inner understanding and inner experience (most importantly, that the audience gets that inner experience), all of these things have to go through a true core of sound. If it doesn't go through a supported core of sound, none of what you're trying to reflect through the text will get out there. It's a difficult task we have.

Meribeth Dayme

One is high use of the imagination of that student, particularly with the text—playing with that text, insisting that they perform even a few lines, without any kind of criticism or stopping and "as if." So it's creating in the mind and in the brain a performance at each practice and at each lesson. These things have to be built in; to me they're part of the technique. If you don't build them in, then they're something "extra" and they often get left out. Your reflexes are built on the way you approach something. So if not, your reflexes have been prepared for performance until the last two weeks or the time period right before performance; then, in a stressful situation, you're not going to be able to rely on them. It's built in. It's part of the package!

Robert Edwin

Again, we must celebrate the rare performer who can create such a powerful performance. It has been my experience, after over forty years of teaching rank beginners to elite professionals, that very few singers are gifted with enough musical talent, emotional insight, and pure grit to achieve that sublime level of art. Our job as teachers is to open doors via challenging vocal technique, repertoire, and performance skills so that a student can be put on a path of self-discovery that may lead to greatness. We should always be looking for the next level in our student's development. Undertraining them or babying them does them no favors. In my studio, I like to use the image of an endless staircase. Don't stop climbing unless you run out of talent, motivation, or desire. Never be completely content with where you are on the staircase, but enjoy the climb no matter what step you are presently on. Learning, growing, and achieving should be serious fun.

Jeannette LoVetri

A powerful performance is one that is memorable. In almost every case that has to do with clear and direct communication of an idea or experience. We all respond to emotion biologically. Can you look away from a loud argument? Do you avoid turning around if you hear a scream? Without emotional honesty, performances might be intellectually interesting or stimulating, but if you want to remember a performer or a performance, emotional impact is the most powerful means to that end. Some singers are afraid of being emotional. That works against them. Training is supposed to allow the voice to be fully emotional in a highly functional way. Then, the rest is up to each performer. They must decide what they want the audience to take away from hearing them. Quite frequently, surprisingly, singers don't really know as they don't ask themselves that question.

Mary Saunders-Barton

My own performing experience has been invaluable in working with vulnerable young actors who are just beginning to explore their emotional imaginations. Once again, I am part of a collaborative team. In their performance studios, students begin the process of integrating singing and acting skills that bring songs to life. In dance classes, they begin to incorporate their acting and movement. I have many opportunities to see this work as it develops in class, in mainstage productions, and even in professional productions as students progress through their training. My goal in applied studio voice training is to help them develop the technical vocal proficiency to follow their heart's lead, wherever it takes them.

Chapter Sixteen

Auxiliary Training

What kinds of "auxiliary training" do you recommend to your students?

The singer seeks to become as complete an artist, musician, and performer as possible. With this goal in mind, the pedagogues were asked to recommend ways outside of voice lessons through which the aspiring vocal artists can "round out" their performing education. The list is presented by reference frequency.

If you are not familiar with the Alexander or Feldenkrais methods, the index provides a brief description of these useful "body-awareness" techniques.

1. Take movement classes: dance, fencing, and so forth. Include rhythm experience such as drumming.
2. Alexander Technique; Feldenkrais Method; Pilates; Havening Technique.
3. Take drama and acting class; get acting experience.
4. Learn to be a good sight-reader.
5. Study piano, in particular, and learn to play other instruments, preferably strings (avoid brass).
6. Read literature, poetry, books on music and performance, drama history, and philosophy, for self-development.
7. Go to museums, plays, and movies—anything to increase your ideas and experiences about life.
8. Study culture in general; travel.
9. Become well grounded in languages.
10. Study yoga, aikido, chi gong, tai chi, and meditation techniques.
11. Gain life experience, and learn about self.
12. Study conducting.
13. Hear and watch lots of singers (recordings, videos, and live performances).
14. Listen to music other than just vocal, as well as other styles.
15. Become well grounded in music theory and history.
16. Walk, swim, and do aerobics for general health and conditioning (but not so much that energy is deflected from singing).
17. Sing in choirs; participate in summer institutes; and attend voice conferences.
18. Learn to love words.
19. "Tank up on beauty."

TEACHERS' REMARKS

Marcia Baldwin

Students should have a background in piano. If they study another instrument, I would say that flute or strings are preferable. Stay away from heavy brass or wind instruments. I've taught some trumpet players, and it's extremely difficult because the diaphragm is so tight. Their voices are big because they're used to pressing the air out.

Students who lack any instrumental background have a hard time learning music.

The profession is extremely competitive. Singers need to know how to sight-read if they want to compete for jobs, especially those that come up "spur of the moment." I cannot tell you how many good jobs I got because I could learn music quickly—roles moved into when somebody got sick at the Met. I would cover major roles because they knew they could rely on me. That kind of reputation gets out very fast—that is, whether or not you have good musical skills.

Other things I advise: Feldenkrais. Pilates, Alexander, and movement for the stage. Languages, languages, and more languages. There is no such thing as diction being too good. Go to Italy, Germany, and France for a summer. Find the money—beg, borrow, or steal it to go. One needs to know all the intricacies of fine diction in order to compete. It's also a wonderful cultural experience to add to one's craft. Take acting, movement, and opera workshop classes, which also offer makeup classes. If you do regional theater, you often have to apply your own makeup—even character makeup, which includes putting on your own wig. They might have gotten the wigs from somewhere, but there's nobody there to help you. You need to know how to do that—become acquainted with your own face and what makeup you need to use to make yourself look the best.

Barbara Doscher

I recommend acting, dance, and stage movement; quite a lot of my singers work out someplace. I believe very strongly in workouts, with emphasis on dynamic range of motion and balance. I don't approve of heavy weight lifting.

I think they should take formal course work or should be reading poetry, drama, literature, philosophy, and history—all the things that they apparently know nothing about. They got through high school somehow, but I'm not sure how.

Jack Coldiron

You might find this unusual, but I like my singers to sing in choirs. I know a lot of people don't, but at least at my school the choral people not only know something about the voice but also are sensitive to the problems of singers and they don't abuse the voice. My own experience has been that choral singing was and continues to be a great joy and something through which I have learned a great deal.

Performing situations—almost anything in which the singer has an opportunity to perform.

Certainly reading appropriate material, such as the NATS *Journal of Singing* and other sources that offer other people's opinions about pedagogy and all the aspects of singing.

There are so many opportunities now to hear and observe fine singers on CDs, on television broadcasts (Met simulcasts), on YouTube . . . all of which can bring about recognition and ownership of fine professional singing. Acting lessons are absolutely suggested.

Joan Wall

I have organized my response by categories:

Movement training and body awareness

- Movement for Performers course (offered at our university)
- Pilates training (offered at our university through the dance program)
- Dance (offered at our university)
- Alexander Technique
- Tai chi
- Yoga

Drama training

- Acting training (offered at our university)
- Performances in musical, opera, and plays (offered at our university)

Literature

- Poetry and literature study

Vocal and musical training

- Foreign language
- Singing diction
- Master classes (team taught by various teachers)
- Reading of journals and texts
- Attendance at live performances (at our university and professional offerings in the area)
- Viewing video performances by great performers
- Listening to recordings of all kinds of music

Leslie Guinn

All students can profit from some movement and acting classes. In addition, I sometimes recommend Feldenkrais classes. Meditation can be very helpful for some, and I suggest they begin with Herbert Benson's highly respected book of some years ago, *The Relaxation Response*.

Bruce Lunkley

If they intend to work on the stage, I encourage movement and dance. We do have some Alexander people in the area here, but I don't see any reason to stress it if it isn't readily available.

I recommend theater training and stage work.

I think reading poetry is very good for them.

William McIver

I think anything that helps students to be healthy and happy can benefit their singing in an ancillary way. I especially stress to young students that they have chosen a profession in which their mental outlook is terribly important. Whatever helps, be it religion, psychology, or meditation, that's up to them . . . but it's important to be optimistic and to be relatively happy with one's self.

The better shape one is in physically, the better off you're going to be as a singer. I do ask the men to be very careful about weight training. I think the jury is probably still out (although they're finding now that maybe it's not as bad as we once thought), but I still stress flexibility, rather than bulk. I'm concerned that if we become muscle bound, we could lose some of the suppleness of the musculature that's needed for classical singing.

Carol Webber

A lot of the available physiological approaches, such as Alexander and Feldenkrais, are really wonderful when they're taught by someone who is innately a good teacher and responsible for the information as it applies to each individual. Yoga is good for mind/body centering.

I recommended modern dance, rather than ballet, because the body in ballet is pulled in and up, and in modern dance, gravity is not always defied. Swimming is a tremendously good partner to singing because of the breath work. Anything you can embrace that really gives a sense of contact with your whole body can be helpful. Given that so many people in our society are really uncomfortable with their own bodies, I believe when you talk about physical fitness alongside singing, you need to find for each person some activity he or she can feel acceptable and confident while doing. Being "fit" is a good term to use, not regarding weight per se.

Piano. I have not enough respect for a singer who cannot play the piano. That is a prejudice of mine. For singers to deprive themselves of the simplicity of finding the notes with your hands seems foolish, given how much we must use our voices in daily life. I have a background in piano and flute. I know a lot of singers who come through woodwinds to voice. I still favor the piano for developing the responsibility of being a good musician. The accuracy factor in pitches, rhythms, and the structure of a piece can be embraced in this way—the skeleton of the musical score is well found in piano playing. Any instrument you want to take on is fine, but I favor starting with piano. When I get calls from parents with talented little kids, I say, "Piano lessons now, voice lessons later."

Music is about life. The song literature is specifically about the largest emotions of human living. The singer has a "story" to tell that involves a real appreciation of human behavior and feeling. Poetry is beauty of language, not only in sounds, but also in ideas. Go to movies, plays, and art museums. I like to assign a project where a student selects a song and then finds a picture in a museum that captures it in some fashion (or vice versa). We singers need to correlate all of our sensorial abilities—touch, feel, sight, and smell. Of course, studying acting increases that ability. A good acting teacher asks these questions: Where did your character come from just before this entrance? What kind of clothing are you wearing? Is the fabric finished, smooth, or rough? What kinds of shoes would your character wear? What time of day is it? What are the light, the weather, and the air like? Singers without that kind of curiosity must have fabulous voices, an extraordinarily beautiful, natural sound. Even then, for me, something is lacking. The imagination factor must be very, very high. I don't do well with students who just want to sound good (singing jocks, I call them). I'm interested in someone who is artistic and at least a little theatrical, whose creative juices run fast and deep. Everyone knows it is rare to find all of that in one person. It seems so often to be a sort of cruel joke that the person with the most imagination and the most curiosity is not necessarily the person with the most ravishing sound (and vice versa).

Edward Baird

I think it's good for them to take some dance, movement, and drama classes. Alexander Technique is very good—opportunities to work with an Alexander specialist have increased, but you have to be careful to find the "real thing." Unless you know the whole system, know what it's good for, and what its limitations are, then you're better off not dabbling in it.

I insist that my pedagogy students read five articles out of the NATS journals that are current for that semester. They pick two of the articles and write a review. Not only are the articles valuable, but also I hope they'll develop the habit of reading the most pertinent periodicals in their area. They can opt to pick something out of the *Journal of Voice*, although that can get very technical for most undergraduates.

Lindsey Christiansen

Alexander is very useful. I insist that my students exercise, by either walking [or doing] something aerobic—swimming is good for singing well, in general. It's good for the chest muscles, especially if you do the breaststroke.

I tell students that they have to "tank up on beauty." You've got to have something to sing about. Because students are so overwhelmed with the amount of work they have to do, they need to go to art galleries, read, or just go and sit [among] flowers some of the time. Maybe that sounds silly and kind of "pie in the sky," but I think that it's absolutely essential for artists.

Students should read a lot of poetry and learn to love it. I think it's really important to understand not only the music of a certain period but also the culture and history. It's also terribly important to have some background with philosophical issues. Classes in movement are very important. The study of languages is essential!

Marvin Keenze

I have experienced the rewards of Alexander training, yoga, Feldenkrais, Dalcroze movement, and the Alfred Tomatis listening program. All of these have helped me to understand the complexities of a coordinated body that enables one to move well and to produce sounds that reflect a holistic coordination. Our voice students at Westminster Choir College benefitted from the strong choral studies program and conducting experiences. These classes enrich their musical lives and their understanding of what goes into music making at the highest levels. The ability to play the piano is a great asset to any singer and teacher. The skill to work with an accompanist and coach must be learned. Academic experiences in collaborative music making are essential.

Singers should be literate. They should love words and languages. They should love just sounds . . . vowels and consonants. They should hear lots of singers. I find my best students love recordings. They should be interested in how singers sound. I encourage them to get really excited about certain singers and to learn to identify those singers' "sound."

Helen Swank

Alexander, aikido, and Feldenkrais—most people who teach Feldenkrais will teach aikido as well. I think anyone ought to have as many experiences in any of these things as they can get. Some will work for them, some won't work for them; it doesn't matter—you learn, you always pick up something.

Laura Brooks Rice

Movement classes. If I find that they have unusual physiological tension problems, I would send to them to an Alexander technician. Yoga and Suzuki movement have been added to Alexander Technique as important ways to find balance and poise in my students.

Dale Moore

I think anything that will ultimately contribute to the student's performance is beneficial. We are dealing with a performing art. I've attended some Alexander workshops and have read two or three basic books about the Alexander Technique. I think that is certainly fine. For male singers, I recommend fencing; for all singers, any kind of movement classes, acting classes. Languages, of course. Also, as much as possible in this age of specialization, general cultural studies.

Shirlee Emmons

I encourage my students to take a lot of acting lessons, not "acting for singers"—real acting courses for real actors. Dance and work with a performance psychologist are very, very useful. Naturally, with our new book, *Power Performance for Singers*, singers can do a lot of performance work by themselves. That's why we wrote it! Alexander Technique work is also extremely helpful.

Cynthia Hoffmann

Body training is essential and invaluable (e.g., Alexander, Feldenkrais, yoga, modern dance, fencing, tai chi, karate, etc.). Of course, one needs acting training as a singer, but it is also helpful to do straight acting work. Playing an instrument is helpful, even if you start late. Other kinds of work include rhythm and movement training—getting the body to feel the music, and certain sports, like swimming. I also recommend meditation as a way of centering and clearing the mind, enhancing the breath, and creating an inner awareness.

Helen Hodam

I recommend movement classes or body fitness classes. Some people are very tense. I think the body movement has been a big help to some of the people who are not very good breathers. Alexander Technique seems to be helpful.

Oren Brown

Of course you can't do anything in music that's not in your head. You've got to get the music in your mind and know what you want to do. You have to really think. Contrary to what most people feel about a singer's brain being a head full of resonance, there has to be some intelligence there, especially if one is to communicate. I like to have a person broaden his mind as much as possible. The more he can understand of language and culture, the richer will be his background in bringing it to interpretation.

As far as the body is concerned, I like to feel that the person is in good physical condition; walking and swimming are two of the best exercises. To exercise in order to perform a physical feat is not necessarily the object of being in good physical condition. If a person exercises to that point, perhaps he or she has gone into the pool of energy that ought to be saved for singing. That takes energy too. One should not do too much and fatigue the body—you need to reserve your energy for singing.

[On the Alexander Technique and Feldenkrais Method:] I feel they're beneficial, although I don't teach them personally. I had a seminar in Amherst (Massachusetts) from 1972 through 1985, and for the last eight or nine years, we had an Alexander teacher as part of the faculty. Classes for everybody were held in the morning and then individual instruction was available through the day for those who wanted it. Everybody who took part liked it.

Edith Davis Tidwell

Several of my students do yoga and I encourage them to continue that. We also have a course at the university called Music Mastery Performance Lab that introduces exercises to help promote relaxation and awareness, and addresses ways to release the problems that produce performance anxiety. An instructor who is also a specialist in "Havening Techniques" teaches that course.

Students have learned so much in intensive and most productive weeks at the SongFest Summer Institute in California. Composers, singers, pianists, coaches, and specialists in song repertoire are there on the faculty. (That personnel varies from year to year.) There are ample rehearsal, coaching, and performance opportunities. That program has been a stimulating experience for my singers.

My students have also had fine opportunities at summer festivals, especially Tanglewood (in the Berkshires) and Aspen (Colorado).

Meribeth Dayme

Lots of things, depending on the student. Rhythm things, such as drumming, dance, and any kind of movement—chi gong. I like chi gong instead of yoga because chi gong is moving and breathing. I recommend meditation.

Theater!—acting, playing with text, and use of subtext. Any kind of performance possibilities. Reading, obviously, but self-development reading—not reading in the field of voice. Looking at any number of wonderful things that can feed the imagination of a performer that are not necessarily coming from music.

Robert Edwin

My students are strongly encouraged to study dancing and acting in addition to singing. The "triple threat" performer is almost a requirement for success in many fields of the performing arts, especially music theater and opera.

Stephen King

We're doing this Young Artists Vocal Academy at Houston Grand Opera that's been wildly successful. We bring undergraduates, most of them rising seniors, and we immerse them for a week in all of the things at the opera house. We give them advice about repertoire, musical and dramatic coaching, voice lessons, and career advice. They get to talk to people at the very top of the field.

Jeannette LoVetri

I want my students to listen to all kinds of music and singers. I want them to hear different kinds of voices and styles, and I want them to begin reading articles and books. I want them to interact with other experts. I expect them to investigate both music and performing in whatever styles they like, but also in styles they do not expect to sing.

My professional vocalists often compose or arrange their own music and often share with me the things and people that have influenced them so I can grow as well. I learn a lot from my students and I enjoy that.

I encourage everyone to attend voice conferences such as the Annual Symposium: Care of the Professional Voice or the Vocology Program of the National Center for Voice and Speech and the conferences by NATS in the United States or ANATS in Australia, the ICVT internationally, and the British Voice Association in the UK. There are also many other conferences now for voice all over the world. Attending any of them is an important thing to do.

Mary Saunders-Barton

Working with preprofessionals in a university setting, all aspects of training are integrated. Acting is the skill that binds the others together. We are singing and dancing "on behalf of" the dramatic context. However, if I notice stubborn tensions that could be helped by added physical work, or music learning issues that might be helped by additional help with music theory, the training "team" is always available to augment and support individual progress.

On the other hand, a private student in New York City might come to me with any number of possible deficits. If a singer has limited training as an actor, I would recommend acting study. There is really no way to proceed without that skill. Lack of dance is also very limiting for a musical theater career. As cast sizes diminish, ensemble performers need to do everything . . . even play instruments. I also frequently encourage students to seek out rock/pop experts for help with certain contemporary styles.

Chapter Seventeen

Successful Attributes

What are some of the attributes you feel contribute to the success of a young professional (or aspiring professional) singer?

This list is not so much by importance as by frequency as the pedagogues made mention. However, a rather natural priority derives from frequency.

Attributes related to the voice/instrument

- Have a secure and reliable technique.
- Know his or her own voice.
- Have an outstanding/distinctive/interesting voice.

Attributes related to intellect

- Have innate intelligence and intellectual mettle (mental toughness).
- Develop musical intelligence and the ability and willingness to learn music quickly.
- Have good concentration.
- Display dramatic instinct.
- Be an imaginative thinker.

Attributes related to application/motivation

- Become well grounded in languages and musical styles.
- Make solid choices about career—roles, direction, whom to listen to, and whose "ear" to trust.
- Be disciplined.
- Bring tremendous dedication and love of the art to singing.
- Have a need to sing.
- Possess a need to communicate.
- Develop musical intelligence and the ability and willingness to learn music quickly.
- Have determination and a capacity for hard work.
- Be very well organized.

Attributes related to musicianship/musical training

- Be an excellent musician.
- Become well grounded in languages and musical style.
- Develop musical intelligence and the ability and willingness to learn music quickly.
- Be an excellent sight-reader.
- Have good keyboard skills.

Attributes related to personality and personal development

- Be professional.
- Be dependable.
- Be prepared.
- Be punctual.
- Display solid work habits.
- Have consistency (both vocal and personal).
- Have resilience—be able to bounce back from both the highs and the lows.
- Show mental toughness.
- Be disciplined.
- Have an understanding of himself or herself as a human being, rather than only as a performer. He or she should develop an inner security to survive professional stresses.
- Have determination and a drive to succeed.
- Display spontaneity, creativity, and ingenuity.
- Make solid choices about career—roles, direction, whom to listen to, and whose "ear" to trust.
- Have good business sense.
- Develop organizational ability.
- Show commitment to hard work and sacrifice.
- Bring tremendous dedication and love of the art to singing.
- Be a good colleague.
- Cultivate sensitivity.
- Have personality.
- Have charisma.
- Have a good appearance.
- Be distinctive.

TEACHERS' REMARKS

Barbara Doscher

The number one attribute that contributes to the success of a young professional singer is, without a doubt, an outstanding natural instrument. You cannot put that in somebody's throat. These people who continually worry about somebody's grade point average and [if] they have good foreign-language diction when they enter the graduate program—all that stuff can be taught. But you can't teach a voice where there's just an average voice.

Second, for success, you have to have good technical training, especially from ages twenty-three to thirty. I think most voices do not mature until a person is about thirty. What to do between twenty-three and thirty is a big, big question. If you go into music theater, you're singing seven or eight performances a week, which is much harder on the voice than doing operatic work.

I think the person should have good stature and a pleasant appearance. By "stature," I mean the tenor shouldn't be five foot four. I had a soprano a number of years back; she's now doing Carlotta in the National Company of *Phantom* [*of the Opera*]. She's six feet tall. Fortunately, when we did *Marriage of Figaro*, we had a baritone who was six feet eight inches tall. So, he sang the Count and she sang the Countess. That's good stature, though, for a big hall. Very few people who are five feet two are going to be singing in big halls.

The fourth thing: an intelligent throat. That's entirely different from brain IQ. I've had some people whose brain IQ was not too swift, but they've had great "throat IQ." The minute you give them an inept vocalize, their eyes get slightly opaque. That is invaluable, because when they leave you and they get with a coach who doesn't know beans about acoustical matters for the voice, they have to know how to protect themselves.

Fifth, excellent musical training, including the ability to sight-read, some keyboard experience, and the ability to learn music swiftly. If you don't have those, you're not going to have a professional career.

Number six is the hardest to pin down: presence. Some people call it charisma, but when a person like that steps out onstage, you know someone has arrived. I don't know how they do that or what it is, but it's almost as important as that natural instrument I was talking about.

William McIver

The vocal talent has to be there; beyond that, I think some things are terribly important: A very strong sense of self. Somebody who cannot be crushed by momentary setbacks. They have to really believe, and they have to really want it. In more than thirty years of teaching, I have seen people that I would not have guessed could make their way as professional singers who have; I've seen others whom I felt quite certain would and have not. Obviously, there are ingredients beyond talent and even intelligence—perhaps a drive to succeed and a belief in one's self and perhaps a higher being. I think all one has to do is read stories of professional singers who have been repeatedly rejected, are finally accepted, and then excel. Only then does one realize that (1) not everybody really wants to expose themselves to that kind of rejection, and (2) not everybody can come through that kind of rejection with self and ego intact. So, hats off to anybody who makes it! I think it's a very tough career.

Marcia Baldwin

Musicianship and the background in that respect. Commitment to extremely hard work and sacrifice. There are years of living out of a suitcase. Years of not being with a family, nor with a loved one. That is the norm. There are exceptions, of course. It takes everything: wonderful languages, style, and musicianship.

Carol Webber

A young professional singer's most important attribute is determination. The kind of singers to whom you can say, "Can't you find something else to do?" and they won't quit. Dogged determination and discipline are the attributes that have to be present for a career to happen. Unfortunately, those two Ds don't always come along with the finest level of talent, and the finest level of talent often does not have the dogged determination and discipline. We get mixed results at the top of the business. Discipline and persistence require a certain strength of ego. The original Greek core word for ego could have been translated as "soul." If you really want to be an artist, the ego must be unified in the soul, not just posturing. The public always knows. If that determination, discipline, and the potential for soul is present, then the manipulation of managers and marketing won't kill the artist because those attributes also include the ability to say no—to know when yes is appropriate and when no is appropriate.

Leslie Guinn

Excellent musicianship, except for the rare extraordinarily gifted singer. If a person has one of these voices (that is, the one every fifty years or so), they might be able to do almost anything they please and get away with it. That's not true for 99.9 percent of the rest of us. I think it's musicianship and the training that accounts for that. Solid work habits. Dependability. By that, I mean both being prepared and being on time—as silly as that might sound, it's a fact. I've seen it happen time and time again, where the less-talented individual gets more and more work because they're prepared. I wish students would learn that early on.

Shirlee Emmons

Mental toughness must be inherited, learned through experience, or acquired by design (i.e., by reading books such as *Power Performance for Singers*). Obviously, a singer must have what some call a "talent for singing." That includes a reasonably good instrument, a built-in sense of how one sings, and a very strong desire to sing—an intense desire that will overcome obstacles.

Although this might seem a strange answer, I think a singer also needs organizational ability (or has been blessed with a stage-mother type of person who will do the organizational things!). From the very beginning, singers are always faced with the problems of organization. To cope, they usually need the help of a more experienced musician. First of all, the singer has to organize practice time; he or she has to organize what was learned in a lesson and apply it during the practice time. A singer must organize for public appearances, of however low an echelon they might be. Once graduated to a "baby professional," the singer has to organize practicing for the next engagement. If the singer is not clever about that, he or she may be practicing too far ahead or too far behind the next engagement. The ability to balance all these balls in the air, being organized and efficient about the use of time, is exceedingly important. All the business details of the various engagements, from local churches progressing up to opera, must be organized by the singer. Even after management enters the picture, the singer cannot hand over all these details to the office; he or she must keep on top of it all. Most managements don't do all this until the singer becomes famous enough for them to worry about maintaining their singer's place in the musical world. If the singer is not prepared for a certain audition because it is interfering with preparation for the next engagement, management will blame the singer. Almost until the singer is a world figure, it is his or her responsibility to be organized.

As far as education is concerned, I cannot see that schools, even graduate schools, are so necessary. Because a school is evaluated for its educational standards, it must have certain requirements, and there must be a way to test whether the singer has passed the requirements. More often than not, the amount of repertoire learned by the singer is the main method used for evaluation. In most schools, the singers end up spending the least amount of time practicing voice and the maximum amount of time passing the theoretical or academic courses because these are easily quantified. Singing is not so easily judged, especially because each voice teacher who sits on the jury has his or her own idea of what good singing is. As a result, many, many singers leave school not yet singing very well.

Certainly a singer must, one way or another, learn languages, theory, harmony, and so forth, but there are, of course, methods other than going to school to do this. The reason for knowing the information contained in theory courses is not in order to transpose or theoretically analyze music but to enhance the interpretive abilities by understanding of music. Often, the young singer doesn't even understand why the study of theory is required. It is sufficient to pass the course. In that way, the young singer is cheated of an advantage.

Usually people go to school because it seems to offer many benefits for the money spent. But frequently it does not. When there is not enough time for practicing the major subject, it puts the singer far, far behind other singers who got on with training their voice. A singer will not be refused an operatic position because he or she lacks a master's degree. It will be either because the singing is not good enough or because the musicianship is unreliable. That's all. Technical skills and performance skills are most important. In point of fact, it would also be very useful for singers to spend time reading and learning to understand a wide variety of poetry to hone their interpretive skills.

Bruce Lunkley

I think young professional singers have to be just that: professional. They have to be vocal technicians, they have to be linguists, they have to know their way on a stage, they have to have personality, and as Vennard said, they must have a certain degree of ego.

Lindsey Christiansen

[Boris] Goldovsky used to call it "multiplication by zero." There are certain things that a singer must have, either a little of it or a lot of it. If they've none of it, it's multiplication by zero, and they ain't gonna have a career. I stole that from Goldovsky, but I think it's really true.

First of all, they've got to have an interesting voice. It doesn't always have to be a beautiful voice, but it certainly needs to be interesting. And there has to be a musical intelligence, and there must be some facility with languages. Along with musical intelligence is an ability and willingness to learn music quickly.

There's got to be a need to sing, a feeling that what they're here for is to sing. That has some real human negative fallout. I think we just have to put up with it and help it be as kind as it can be. I think the need to sing has to be there. They also need intellectual mettle.

I think they have to look good and have to worry about looking good. They need to have dramatic flair—a need to communicate.

They have to be willing to put up with sacrifices on a human level in terms of lifestyle and concentration.

They must have charisma. There has to be something in a singer that separates him or her from everybody else, something in the sound of the voice, in the way they express words, in their feeling about language, their ability to make a phrase, their exquisite high notes, and their lovely soft notes—there's got to be something that makes them distinctive. They need to have an incredible capacity for hard work.

I tell you, the older I get and the longer I teach, the more I'm convinced that a good voice is maybe 10 percent of the mix. It's an essential 10 percent; you can't have it without it, but I have seen too many good voices not be able to pull it off, and I've seen what would be considered average voices make a career.

You have to have good technique, obviously—that's a given. You have to develop a workable, totally reliable technique. One of the marks of a good technique is one that holds up even when you're feeling at your worst.

Marvin Keenze

Successful young singers need to give the impression of confidence and a sense that they know their voice strengths and limitations. They need to be well trained in languages. This does not mean just the correct pronunciation but also the true essence of the energy and frequencies of the languages. They must be good musicians and quick learners. They need to know that there is more to the art than just a beautiful voice. Successful singers need to know how to follow a conductor and a director. They need to know whom to trust about vocal instruction and the assigning of opera roles. They need to know when a change of teacher is necessary and that too many changes can result in technical confusion. They need to know how to take care of the voice and keep it healthy and flexible. They need to know when and where to audition.

Helen Swank

One thing that is important for the professional singer is to have an understanding of themselves as human beings, rather than just as performers. All of life is not lived on the stage. They've got to become "whole" people—they're going to be better able to stand the professional stresses if they have inner security to fall back on. They need to realize that failures happen and successes happen; life goes on, and that's the name of the game. I have one gal who's on the professional circuit who has such a healthy, wonderful attitude about it all, and I don't worry about her. She's going to be fine vocally. When she isn't, she comes back for lessons. The internal strength becomes very important, and I think it's something we can help our students develop.

Acting experience and dance—especially as Broadway musical and opera come closer together. It would be wise for students to have experience in both. Being able to move (and act) well onstage becomes all the more important as an ingredient for selling "the package."

Laura Brooks Rice

Luck, who you know, and of course, how well you sing.

Dale Moore

It's so complex. Growing up in a musical atmosphere is of incomparable value. I find that the students who have grown up in a musical household where there's good music heard, where they were taken to concerts, are light-years ahead. A student who can't read music starts from so far behind that it takes an innately intelligent and disciplined person to overcome that background.

Intelligence is tremendously important. I'm not talking about intellectualism. I'm talking about innate intelligence and sensitivity. I think these are all factors.

Early on, the love of the art. I find the students who bring a tremendous dedication and love of the art to their music are the standouts—that carries to an audience, to managers, anyone.

The student must have the desire to sing. I don't think Margaret Harshaw would have shot me for quoting her: "It's got to be sing, or die." That need is the bottom thing. Loads of people should sing and should always be encouraged to sing for the enjoyment of singing, but in terms of a having a career or anything important, it must be "sing or die."

Cynthia Hoffmann

I think most colleagues in our field would agree that singers aspiring to a professional career need to have the desire and the drive to do it—they have to believe in themselves and what they have to offer. It is hard to sustain the path toward a career if they do not have or develop these qualities because many difficulties and disappointments come along the way to and during a career. Important attributes are being able to communicate personally—music making by breathing new, individual life into the pieces and roles performed. They need, at least, a good voice (a distinctive timbre is a plus), and they need to be a good colleague (and a prepared colleague). They will need these attributes to be rehired and to sustain their career. Along with the above goes consistency, both vocal and personal, an ability to "stay the course" and bounce back from both the highs and the lows.

Joan Wall

I think American singers receive excellent training in the universities, where they get a wide scope of learning as musicians, vocal technicians, and performers.

In addition to these qualities, however, a young singer needs training in the business aspects of a singing career. Many young singers lose out in this area, and it is an area that needs further development in the universities.

Richard Miller

It's not just the vocal instrument itself; it's a combination of factors. A successful singer has to be someone who's musically well trained, someone who has the ability for imaginative thinking and with dramatic instinct. All of that is highly dependent upon reliable technique. If you don't have a reliable technique, none of the rest of it counts.

Helen Hodam

I think they have to carefully choose and decide whom to trust and listen. They have to have at least one person they can talk to whom they can trust. It is hard.

Oren Brown

They've got to have the voice. They've got to have the personality. One has to have a good appearance, stage presence and personality, technique, and something to say. I remember a student who sang beautifully but didn't communicate anything. She was not admitted to one of the fine schools that she wanted to go to because they said, "Well, she's not saying anything." One has to really communicate.

Edith Davis Tidwell

My list: A strong work ethic with the desire to improve, explore, and keep learning. Musicality. Excellent musicianship skills. A passion for music (not just performing). Healthy lifestyle. Confident yet humble. Authentic in own being and in presentation. Respect. Cooperative and generous in spirit. Maturity. Integrity.

I think it is very important for the young professional singer to have a reliable support group or a support system—perhaps a mentor, teacher, or someone in the community or family—readily available for providing counsel.

Stephen King

[Know your strengths:] We had a student here (at Young Artists Vocal Academy, Houston Grand Opera) from a major school that we would all know. I asked him, "Why are you singing this particular music? You are a classic musical theater guy. You look like that, you move like that, you sound like that. Why are you trying to do this?" And he really didn't have an answer for me. He would be really successful not trying to sing opera—and he's at one of the most important schools in the world! It's such a complicated world out there right now, and we need to make it as uncomplicated as possible, be honest with people at the beginning, and help them get on the right path.

Chapter Eighteen

Professional Singers

What is your opinion of today's professional "career-track" singers?

Teachers were asked for their opinion of the American singer and were also asked to give reasons for their assessment. Through public expression of their viewpoints, this informed sample helps clarify and document perceptions regarding the current status of the professional, American-trained singer. Most agreed that American singers were well trained, but many expressed concern about deficiencies in preparation, perseverance, quality, and so forth.

TEACHERS' REMARKS

Dale Moore

I feel they are very high caliber. I get a little out of patience with all the talk of the various golden ages and that we don't have voices like we used to have. I think we have a lot of very fine young singers. Of course, there is always some concern as to whether or not the "career-track" singer gets the right instruction at the right time. Will he or she realize soon enough how important it is to have a systematic technique? Will he or she have wisdom enough to turn down what might be tempting opportunities if they are not ready for those opportunities?

We do have too many ten-year careers, when they should be thirty-year careers. Part of that I lay at the feet of managers; at the feet of opera directors who will not stage singers so that they can sing advantageously. We can also blame those conductors who do not know they have a left arm in order to keep the orchestra down. We are currently going through the "heaviest" craze, at least in my lifetime—by that, I mean roles are being cast toward too much heft. As I said in a NATS *Journal of Singing* article a few years or so ago, I am convinced that people like Luigi Alva, Cesare Voletti, and Ferruccio Tagliavini would not probably even have careers today; they would be told their voices are too small for professional careers. Would Elizabeth Schumann, Lily Pons, would any of the voices that we prized so in the forties and fifties have had a chance? That is my concern for the young singer—it is so tempting to try to make your voice do what you think will sell. We have to constantly remind them, "Train your voice to be as good as it can be." Get it free, adjusted, and resonant—rather than make it into something you think will get you a role.

Leslie Guinn

America turns out a terrific product in its young professional singers, many of whom are heard in our regional opera houses. They move, act, and sing quite well, with a healthy approach to providing generous amounts of sound. These singers who endure beyond the first engagement or two have demonstrated, beyond the basic vocal gifts, good discipline in staying technically secure through repeated auditions and rehearsals, tenacity in pursuing their goals, and good musical intelligence. I'm very sorry to see the decline in recital offerings. It has become very difficult for the younger artists to get bookings for recital work in general.

I share the concern of many who believe that some young singers sacrifice a degree of vocal health and longevity by pushing their voices beyond its optimal size. Patience with one's vocal development is a must for a long, healthy singing life.

Cynthia Hoffmann

I believe we are producing many well-trained singers who have a good understanding of their instrument technically, and their dramatic and language training enhances their work and versatility. However, I also feel that we are not creating enough artists. Because of economic necessity (earning a living performing), singers have to work mainly in opera, which has grown in popularity in the United States. They want and need to do it well in order to be hired, and preparation involves many facets—it takes time. So, they often do not have much time left to focus on song or concert repertoire—on the smaller, more intimate forms that contribute so much to personal and musical expression. I feel it is important for a singer to have a balance between recital and operatic experience for artistic growth and development.

Unfortunately, the recital medium is not as prevalent today as is opera. Recently, however, there has been movement to support recital and concert opportunities for young artists (the Marilyn Horne Foundation recitals, for example, and also opera companies that include concerts of song repertoire in addition to opera performances during their season).

Edward Baird

I really think the American-trained singer is the best prepared of anybody in the world and the best rounded. They're the best vocally trained people, they're the best musically trained people, they're the best musicians, and generally speaking, I think they're the best onstage too. The competition, of course, gets keener all the time, but I think the Americans are the ones who go out there and really stand up to it. Sure, it can be better, and not everyone is excellent, but generally speaking, I think the American-trained people are the best. I think most people around the world would tell you the same.

I really feel that it has come from our sharing of ideas, like we're doing right here [at the International Congress of Voice Teachers in Philadelphia, summer of 1991] and for which I give NATS the biggest credit. I think our association is the one that really started this sharing of ideas. So, I think the whole business of why our singers are better is because we have been more willing to share. It's the openness . . . of course, they get a more rounded education in our universities too. They get dramatic training and they get liberal arts training.

The American character is very open. The whole idea of sharing comes from that sort of thing; that they are very open—willing to share. They're willing to take more chances with that kind of thing.

Helen Swank

I think we probably have some of the most talented singers who are without jobs than at any time in history. There are some very fine singers who, for one reason or another, have been in the wrong place at the wrong time, should be employable, but just aren't. Maybe it has to do with the business of agents and management, of marketing these singers, and of networking within the vocal area so that these well-educated, capable people get heard.

I think that the development of opera in the colleges and universities has been an important aspect for the development of the singer. Now you need experience. Where do you get experience? To be hired, you need experience. College productions give them that, and then regional opera, which usually follows.

I have concerns about some of the "audition programs"—not those like Houston [Grand Opera], Chicago Lyric's, and Santa Fe's [apprentice programs]. Those are wonderful. But there are some "name" audition programs that I believe don't really serve to do much, except get their name on some publicity. Unfortunately, I see a lot of students spending a lot of money when there's almost no guarantee for results. As professionals in the music area, we should do something to start policing these programs.

Yes, [I think that American singers are of generally high caliber]. I think we have more teachers now who are better educated as to how you maintain voices and don't abuse them—don't misuse them—than we have had. I think a lot of that is thanks to organizations such as NATS and the Voice Foundation and that kind of thing. I think college teaching [has improved]—I've been at Ohio State for twenty-five years, and I've watched the caliber of teaching improve with every turnover.

Maybe this is a period when, for the first time, voice teaching has been a professional entity in itself, and not a lot of performers doing teaching because they quit performing. I really think there's a different direction.

Marvin Keenze

Everywhere I go in the world, I hear that American singers are the best trained. What is meant is that we give our singer-students a well-rounded education that is usually done in a sensible and progressive way. We guide our students in areas of musical skills, health, psychology, and pedagogy, and offer opportunities for performance. I hear fine singers in every country that I visit, but often there are not enough opportunities to perform for them. I think that we American teachers have truly benefited from the best of international teaching and have been able to incorporate these best features into our teaching. The areas of voice science, voice medicine, and pedagogical thought have greatly improved our teaching. The development of the International Congress of Voice Teachers and the formation of national associations have brought us all together in a way we could not have imagined.

Shirlee Emmons

I think American singers are the cream of the international crop. Totally superb. They are extremely well trained musically; they possess phenomenal voices; they are linguistically talented; they have great flair for the stage and take their acting seriously. The only possible drawback is the emphasis placed on marketing assets by administrators and managers has shifted to youth as the prime quality. This results in a situation somewhat like that of the so-called golden age. (I once had a great friend who, in her eighties, told me that we all have the idea of the golden age wrong. She herself was a part of the golden age and coached with Mahler and Schoenberg. She insisted that the method of making a career in those days was to study for six months and then go on the stage. Those who survived were physically and vocally the fittest and became famous. The others we have never heard of.)

Nowadays, it is virtually the same. The ones that survive the rigors of a career to become renowned are those who had mental toughness and physical abilities at an early age, and probably a very good first voice teacher.

Bruce Lunkley

I think the American professional career-track singers are probably as good as there are around. The demands made on them in this country are broader than the demands made anywhere else. I'm referring not just to languages but also to styles and that they have to sing outside of a single Fach. I think the whole Fach system is suspect anyway. I remember hearing a recording of Lucrezia Bori singing Mimi in *La Bohème*. Today, people would snicker at someone that small-voiced singing such a role. Today, several factors have forced us to create monster singers: the size of the halls and the enormous orchestras. But I think, overall, American singers are well trained.

Richard Miller

I would say that American singers as a group are in general technically far more natural than any other group. I spend a great deal of time in Europe, and there is no doubt that, technically speaking, American singers tend to be far ahead of their European counterparts.

What characterizes American singers is that they generally function better technically than many European singers because they are less bound by the regional and national traditions that often plague the European. In other words, there are certain kinds of problems for English singers because of their choral tradition, for example, particularly in the soprano voice, where many English sopranos begin to sound like treble boy voices when they sing. If they want to get into the international scene, they have to get away from that. Then there's what I call the "tube tone" of the German school, which is very often something considered desirable in certain kinds of music but which is not appropriate to operatic and internationally acceptable singing. And the French have their own particular tendency with their absolute involvement in the word, to the detriment of vocalization. But in America, there is a more eclectic situation. You can find all of those strains in America, but we are not riveted to some single one. Most American singers have, over a period of time, been subject to a variety of ideas. Americans are pragmatists, much more so than are European singers. I am quite convinced of that. An American will see a colleague who handles a certain part of the voice very well and will say, "Hey, what do you do?" And they might change to a more favorable approach.

In a way, America, by not having had an early, great historic vocal tradition of its own—it had a Germanic/Nordic choral tradition, it had the Italianate tradition in opera, and that was basically it—but, in a sense, not having had a great historical national school of singing here, we've been in better shape to take a more eclectic approach to round off the corners of parochialism.

William McIver

One of my advisees wrote his dissertation on this topic. He is a tenor currently singing in Germany. His topic is "The American Singer in the German Opera System." He developed a questionnaire that was sent to intendants, to agents, and so forth, in Germany. He got back a lot of useful information about how they perceive Americans. It's quite revealing; they think very highly of Americans in terms of preparation. They feel they are better prepared musically, vocally, and linguistically than their European counterparts. In some cases they find American singing is too homogeneous, not quite personal enough, unique enough, or maybe even temperamental enough—but eminently well prepared. I would trust their judgment on that; their criticisms are probably valid, and their approbation is probably deserved. I think the colleges and conservatories are, in general, doing a good job developing integrated singers. It's always a problem for such programs to find the correct balance between academics and performance. Some students don't want any academics, and some students thrive on them. That's a problem, but I think the American singers hold their own in comparison with singers from other countries.

Jack Coldiron

I spent three sabbaticals in London, England. I've heard many, many singers. I remember my second-to-last trip: I went to Wigmore Hall, where I saw a flyer on Thomas Hampson. I didn't know who he was, but I bought a ticket to hear him because I liked his program. Only after I got there did I realize he was an American! I just had to say, I thought that was the best singing I'd heard all year.

What I like about American singing is, first of all, the solid technique and a very direct kind of presentation. There is a personality and approach to singing that is very direct and open—I like the basic quality of American singing.

I think the caliber of American singing, vocally, is excellent. Perhaps we are not as intellectually prepared as some in the areas of literature and language, but we have solid technique and very good, strong dramatic ability. I hear this opinion reflected by English teachers; they think very highly of American singers. I believe that American singers are considered around the world to be the best prepared examples of professional singers.

Lindsey Christiansen

I have enormous respect for them. It's such a difficult "row to hoe." The kind of perseverance, the kind of deprivation in a way of what they have to have in order to be able to afford what they like to do—I just have enormous respect.

Whenever there is anything that's a very intense career decision, it requires a focus that doesn't allow for some broadening things that are tough on a human level. That's why I tell my students to go to the museum a lot and read a lot. I think it's very, very important that the life of the mind not be neglected. I think there are more dangers than there used to be of doing too much too soon, of being discouraged too quickly, and of knowing exactly what is right when. They have to know ways to help get the experience and keep the sense of what it is they're supposed to do.

As to the general caliber [of the American singer], I think it's mixed. I think there are some wonderful singers right now, although I think we have a dearth of big voices. Because they're being required to do things early, I don't think the voice necessarily has the opportunity to mature to the bigness it could have.

On a vocal level, it's hard. Lots of singers are not ready after four years, and lots are not ready after six; they have to invest a lot of money and time.

I think training is very spotty; when I judge or hear competitions, I'm often horrified by what I think is [the result of] inappropriate teaching. Yet I also hear [the results of] some very fine teaching. I think it's a mixed bag.

Barbara Doscher

The ones I have had direct contact with are of very high caliber and have dedication and motivation. In general, I think that American singers have very good technique. It's technique that will permit them to have long-lived singing voices. The thing that does disturb me is that many of them do not have enough training in acting, whether it's for opera or for recital work. A lot of them think that having a beautiful voice is enough. They don't have a care for the words, for what the poem is about. You ask them what the poem is about, and they look at you as if you asked a strange question. Many of them try to spread themselves too thin or attempt to sing roles that are too heavy too soon. One of my favorite sayings is, "rather a month too late than a day too soon."

Carol Webber

I think the American singer is trained as well or better than the European singer but that the time it takes to develop artistry is not then allowed, and the pressure to compete and win early is the "American way." If they're successful early on, many singers wash out early because they are pushed too far before they are really ready. A few of them hang on and survive to become great artists. You can see it in every decade—some of the young artists in *Opera News* that are listed as stars of the future and then are never heard from again.

Zinka Milanov said just before she died that this is the age of the five-year career. In a second five-year period, the inner loop gets tighter. The number who pass through that loop to the ten-year mark will drop to half or less than those who last fifteen years and more. I think our initial early career talent pool is terrific. What's done to them in the name of career success and ambition isn't always terrific.

Helen Hodam

I think many of them have been trained very well and have beautiful voices. It's the things that they have to do to have a career that I don't like: I have a beef against some of the opera companies that don't take care of the young singers, particularly in apprentice programs. They finish school and hope to get into an apprentice program, where they earn maybe $145 a week with room. Some companies give them unsuitable roles and overwork them. I resent this! Some also charge them a sizable audition fee that is not refundable. The young singers have to do it to get experience, but the people who run some of these apprentice programs have little thought or regard for these young singers and their preservation.

The same thing happens in Europe; there it is just as bad and maybe even worse. It is true that if you get into a small opera house, you are at least paid fairly well, but they throw everything at you. You work hard, and the Germans are screaming at you, if you're American, about your German. It's a very stressful situation. I tell my students never to go to Europe unless they have had some experience and can speak German accurately.

I think we have a lot of beautiful voices and a lot of people who sing really well—then they launch a career; pretty soon the voice begins to get frazzled unless they are nurtured and handled wisely. One has to learn the art of self-preservation—how to protect your voice. Orchestras are bigger, they're louder, and houses are larger. The tendency is to now have bigger voices do the roles that lighter voices use to do. Licia Albanese said that too many of the conductors in the opera houses are actually symphonic conductors and not opera conductors.

Marcia Baldwin

It seems many of today's singers have a generic sound—nothing sets them apart. There is almost no personal involvement in what they're singing about. In every contest I've judged in the last few years, this has been the case. You assume they do their homework, so they know what they're talking about, they know what they're saying, and they know the story of the opera, and so forth, but they don't impart that. They are on the outside looking in and singing oh so prettily, but so what? That doesn't mean anything. I want to be moved. I think anybody who is adjudicating or is hearing singers to hire wants to be moved. There is so little shading and coloration. It's good singing, and it's pretty healthy singing for the most part, but it's very monochromatic. We don't read, especially we don't read poetry; we don't develop our imagination. In that regard, many young singers don't understand what is needed to become a "complete" singer.

Oren Brown

I think we have fine talent. [However,] I think it is rather rare that we hear that talent used to its optimum. My opinion reflects what I was saying earlier of the sensitivity of our teachers to really hone in on the essentials and to allow the voice to grow at its own rate, rather than lead a voice through to do things it wasn't ready to do. If voices are used well, they can go on for a very long time.

Edith Davis Tidwell

I taught undergrads and graduate students. When the graduate students came to our program, they were always in a rush to get on to the next phase. Things today seem so quick and accessible, and I think it's good and also necessary to have goals in mind; however, technique is still developing, and focus must be kept on the process. Development is really crucial. Graduate students often come with this in mind: "I'm going to do this audition . . . ," and they get their mind set on that repertoire, the five arias, and so on. Sometimes I feel it's as if "we're going to flip this house—we're going to make it look really pretty quickly—on the outside"— and what is the true growth? I find myself facilitating the repertoire required for competitions and auditions rather than teaching the repertoire I perceive will take them to the place I see they could be. I want to encourage them, but I want them to slow down and, of course, with an eye on the goal, work in the present, to be able to deliver in the future.

Meribeth Dayme

Today there are too many professional career-track singers who have been trained to be overly analytical about their voice and performance. They are losing the message, and the passion is blocked. I want a compelling performer—I want a performer to demand that I listen. Today's singers are too intellectual, and as a result, I miss a certain presence: presence of sound and "presence of being" onstage. The ones that are really good are truly lost in the music, the text, and their performance. Obviously, throughout history, we have had only a handful of compelling performers. I think that's too bad. We can have more. We can have more compelling performers when we learn to teach it—and a lot of it can be taught.

Right now, I'm hearing intellectual singing. I hear it on the master classes that are being presented to us on television. The teacher working with them (for example, Joyce DiDonato) is always asking for more passion from these singers. And they have strange, quirky mannerisms. Well, why does any teacher allow that? That student can't be so stubborn that they continue to do such strange things if the teacher doesn't want them to, especially if they've been videoed enough and can see for themselves what they are doing.

To me, we are missing some things in the way we teach, and that is creating a vacuum in the number of compelling singers.

Robert Edwin

The elite singing artist, like the elite in any competitive field, is rare. One can be a professional career-track singer and not be an elite singer. There are professionals working in dinner theater and on Broadway, and in local opera companies and at the Met. It's safe to say the more highly esteemed the venue, the higher the level of competition, and the more elite the artists.

Stephen King

We definitely have gotten away from what "career-track singing" used to look like. I think that's because of all the compression in the singing business. There are so many less jobs, fees have gone down and not up. People who normally could make a living in the business are having a harder time doing that. You can't sing in the regional circuit forever. If you can't graduate (to the bigger houses), they're not going to hire you ten years later to sing the same role, because there's somebody who's cheaper and younger.

Mary Saunders-Barton

In the eighteen years that I have been on the musical theater faculty at Penn State, we have seen a substantial increase in the number of gifted and well-prepared applicants to the program. Out of approximately seven hundred auditions, we accept a class of twelve to fourteen students, so the competition is very stiff. Musical theater is a young person's profession—four years has to be enough to prepare them to compete in the industry. Most of these young performers find work immediately after graduation, and a good percentage go on to significant careers.

Any rigorous BFA musical theater program provides volumes of feedback and practice in audition techniques and professional conduct. By senior year, most of these young people have impressive skills, each with a unique set of attributes. Beyond talent and skill, I think what sets any performer apart from the pack is an unwavering commitment to professional ethic, artistic discipline, and a spirit of generosity and genuine kindness. These are the qualities that attract industry professionals and keep a career going.

Chapter Nineteen

American Vocal Stamping

In your opinion, do you think there is an "American sound" or "vocal stamp" characteristic of American-trained singers?

The teachers were asked if they thought American singers could be identified by a characteristic "sound" or "vocal stamp." This could be described as a sound that distinguishes American singers from those of other nationalities.

A few answered definitively "yes" or "no." Most of the pedagogues pondered the question before answering "perhaps" or "maybe." Some teachers clarified their remarks by saying that the finest American singers have what they would call an "international sound" (a term that Dale Moore attributes to Richard Miller's nomenclature).

TEACHERS' REMARKS

Leslie Guinn

I sometimes can tell if a singer is American, if only hearing them on the radio, without knowing a name or context. There is often an openness in the act of singing that is American sounding to me. The comfort level with the style of American music, such as Foster, Ives, Copland in his *Old American Songs* arrangements, some Rorem, and others will alert me. However, there is an intangible something else that helps me make the identification, for which I don't have an explanation.

Edward Baird

I don't know. That's an interesting question. If there is, it's what most people refer to as the "Italian approach."

Helen Swank

I doubt if I would [be able to identify a singer as "American" by sound alone]. If you were able to do that, I think what I would be identifying would be the voice that isn't overcome by vibrato. It's a more "natural" sound, perhaps. I'm not sure that I could ever do that; I'm not sure there are that many differences, but my mental idea of what is a good American sound is just a healthy, lacking in tension, free, bubbling sound, a vibrato that is an asset, rather than a noticeable liability, perfectly pitched, intonation perfect, well placed, even scale . . . but that's what everybody's after, so I'm not sure that I could identify it.

Marvin Keenze

Perhaps there is a kind of freshness to their voices. Perhaps we are open to a wider variety of acceptable sounds that give the voice more choices of colors. Could this be the influence of the musical theater?

We like a generic sound that has a balanced harmonic spectrum. We don't like to hear any throat tensions or an excessive or slow vibrato. We want to hear vocal freedom and a voice that knows its limitations and is respected by the singer. We want to hear the voice in the proper repertoire. All of this contributes to a healthy, flexible production. There is some danger in a homogenized kind of singing, where everyone sounds pretty much the same. I have heard criticism of this recently: a kind of all-purpose teaching that does not recognize the importance of the singer's contribution to the total sound can diminish the uniqueness of a voice.

I am grateful to have the opportunities to hear and teach singers in many parts of the world. I do hear fine singing and observe excellent teaching wherever I go, and I always learn from these experiences.

Richard Miller

Is there an American sound? A lot of Europeans think there is an American sound, but a lot of them will say, "Well, what is true about most Americans is that they sing better overall." All you have to do is look at the German theater itself. In almost every house, you'll find three or four—not just Americans [but also] Canadians—North Americans. It's almost always the case. My French students and my German students will say, "Oh, of course, we know the Americans are the best singers in the house."

My life over there as a voice teacher is in part enhanced by virtue of the fact of the general reputation of singing in America. In France, singers feel very often that there is a prejudice against them; they say, "Well, they always hire Americans." Then if you really talk to them about it and get to know them a little better, they'll say, "Well, but of course, she sings so well." There are also more of us, and there are more of us who study.

The other thing is that the advanced musical educational system in America is better organized. You can't even get a catalog from an Italian conservatory; it often has no course catalogs. The same is true in France. There's no real course of study. It's all free—you don't have to pay anything for it; you can be a conservatory student from the age of eighteen to the age of thirty and do nothing else, and very often [you can] even get a subsidy for doing very little! So, initiative is entirely different. I'm very much opposed to certain kinds of competitiveness in general, and to a materialistic society, but when it comes to vocal study/musical study—competition is a real incentive!

Shirlee Emmons

I don't know if there is a characteristic American sound. I guess I wouldn't be able to say that. The Germans do a lot of barking, perhaps because they are so worshipful of consonants. My singers who are placed in German houses all say that the German singers are generally the worst singers on the roster. The former East Germans are a little better. The Slavs are very good. They must have very good teachers. The French are worshipful of their language and are not anxious to modify any vowel, no matter on what pitch it is found. Each country, I suppose, has what you might call a characteristic sound, almost always determined by the language of that country. Russian, Scandinavian (except for Danish), and Italian languages do help vocalism a lot, in my opinion.

Bruce Lunkley

I'm not sure there's a "vocal stamp" or an "American sound" as much as I'm sure there are other national sounds. I think our sound is a little more all encompassing; it's a more open, less fused sound. It might be our language. Our language is not as precise as Italian, Spanish, French, or German. There certainly is no "high English" (as opposed to high German). That might mean an easier general sound—even in the foreign languages. I suppose you could say, yes, you can identify an American singer, but I don't think it's by the sound; I think it's what the sound doesn't have. I think the over-brilliance of many Italian singers, the over-darkness of many German singers, and the over-lightness and purity of a lot of British singers can be recognized. I teach in Europe—I hear and know about that. I think American singing is a little more full blooded and full blown, without being an exaggerated "blow 'em out of the hall" sound.

The American singers as a whole do not take themselves quite as seriously as other nationalities. They seem to have more of a sense of humor, a balance about it. They are more colleague oriented. They seem to have some kind of unity. There are exceptions, but basically they seem to think of music as being communal. They're looser, I think.

Joan Wall

I don't have a strong opinion about this question. If anything, American singers have higher expectations of themselves as total performers. The style of vocalization that is more often heard in America might be classified as the "Italianate style" of singing—a brilliant, full sound, with well-developed female low range and strong male high range.

Carol Webber

Because a lot of our teaching is in the European tradition, I would hesitate to say that there is an American sound. I think if there is an American sound, it is the American musical theater sound. Basically [in classical voice], we are still emulating the vocal tradition of Western Europe. I wonder if the American sound is brighter? I'm not sure. A question to the question: If there is an American sound, is it because our theaters are so huge? That actually takes us back to the young American singer. Not only [is there] manipulation by the business, but also the early opera career in three-thousand-seat halls (as opposed to the early opera career in smaller German and Italian houses) can wear out a voice. By the time European singers shift up to the Munich or Vienna state opera houses, they've immersed themselves in the trust of their own human, fragile voices in smaller halls. Many regional opera companies in America still use huge halls.

Helen Hodam

I think we have an "international sound." I think we're a blend, and that's what makes us sing above them. We're not a narrow, traditional German sound—well, there are plenty of Germans who don't sound like that either. I think perhaps the majority of our teachers are more oriented to the traditional Italian method. We like a good ringing sound. But I think the Germans themselves have changed, and I think we have more and more an international sound. I think that's the reason we turn out so many fine singers.

Dale Moore

I slightly prefer the way Richard Miller would put it in terms of an "international" sound. I think because so much is expected of the American singer in terms of languages, varieties of style, that yes, there is. But I would say American/international or international/American.

At the congress in Strasbourg several years ago [the first International Congress of Voice Teachers], we heard master classes with many different singers of many different nationalities, and Thomas Hampson walked onstage and sang the closing event of the thing (even though he had studied recently with Horst Günter in Germany, because that's where he was singing). He [had been] trained by a nun in Spokane, Washington, and this was American singing. This typified a command of all of the languages, the ability to sing and project a Wolf song, a Samuel Barber song, or a Debussy mélodie. Yes, I think there is an American singer in that sense.

Oren Brown

I don't think there is an American sound, or a "black" or "white" sound. I listen to the radio in the car, and I don't know who I'm listening to. There are certain schools of singing. I think it's a cultural preference.

[Do you think American singers fit into any particular category of sound?] No, and I think that's one reason they are so universally useful. They like the American singers in Europe because they can sing any of the repertoire—the French, German, or Italian—but some singers are better suited to one type of repertoire than another, of course, depending on the voice.

Lindsey Christiansen

In a way, Americans are the most versatile singers in the world. When I was in Europe, it was, "You're an American?" [sense of awe in the voice].

Because we have to pay for our education, we have a clear sense of what the Germans don't. I think there is more versatility in American sound. There probably is a sound. There's certainly a German sound, there's certainly a French sound, and there's certainly an Italian sound. I think we do some of it. I don't know whether or not there is an American sound. Maybe there's an influence of musical theater. I think the versatility is what distinguishes the American singer.

When I think about American professional singers, there was Arleen Auger on one hand and Marilyn Horne on the other. I think there's a certain affability, a certain openness. I think in the best American singers, there's a simplicity. I guess I have to keep getting back to versatility: the ability to do many, many things and a willingness to do many kinds of things. I think the singer-actor is a stronger characteristic in many American singers—acting, being good onstage, and believable as a character. [But] is there an American sound? I just don't know.

William McIver

I don't think so. Most of our teaching in this country is derived from the national schools (as Richard Miller outlined in his book *Techniques of Singing*). We find teachers who teach with a Germanic orientation and others with a more Italian orientation. Some are a mishmash of other things—to that you can throw in the influence of people like Cornelius Reid. To my knowledge, none of what Reid teaches is prevalent in the national schools as outlined by Miller. It's easier to point to attributes that epitomize the American-trained singer. Those are good linguistic preparation in terms of the sound of language. (Often though, [it is] not prepared deeply enough in terms of language comprehension. It is difficult if you want to be absolutely fluent in five languages. Not many people have either the time or the skill to do that.) Americans are, in general, musically well prepared. They are also generally reliable, and they learn pretty well. Still, I'm not sure that one would say there's really an American sound. What I hear is too mixed to qualify as any kind of unified American sound.

Jack Coldiron

People I think highly of are Thomas Hampson, Jerry Hadley, Frederica Von Stade, June Anderson, and so on. They are excellent singers who have marvelous vocal sound. I don't know whether you'd call it American, but perhaps it definitely reflects some American ideas. Adjectives to describe those ideas would be free, warm and rich, and direct (not without nuance but not a mannered kind of singing)—natural. I think it really reflects the American personality. I remember once I was attending a workshop on auditioning, which was being done by one of the coaches from the English National Opera in London. The man was urging this male singer on to explore certain open, dramatic kinds of things. The singer stopped and said, "You know, I don't understand why it is, but I see American singers just get up and wail away at things, and they just do it, and I find that difficult." I think there is a certain thing about the American personality. Sometimes we get branded for it because they say we're too brash and forward—but it's our open society, and generally, when we sing, we reflect that in the professional world. I don't find anything very "precious" about American singers and their presentation! I approve of that.

Barbara Doscher

Is there an "American sound"? No. The best American-trained singers use the traditional Italian or bel canto method, and have the same aesthetic values as that school of singing: a fluid, bright timbre with a legato based on an even scale and a focused middle voice. I think the great majority of well-trained American singers sound just like that. The ones who sound "American" are singing American music, and by that I mean Gershwin, Porter, Kern, all those "tune-smiths." What we're talking about, then, is music that is very melodic. That's American music. I think we've mixed up the "American sound" with "American music."

Marcia Baldwin

Yes, I do believe there is something that marks an American sound. It's a forward, bright sound easily produced—with the languages being less than exemplary.

Laura Brooks Rice

In terms of a characteristic American sound, I guess it would have to be based on the approach to the language.

Edith Davis Tidwell

Well, there's a lot of talk about that. I do think there is (in the professional American singer) a clean sound. It's accurate, rather sparing with portamenti, it's versatile, and there's a lot of use of color, and there is clarity of diction, no matter the language.

Sometimes, in English presentations, there's a casual sound . . . music theater . . . a sound that's not quite as opulent when we sing in our native language.

Now (this has to do with students)—the idea that recitative goes lickety-split. I find that is the tendency now. I think the students can get caught up in trying to make it sound easy and conversational and then move it so fast that it doesn't show the line, the direction of speech, the intent, or the language.

Meribeth Dayme

After all that I've said, American singers are still far more open than most others. The European teaching—and this is very general—is still intellectual and pedantic in lots of ways with too many remnants of old-school teaching. Sometimes this is good, because it gets people singing with correct diction and articulation, and so forth. On the other hand, the performance loses something.

The Americans have had "pedagogy" since the 1930s and early 1940s, and it has been useful in developing good teachers. Vocal pedagogy is still not common in Europe. In Europe, certainly in England when I first went there, they didn't want anybody having "pedagogy" with anyone other than the teacher with whom they were studying, for fear they might learn something that might interfere with the singing. That was that old bias that "if they know too much, they can't sing." It took a long time to change; now England is catching up—they are very involved in the science of the voice.

Robert Edwin

Personally, whether listening to classical, music theater, or CCM singers, I usually cannot distinguish the singer's national origin of training. However, one major point about American training is that singers are taught to sing authentically in languages foreign to them. I often hear foreign accents when English or American is sung by nonnative singers. The Three Tenors concerts, for example, showed a clear lack of respect for my native tongue.

Stephen King

Actually, I do think there is an American sound—and I think there are a lot of people in the industry who wish that it would go away.

It's an overtrained, overcoached, generic (as one of my colleagues says), "white-bread, no-grain" sound. I think a lot of the technical foundations are good and correct, but it's lost its soul, its uniqueness. As another colleague says, "There's not a distinct sound here." They're just mimicking what they hear on YouTube. They haven't gone in, worked it out, and found their sound. I think that's the thing you hear, that's really the difference in European (what I call "Old World") singers and so many of the American-trained college/conservatory singers.

I'm looking for people who don't sound like everybody else, who have unique, distinctive characteristics in their voice, even if I don't necessarily like the sound. I don't find it compli-mentary when people say, "That's the American sound." Conversely, I don't think we should put those labels—the Italian school, the German school, and so forth—on people. Teach singing, and help them find the unique characteristics in their voice, based on teaching the facts of singing. If you teach the facts of singing, nobody is going to sound the same if they are truly finding the honesty of their instrument.

Mary Saunders-Barton

This is a funny question applied to musical theater, which is a quintessentially American art form. I have had conversations with British colleagues who speak of the difficulty their students have emulating the bright forward American vernacular [a]. The skillful American belter, male or female, takes full advantage of the "trumpet acoustic," as Ingo Titze calls it, and it certainly defines an "American sound." Voice training techniques have lagged behind the profession for years, but happily, we are finally catching up.

Part 3

Teachers' Professional Training

Topics in this section include the following:

- Teacher's own training
- How these teachers stay current
- Teachers' personal goals and priorities
- Teachers' viewpoints regarding attributes in an "outstanding voice teacher"

What makes a teacher "outstanding"? What special qualities elevate a teacher's status from "average" to "superior"? How do teachers keep their teaching fresh, energetic, and vigorous?

Will scrutiny into the background, education, and experience of a group of "exemplary" teachers reveal a common thread?

These questions prove significant. They summarize all that has come before and crystalize the intent of this book, that is, How can we best direct our own development in the field of vocal pedagogy? What are the standards of excellence embodied in these role models?

Chapter Twenty

Schools of Singing

Do you think there is what could be called an "American school of singing" similar to the existence of an "Italian school," "German school," "British school," and so forth?

The teachers were asked if they felt American vocal training could be said to constitute a "school," that is, a fairly unified national approach to teaching voice and voice performance.

Most of the pedagogues interviewed felt there was not a distinctly "American school." Several stated a flat no; others were unsure. A few compared American training to an "international school" that has evolved in recent years. The profession has become more blended as the international community shares global ideas and knowledge concerning singing and pedagogy.

TEACHERS' REMARKS

William McIver

I don't think so. Most of our teaching in this country is derived from the national schools (as Richard Miller outlined in his book *Techniques of Singing*). We find teachers who teach with a Germanic orientation and others with a more Italian orientation. Some are a mishmash of other things.

Laura Brooks Rice

No, I think it's very much like this country is. It's amalgamated. I certainly can't say that my singing isn't American, because it's based on the Italian bel canto, and it's also very German influenced: the back breathing. It's a homogenized version of all styles of singing. I guess that's the way I'd put it.

Bruce Lunkley

I don't think there is an American school of singing. I just think we teach generally very well. I think American singing teachers know a lot about the voice, how it operates and how to make it work well. We have systematic courses that teach vocal pedagogy. The number of pedagogy classes in foreign conservatories and colleges is nil. Where do they learn to teach?

"I'm going to open a studio—what do I do next?" Even undergraduate schools in America will often offer an introduction to vocal pedagogy for the majors.

Marcia Baldwin

I believe the personality and soul of the singer make the sound what it is. Americans are a more casual society than many others, our language is more colloquial than British English, and we have many regional dialects. Of course, we work for consistency and purity of vowels, but the spirit of the American comes through the sound.

Richard Miller

No. [Our country] has the highest percentage of persons who are interested in what I like to call the "international sound." In other words, what we want is a sound that is acceptable in Tokyo, Munich, Paris, New York, San Francisco, and Rio de Janeiro. It should not be a sound that is only pleasing to a certain kind of national coterie. I'm talking about a specific kind of cultivated singing, what people call "classical" singing, but I would rather call it "serious vocalism."

Now, of course, we have historically "informed" performance movements in which people try to make sounds that they assume were made in former centuries. I read incredible things about vibrato-less sound, none of which is historically provable. In fact, the opposite is the case. There is room for a variety of vocal niches in this country, but if you're talking about main-route vocalism, the kind that basically we are involved in, in conservatory work, in NATS, and so forth, there is an international sound. Good Italian singers use that sound, and good French singers use that sound. And it isn't a uniform sound; it means that freedom of function permits the free sound to emerge. It isn't marked by trying to make a tube tone, a thick sound, a pushed sound, a tinny sound, a sharp sound, a rigid sound, or a soft sound. It is the result of good coordination between the breath management, the larynx, and acoustic factors. When all of these are coordinated, an international sound emerges. I think America comes closest to all of the countries in the world today in achieving that goal.

Leslie Guinn

If I had to describe it, I would say that it's probably an aggressive approach to performing and singing that is generally free of a romanticized approach, both to interpretation and production. It's hard to define, but American singers seem to have more of a business, no-nonsense approach than some of their colleagues in Europe might have.

Jack Coldiron

There have been so many well-known American teachers and pedagogues who have produced concrete teaching methods that have been widely accepted as fundamental (William Vennard, Richard Miller, James McKinney, and Scott McCoy, to name only a few). I think it is possible to believe there is an American school of singing. Also important is the American interest in knowing the newest research and scientifically accurate background for technical singing skills that is generally reflected in American singers.

Shirlee Emmons

I don't think there is an American school of singing. We all seem to disagree with each other. To our credit, however, most of us are really interested in knowing the newest research and the scientifically accurate background for technical singing skills.

Helen Swank

I think there probably is not. I have known many teachers who were of basically German background because we sent so many over there the generations before mine. When they came back, they were basically oriented in that particular way: the breathing and a kind of a gutsy approach to singing. I think that in America, if we have an American school, it's one that has tried to move away from much of a localized kind of teaching, from a country-locale kind of teaching, and is trying to take the best of all the world's and maybe has tried to relate first to what works for a student, rather than put on them certain limitations or certain rules and regulations. I find that I teach a little differently, depending on the individual student. Some of them need to work in a very high-placed, Italian-French kind of way; some have a little gutsier, even a lower, breath. You just kind of work with the student to bring out the voice so that it's free.

Pragmatism—I guess when you get right down to it, that's the basis of my teaching technique (snaps fingers and laughs)—whatever works!

Carol Webber

I think singing is international, human. The world is much too small a place these days to engage in nationalistic fervor about the arts, so I hope we don't.

I think there's enough of an array of training going on in America that it is impossible and unnecessary to categorize.

Singing is ultimately human, soulful, and therefore individual and unique to each singer. We should be encouraging healthy, honest, and beautiful singing without categorization or competition regarding source. America is a melting pot; we inherit the wisdom of all cultures and the flavor of many languages.

Meribeth Dayme

In general, the American singers are far better than their European counterparts. We have a better "middle class" of singers but not necessarily stars. However, there are a lot of fine young singers all over the world that we don't know about because they haven't yet become household names. The Chinese and Russians are developing some marvelous singers.

As for an "American school"? I don't know. Certainly the American language and the American approach are going to give it the sense of having an "American school." Right now, with all of the different things going on and all the different influences that are happening— the influence of science, and we're just beginning to get the influence of sport—there are new threads coming into the teaching. It is still too overwhelmingly "science."

Chapter Twenty-One

Personal Voice Training

Where and with whom did you receive your own training?

Asked about their own vocal education, nearly all the teachers responded that they were trained in America, primarily by Americans. Several of the interviewees began their voice training with a private teacher in high school. All were educated through the American university or conservatory system, or both, and then began to teach within the same system. Several continued postgraduate training with private teachers in America. A few spent time in Europe for further training and professional experience.

TEACHERS' REMARKS

Carol Webber

I studied in high school with a woman in Ottumwa, Iowa, named Margaret Stolz, who was the "dowager empress" of the cultural life of southeastern Iowa. People liked to criticize her because she was bossy. Most folks thought she took herself too seriously and was haughty. The truth is, she intervened in my life and changed it. She heard me sing with the junior high school choir and called my parents to say, "You don't know it, but you have a singer in your family and she should be studying." I went to her my senior year in high school. She found ways to involve me in all her other lessons. Money for lessons was a problem for me, so she would have me come and do dishes, or arrange flowers, so that I was in her house while she was teaching; I listened and learned.

My high school music teacher led me to the Oberlin Conservatory; Daniel Harris was my teacher there. I've learned a lot from many gifted, well-trained people since, but Mrs. Stolz and Dr. Harris planted in me a certain belief system about the completion of a person in the arts (regarding responsibility for being a good linguist and good musician and so on) that has stood me in incredibly good stead. I have studied for short periods of time in several locations. I've had good experiences; basically I've had good influences, and when they haven't been good influences, I've had enough experience to omit what wasn't good while keeping what was good.

Bruce Lunkley

My teachers were Roy Schuessler (at the University of Minnesota), Aksel Schiøtz, and Horst Günther. From Schuessler, I learned freedom from tension. He taught loosening the voice and loosening the physique. He was nondirective: there was no thought of placement, no effort to make you do anything with your voice—always let the voice do it. Schiøtz stressed clarity of sound. He discouraged the student from "putting on" or adding anything artificial to the sound. I learned how to approach art song and to "get inside" the songs.

I met Günther at the original AIMS [American Institute of Musical Studies] winter institute in 1972. I went to him because I found I just didn't have enough low range. I was pressuring things, and he released that. It was remarkable what happened—before I worked with him, I was a baritone with a low Bb to a reliable F#; under his guidance, my range increased. I developed a low G to a high A, and even higher in vocalizing, with a lot of freedom. He built on the idea to not "push" air at the voice and not "grab" the voice with anything but "allow" the air to become the voice. The air reaches the vocal cords and is transformed to a new form of energy called sound. That idea has been very, very helpful and is one I use a lot with students.

Helen Swank

I studied with Dale Gilliland. He was head of the voice area at Ohio State University for many years. I have to give Dale credit for being willing to let me go my scientific route as a graduate student. There was such a difference in approaches at that point. A voice science approach was fairly uncommon then, but I had free license to go ahead and study whatever I wanted. That was wonderful, and I really appreciated it. He favored what I was doing and supported me in going ahead with my work.

I'm an avid reader. Since I watch a lot of master classes, I've begun to wonder which is mine and which is somebody else's idea at this point. You really do become an amalgamation when you've been teaching for X number of years. And that's good.

It's important for a teacher to have sung or be a singer because you've got to try out things. They have to work for you if you're going to be able to teach them to somebody else.

Richard Miller

I have been exceedingly lucky with teachers in my lifetime. My mother was a singer, not a great singer, but she was a singer. She taught me how to breathe to sing when I was a child, and I sang a lot as a child. In a sense, it was the same breath management that I use to this day.

Next, I had an excellent high school music teacher, Ruth Cogan, who was an exceptional woman. She dealt with the sound itself. It was not just participation; vocal timbre and vibrant singing were important.

I feel I owe a great deal to my next teacher, Harold Haugh, who was professor of singing at the University of Michigan and a member of NATS. I studied with him for two years, and it was largely from him I learned about an agility factor that I'd not previously known. This was around 1946, and already he was involved in vocal physiology. He was quite knowledgeable. He knew how the vocal folds worked, he knew what airflow was. He knew the international IPA. I used the IPA from the very beginning as a college student. He knew what vowel definition was. He was a very fine pedagogue and a wonderful person. He was also a tenor and a very good vocal model for me, so I was very lucky.

On the basis of that training, I was awarded a Fulbright and went to Italy, where I was fortunate to study with two marvelous teachers. One was Luigi Ricci. Most people considered him a coach, but he made it very clear that if I wished to, I could also study voice with him. I had a voice lesson every day, five days a week, in addition to coaching sessions. He had been associated with [Antonio] Cotogni, a pupil of Giovanni Battista Lamperti, so a lot of the information that came through him was from that school. I was there in a course called Perfezione della Voce (Perfection of the Voice), concluding with an artist diploma from L'Accademia di Santa Cecilia. We began every private lesson with one of the aria antiche— not just the usual twenty-four but all from the original Parisotti version. We coached and studied opera roles but also worked a lot technically.

The next teacher was Mario Basiola, who was in Milan. When I had a few days off from the Stadttheater in Zürich, Switzerland (where I was singing for a period of years), I would go down periodically and study with him. He too was a singer and a Cotogni product. (Ricci was a wonderful coach and teacher, but he was not a singer.) Basiola had had a great career. While I worked with some other people off and on, these were my main teachers. I think my background has been almost entirely of the historic Italian school. During my years in Europe, I had wonderful Lieder coaches in Switzerland and Germany, but I didn't study voice with them. All of the time I was in Zürich, I did not want to study with a German-oriented teacher; I wanted to study with an Italian teacher.

William McIver

I studied with Richard Miller and Harold Brynson at Oberlin, Grace Wilson at the University of Illinois (who was a wonderful teacher), and John Crain at West Virginia University, a very fine tenor and singer at both the Met and New York City Opera for a number of years. I've also been influenced by the writings of Herbert Witherspoon.

Barbara Doscher

I studied with Berton Coffin. I have incorporated his approach to the acoustics of the singing voice. He had absolutely unbelievable ears. He didn't pay a lot of attention to his chart if someone was singing the right vowel. They could sing anything within the ballpark of that vowel and get away with it, but if they hit a clinker, he would notice it right away.

Shirlee Emmons

I studied in college with a man whose teaching I don't remember at all. I don't remember him as effective or not. I think he was probably more a coach than anything else. I left school with many technical skills not yet under control. Then I went to Curtis Institute and studied with the great Elizabeth Schumann, who was a disastrous teacher, although an angel of a singer and a delightful person. I faked a nervous breakdown to get out of Curtis without offending anyone. Then I went to New York and studied first with a woman that I do not remember at all. Finally, I found William Herman, teacher of Roberta Peters, Jan Peerce, and many others. He managed to change me into a soprano, something no one else could do.

[Asked if she had been a mezzo before:] Yes, there had been general agreement that I was a soprano, but no one could make me function as one until Mr. Herman. Meanwhile, I began a career, heaven knows how! Then I went to Italy with a Fulbright scholarship and studied with two teachers there. Neither one could do anything for me. All my problems were still my problems—high notes and pianissimo. I was a kind of short soprano.

When I returned to New York, I studied with an assistant of Herman, Evelyn Hertzmann. She was perhaps my best teacher. But I still got into vocal trouble, mainly because the same problems were pasted over but still not really solved.

When *The Art of the Song Recital* was about to be published, I went to the NATS convention in Houston. Berton Coffin recognized me from our Robert Shaw days, although I did not recognize him. He presented me with a hand-colored acoustical vowel chart, which I didn't know how to use. He and his wife Millie were so generous in sharing their knowledge of how to handle book publication!

By this time, I was in great vocal trouble and had stopped singing. I made a resolution to restudy my own voice by working with one vocal technique book at a time. I began with Appelman's book and followed that with Coffin's *Overtones of Bel Canto*. The light dawned! At that age, and with the disaster that my voice had become, I put myself back together with the help of Coffin's book.

I began to follow him, taking down every word he said with a tape recorder. I even kept a tape recorder in my lap at dinner parties when I sat next to him, asking questions and learning. I began to understand the acoustical vowels while I was teaching at Princeton University and continued to teach the Coffin information when I moved to Boston University. The best part of the story is that I taught myself at the age of sixty to have easy high notes and a reliable pianissimo—all by means of the Coffin books.

Edward Baird

I studied in high school, beginning in the spring of my freshman year. My first teacher was Robert Milton, head of public school music in all the Kansas City schools. He replaced Maybell Glenn (a well-known music educator) when she retired. He had started out as a choral director in one of the big Kansas City high schools.

When I went to University of Missouri, Kansas City, I studied with Hardin Van Deursen, with whom I did my bachelor's and master's degrees. He had a bachelor's degree from Northwestern and a master's from Michigan.

While studying for the doctorate at the University of Michigan, I started with Chase Baromeo. When he retired, I studied with Ralph Herbert. He was originally Austrian but lived and taught in the United States for many years. He was a baritone and had been a stage director at the Met.

Oren Brown

I began voice studies in my last year of high school with a couple of local teachers. Next, I worked with Arthur Wilson, a highly respected teacher in Boston. He had a very fine group of students winning prizes in those days, but I don't believe he ever taught a student who became a famous singer. Sometimes it works this way. If you get a great voice in your studio, then you can be a great teacher. But it's much more important to be a great teacher and teach people how to use their voice well, even though you don't produce some great internationally known singer.

From Wilson, I learned many of the relaxation techniques, and to allow the breath to do the work. He eradicated many of the incorrect things I'd previously learned. That was a big influence. It was correcting those things that eventually led me to work in voice therapy. I eventually joined Barnes Hospital as a member of their staff from 1952 to 1968. There, I worked with all sorts of people who had functional throat disorders. Many people with various problems came to work with me. Of course, this made me more sensitive to obstacles that interfere with the free function of the voice. I was very grateful for the opportunity to work there; it made me more sensitive as to what can interfere with the free function of all voices. I worked with thousands of people. Most of them were not singers, but what is healthy for the speaker is healthy for the singer. You have one set of vocal cords.

Cynthia Hoffmann

I began vocal study as a junior in high school, having already studied the piano since the age of eight, beginning with Clarice Lepton from the Milwaukee Conservatory of Music. My first singing teacher, Winifred Sloop, was a colleague of my piano teacher, Madame Margaret Buttree. Undergraduate voice study was with Larra Browning. In New York City, I worked with Daniel Ferro, Oren Brown, and later with Beverly Peck Johnson. During the summers in California, I began a long association with Margaret Shaper, who chaired the voice department at the University of Southern California. Shaper studied with Metropolitan Opera tenor Paul Althouse and with William Vennard at USC. I also worked with Margaret Harshaw, who studied at the Juilliard School with Madame Anna Schoen-René (who was a student of Pauline Viardot-Garcia and of Manuel García). I have also worked with Vera Rózsa. My coaches have included Hugues Cuénod, Judith Raskin, Gérard Souzay, Ralf Gothóni, Robert Evans, Martin Katz, and Margaret Singer. I owe a great deal to these fine teachers and others from whom I have learned so much.

I should also mention that I studied acting with Sanford Meisner (former director of the Neighborhood Playhouse and member of the Group Theater), Wynn Handman (the American Place Theater), and Suzanne Shepherd. In addition, I have studied the Alexander Technique for many years with teachers with various training backgrounds including Troup Matthews, Misha Magidov, Richard Levine, Judah Kataloni, and Ann Rodiger, with whom I also trained for one year. I am currently working with the training course of Joan and Alex Murray. Their work, along with others, has had an immense influence in my life, my singing, and my teaching.

Marcia Baldwin

I was fortunate. When I was fourteen, my first voice teacher was Esther Malmrose. She taught in Rock Island, Illinois. We did a lot with breathing; she would light a candle, put it on the piano, and have me stand two feet away. I would have to keep the flame flickering steadily with my breath. That's very hard to do! She was very careful with repertoire and avoided any that was too heavy for me. Of course, I had been studying piano already since I was seven. I also studied cello and clarinet in my high school years.

At Northwestern University, I studied voice and piano. I went to New York and studied with Marinka Gurewich. That's when I really learned how to sing. I studied with her all the time I was in New York City, including the years I sang at the Met. She didn't talk a lot about physiological concepts. She did use some imagery. She emphasized frontal resonance, which, no doubt, is why I do also, and she taught me how to sing a beautiful pianissimo. Gurewich was of the old school. She had studied with a descendant of the Garcia/Marchesi line. She stressed vocalizes and would create them for me as we went along. I had an entire book of staff paper with vocalizes in it.

Jack Coldiron

Early private teachers gave me a solid foundation. They taught me many things that, even now, I hang on to. Forward tone: I still see my first teacher sitting on the piano bench, open mouth, motioning with her fingers right at the teeth and saying, "This is where it belongs, right here behind your teeth."

I remember one teacher I had when I was young; she was a Julliard graduate, and she spent most of the time making me learn to breathe. I am in her debt for that. She spent time making me count out loud on pitch, walking about the room doing the same thing, and teaching me things like the "dog pant" and the "hiss" exercise.

I was twenty-three when I went to college. I had studied voice a good bit before that and had some very good teachers with excellent educational backgrounds (i.e., Eastman School of Music, Julliard, and Boston University). My college teacher had an outline of the "ten points of singing," most of which I still remember. It listed the basic points of singing and suggestions like "now add yourself."

Later, I studied some with William Vennard. I still use his "yawn-sigh" idea with students. The "bouncing epigastrium," work in the middle voice, and vowel modification—those are all things I particularly remember from his teaching.

I had the opportunity to study with Horst Günter. He was constantly thinking, learning, and coming up with ideas—an exceptional man who lived to age ninety-nine. His auditory and sensory awareness was remarkable. He had a little chart of the progress of sound and where it goes from the minute you begin phonation in the mind, outward and around again into the mind. He emphasized imagination and the importance of the brain in singing; I find that fundamental, but I think at times it is bypassed.

Graduate study with Mack Harrell was valuable—especially in the area of musicality and artistry.

Leslie Guinn

Three very important teachers for me, for very different reasons at different times in my life, were Todd Duncan, Cornelius Reid, and Margaret Harshaw. Duncan provided a sense of direction, inspiration, and discipline at a very early and important time for me. Cornelius Reid taught me one of the most important things I even learned as a teacher, which was to listen to how a voice functions. Many listen to the aesthetics, which to me are severely limited if the function itself isn't healthy. Reid offered the tools to change a voice's function through his work on registers and bringing them into a state of healthy coordination. Over the years, I've gone my own way with these concepts, but functional listening has remained the core of all my work as a teacher. He is a wonderful gentleman with impeccable integrity. In my late forties, I began several years of work with Margaret Harshaw who helped me increase my voice size, depth of sound, and stamina by leaps and bounds. She taught me a great deal about the importance of intensity, concentration, and strong physical work.

Lindsey Christiansen

I had a very odd pilgrimage into this profession. I did my undergraduate work at Westhampton College of the University of Richmond, where I had a wonderful liberal arts education. My major was in music history with a major performance area in organ, although I sang a little. I studied with Grace Wilson, an extraordinary woman who had been a student of William Vennard. She was one of the giants in my life, a complete musician. She was also a wonderful keyboard player and just an incredible human being. I was only with her for those two years.

I went to the University of Illinois for a masters in organ. While I was in graduate school, I decided to be a singer too. In two years, I had master's degrees in both organ and voice. I started teaching right away at the University of North Carolina. I was hired for both voice and organ, but I ended up just doing voice. I also studied at that time and had several teachers. Charles Lynam (a wonderful teacher at University of North Carolina, Greensboro) gave me the most.

Then I got a grant to study for a year in Hamburg at the opera school. I studied with Maja Stein there, had coachings, and did a couple small roles at the state opera. When I came back, I got married and moved to this part of the country (Princeton, New Jersey). I studied in New York with Margaret Hoswell and then with Shirlee Emmons.

Joan Wall

First, I'll list my teachers. They were as follows:

- Ralph Errolle at LSU
- Earl Redding at LSU
- Claude Wise, also at LSU
- Marinka Gurewich, NYC
- Martin Rich, NYC

Errolle, Gurewich, and Rich were superb musicians and had impact on my growth as an interpretive artist. Wise was a teacher of English diction who taught me the International Phonetic Alphabet and to love words and precise diction.

The greatest impact on my teaching came from Earl Redding, with whom I did my undergraduate vocal work at Louisiana State University. He shaped my early learning and formed the foundation for my later outlook on vocal technique. He was mechanistic in his approach to technique. By explaining specifically how and why the voice worked, he gave me vocalizes to train the different parts of the instrument. We worked most specifically on articulation and resonance. His specific, kinesthetic instructions helped me improve rapidly, and I found I could clearly remember what he had said, even years later.

In my teaching, I have combined a multitude of ideas from many fine pedagogues. From reading the vocal literature and attending master classes, I have expanded my knowledge and feel that I owe so much to so many that I cannot even list them. I do feel I have been influenced in my teaching of vocal technique by William Vennard and Berton Coffin. But vocal technique is only one part of my teaching. I spend considerable time with musical, imaginative, and performance aspects. I owe my musical training to my early piano and choral teachers. The performance teaching comes from drama classes and what I have learned in life as a whole.

Laura Brooks Rice

I studied with Margaret Harshaw and consider her my first and only teacher. I studied with her consistently from 1977 to 1981 and continued to study with her whenever I could until her death. In a nutshell, I learned correct breath management, a sense of where the voice needs to be placed, how to sing over an orchestra, and how to be an opera singer. That's what I really learned from her. I credit her with not only shaping my voice but also shaping my character through that. It's hard to describe what she did, but it's a total understanding of the voice. She taught good, low breath management; a high forward placement; and everything that affects that.

Marvin Keenze

I began as a pianist at the age of four in Louisiana and made good progress technically and musically so that as a teenager I performed with the New Orleans Philharmonic Orchestra. My interest in choral music brought me to the Westminster Choir College in Princeton, New Jersey, where I majored in piano and studied conducting and voice.

After receiving my master's degree, I joined the army chorus in Washington, D.C. It was there that I met the great influence of my life, Todd Duncan, the distinguished baritone and teacher. I started in his studio as an accompanist and soon became a student of his. I saw teaching that was so inspiring I became hooked into this world of singing and pedagogy. I was a regular in his studio for thirty-five years, and these lessons provided me with ideas and stimulation that led me into the profession that I have now. To Todd Duncan, singing was boring if it was not connected to the whole person and when the sound did not reflect the text. He was insistent that the pitch and vowel be reconciled in such a way that there was always an emotional result. He introduced me to books on voice pedagogy, and he himself was interested in the latest research and information about the physiology and acoustics. One time I was visiting him at his Annapolis home, and we sat outside and looked out at the beautiful bay. He said to me, "Keenze, what do you think of subglottal pressure?" He was always the pedagogue and yet also the artist/performer. I observed him on many occasions teaching master classes. There is not a class that I do that has not been influenced by observing him.

Helen Hodam

The teacher who most influenced me was Grace Perry Polanski. I studied with her in New York. I thought she was the best, most practical, and the clearest of any teacher I've had; I really learned how to take care of my own problems. I also had two teachers of German background and one Italian, but it was with Grace that I really best learned how to handle and take care of my own voice.

Dale Moore

I began voice studies with William English, now retired as head of the music education department at Arizona State, Tempe. That was at the end of my sophomore year in high school, and he was my high school music teacher. As I look back, I realize he was a very sound teacher. He himself had studied with Louis Nicholas, one of the grand men of the profession.

In my senior year, English left my hometown, so I worked with Glenn Peterson. He taught at Baker University, close to my hometown in Kansas.

I entered the University of Kansas and did both my bachelor's and my master's with Reinhold Schmidt. During the years of my master's degree work, I had a Fulbright to the Mozarteum in Salzburg, where I had coachings and sang in some of the operas. When I returned, I finished my master's with Schmidt.

Next, I studied with Burton Garlinghouse every two or three weeks between 1962 and 1965. At that time, he taught in the Cleveland area; later, he had a big studio in Los Angeles. I had several lessons with Cornelius Reid during the summer of 1971. I gained an understanding of certain concepts from Cornelius that I respect and continue to use in my own singing and teaching.

Edith Davis Tidwell

Please see her bio for teachers and training.

Meribeth Dayme

I studied singing with Joan Jacobowsky at Salem College in Winston-Salem, North Carolina. She's still alive, and I believe she's still teaching at age ninety. And then I studied in New York with a man named Bud Remley who was at Teacher's College and at Union Theological

Seminary. I got my master's in church music there, and then I worked with William Vennard for my doctorate.

When I first started teaching, I was hugely influenced by these people, because I knew nothing else—this is typical. When we study singing with someone, we're bound to use what they do because that's what they know. I was in their pedagogy classes (not for my master's but for my undergrad and for my PhD). I was heavily influenced by that. But I have also always been imbued with a huge amount of curiosity—that's just me! There was always a sense that there was more, so I personally explored a lot. I also had had a background in dance and, by the time I got my doctorate, a background in anatomy. I had a background in so many things before I went to London to study. I studied with a well-known singing teacher in London, Audrey Langford—she's not alive anymore.

When I went to London to study, I had an opportunity to look at a lot of alternative healing, a lot of work with energy, all kinds of things. I did huge amounts of reading; it's like I was let loose to do research and ended up having a great time learning and playing. . . .

Ultimately, I'm going to experiment with anything, so I say to myself, "Okay, how would this work for singing? What would happen if we did this? I've had that approach for most of my life, and recently CoreSinging became a solid approach—and CoreSinging wasn't created; it was more of an evolution—it was a culmination of all that exploring. I found when I was trying it out in various seminars and workshops, it was working. Finally, it became its own entity after I had done enough exploration with it to know that it was going to work practically and theoretically. It became an approach to singing that gradually replaced almost everything I learned from my old teachers. In all honesty, I found that so much of our traditional teaching actually blocks the energy of the singer. We have a tradition of saying singing is hard, and blocked energy is a very good reason for it to be difficult. Some of our old-fashioned ways of teaching singing tend to block the singer's energy, and then we tell them it's hard. Without that energy flow, it is. For me, singing needs to be easy, and CoreSinging is an approach that makes it that way.

Robert Edwin

My primary voice teacher for over fifty years was my mother, the late and noted New York City singing teacher Helena W. Monbo. She both taught me how to sing and how to teach singing. She called her method "Voice and Speech Dynamics in the Total Personality," in which all aspects of the human voice and psyche were explored and integrated. My father, the late Edwin R. Steinfort, was a professional singer and voice researcher. My pedagogy is heavily based on her and my father's pioneering efforts to incorporate the sciences into the art of singing.

Stephen King

I started my training as a biochemistry major at Auburn University. I grew up in the country in Alabama. I had no idea what an opera singer was. Fortunately, my parents believed that we all should do whatever we wanted to do. We five kids took piano, and we all played an instrument. I would play my trombone and take my piano lessons and played whatever sport was in season.

I didn't go to Auburn for music; I went there because I wanted to go to Auburn and be close to home. I wasn't doing anything in music, but I ended up playing my trombone in a kind of jazz band. Somebody got me to sing for the Auburn Singers, which was a show choir. Then I started taking lessons. I spent one day in music education. We sat on the floor and played with rhythm sticks in class. I went back to my teacher and said, "I'm not going to be able to do this." And he said, "Well, hang in there, take these lessons and then sing for the voice faculty in the semester juries, and we'll advise you."

I had grown up singing in church but nothing formal, no lessons. I had no idea what that was about. But I got into it, and two semesters later, I was singing Bob in *The Old Maid and the Thief*; then, the next year, *Gianni Schicchi* (which I probably shouldn't have been singing!). After three years, I was good enough to get a scholarship to Florida State. That's where I began to take it seriously. People said, "You should do this, you should be a singer." I started to study more seriously. I had met my wife, a pianist, by then. We got married and went to Florida State.

When I graduated, I think there may have been only one young artist program in the country. I was not about to leave and go to Europe with my new wife and get so far away from our families, both of which were in Birmingham. So I started taking singing jobs and part-time work . . . and then started to consider that I might want to teach in a denominational-related school. I had grown up in Birmingham, so I knew about Samford, Baylor, schools like that, and I thought, well, that sounds good.

I had studied with Roy Delp [a former NATS president] at Florida State. Somehow I connected with Jay Wilkie and the dean at Southern Seminary in Louisville. So I went there and kept doing professional jobs and started my DMA [doctor of musical arts], thinking that this would be a good backup plan. I hoped to sing and get a job to support my family if needed.

About halfway through the degree, the dean told me there was a part-time job at a nearby college and would I want to look into it to gain some experience. So I commuted there for a couple of years, and then they hired me full-time. I made more money singing than I made teaching for the first two or three years . . . my full-time salary was pretty pitiful! I had a little office with a window air-conditioning unit—it was pretty primitive.

We eventually moved there, and I stayed there four years. I was always singing somewhere. University of Kentucky heard me and hired me. I had been teaching for four years, and I knew about nothing, but I did the NATS Intern Program during that time, and Shirlee Emmons was my mentor. Looking back on it, I was around some good people who were on the cutting edge for the time. They were good teachers, and they had good students and had success at helping them get better. I found that inspirational. But certainly I didn't know much about teaching singers except, "here's what I do . . . do this." So I learned pretty quickly that, for me, that was not a good way to teach.

I started teaching at Kentucky, and we were able to attract some talent there. There are people from that era who are still working professionally today. I really, honestly believe, in my heart of hearts, that great talent and great singers are why we think there are great teachers. It's like the forthcoming book, *Great Teachers on Great Singing* [by Robin Rice]. I told Robin, "There are no great teachers without great singers, right?"

You could go out in the middle of nowhere and find a great teacher, but they're not in a place that attracts great talent, and therefore nobody knows about them. But if you're teaching someone who sings at the Met or is winning all these big competitions, by inference, everybody thinks you know something . . . and really, you know the same thing that is out there to which everyone has access. If you're fortunate to be in a place where you are around a large body of talented people, whether it's New York City, Houston, San Francisco, LA, or Chicago, it increases the odds that you will attract talented singers.

So I've been really fortunate that way; being around people who were successful where they were and then not copying anything they did but trying to find my way of doing it. I think my students have taught me. I've learned by observing them, seeing what works, what language works, what concept works with certain personalities and certain types of singers and then trying to "stick to the facts" and mold my language to help the singers understand what they need to do. I'm always trying to understand the facts better. I'll go through phases where I'll read about the latest stuff and I'll think about that. Some of that sticks in my own pedagogy, and some of it doesn't. I think generally at the top levels, there are a lot of people saying the same things, but they may not be saying them in the same way, and so that leads to some confusion if people don't understand what you're talking about.

Jeannette LoVetri

By the time I was twenty-nine I had had eight singing teachers and numerous coaches, all classical, some very highly regarded. I was a confused mess. I studied with many experts, but I ended up very discouraged. My last teacher did not recognize that I had probably developed nodules due to his insistence that my voice be "bigger and fuller." I am a light lyric soprano, but my vocal function was chest dominant in my middle voice, and he didn't recognize that. Consequently, my upper range really didn't go where it should have. I fixed it myself decades later, but by then I was no longer performing professionally.

I had one year of college at Manhattan School of Music with a Wagnerian soprano who disliked my little bird-chirp voice. I quit after that, and all my study since then has been privately. I have worked with other coaches, both classical and music theater, but all my vocal work I did alone. I also bumped into voice science in 1978 at the Voice Foundation's Annual Symposium: Care of the Professional Voice, and through that organization I have been able to collaborate with internationally recognized experts in every voice discipline. I have written pedagogy and scientific articles on CCM and am still involved in research.

I currently share what I have learned in forty-five years of teaching singing through my course, Somatic Voicework, which is newly in residence at Baldwin Wallace University starting July 2017. We have had more than 1,200 people from all over the country and the world during the past thirteen years attend to learn about vocal pedagogy for today's CCM styles. I also teach under the auspices of the University of Illinois Medical Center's Chicago Institute for Voice Care and have been at several other internationally recognized medical centers as a guest expert lecturer and clinician. Because my education was largely "in the trenches," working with Broadway performers beginning in 1980, and in dealing with many artists and many styles, I do not have the kind of background that those who have learned primarily through academia have. This allows me to bring a different perspective to the work.

I also continue to sing publicly, even though I was diagnosed in 2013 with a left vocal fold paresis. I have sung classical, jazz, and rock songs in performance, and although the sound is not flawless, I have overcome most of the obvious issues only through my own vocal exercises.

I have been influenced by William Vennard, Cornelius Reid, Meribeth Dayme, Richard Miller, and by many voice science researchers including Drs. Johan Sundberg, Ingo Titze, and Jan Svec; medical doctors Robert T. Sataloff, Peak Woo, Jason Surow, and Markus Hess; and many, many others. My background and influences are a "salad" from all the disciplines and from many authors, medical experts, researchers, and artists, and from my own investigations of all styles of music as a singer.

Mary Saunders-Barton

As a singer and a teacher, I stand on the shoulders of many who have gone before me.

I began studying singing in high school with Jean Ludman who, I later discovered, was the first woman president of NATS! She took me to the first Met auditions I ever attended and was a kind and helpful guide. During graduate study in Paris in the late sixties, I studied with Pierre Bernac, who inspired me artistically and whose manner with students I admired and now try to emulate. When I threw my hat in the ring in NYC as a performer, I studied with Marge Rivingston. Learning to belt and mix, however, was something I had to learn by trial and error and by emulating performers I admired. There were no musical theater training programs where all skills were taught in one place. We took dancing, singing, and acting "á la carte," and most of the voice training was classical. We were still working from an essentially classical model, and belting, if attempted at all, was considered a strictly chest quality.

As I began to teach myself how to belt back in the early seventies, my vocal role models were Barbra Streisand and my friend and colleague, Broadway actress Alix Korey. I was amazed by both of them. They had the ability to sing so effortlessly and powerfully in a high, buoyant, soaring belt. They seemed to have complete dynamic control of the middle range of their voices. These two singers were in fact my introduction to the concept of mixed speech and the famous Broadway belt sound, and I have never looked back.

I also owe a debt to Joan Lader and my beloved colleague Marianne Challis, who introduced me to some of the fundamental concepts of Jo Estill. I deeply appreciate Jo's flash of genius with regard to accessing vocal "qualities" in a conscious way.

Another stroke of good fortune for me was being invited to join the voice faculty at Penn State as a musical theater specialist in 1999. I became part of a community of dedicated voice teachers who welcomed me with open minds and hearts. A powerful synergy was created that has enriched us all. I finally joined NATS and participated in a workshop, Music Theatre and the Belt Voice, in New York City, spearheaded by Norman Spivey. NATS has been a powerful force in creating a vital progressive voice community that embraces all styles of singing, and we are all the better for it.

Chapter Twenty-Two

Staying Current

How do you stay current in your field?

"In-service training," "professional development," and "professional advancement"—in the business community, these traits are recognized as essential for upward growth. It is equally important to vocal pedagogy. Dedicated voice teachers strive to stay current, stay involved, and advance their own knowledge. Voice research has had a great impact on our understanding of the vocal mechanism. In talking with these teachers, it was clear that they strive to stay "up to date" in several ways: through membership in professional organizations (notably NATS and the Voice Foundation), through informative reading, by listening and observing singers, by actively performing themselves, and by teaching.

TEACHERS' REMARKS

William McIver

I read. I read as much as I can: *Journal of Singing*, the *Journal of Research in Singing*, and the publishings of the Voice Foundation. I hold memberships in MTNA [Music Teachers National Association] and NATS; I'm on the executive board of NATS as national president.

Jack Coldiron

I had a most fortunate situation where I worked for more than thirty years and I had four sabbatical leaves. I studied in Germany and in England, and had great encouragement to study in the off summers. I've done a lot of continuing study. I read, talk with teachers and singers, listen to singers, and go to conferences.

Coachings, of course—I'm open to advice and always want to learn. I still perform. I think the way to stay current in your field is to do it. You find out whether you can or cannot.

Laura Brooks Rice

I stay current because I'm out there. I sing a lot. In fact, I do a lot of workshops for our students—what apprentice programs are available, what roads to take, and what to do after graduate school.

I attend conferences, master classes; I read voice journals. I have a project to eventually read every voice-science book there is, just to recharge my batteries. In the process, I put together my own little handbook for my students. I read the NATS and Voice Foundation journals.

In addition, we have a vocal pedagogy laboratory at Westminster, with all the new electronic equipment. I find it interesting.

I have been active on panel discussions at Opera America with the Singer Training Council. Through those conversations with professionals in the field of opera, taking their important input to heart, I created a program at Westminster called CoOPERAtive that is a complete opera training program for young professionals. While no longer an active singer, I have kept abreast of the field through these conferences and through the invited faculty to our program who regularly work in major opera houses around the world. I also teach the young artists at the Washington Opera Domingo-Cafritz program as well as the Lindeman program at the Met. This keeps me current in terms of the demands of an operatic career in the twenty-first century.

Oren Brown

I'm a member of NATS. I've also been a part of the Voice Foundation since it started in 1972. I attend as many conferences (including those of the International Congress of Voice Teachers) as I am able.

I teach in Scandinavia and have every summer since 1980.

Helen Swank

I read the NATS *Journal of Singing* and the Voice Foundation's *Journal of Voice*. I've utilized them as much as possible in our vocal pedagogy course. Research is an important part of keeping students current, and certainly such material keeps me up to date. I also stay current with master classes, the national NATS conferences, and new books. It's my goal to check out all the new books so that I have the most current good text for the pedagogy class. That's a way of keeping up to date.

Edward Baird

For seven or eight years, I was the workshop director for NATS. Not only was I at every workshop, but also I helped put together every one from 1977 to 1984. I am also a past president of NATS, and of course I'm at all of the NATS conferences.

Richard Miller

I stay current through teaching, through NATS, and through my own voice laboratory; I am an adjunct staff member at the otolaryngological department of the Cleveland Clinic, where I have observed operations. I have participated in many research projects with fiber optics. I've visited Sundberg's laboratory in Stockholm and have done research in Holland and France. We have conducted a great deal of vocal research at the Otto B. Schoepfle Vocal Arts Center at Oberlin.

Barbara Doscher

I subscribe to professional journals. I particularly like the *Journal of Voice*, which keeps me fairly current about what's being done in the voice science labs. I wouldn't think of having a voice science PhD at the University of Colorado because I think being a vocal pedagogue and being a voice scientist are two different things. I admire these people a great deal. I do admire the work they do, and I think it's very helpful for us. I don't think we should call ourselves "professional" if we keep doing the same things we've done for the past twenty-five years and never read about something that might change the way we are doing things. I don't find that professional. I would not want to go to a doctor who is still reading journals from twenty-five years ago.

Carol Webber

I stay "current" by performing as much as possible. I collaborate whenever possible with other teachers. Schooling for myself as well as my students must include the stage.

Bruce Lunkley

I stay current in my field by participating in NATS in every way: the intern program, the workshop program, the national convention level, and auditions (regional and chapter). I teach many master classes throughout the United States and Great Britain. That gives me the opportunity not only to teach but also to converse, talk with, and learn from colleagues. I have found that, over the years, these have been the most fruitful opportunities. I also read the journals and the other publications (the Voice Foundation), and so forth.

Dale Moore

I've been active in NATS for twenty-seven years and am a past president. I feel the *NATS Journal* (now *Journal of Singing*) is not only the most important thing that NATS does but also still the most underestimated and (unfortunately) least-used aid put into the hands of singing teachers. I've attended the Voice Foundation symposia and have taught there. I feel the scientific side can be very, very important. I get lost in some of the medical things but always get something from it.

I try to keep up with every new book on singing, at least look it over and see whether it's something I want to own and read.

I listen to as much music as possible in terms of modern-day performance, although I don't have as much time for it as I would like. Every voice teacher should be able to spend a week each year at the Metropolitan Opera, just to see what's selling nowadays and whether we agree with it or not. I try to keep up, especially when working at places like Eastman or Indiana University, where some of our students do move right into major regional opera or on to the Metropolitan. We have to know what is going on there. That doesn't mean that we change our teaching methods in order to make them fit that standard, but at least we should know what the Met is looking for.

Marcia Baldwin

I am always talking with colleagues around the country. In the summertime, I try to see and hear as many vocal events as possible. I read the NATS *Journal of Singing*, *Opera News*, and the *Classical Singer*. I have kept in touch with former and current students. I also attend many symphonic, chamber music, and opera events during the season.

Marvin Keenze

I have learned from my association with voice specialists and teachers at NATS conventions, workshops, and symposia, and from my own colleagues and students. I cannot imagine teaching without these influences that constantly challenge me to be better at what I do. NATS and the Voice Foundation have had an enormous influence on my teaching. As NATS coordinator of international activities, I have met with teachers in all parts of the world. I have attended meetings of the European Voice Teachers Association and helped to plan international congresses and conventions. I have had a rich professional life from which I have gained knowledge, confidence, and humility.

Lindsey Christiansen

I read the NATS *Journal of Singing* and occasionally read the *Journal of Voice*. I share ideas with my colleagues. I go to a lot of concerts but not just voice concerts. I hear a lot of music, listen to recordings, and I read.

In the last four or five years, I have spent a good deal of time studying Schubert and other aspects of German lieder.

Leslie Guinn

Vocal pedagogy and its application to other areas of vocal work are fascinating to me. The constant search to better understand the often-mysterious ways of vocal function will always hold my interest. For some years, I have worked closely with otolaryngologists who had a special interest in performing artists. At present, I have an appointment at the University of Michigan Vocal Health Center, where I work with an otolaryngologist and speech pathologist treating professional voice users, such as teachers, attorneys, and ministers. They experience difficulties caused by injury, disease, allergy, years of bad speaking habits, and so forth. Observing the patients' exams and discussing the patients' vocal problems with my colleagues at the clinic is a constant resource for new insights. I also discuss pedagogy with teacher colleagues, attend quite a number of conferences and symposia, and read a great deal of related material.

Helen Hodam

I subscribe to the trade magazines: the NATS *Journal of Singing*, *Opera News*, *Opera America*, the *New York Opera Newsletter*, and *Classical Singer*. I attend conferences when I'm able, although it's hard for me because I'm busy teaching myself. I make an effort to go hear my students sing, whether at City Opera, or Glimmerglass, or Cleveland.

Cynthia Hoffmann

I have attended the Annual Symposium: Care of the Professional Voice for many years and have participated frequently as a demonstrating teacher and as a panelist. I subscribe to and read professional magazines (NATS, *Opera News*, BBC, etc.) and have a good library to which I always seem to be adding. I like the idea of looking back historically and relating past information to that of the present. I still sing a bit—now if only to vocalize and demonstrate occasionally for my students if I feel it would be helpful.

I began teaching voice in tandem with singing and so have been able to sit in on lessons and coachings taken by friends and colleagues. I have observed Cornelius Reed on several occasions, as well as Armand Boyajian, Regina Resnik, and Judith Raskin, to name a few. In addition to listening to recorded performances, I attend vocal master classes regularly, as well as live performances, including those of my students both in and out of school. I always learn something about their singing and performing outside of the studio.

Shirlee Emmons

I am an assiduous reader of the *Journal of Voice*, the *Journal of Singing*, the *Classical Singer*, and the new technical books. I have recently reviewed Richard Miller's newest book, *Training the Soprano Voice*, which I find to be superb in every way.

Joan Wall

I read journals, new books; I attend master classes and performances. I also stay current by talking with colleagues.

Meribeth Dayme

First of all, I am fascinated by observing the trends. I spend a lot of time on the Internet, I read all I can get my hands on, and I love to look at the forums where people are discussing the different issues with singing, whether that's on Facebook or LinkedIn, because that tells you where people are at the moment. I watch *American Idol*, *The Voice*, and the like, because I feel it's my duty to know what's going on, not to criticize, but to stay in touch with what's happening in the world of voice. I look at the scientific things that interest me, but right now my attention is drawn to various strands of physics, self-development, creative learning, use of imagination, the spiritual, and the alternative subjects that feed the spirit of the singer.

Robert Edwin

If voice teachers just read the NATS *Journal of Singing* and nothing else, they have a good chance to be well informed and up to date in the field. I read the journal as well as books on pedagogy, repertoire, and voice science. I'm especially interested in neuroscience and anything about the brain since I believe it is the center of the universe for us all. Nothing happens in the singing system without brain activity, and the better we understand it, the better chance we have to improve our singing and our pedagogy.

I also participate in the Voice Foundation's Annual Symposium: Care of the Professional Voice and try to attend as many singing-related conferences, workshops, and seminars as time allows. As a member of the Internet world, I do Skype and phone lessons, although I much prefer "live and in person" studio work. My studio is well equipped with recording devices, performing mics, speakers, amps, and literally Bach-to-rock repertoire and recordings.

Stephen King

As busy as I am, I try to stay current. What keeps me current is being around singers and being in it with them (and relying on other people to write things and research things; that's just not what I do). Someone asked me if I were ever going to write a book, and I said, "Nope!" There are plenty of books about how all this works, and all I can do is tell you it is about what I do with it. Since I don't have a system, it's not as if I can publish "Ten Easy Steps to Learn to Be a Great Singer." I don't have a method. You just accumulate a lot of stuff and then you have to sort through it and figure out how to use it. I try to keep it simple. (Although I'm more a Garcia guy than a Lamperti guy, I'm always using that Lamperti quote: singing is simple, but it's hard to be simple.) Sometimes it's not simple, and you have to simplify it and figure out what's wrong.

Jeannette LoVetri

I read articles and books, I attend conferences, I talk to colleagues, and I continue to do research. I attend concerts, performances, shows, gigs, and recording sessions. I sing. It all keeps me on my toes.

Mary Saunders-Barton

I have maintained my NYC studio since coming to Penn State in 1999 and teach there twice a month. I knew it would be important to keep my eye on what was happening in the industry. During the thirty-five years I have been teaching, musical theater has continued to reinvent and renew itself by absorbing contemporary styles of singing to tell its stories. Rock, pop, hip-hop, country, operetta, golden age, and classical styles are all fair game for musical theater composers today.

The astounding success of Lin-Manuel Miranda's *Hamilton* on Broadway has given new life to the art form and new hope to our underrepresented artists of color. This is an example of the power of theater to effect cultural change.

As vocal demands escalate, teachers have a unique and unprecedented challenge to monitor the vocal health of their students in a multitude of unpredictable circumstances.

Chapter Twenty-Three

Objectives and Priorities

What are your personal goals and objectives in your own teaching? What are your priorities?

A ship captain calculates the best and safest navigation; travelers "Google" directions using GPS for the preferred route to a destination; and an equestrian competitor "walks the course" to determine the best approach to fences. Similarly, educators can define "goals and objectives" in their own teaching to ensure clear vision to keep themselves and their students on course.

These teachers clearly hold high standards for themselves as well as for their students. Taken as a whole, their priorities can be compiled as follows:

1. Foster independence in the student. Instill vocal and musical security so the student can become a completely independent musician.
2. Implant a healthy, reliable vocal technique that will promote longevity.
3. Encourage free, joyful, spontaneous music making.
4. Help the student develop the ability to be a communicative artist who is responsive to the demands of the composer and poet. Inspire that extra dimension crucial to compelling performances.
5. Give students an excellent command of languages.
6. Introduce the student to new and varied repertoire and styles; help them understand the demands of different styles and periods; and show them how to find shades of meaning.
7. Give the student confidence in what they do to progress to the next level.
8. Be clear and articulate as a teacher in goals and explanations.
9. Be honest as a teacher.
10. Fix any technical problems.
11. Have variety in teaching and not be locked into a rote formula.

TEACHERS' REMARKS

William McIver

My goals are as follows:

1. to facilitate development of vocal technique, which supports communication for the students;
2. to help build the confidence of the students so they can become independent of me;
3. to give them the confidence through what they do to progress to the next level, whether that is proficiency as a public school teacher or a professional singing career, or acceptance into a prestigious master's or doctoral program.

In terms of technical development, my goal is to help them develop a technique that will be efficient and serviceable over a long period of time. It's possible to make huge changes in a young voice during the freshman year, not all of which I think are appropriate. One has to be careful of that trap. It's best to lay the groundwork for something that will be serviceable in the years to come and that will give the student longevity and freedom in terms of what they're doing.

Helen Swank

My personal goals and objectives are to allow all my students to be the best they can be as a performer, to help them maintain wholeness of spirit while they are doing this, and to give them the vocal/technical tools that will allow them to self-monitor their singing—to know when things are good or when things need help (their own or someone else's).

My priorities lie in keeping the vocal instrument sublimely healthy and in allowing the student to really enjoy this business of sharing emotions, feelings, and beauty with others.

Jack Coldiron

My priorities: to assist the student toward free singing; to develop acceptable diction; and to encourage enjoyable music making—to have the singing experience be an expressive and joyful experience.

If singing can't be joyful and fulfilling, then I think one must reassess. I am most interested in singing that promotes longevity, a technique that will serve that singer for a long, long time. My last public recital was in 2014, at the age of eighty-eight years, at Texas Christian University in Fort Worth, Texas.

Laura Brooks Rice

My first priority is to shape and begin to define a student's voice and to bring out their individual sound. I emphasize "begin" because, once again, we're talking about a four-year program. I'm very quick to emphasize to students that by no means do I feel they are finished after four years of college. They're all in such a big hurry and think they need to get out there immediately.

Since this book was first published, most of my teaching is now at the graduate and young professional level. My goals for those lessons have not changed but perhaps need to be able to help those singers find a technique that serves them well and that inspires quicker independence from me, their teacher. Two books that I refer all of my students to are *The Practicing Mind: Developing Focus and Discipline in Your Life; Master Any Skill or Challenge by Learning to Love the Process* by Thomas M. Sterner and *The Talent Code: Greatness Isn't Born. It's Grown. Here's How*, by Daniel Coyle. Both books encourage short, focused, repetitive practice sessions that encourage a visceral memory of the physical act of singing.

Helen Hodam

As a teacher, my goal is not only to teach them to sing correctly and to develop their voices but also to be sure they will know how to take care of themselves when they get out in the professional world. It certainly is a case of self-preservation out in the big, wide world, particularly in Europe. Singers might have to go quite a while without a teacher, and I want to be sure they know how to take care of themselves. They'll always need someone, they'll always need another ear, but they must have a clear idea of their own voices, what works for them, and what to do when it doesn't feel right.

Lindsey Christiansen

My goal is to help the student be a completely independent musician with a thorough and completely reliable technique. They should understand their technique so they can be responsible for its continued growth. I want to help students understand that technique and singing cannot be disconnected from the music. Technique is the means that allows them to fully realize the music. An important teacher I had once said, "The smallest unit in music is the phrase. Anything smaller is only sound"—so true!

I guide my students to learn a great deal about repertoire and to know what repertoire is appropriate for them; to have excellent command of languages; to understand of the differences of style; and to appreciate a wide number of kinds of styles. I'm a real stickler for working in diverse periods and styles: singing Baroque music or always working on something from pre-1750 and something post-1930.

I want my students to become independent, expressive musicians, able to unleash and unlock their expressive selves. I want them to have the musical and vocal tools to do that. I also want them to have a sense of the possibilities. I believe it's my responsibility to have a vision for what they could be. It's a matter of holding that out and helping them move in a direction that allows them to realize that vision.

Again, I think a big priority is that they learn to practice, that their practice time is as important as everything else. They must learn to regard the time they spend in the practice room as useful time. I want them to know what they're doing so they could teach somebody else. I have my entire studio in at least once a week to sing for each other. We talk a lot about technical things. We learn to verbalize. Not all have "vocal ears"—just because they sing well doesn't mean they always hear well. So, we try to train those a little bit.

Marvin Keenze

In my retirement from academia, the private studio is a different challenge. I have become especially interested in helping my singers retain a youthful and flexibly expressive sound. My priority is to help the students learn to know their instrument, and to respect it. I want them to become aware of its potential and its limitations. I train the voice as a musical instrument, one that responds to thinking and imagination. In our technique, we're trying to discover the uniqueness of each voice. Our goal is to make the voice responsive to the demands of the composer and the poet. We learn to reconcile the music with the word so that they complement each other.

I introduce the student to new repertoire, new styles. I help them to understand that each style puts different demands on the vocal instrument.

I want to develop the full, practical range of each voice. I guide my students to realize that the art of singing is a discipline but one that must be connected to the joy and spontaneity that made them want to sing in the first place. Whatever technique we work for should not destroy this spontaneous spark of creativity.

I have all kinds of students. I have some who are more interested in the spontaneity than in the precision. I take them from where they are. How much I emphasize technique depends on what they want from me. I sneak it in with some of them. In other words, the technique comes from making the music work. I stress the literature more than the discipline. Most of my students are really interested in the technique of singing and know I have the information about how the voice works physically and acoustically. They want specific information.

Cynthia Hoffmann

One of my goals is to make the student aware of what they are or are not doing to make their singing and music making effective, joyful, fluid, and so forth. Nellie Melba said it well: "One needs to be conscious of self, but not self-conscious."

Another goal is to help the students become independent by giving them the tools so they can teach themselves technically and artistically to plan their own work and feel they have a good sense of what they are doing.

I want to keep growing, both personally and in my work, and keep my enthusiasm for the student, the learning process, and the music.

Shirlee Emmons

Most of all, I want to be able to fix any technical thing that needs improving. I want to be able to hear the problem and know several ways to alleviate it. I want to understand vocal problems and their genesis, with solutions ready to solve them. To that end, I must continue to study, read, and ruminate about hidden connections between problems and their solutions. I want to be able to impart consistently good technical skills. I want to be able to show singers how to unearth meaning in their repertoire, to teach them how to see more and hear more in their music, to encourage them to do at least some of the work that is now allocated to coaches. (Singers are the only musicians who are automatically presumed to be incompetent at making musical decisions about their own repertoire.) Then I want to be able to inspire singers to learn the mental skills that will make them into consistent and elite performers.

Leslie Guinn

My first priority is to train the student to understand the principle behind all our work so they may become less dependent on me as soon as possible. My teaching goal is to help the student sing as freely as possible, which goes a long way to unlocking musical ideas. I've found that when vocal technique is inadequate, one knows on a subliminal level to avoid certain musical gestures. The idea never even surfaces. Musical imaginations are freer when voices are released from conflict.

Marcia Baldwin

My goal is to serve the needs of the student instead of my own ego. My main objective is steady (even if, at times, slow) improvement of all facets of singing. The central priority for me is probably the quality of the sound.

Bruce Lunkley

I try to get the most out of the students that I can for their sake. I want their instrument to be the best instrument it can be for them. I want it to be self-fulfilling for them. I want it to bring them an understanding of how special it is to have a talent like singing and that millions of people don't even understand what it's like to be able to do that. That translates itself very quickly in relationships. I bond very strongly with my students, perhaps more that I even should sometimes, but then there's a good exchange, a very honest exchange of feeling about singing. They know that if I'm saying how something sounds, it's not negative but direct; it's only that way because I know I can trust them to take it that way. It's important that it be said; it's always straightforward, and they know within a semester or two exactly what I think their potential is. I never tell them that they're going to be a professional singer. Never. I've had two students compete in the Metropolitan Opera competitions, and they begged me to tell them if I thought they were going to make a career, and I said, "I can't tell you that. I have you for four years, how do I know what you're going to do? I know you have fine voices, and I think you're going to sing well, but that's years from the Met." I do encourage them. When they do well, they know I'm enthusiastic, and when they do badly, they know I will tell them how to do it better next time. I'm not aware of doing that (being positive); you just have your own style, and you do it and you don't define its boundaries or direction; you just do your thing. The whole point of teaching is the student; it is not the teacher. This is not a glory trip; this is not an ego trip. I don't think every teacher can teach every student. I think a good teacher can teach most students and take great pride in what they do without becoming an egomaniac about it.

Barbara Doscher

Although it doesn't always happen, I want students to have enough technical independence to be able to protect themselves from dire things happening to their voices. To do that, a student has to know what he or she is doing to some extent, and why.

I have a thirty-three-year-old student who has been doing some concerts with Pavarotti. She called me two or three years ago and said, "I'm having some intonation difficulties around B4, C5, C#5." I asked, "Are these difficulties on front vowels or on back vowels?" There was a long, long pause. "Now why didn't I think of that!" she said. "They're on back vowels. I'm too open, aren't I?!"

If that wouldn't have worked, she at least had some idea of where to go with it. I think it happens better for those people who have that throat IQ. I didn't have that. That's why I'm a good teacher because I went through all the struggle.

The last goal is to encourage creative development, discovery, the use of imagination, and so forth.

Edward Baird

Establishing a good vocal technique is certainly one of the main goals. I tell my students I'm trying to work myself out of a job! In other words, I strive to teach them not only to sing well but also to know their own voice; to know how to approach and deal with their own problems so they can carry on by themselves. That is my primary goal.

Developing the ability to communicate is important—that would be visual and vocal, through tone color and intensities—all of those things. That is a second goal: to develop their ability to communicate.

Another goal is to inspire that extra dimension in a performer, that ability to have extra excitement or extra charisma. That would certainly be one of the goals too.

Richard Miller

Everyone has a right to sing. However, professional aims far exceed those of amateur goals. Student and teacher must objectively assess them. My chief priority is to provide a student with the tools with which he or she can fulfill the promise of the potential of that voice, whatever it might be. In the process, I want to stress the great satisfaction of accomplishment (at whatever level) that accrues from vocal discipline. My second priority is to build student independence, based on verifiable principles so the singer has a basis for meeting all career challenges that lie ahead.

Oren Brown

I like to establish in all my students a solid technical approach for the release of the voice. It has been said that an artist without a technique is muted. I feel this applies especially to voice. I work with exercises that will find the complete range of the voice and do things that will stimulate responses, build reflexes, and awaken kinesthetic responses. Eventually, you use all of these kinesthetic responses for your thoughts.

Joan Wall

My highest priority is to teach in such a way that students are enriched emotionally and spiritually. I hope to help students define and reach their goals as singers, to amplify their love of music, and to inspire them to seek an increasingly high level of artistry.

As a teacher in a university, I want our curriculum to adequately prepare our students for a future in music. It is important to me that, before our students leave the sheltered environment of our music school, they have a rich understanding of their voice and their artistry, and that they have the necessary skills to continue to grow as fine singers and teachers. If in the future they find their voice is not working as well as it did when they had the full support of the university faculty, I want them to know what to do. I want them to know the functioning of the voice and how to correct problems, to seek excellence in singing, and to understand the anatomy and physiology of the voice.

It is also important after they leave the university that they are able to prepare themselves musically, to create their own interpretations and characterizations, to work with stage directors and musical directors, and "to present to the audience a fully developed, congruent human experience, so that the audience can have an emotional experience that they might not have had if they had not come to this particular performance" (Caldwell, *The Performer Prepares*).

For students who are future voice teachers, public school teachers, or choral directors, it is my desire that they have a strong academic and artistic foundation to prepare them for teaching voice, music, and performance. I hope they have many efficient ways of communicating musical and vocal ideas and that they can guide their students into compelling singing performances.

Carol Webber

My goal is to get better. I think I am a better teacher now than I was five years ago; I think the same could have been said at that point. When I look back to the very first teaching I ever did, I always feel I should write those people a letter and say, "Ah . . . get yourself some new information!" Because my information has changed a lot. I also have to say that I am a singer;

my experience is as a performer and a fairly long experience as a teacher. I think teaching is about understanding how another person thinks. The means to my goal of getting better includes not just concentrating on singing, the subject of singing, and the subject of vocal physiology, languages, all the things we deal with; I feel it's more and more that if I can teach a person to focus and concentrate well, then I'm helping liberate him or her to learn anything. So I'm doing a lot of reading and looking for classes I can take in the new discoveries about how the brain works: neurotransmitters, neuropeptides, what we know now about how cells communicate, how the brain actually works, and the fact that how we feel can now be shown with objective scientific data to affect the quality of our thinking and the process of how we think. So, [I see] a larger view of issues about learning not just issues about singing.

Dale Moore

My first and almost only priority is that any student who works with me will sing better six months from now than he or she sings now.

Edith Davis Tidwell

Witnessing the progress and success of a student is thrilling and invigorating and brings joy and reward beyond measure. For each singer, I have always worked to enhance the voice and performance, and to instill confidence with honest and candid assessment. I often use prompts such as allow, release, pour, nourish, spin, motion, line, direction, and deal. You deal it! You engage, you commit, you put it out there, you invest it, you work through it, and you stay with it. It is a positive endeavor—focusing all the energy and concentration to see it through. You own it.

Meribeth Dayme

My first priority is that the students become strong as a person, that they do not give their power away to the music, the teacher, or the learning. I want them to become confident so they are standing on their own two feet and that the teaching manifests as a coresponsibility and not a guru-student relationship. Ideally, it is a win-win situation for both.

Robert Edwin

My personal approach to voice pedagogy is fact based and gender neutral. Modern voice science research has revealed how the human singing system actually works and, in so doing, has revolutionized the teaching of singing. No longer do pre-science phrases such as "sing from the diaphragm," "place the voice in the sinuses," or "fill your stomach with air" have any validity in today's voice pedagogy. Likewise, gender bias in teaching has been questioned because the male larynx and female larynx are functionally the same. Simply put, male voices and female voices can and should function in very similar fashion.

My personal teaching goals and objectives are very simple: I try to do everything in my power to help students become the best possible singers they can be. I train my students individually (no "one size fits all" training in this man's studio) so they have their own unique sound and emotional base. My priority? I want students leaving my studio to be measurably better singer-actors than when they first arrived. As long as I have the motivation and energy to do that, I will continue to teach.

Stephen King

I'm definitely a "bloom where you're planted" guy. Since I've never applied for a job (laughs), I just kinda roll with it if it's something I think I can do and be useful. "Bloom where you're planted; success is the journey"—the journey is going to have some ups and downs, but the success is going to be the taking the journey.

I try to get my students to believe that nothing is wasted, that it's all going to lead to something that is good if we put ourselves into it. That means you've got to learn how to fail well and trust that making mistakes is not the end of the world. [You must] not try to be a perfectionist, which generally just ends up being the enemy of anything good.

My personal goal is to try to help people get better, and it's not even so much about the singing; the singing is just the vehicle for it. Having that relationship where you're working with somebody—you could be a golf coach or a swimming teacher, or a voice teacher—it's helping somebody achieve what he or she has the talent to do. That's really my goal. I know that's what is motivating me right now, because I don't need to work any harder! It's really the relationships I have with these singers. I enjoy it. I get a kick out of it, like trout fishing, chasing those trout up and down the river, and chasing that little white ball around the golf course. I love those kinds of goals, and whatever that "sickness" is, I love helping a singer get from A to B and B to C. At some point, it's not even the voice stuff. It's really about the relationship. Our communication method is the voice and music. Anything you do, if you like it, it's about the fulfillment. I didn't set out to do this or plan to do any of this. It's not as if I had this career goal and it's always happened. For better or worse, one thing led to another; there are bumps along the way; there are difficulties, but none of it is wasted. It's all worked out well.

Jeannette LoVetri

My goals are to serve the student's needs both vocally and as an artist. I strive to correct vocal problems, to develop vocal strength and freedom, to help the vocalist sing in a free and authentic manner, and to serve the music she or he wants to sing honestly and personally. I strive to stay focused at all times in the lesson on the students and their voice. I strive to keep my explanations simple and clear. I strive to stay away from "voice teacher jargon" that means something only to me. I am not interested in impressing the students; I am interested in giving them my full attention throughout their lesson.

The priority is always vocal health, which is made much more possible by developing the instrument to be both strong and flexible, connected to the body, and to cultivate clear aural and physiologic understanding of what happens while sound is being produced. Sound for sound's sake is useless, so conscious awareness is always necessary. There is a lot of unconscious, mindless singing in this world. Ugh.

Mary Saunders-Barton

My primary goal in training young musical theater performers is to instill in them a respect for their budding artistry. We tell our students to "trust the process" as they train. This includes the care of the entire instrument, mind, voice, and body as inseparable parts of a whole. They would treat a Stradivarius with respect. No Stradivarius is as precious as they are.

Chapter Twenty-Four

Outstanding Teacher Attributes

What attributes do you feel typify the "outstanding" or "exemplary" voice teacher?

The exemplary voice teacher

- has "good ears," that is, is sensitive to tonal sound and consistency;
- has good eyes to see problems;
- has a sense of vision about the voice when it is a "diamond in the rough";
- has the ability to analyze sound per

    a. a sense of tone,
    b. diagnose faults, and
    c. communicate techniques for successful improvements;

- is able to articulate clear goals in clear, direct language;
- inspires the students and propels them forward;
- has a depth of knowledge about the voice, the vocal mechanism, and how it works;
- is passionate about music and has high standards regarding music;
- is an excellent musician;
- knows languages;
- has good piano skills;
- is honest and truthful but sensitive;
- is flexible and open-minded;
- teaches creatively;
- is able to adjust to the student's needs and personality (teaches to the person);
- has a strong desire to help the student;
- is curious, keeps learning, keeps listening, and continues to grow;
- has a positive, supportive teaching approach;
- is patient, kind, and generous;
- is empathic;
- is honest;
- has a good sense of humor;
- has "vocal empathy";
- tries hard and perseveres;

- challenges while encouraging the student;
- uses variety in teaching, is not harnessed to a "method," and does not teach by rote;
- has a fascination with the human voice, with singing, with the history of voice, and with voice teaching;
- stays current and informed in the field;
- enjoys associating with colleagues and shares knowledge;
- has integrity, is ethical;
- allows the students to have their own personality and to blossom;
- is a role model;
- understands the real function of the vocal mechanism and can marry voice technique with emotionally connected expression;
- gives a singer the ability to find personal meaning in music and text;
- helps students to achieve self-discipline, self-control, deserved self-confidence, and self-realization;
- knows his or her own voice;
- loves people;
- loves the profession of teaching;
- prepares the student for the next phase; and
- knows when to let go.

TEACHERS' REMARKS

Barbara Doscher

1. By far, at the head of the list, is to know your field. Know how the instrument functions. There are many different methods and ways of using this knowledge, but if you don't know that, you can be the nicest person in the world, and it won't make any difference.
2. Love people and the profession of teaching. I think it's terrible when someone who is an introvert, and would rather not be doing this, is trying to teach (although I would rather meet someone like that who knows the field than a very nice person who has caught a whole bunch of people in his or her web and doesn't know a damn thing about what he or she is doing).
3. I think the outstanding pedagogue continues to grow, to improve, and to learn new things. Never close your mind!
4. In our field, you need to love music with all your heart. There's no halfway attitude.
5. You have to have a lot of patience, and I think you must have a supportive approach to the learning theory. Too many people are using phrases like "get out of the kitchen if you can't stand the heat." I don't believe in that, either at the training level or at the professional level. I don't think that's the way human beings behave, and I think encouragement and support is the best thing you can do. I don't mean you let them get away with anything, but I think you have to understand that people move at different paces.
6. The ability to let each instrument reveal itself. Don't impose your own aesthetic tastes on an instrument that is entirely different from what you like. I've been accused of saying that every instrument is a beautiful instrument. Well, if it's operating right, it will be.

Marcia Baldwin

Love, support, technical information, and aid in career direction—for me, those are the attributes of an exemplary vocal pedagogue.

Helen Hodam

First, they absolutely must have to have a good set of ears. They must be able to fine-tune. That never stops until you get the kind of tone you want. It may be present only on one or two tones, but it is there. Some teachers can begin with a singer and then not know what else to do. They cannot guide the tone to improve or hear and realize the full potential of the voice. They can't hear beyond the present sound.

No teacher is really very good unless he or she can articulate. It's critically important to be able to explain things in a clear fashion without overexplaining.

Excellent teachers have to be good musicians, and they must know their languages, and so forth.

A good teacher must persist. Maybe that is all that voice can produce, but you never know. If you hear just one tone, you think, "Now, that's the fundamental tone of this voice," and you keep after that. As my teacher said, "You persist and you insist." I would say that's what makes a good teacher. Many teachers sing well, but they can't analyze another person's voice, nor do they know how to tell the student what to do.

Edward Baird

Number one is the ability to diagnose a voice and diagnose its vocal faults. If a teacher is unable to identify and diagnose what is wrong, he or she can't possibly figure out what to do with it; you're shooting in the dark. (I guess at some time or another we're all doing that!)

One must communicate successful techniques to improve those faults you've diagnosed. Communication is extremely important. I've had a lot of students say to me, "You make it so clear!" Many times I observe other people, and they talk around in circles. If they would just use such and such a word or such and such a phrase, they could cut to the heart of things a lot quicker. I think communication is extremely, extremely important.

A good teacher has to have a very sensitive ear in order to fine-tune a student's voice. Once you've diagnosed and communicated to them what you want them to do, you have to listen very carefully and fine-tune the whole voice. I think that is what characterizes a good teacher.

The ability to be flexible and to adjust your approach to different personalities and problems is important. Some teachers put everybody through the same mold, but I think you have to be a different teacher with each student. You might be after the same kinds of things, but you might have to calm down hyper students while others you might have to crank up. It's also important to be encouraging but with realistic goals. A lot of people lead students to think they're better than they really are. They head for disappointments down the road.

Richard Miller

The main criterion for successful teaching is the ability to produce recognizable results in those being instructed. This does not mean the inducement of immediate, dramatic changes (although they sometimes occur) but in establishing durable principles that will last a performance lifetime. Teacher perseverance is a high priority. It is not enough to explain a concept to a student but to stick with it until it has become routine. Nondestructive teaching is the only real instruction. Negativism is out. Teaching voice is teamwork between the teacher and the student, and should be equally rewarding to both because voice is the ultimate musical instrument, uniting body and spirit into the art of communication.

Bruce Lunkley

An outstanding voice teacher has knowledge of the voice, the mechanism and how it works, willingness to use any approach that seems applicable to the individual students to make them sing with greater ease and more fully find their whole voice. Sometimes I've taught very mechanically, sometimes I've taught very imaginatively, and sometimes very pointedly and scientifically. It really depends on the student.

I think an outstanding pedagogue is one who is not harnessed to a precise method or a precise set of vocalizes and can vary that when the situation obviously calls for something different. I think great teaching is informed teaching, I think it's creative teaching, and I think it's person-oriented teaching.

Excellent voice teachers see singing in the perspective of something that humans do that's special but not life consuming for everyone. I've also had colleagues who would say that every student was going to be the next Beverly Sills. I just hope my students will go on and sing happily in choirs and churches, and so forth, for the rest of their lives and enjoy it. If they have a career and make some money, that's great. It becomes something that's part of their life that is, for them, very special.

Laura Brooks Rice

It is someone who has an excellent ear and eye, someone who has a clear understanding of his or her own voice and can effectively relate the sensations of singing to a student. The person hears students as they are, as they might be, and as they should be.

An exemplary voice teacher can clearly diagnose and solve vocal problems—the second part is obviously the most difficult.

They should be someone who can adjust himself or herself to the talent, intelligence, and temperament of each student. That's difficult.

It is one who teaches voice training as an ongoing process. Learning to sing involves patience, practice, and, eventually, independence.

It's very important that the teacher of voice also sings. That's the approach I take. I'm a performer/teacher. On whatever level, they must sing if they teach voice.

Voice specialists should have a complete understanding of the physical anatomy of singing and be able to present that knowledge clearly to each singer. Every singer has the same physical anatomy (larynx, lungs, soft palate, ribs, sternoclytomastoid muscles, etc.), but each body and each throat are unique. Having the understanding of the basic anatomy but being able to help each singer make a success of that knowledge in his or her body is essential. It is not "one size fits all."

Carol Webber

An exemplary vocal pedagogue needs to accept each individual completely, applying his or her own knowledge and experience to each person as can be best received by each person. A responsible and excellent pedagogue will constantly increase his or her own base of knowledge and experience, and not "drift." At the same time, knowledge by itself is not very helpful if the means of communication is not completely developed, and regardless of personality type, the famous or not famous teachers need to constantly hone their ability to deal one-on-one with the most exposed part of another human being: the desire to be truthful and honest in expression. While there are years and years of lessons' worth of information to deal with, singing is a sport, and it's a sport in which you're trying to tap into the involuntary muscle system through the best use of the voluntary muscle systems. This means mind-body-spirit. So, I like to see a teacher who isn't careless in any of these ways, who might be more specially gifted in one area than another, but who makes a genuine effort to cover all the bases.

Leslie Guinn

I believe an exemplary vocal pedagogue must have honesty, compassion, humor, integrity, and a prodigious quantity of vocal empathy. Though I am sure there are successful vocal pedagogues who are not paradigms of integrity, it is a given that they should have expertise in their field, and always a plus if they possess nonthreatening communication skills.

Cynthia Hoffmann

An exemplary voice teacher has

- an ear for both sound and consistency in sound;
- musicianship, musicality, and an ear for language;
- knowledge of the instrument—technical and in regard to repertoire;
- clarity—an ability to convey what the student needs to do and how to do it; and
- a positive approach—the studio needs to be a safe and fair place. There are too many places in our business where it is not safe, and the voice studio should not be another one of these places. The teacher should be honest and forthright—not overly protective of the student, but the overall atmosphere needs to be positive.

I believe good teachers should support their students, tell the truth, and set the standard to be achieved. One of my young students said, "Ms. Hoffmann, if you don't tell me, who is going to? No one ever tells you anything." This may not always be true, but if the studio is a safe place, they can build confidence in their work there and take that into the professional world.

Marvin Keenze

An exemplary pedagogue should have a fascination with the human voice and, of course, with music itself. We must have knowledge of voice structure and function and how it all works together for communicative and healthful singing. One of our greatest talents is to be able to hear a sound and to know why it is what it is. We need to have a definition of good tone qualities and to know when certain sounds are appropriate and when not.

A singing teacher must like people and enjoy relating to singers at various levels of accomplishment and personal growth. We must possess a confidence about what we know and be able to express it clearly. We need a teaching language based on fact and yet rich in imagery and expressiveness. We need patience and a certain order in our lives that allow us to give undivided attention to our student during a lesson or class. We need to know literature, repertoire, poetry, and history, and to always be a student ourselves. We need to explain to our students just how we work the best and what they need to do to get this from us.

William McIver

A voice teacher should appreciate the past; a voice teacher should know the history of singing and the writings of those teachers who turned out the best singers in the eighteenth, nineteenth, and twentieth centuries. A voice teacher should stay current with things that are being done now to advance vocal knowledge. A voice teacher should participate in and support professional singing organizations.

Vocal research by itself does not necessarily translate to better singers in the studio, but I do think it's very important for vocal pedagogues to converse with voice researchers. That way they keep one another on track. Subjective opinions in the studio can be either validated or rejected by good vocal research. The vocal researcher comes up with information that either can or cannot be verified through experience in the studio. Although some people are overenamored of what vocal research can do for the singer, I think it's an exciting, important time. On the other hand, some people keep their heads in the sand and say, "We don't need research because people have sung without the wealth of information now available so there is no reason for it." I think that's equally wrong. If you look at the history of singing, most of the great teachers were also among the most knowledgeable of their time regarding the physiology and acoustics of the voice. The best teachers were those who took the time to learn their craft, not the ones who relied on some personal, intuitive system.

Some people understand the singing voice but lack the skills, patience, and perseverance to help someone else sing well. That's the teacher's job; in some way, you have to get them to do it. That can be through verbal or nonverbal instruction demonstration. It serves no purpose to just lay out before a student everything he or she is doing wrong. The teacher's job is to bring the student to where the right things happen. Then it's how skillfully the students use the information that determines whether or not they become a good singer.

The teacher needs to have vast knowledge about the physiology and acoustics of singing, repertoire, and languages. People who are starting out (to become voice teachers) should develop piano skills. It's possible to be a wonderful teacher without that, but it's definitely an asset to have them.

Perhaps the most important asset is hearing acuity: an ear that can hear gradations in timbre, vowels, vibrancy, and pitch. The very good voice teachers have an acute sense of hearing that guides them in what they do to bring the student's voice into line.

Teachers should be role models for students. Teachers should create an environment where students want to learn. At a certain point, you might have to discipline students in order to hold high standards in front of them. Your role is not always to compliment. But if you are consistent and impartial in relating to students, they will respond positively to criticism.

If you look at the profession of voice teaching, you see a huge disparity—from authoritarian to the mother (or father) figure who becomes highly involved in the personal life of the student. Each teacher has to find a way of relating that's in tune with his or her own inner self-nature. Love and respect for one's students and honesty in relating to them will provide a positive environment in which learning can take place.

Oren Brown

One thing is a very strong sense of empathy with the individual qualities of each student. It's very important that teachers have a strong sense of the musical values in the selection being studied and that they open the way for the students to grow into their own identity with the words and music.

In our day and age, it's important for a teacher to have a solid knowledge of the anatomy and physiology of the voice. One must understand the physical laws that apply to sound making as a foundation for what to expect from the voice. It also helps to have some idea of how the nerves function and how we hear with our ears. Having some idea of how the ear responds can be valuable.

It is most important to be aware of the psychological implications, both as they apply to the student's individuality and how they feature in the music. You must get the whole psyche involved in the interplay.

Shirlee Emmons

Exemplary vocal pedagogues do not limit their teaching to what they did as a singer but understand the real function of the vocal mechanism and have the ability to impart this to their singers in a specific fashion. Exemplary vocal pedagogues can give singers a system by which they can find personal meaning in music and text, not just rely on a spoon-fed, predigested "correct" interpretation, but unleash their own imagination. Exemplary vocal pedagogues teach their singers to expand their creative thinking and their personal response to the music and text. Exemplary vocal pedagogues help their singers to achieve self-discipline, self-control, self-confidence that is earned, and finally self-realization.

Jack Coldiron

An exemplary vocal pedagogue should be a critical listener (i.e., someone who has a good ear). If you can't hear the problem, then you can't do anything about it. No matter how much you know, you have to know what the problem is.

Technical knowledge: you have to know something about the vocal instrument. Then, if you know something about it, you have to be able to communicate your ideas. Listening, knowledge, and the ability to communicate are absolutely fundamental.

Other attributes include enthusiasm for your job and knowledge of literature.

A very important asset is a strong desire to help the student. So many teachers just go through the motions and don't really care about the student. The teacher is dealing with a person's most personal life. As a teacher, you just can't afford to stand off, be uninvolved, and not care. Don't treat the students like some sort of chattels; they are individuals; they are worth something. In summary, the outstanding voice teacher

1. is a critical listener;
2. has technical knowledge;
3. has an ability to communicate;
4. has enthusiasm for the job;
5. has a strong desire to help the student; and
6. emphasizes the worth of the student.

Helen Swank

The outstanding or exemplary vocal pedagogue has the following attributes:

1. cares about the student as a whole person;
2. will not harm the singing voice;
3. understands the physiology of the vocal mechanism;
4. is a great communicator;
5. understands teaching techniques and approaches that all lead to student understanding;
6. is an expert diagnostician;
7. can help the students develop themselves;
8. is a consummate musician himself or herself;
9. knows what makes a voice outstanding;

10. can identify where a voice is headed as to quality, style, and impact; and

11. is free to share experiences, techniques, and wisdom.

Dale Moore

Patience, patience, and then patience. We all aim to know as much as is humanly possible about the workings of the human voice: about the repertoire, the singers' languages, and the rudiments of acting and stage craft in order to help them be prepared.

Certainly one of the most important things is the ability to diagnose vocal problems and have a solution for them.

One must have tremendous drive to challenge the students while you encourage them.

I have found that for myself only a positive approach works unless students are just so cocky that they need to be knocked down a bit before you can teach them anything. I have always found that encouragement helps more than verbal abuse of any kind. If a student is going to be able to sing at all, it must be a joyful thing.

Lindsey Christiansen

In my experience, outstanding teachers were people of great integrity who had a sense of vision of what a voice could be and how that person could be his or her best self.

The outstanding pedagogue understands, first and foremost, that the voice is the servant of the music. He or she also understands the physiology of the voice, the anatomy of the voice, and the physics of the voice, and has a terrific ear. Without that terrific ear, you might as well do something else; you just have to have that. Terrific ears and good eyes, so you can see what's going on. It's essential to have the verbal skill to be able to translate what one hears and see into instructions that will allow the student to make positive changes in his or her singing. Many teachers can identify vocal faults. Those with effective remedies are rarer.

The most outstanding pedagogues I have known have been wonderful musicians who have loved music; they have passion for music and have never lost their passion and excitement for poetry and drama, for going to theater, and for going to hear music.

The best pedagogues get excited about other singers. I think the best pedagogues do not talk disparagingly about other students or about their colleagues. I find that so unpleasant, and it really does mar what could be fabulous pedagogues.

It's very important to build a systematic technique. If the teachers don't have understanding of what a fine technique is and the ability to build it, then no matter how wonderful they are as people, how great as coaches, or how good their ears, they can't be what I would call great pedagogues.

I also think a great pedagogue keeps learning, keeps listening to singers, and keeps listening to the way people talk about singing and voice.

Joan Wall

An exemplary pedagogue is a knowledgeable vocal technician, musician, performance coach, and linguist. However, I do not believe that an exemplary pedagogue can be defined by academic knowledge alone.

A truly outstanding pedagogue is a respectful, positive, nurturing teacher who can guide and hone students' self-discovery, who can challenge them to reach deep into their emotions and souls to express music, and who can tap into a wide variety of pedagogical methods. An outstanding pedagogue elicits the emotions and creativity of the singers, lifts them to ever higher artistic performances, and enriches the spirit.

Edith Davis Tidwell

The sound of the human voice in music making ignites the passion of soul and spirit. The voice is the most personal of all instruments, and finding success as a teacher of singing goes far beyond the technical aspects of vocal production.

Teaching voice . . . teaching singing . . . is the training of the entire body—the physical, the psychological, the emotional, and the cerebral. It is a delicate balance. The teacher of singing must critique without destroying confidence, encourage without projecting unrealistic goals, nurture without becoming possessive, and instill a competitive spirit while maintaining objectivity.

It is the responsibility of a teacher of singing to enhance this instrument by providing guidance to develop and instill knowledge of the vocal process, repertoire and style, discipline in study and practice, commitment to the text, and respect for the integrity of the music and joy in performance.

Meribeth Dayme

I like to see a voice teacher grounded, aware, open-minded, curious, and dedicated to serving humanity through work with the voice. Teachers need various musical skills as well as understanding of human behavior and the arts. Very important for me is the pursuit of new ideas and the ability to understand how they fit with teaching and performing.

Robert Edwin

Robert Caldwell in his book *The Performer Prepares* describes what should be the end result of good pedagogy: "Performance work—the time spent to craft a rich inner experience to take into the performance—is essential because a correct interpretation played (or sung) with correct technique is simply not enough to build a powerful performance . . . the performer must build compelling inner experiences beforehand and take them into performance."

An outstanding or exemplary pedagogue is one who can help the student marry voice technique with emotionally connected expression. I see too many vocal robots who have been taught technique in a vacuum—mechanical exercises done with no human context, no reason to "be." I also see and hear incredibly expressive singers who are vocal train wrecks for lack of voice technique. Teaching one without the other—technique without an emotive base, or emotion without systematic structure—is simply bad pedagogy and should be avoided at all costs.

Stephen King

One who tries hard. Are you willing to expand? Not just keep doing the same thing, but are you willing to take all your information, listen to things differently, and be malleable, or do you have this way of doing things and everybody has to fit into that way? If you do that, for me, there are going to be some pretty big flaws. I try to find it the other way, where you take the facts of singing and then you try to help everybody understand that—let it be their idea, make it their perspective. As they understand it, if they're getting better, they begin to crave that more. In other words, find a way to help them get better, whatever that is within your area of expertise. If there are external issues, you may have to send them to someone else. If somebody has personal issues, I refer them to someone who can talk about that, because I don't think that's any of my business.

Trying hard and blooming where you're planted is paramount to being good at anything. It's not so much talent as it is effort. Sure those people who are singing (at the highest level) have to be extraordinarily talented beyond everybody else, but there still has to be extraordinary effort. But what do we [teachers] do? Anybody can learn the facts of singing, and most people can cultivate their ears if they make the effort. Then, once you cultivate your ears, you have to know how to prescribe something that's actually going to help somebody, based on what you hear. You must get past the superficial "Oh, they're out of tune!" Why [are they out of tune]? And how do you fix it? Those people are the ones who are going to be the best, because they will work relentlessly to find a way to help somebody.

Mary Saunders-Barton

The voice teachers I most admire are always learning as they go. They share their knowledge eagerly with students and colleagues but are open to new information. They celebrate a community of shared experiences and a free exchange of ideas.

The voice teachers I most admire exemplify kindness, generosity, and empathy in all their interactions with students and colleagues.

CODA

It's very difficult to talk in clear, objective, and descriptive terms about voice and singing; it's even harder to discuss how to teach this most personal, often intangible art. In presenting the collective statements of these teachers, I have attempted to retain each one's personal "voice" and characteristic stamp. Even given the orderly framework of the categories by which the book was organized, differences in teaching manner and areas of emphasis clearly shine through. Such is the nature of teaching voice and voice performance: there is room for a variety of approach, teaching style, and emphasis. In the hands of a quality teacher, all can be validated when the student benefits. Every student has the potential to learn, grow, and develop to his or her fullest capacity; in the hands of a gifted teacher, the gifted student can evolve to levels of distinction and artistry.

Clearly, teaching voice performance is far more than an occupation—it's a profession, requiring exceptional skills, creative imagination (one could even say intuition), and unwavering high standards. No longer can it be perceived as something that retired or "failed" professional singers succumb to when they can no longer perform. None of the teachers quoted here perceive teaching as anything less than a calling—a legitimate and demanding discipline. Teaching voice and vocal performance is a science that deserves (and is finally recognized for) its own arena of importance and excellence. Helen Swank expressed this well in her comment: "This is the period when, for the first time, voice teaching has become a professional entity in itself, and not a lot of performers start teaching because they quit performing. There is now a different direction."

Not every great singer is necessarily a great voice teacher; such experience provides no guarantee for knowing (or caring) how to teach. At the same time, it is fair to say that a voice teacher ought to have personal experience in performance themselves. Without that firsthand knowledge and empathy, a teacher cannot truly identify and convey relevant information and insights to the student. Some of the teachers in this project had retired from active singing, but they had been singers. Such a performance background is essential to teaching excellence. Recall Laura Brooks Rice's words: "It's very important that the teacher of voice also sings. . . . On whatever level, they must sing if they teach voice. . . . [An outstanding voice teacher] is someone who has a clear understanding of his or her own voice and can effectively relate the sensations of singing to a student. The person hears students as they are, as they might be, and as they should be."

The introduction to this book began with a quote from one of the first great voice teachers on record, Pier Francesco Tosi. It seems fitting to give him the final word on this subject.

It may seem to many that every Singer must also be a perfect instructor, but it is not so; for his qualifications are insufficient if he cannot communicate his Sentiments with Ease, and in a Method adapted to the Ability of the Scholar and in a manner of instructing which may seem rather an Entertainment than a Lesson, with the happy talent to show the ability of the Singer to advantage; to conceal its imperfections, which are the most principal and most necessary instructions.

Recommended References

Alderson, R. 1979. *Complete Book of Voice Training*. West Nyack, NY: Parker.

Alexander, F. M. 1974. *The Alexander Technique: The Essential Writings of Mattias Alexander*. London: Thames and Hudson.

Ames, K. 1990. "Here Come the Divine New Divas." *Newsweek*, April, 82–83.

Appelman, R. 1975. *Science of Vocal Pedagogy*. Bloomington: University of Indiana Press.

Balk, H. W. 1977. *The Complete Singing Actor*. Minneapolis: University of Minnesota Press.

———. 1985. *Performing Power*. Minneapolis: University of Minnesota Press.

Bartholomew, W. 1983. "Terminology in Voice Teaching." *Journal of Research in Singing and Applied Vocal Pedagogy* 6 (2): 1–6.

Battaglia, C. 1987. "A Joyful Noise: The Gospel of Singing Well according to Five New York Voice Teachers." *Opera News*, January, 10–15.

Benson, H. 1975. *The Relaxation Response*. New York: William Morrow.

Berliner, D. C. 1986. "In Pursuit of the Expert Pedagogue." *Educational Researcher* 15 (7): 5–13.

Blades-Zeller, E. 1994. "Vocal Pedagogy in the United States: Interviews with Exemplary Teachers of Applied Voice." *Journal of Research in Singing and Applied Vocal Pedagogy* 17 (2): 1–87.

Bozeman, K. 2013. *Practical Vocal Acoustics: Pedagogic Application for Teachers and Singers*. Hillsdale, NY: Pendragon.

Brodnitz, F. S. 1959. *Vocal Rehabilitation*. Rochester, MN: Whiting.

———. 1983. *Keep Your Voice Healthy*. New York: Harper & Row.

Brown, O. L. 1996. *Discover Your Voice*. San Diego: Singular.

Bunch, M. (1982, 1993) 1995. *Dynamics of the Singing Voice*. New York: Springer-Verlag.

———. 1999. *Creating Confidence: How to Develop Your Personal Power and Presence*. London: Kogan Page.

Burgin, J. 1973. *Teaching Singing*. Metuchen, NJ: Scarecrow.

———. 1978. "Contributions to Vocal Pedagogy." *NATS Bulletin* 43 (3): 13–22, 247.

Caldwell, R. 1990. *The Performer Prepares*. Dallas: PST (video also).

Caldwell, R., and J. Wall. 2001. *Excellence in Singing*. Seattle: PST.

Caruso, E., and L. Tetrazzini. 1909. *The Art of Singing*. New York: Metropolitan.

Christy, V. A. 1974. *Expressive Singing*. Vols. 1 and 2. Dubuque, IA: Wm. C. Brown.

Christy, V. A., and J. G. Paton. 1997. *Foundations in Singing: A Basic Textbook in Vocal Technique and Song Interpretation*. 6th ed. Dubuque, IA: Brown and Benchmark.

Clippinger, D. A. 1929. *Fundamentals of Voice Training*. New York: Oliver Ditson.

Coffin, B. 1980. *Overtones of Bel Canto*. Metuchen, NJ: Scarecrow.

———. 1987. *Sounds of Singing*. Metuchen, NJ: Scarecrow.

———. 1989. *Historical Vocal Pedagogy Classics*. Metuchen, NJ: Scarecrow.

Collins, M. E. 1983. "Goal Identification and Systematic Instruction in Private Voice Lessons. *Journal of Research in Singing* 7 (1), 56–66.

Coyle, D. 2009. *The Talent Code: Greatness Isn't Born. It's Grown. Here's How*. New York: Bantam Dell/Random House.

Curtin, P. 1991. "The American Singer." *Opera News*, July, 29.

Dayme, M. 2005. *The Performer's Voice: Realizing Your Vocal Potential*. New York: Norton.

Dayme, M, and C. Vaughn. 2014. *The Singing Book*. New York: Norton.

DeYoung, R. 1958. *The Singer's Art*. Chicago: DePaul.

Directory of Music Faculties in Colleges and Universities, U.S. and Canada. 1988–1990. Boulder, CO: College Music Society.

Doscher, B. (1988) 1994. *The Functional Unity of the Singing Voice*. Metuchen, NJ: Scarecrow.

Emmons, S., and S. Sonntag. 1979. *The Art of the Song Recital*. New York: Schirmer.

Emmons, S., and A. Thomas. 1998. *Powerful Performances for Singers*. New York: Oxford University Press.

Estill, J. 1995. *Voice Craft: A User's Guide to Voice Quality*. Estell Voice Training Systems.

Feldenkrais, M. 1972. *Awareness through Movement*. New York: Harper & Row.

———. 1977. *The Case of Nora: Body Awareness as Healing Therapy*. New York: Harper & Row.

———. 1984. *The Master Moves*. Cupertino, CA: Meta.

Fetterman, D. M. 1989. *Ethnography Step by Step*. Newbury Park, CA: Sage.

Field-Hyde, F. C. 1950. *The Art and Science of Voice Training*. London: Oxford University Press.

Fields, V. A. 1947. *Training the Singing Voice*. New York: King's Crown Press.

———. 1984. *Foundations of the Singer's Art*. 2nd ed. New York: National Association of Teachers of Singing.

Fowler, C., ed. 1988. *The Crane Symposium: Toward an Understanding of the Teaching and Learning of Music Performance*. Potsdam, NY: Potsdam College of the State University of New York.

Fuchs, V. 1967. *The Art of Singing and Voice Technique*. London: Calder and Boyars.

Garcia, M. 1894. *Hints on Singing*. Translated by Beata Garcia. London: Ascheerberg, Hopwood & Crew.

Gollobin, L. B., and H. White. 1977. "Voice Teachers on Voice, Part 1." *Music Educators Journal* 64 (4): 40–51.

———. 1978a. "Voice Teachers on Voice, Part 2." *Music Educators Journal* 64 (6): 46–59.

———. 1978b. "Voice Teachers on Voice, Part 3." *Music Educators Journal* 64 (8): 40–47.

Gorman, D. 1983. *The Body Moveable*. Guelph, ON: Ampersand Printing.

Green, B., with W. T. Gallwey. 1986. *The Inner Game of Music*. Garden City, NY: Anchor/Doubleday.

Henderson, L. B. *How to Train Singers*. 2nd ed. West Nyack, NY: Parker.

Herbert-Caesari, E. (1951) 1963. *The Voice of the Mind*. 2nd ed. New York: Crescendo.

———. 1969. *Vocal Truth*. London: Robert Hale Limited.

Hines, J. 1974. *Great Singers on Great Singing*. New York: Simon & Schuster.

Jones, F. 1979. *The Alexander Technique: Body Awareness in Action*. New York: Schocken.

Jones, W. E. 1989. *Sound, Self, and Song: Essays on the Teaching of Singing*. Metuchen, NJ: Scarecrow.

Kagen, S. 1950. *On Studying Singing*. London: Rinehart & Company.

Koster, R. 1984. "Some Thoughts on the Teaching of Singing." *Journal of Research in Singing* 8 (1): 39–44.

Kreuger, P. J. 1987. "Ethnographic Research Methodology in Music Education." *Journal of Research in Music Education* 35 (2): 69–77.

Lamott, A. 1994. *Bird by Bird: Some Instructions on Writing and Life*. New York: Pantheon.

Lamperti, F. n.d. *The Art of Singing*. Translated by J. C. Griffeth. New York: Schirmer.

Large, J., ed. 1973. *Vocal Registers in Singing*. The Hague, Netherlands: Mouton.

———. 1980. *Contributions of Voice Research to Singing*. Houston: College-Hill.

———. 1986. "How to Teach the Male High Voice, Part One: The Tenor." *Journal of Research in Singing* 9 (2): 3–20.

———. 1987. "How to Teach the Male High Voice, Part Two: The Baritone and Bass." *Journal of Research in Singing* 10 (2): 17–29.

Large, J., and Murray, T. 1978. "Studies of the Marchesi Model for Female Registration." *Journal of Research in Singing* 1 (1): 14.

Lehman, L. 1902. *How to Sing*. London: MacMillan.

Leyerle, W. 1985. *Vocal Development through Organic Imagery*. New York: Leyerle.

Lindsey, C. E. 1985. *Fundamentals of Singing for Voice Class*. Belmont, CA: Wadsworth.

Linklater, K. 1976. *Freeing the Natural Voice*. New York: Drama Books Specialists.

Malde, M., M. Allen, and K. Zeller. (2009) 2012. *What Every Singer Needs to Know About the Body*. San Diego: Plural.

Marchesi, M. 1970. *Bel Canto: A Theoretical and Practical Vocal Method*. Edited by P. L. Miller. New York: Dover.

McClosky, D. B. 1972. *Your Voice at Its Best*. Plymouth, MA: Memorial.

McCoy, S. (2012) 2004. *Your Voice: An Inside View*. Delaware, OH: Inside View.

McKinny, J. 1994. *The Diagnosis and Correction of Vocal Faults*. Rev. ed. Nashville: Genevox Music Group.

Miller, K. E. (1983) 1990. *Principles of Singing*. 2nd ed. Englewood Cliffs, NJ: Prentice Hall.

Miller, R. 1977. *Techniques of Singing: Italian, French, English and German Schools*. Metuchen, NJ: Scarecrow.

———. 1983. *The Structure of Singing: System and Art in Vocal Technique*. New York: Schirmer.

———. 1993. *Training Tenor Voices*. New York: Schirmer.

———. 2004. *Solutions for Singers: Tools for Performers and Teacher*. New York: Oxford University Press.

———. 2008. *Securing Baritone, Bass-Baritone, and Bass Voices*. New York: Oxford University Press.

Nair, G. 1999. *Voice: Tradition and Technology*. San Diego: Singular.

Nelson, S., and E. Blades-Zeller. 2001. *Singing with Your Whole Self: The Feldenkrais Method and Voice*. Lanham, MD: Scarecrow.

Patton, M. Q. 1987. *How to Use Qualitative Methods in Evaluation*. Newbury Park, CA: Sage.

Phillips, K. H. 1984. "Child Voice Research." *Journal of Research in Singing* 8 (1): 11–26.

———. 1992. *Teaching Kids to Sing*. New York: Schirmer.

Phillips, K. H., and W. P. Vispoel. 1990. "The Effects of Class Voice and Breath Management Instruction on Vocal Knowledge, Attitudes, and Vocal Performance among Elementary Education Majors." *Quarterly* 1 (1): 96–105.

Pleasants, H. 1966. *The Great Singers: From the Dawn of Opera to Our Own Time*. New York: Simon & Schuster.

Reid, C. 1950. *Bel Canto: Principles and Practices*. New York: Coleman-Ross.

———. 1965. *The Free Voice*. 3rd ed. New York: Coleman-Ross.

———. 1975. *Psyche and Soma*. New York: Patelson Music House.

Reinders, A. 1988. "Teaching the High Female Voice." *Journal of Research in Singing* 12 (1): 43–46.

Ristad, E. 1982. *A Soprano on Her Head*. Moab, UT: Real People Press.

Rosenberg, M., and W. LeBorgne, W. 2014. *The Vocal Athlete: Application and Technique for the Hybrid Singer*. San Diego: Plural.

Rosewall, R. B. (1961) 1984. *Handbook of Singing*. Evanston, IL: Dickenson.

Ross, W. E. 1959. *Secrets of Singing*. Bloomington: University of Indiana Press.

Rushmore, R. 1971. *The Singing Voice*. New York: Dodd, Mead.

Sable, B. K. 1982. *The Vocal Sound*. Englewood Cliffs, NJ: Prentice Hall.

Sataloff, R. T. 1997. *Professional Voice: The Science and Art of Clinical Care*. 2nd ed. San Diego: Singular.

———. 1998. *Vocal Health and Pedagogy*. San Diego: Singular.

Schiotz, A. 1970. *The Singer and His Art*. New York: Harper & Row.

Schmidt, J. 1998. *Basics of Singing*. 4th ed. New York: Simon & Schuster/Macmillan.

Shafarman, S. 1997. *Awareness Heals: The Feldenkrais Method for Dynamic Health*. New York: Addison-Wesley.

Smith, W. S. 2007. *The Naked Voice: A Wholistic Approach to Singing*. New York: Oxford University Press.

Speads, C. 1977. *Breathing: The ABC's*. New York: Harper & Row.

Sterner, T. (2005) 2012. *The Practicing Mind: Developing Focus and Discipline in Your Life; Master Any Skill or Challenge by Learning to Love the Process*. Novato, CA: New World Library.

Sundberg, J. 1987. *The Science of the Singing Voice*. DeKalb: Northern Illinois University Press.

Titze, I. R. 1994. *Principles of Voice Production*. Englewood Cliffs, NJ: Prentice Hall.

Todd, M. E. 1988. *The Thinking Body*. Pennington, NJ: Dance Horizons.

Tosi, P. F. 1743. *Observations on the Florid Song*. Translated by J. E. Gaillard. London: J. Wilcox. Reprint, London: William Reeves Bookseller, 1926.

Trusler, I., and W. Ehret. 1972. *Functional Lessons in Singing*. 2nd ed. Englewood Cliffs, NJ: Prentice Hall.

Vennard, W. D. 1967. *Singing: The Mechanism and the Technique*. New York: Carl Fischer.

———. 1973. *Developing Voices*. New York: Carl Fischer.

Wall, J., and R. Caldwell. 1992–2005. *The Singer's Voice*. Video series. Seattle: PST.

———. 2000. *Excellence in Singing Series*. Redmond, WA: Caldwell.

Wall, J., R. Caldwell, T. Gavilanes, and S. Allen. 1990. *Diction for Singers*. Dallas: PST.

Wall, J., and P. Stout. 1999. *Sing!* Seattle: PST.

Ware, D. C. 1995. *Adventures in Singing*. Text/song anthology. New York: McGraw-Hill.

———. 1998. *Basics of Vocal Pedagogy*. New York: McGraw-Hill.

White, B. 1989. *Singing Techniques and Vocal Pedagogy*. New York: Garland.

Whitherspoon, H. 1925. *Singing*. New York: Schirmer.

Wormhoudt, P. S. 1981. *Building the Voice as an Instrument*. Oskaloosa, IA: William Penn College.

Yin, R. K. (1989) 1984. *Case Study Research: Design and Methods*. Newbury Park, CA: Sage.

Glossary

abdominals (abdominal muscles, abs). Specifically, the external and internal oblique muscles, transverse abdominis and rectus abdominis.

aikido. Japanese martial art that focuses on energy, motion, and the dynamics of movement. Of equal importance is the emphasis on spiritual enlightenment, physical health, harmony, and peace.

Alexander Technique. Named for Frederick Matthias Alexander (1869–1955), a Shakespearean actor who developed chronic laryngitis. By careful observation, he determined his problem to be muscular tension; he developed the Alexander Technique, a hands-on process that teaches the body processes to work more efficiently (from the 1996 North American Society of Teachers of the Alexander Technique Directory).

alveolar ridge. The bony ridge of the hard palate, just behind the upper front teeth.

appoggio. Derived from the Italian verb *appoggiare*, meaning "to lean." Refers to the coordination of a dynamic balance of respiration, phonation, and resonance in singing.

arpeggi(o). A musical chord that is played in succession of notes, rather than at one time.

articulation. Production of consonants in speech and singing.

articulators (muscles of articulation). The parts of the vocal tract that are responsible for speech and language sounds (i.e., the lips, teeth, tongue, soft palate, hard palate, and jaw).

chi gong. Literally "life energy cultivation," chi gong is a holistic system of coordinated body posture and movement, breathing, and meditation used for health, spirituality, and martial arts training (*Wikipedia*).

contemporary commercial music (CCM). The body of nonclassical styles including blues, jazz, country, pop, folk, rock, and so forth.

cords (vocal cords). *See* vocal folds.

cricothyroid. In the larynx, the four muscles attached to the front of the cricoid cartilage. The action of contraction pulls down the thyroid cartilage and adjusts the vocal folds for pitch changes.

diaphragm. The partition of muscles and tendons between the thoracic (chest) cavity and the abdominal cavity. Functions as a partition between the two regions and is an important muscle for respiration.

diction. The articulation, pronunciation, and style of speaking a language according to defined criteria.

dynamic. Musical concept dealing with degrees of loudness and softness.

epigastrium. In anatomy, the upper middle portion of the abdomen, particularly the area encompassing the solar plexus (from the base of the sternum and outward) to just below the ribs.

extrinsic (muscles). Muscles on the outside (external), as opposed to inside (intrinsic); an anatomical structure (i.e., intrinsic muscles vs. extrinsic muscles of the larynx).

falsetto. Vocal register in the male voice, imitative of the female voice; produced by applying only medial vocal fold compression.

Feldenkrais Method. Named for Moshe Feldenkrais (1904–1980), who developed a self-discovery process using movement. Its aim is to produce an individual organized to perform with minimum effort and maximum efficiency.

formant. A point of concentrated energy within the vocal sound wave. According to researcher Johann Sundberg, the "singer's formant (labeled the 'ring' by William Vennard) occurs between 2500 and 3200 Hz."

frequency. The number of vibrations or cycles per unit of time. *See* hertz.

fundamental. In a sound wave, the lowest frequency.

glottal. Action involving the glottis.

glottis. The space created when the vocal folds are apart (abducted).

harmonics. In acoustics, overtones (or upper partials) of a complex sound. It is an integral multiple of the fundamental frequency.

head register. Laryngeal adjustment related to upper vocal register; often accompanied by vibratory sensations in the head.

hertz (Hz). In acoustics (sound physics), the number of vibratory cycles per second. The greater the number of vibrations, the higher the pitch.

inspiration. Inhalation; the action of taking air into the lungs.

intercostal (muscles). Short external and internal muscles between the ribs.

intrinsic (muscles). Muscles on the inside (internal), as opposed to outside (extrinsic); an anatomical structure. *See also* extrinsic.

IPA (International Phonetic Alphabet). A system utilizing letters and symbols to represent sounds of human speech.

Jacques-Dalcroze, Dalcroze Emile (1865–1950). Developed a system of music education commonly known as eurythmics, which incorporates learning through movement.

kinesthetic awareness. The ability to feel and monitor changes in the levels of tension and movement of the muscles and joints.

labial. Having to do with the lips (labia).

laryngeal. Having to do with the larynx.

larynx. The structure of muscle and cartilage at the upper end of the trachea, containing the vocal folds; it serves as the human organ of vocal sound.

lingual. Having to do with the tongue (lingua).

neuroplasticity. The brain's ability to reorganize itself by forming new neural connections throughout life. Neuroplasticity allows the neurons (nerve cells) in the brain to compensate for injury and disease and to adjust their activities in response to new situations or to changes in their environment (MedicineNet).

onset. The initiation of vocal sound (also called an "attack").

palate. The roof of the mouth (buccal cavity). Consists of the alveolar ridge and the hard and soft palates.

passaggio. Italian term for register transition at the level of the larynx; literally means "passageway."

pedagogy. The science and art of teaching.

pharynx. The throat, specifically the vocal tract from the mouth to the top of the larynx; includes the nasal cavities (nasopharynx).

phonation. The production of vocal sound by laryngeal (specifically) vocal fold action.

Pilates (the Method Pilates). A series of controlled movements created by Joseph H. Pilates (1880–1967), performed on special exercise machinery and designed to engage mind and body.

proprioception. The sense that is concerned with knowing the position of a body part without having to see it.

psoas muscles. A long fusiform muscle located on the side of the lumbar region of the vertebral column and brim of the lesser pelvis. The psoas joins the upper body and lower body, the inside to the outside, and the back to the front (*Wikipedia*).

qualitative research. Method of scientific research where data is collected through in-depth, open-ended interviews, direct observation, and written documents. It is a holistic approach that assumes that the whole is greater than the sum of its parts and stresses the importance of the "why" and "how," rather than the "how much."

register. A part of the range in which all the tones are produced in a similar manner and of a similar quality.

resonance. Acoustical amplification and reinforcement of sound vibrations.

solar plexus. The upper middle part of the abdomen; lies just below the sternum.

sostenuto. Italian for "sustained."

staccato. A detached note, separated from successive notes and quickly released.

sternum. The breastbone; a thin, flat-structure of bone and cartilage to which most of the ribs (except the bottom two pairs of "floating ribs") are attached at the front of the chest.

subglottal. Below the glottis.

supraglottal. Above the glottis.

TA. *See* thyroarytenoid muscle.

tai chi. Chinese discipline that uses a sequence of movements, performed at a slow tempo. Called a moving form of yoga and meditation, tai chi aims to "foster a calm and tranquil mind. Balance, alignment, fine-scale motor control, rhythm of movement, and the genesis of movement from the body's vital center" (from the International Taoist Tai Chi Society).

tessitura. Area within a singer's vocal range produced with least strain.

thorax (thoracic cavity). The chest cavity, containing the heart, lungs, part of the trachea, and the esophagus.

thyroarytenoid muscle. The broad, thin muscle that forms the body of the vocal fold (*Wikipedia*).

timbre. The characteristic quality of sound, determined by the harmonics, that distinguishes one voice or instrument from another.

TMJ (temporomandibular disorder). Now preferably called temporomandibular joint disease disorder. According to the American Academy of Craniofacial Pain, it is a disorder of the jaw joints or the muscles that control the joint.

tonicity (tonus). A state of partial contraction characteristic of normal muscle.

uvula. Pendular muscle at the posterior of the velum; it hangs like a sac.

velum. The soft palate, that is, the soft posterior portion of the roof of the mouth.

vibrato. A pulse produced by alternating perceptible variation in pitch.

vocal folds. Part of the larynx, comprised of the vocalis muscle, the vocal processes of the arytenoid cartilages, and the vocal ligament.

vocalize. A vocal exercise, usually a repeated pattern. The purpose is to train specific vocal, musical, and physical coordination.

vowel modification. Also called aggiustamento. Process of adjusting the vowel to pitches in order to equalize the tone.

Index of Teachers' Remarks

General Index

abdominals (abdominal muscles, abs), 15, 241

acoustics, 75; personal voice training in, 201, 202

acting, 145, 203; in auxiliary training, 163, 166, 167, 168

adjustment, 61

aesthetics, 142–143, 152

age, 126, 127, 138

aikido, 4, 8–9, 78, 241

Alexander Technique, 4, 11, 80, 161, 241; personal voice training and, 203; for posture, 4, 5–6, 7–8

alignment, 7, 38, 76

alveolar ridge, 241

American music, 189

American school of singing, xiii, 195; approach of, 196, 197; disagreements related to, 195, 196, 197; freedom in, 196, 197; "international sound" and, 196, 197; language and, 196, 197; pedagogy and, 195–196; science and, 196, 197

American vocal stamping, 185, 186, 187, 188, 190; American music and, 189; auditions and, 189; disagreements related to, 188–189; generic sound and, 186, 190; identification of, 185, 189; "international sound" and, 185, 187, 188; "Italian approach" as, 185, 187, 189; language and, 186–187, 188–189, 190; in musical theater, 187, 190; musical theater sound and, 187; pedagogy and, 190; quality in, 186; uncertainty about, 185–186, 187, 188, 189

analysis of sound, 225

appearance, 171

Appelman, Ralph, 15

application, 169

appoggio. *See* breath and breath support

apprentice program, 182

arms, 7

arpeggio, 24, 54, 241

articulation, 63–64, 241

articulators (muscles of articulation), 241

artistry, expression, communication: imagination and, 141, 142; love and, 142; observations on, 141; technique and, 142; thought and, 141

The Art of the Song Recital (Emmons), 142

audition programs, 179

auditions, 189; in first lesson, 117, 121; self-discovery and, 148–149. *See also* student auditions

authenticity, 58, 177, 190

auxiliary training, xii, xiii, 162; acting in, 163, 166, 167, 168; body awareness in, 161, 164, 165, 166, 167; conferences in, 168; culture in, 161, 164; dance in, 163, 164, 167, 168; energy techniques, 161; happiness in, 163–164; instruments in, 161, 162, 164, 165; journals in, 162, 163; languages in, 154, 156; literature in, 162, 163; meditation, 163; movement in, 161, 163, 166, 167; piano in, 161, 162, 164, 165; research question on, 161; sight-reading in, 161, 162. *See also* exercise

awareness board, 28, 29

Baird, Edward. *See specific topics*

balance, 7, 37–38, 187; in breath, 16, 21

Baldwin, Marcia. *See specific topics*

Basiola, Mario, 201

body as instrument, 3, 5

body awareness, 161, 165, 166, 167; chi gong, 241; tai chi, 242; yoga, 8, 81, 84, 112, 164, 167. *See also* Alexander Technique

body use, for posture, 5–6

"break points," 46

breath: abdominals and, 15; balance in, 16, 21; connection of, 18; description of, 13; diversity and, 23; drinking straw and, 22; dynamic tension and, 17; imagery for, 92, 93, 95, 96; Miller on, 14–15; muscles of, 20; in personal voice training, 203–204; with phonation, 28–29; posture and, 4, 5; push-pull for, 19–20; in range evenness, 58; in

About the Author and Contributors

Elizabeth L. Blades is a Phi Beta Kappa graduate of Skidmore College who also holds an MS degree from the University of Kansas and a master of music (MM) and a doctor of musical arts (DMA) from the Eastman School of Music. An active performer in opera, musical theater, recital, and oratorio, she is a Certified CoreSinging teacher and adjunct associate professor of music at Shenandoah University in Winchester, Virginia. Blades is coauthor (with Samuel Nelson, CFP) of *Singing with Your Whole Self: The Feldenkrais Method and Voice* and frequently presents national and international workshops in Feldenkrais application as well as on research in vocal performance pedagogy. Blades is the founder/director of Harmony House Music Studio in Berryville, Virginia, and of Vocalhealthworks, dedicated to advancing healthy vocal technique.

* * *

Edward Baird (posthumous) earned both bachelor's and master's degrees from the University of Missouri at Kansas City. In 1962, he received a doctor of musical arts degree in voice from the University of Michigan, the first vocalist to do so. Later that same year, he joined the faculty of the University of North Texas in Denton, where he taught for thirty-nine years as professor of voice and, ultimately, director of graduate studies.

A bass, Baird's performance career included oratorios, concerts, recitals, and appearances in more than sixty operatic roles. Former students include John Carpenter, Frances Ginzer, and Timothy Jenkins, as well as many other artists singing in major opera houses around the world.

Baird served the National Association of Teachers of Singing (NATS) for more than thirty-three years in a number of different capacities. From 1985 to 1987, he was president of NATS, a term marked by impressive membership growth and an increased international presence. Baird continued to serve the organization after his term as president, as national convention site coordinator (seven years), and with the NATS Intern Program as a master teacher; he was also instrumental in helping the British singing teachers association, AOTOS (Association of Teachers of Singing), create a similar intern program. Baird accepted the presidency of the NATS Foundation upon the death of his good friend, Bruce Lunkley, a post both held at the times of their deaths. Baird was working on the revisions to his interview transcript for this book while hospitalized for an operation from which he did not recover.

Marcia Baldwin (posthumous), mezzo-soprano, was professor emerita at the Eastman School of Music. Prior to her tenure at Eastman, she was professor of voice at Indiana University and also taught at the American Institute of Musical Studies, Graz, Austria. Upon her retirement from the Eastman School, she relocated to the northwest, where she served on the voice faculty of Pacific Lutheran University in Tacoma, Washington, as well as at Loyola University in New Orleans.

Baldwin performed nearly forty roles in more than five hundred performances at the Metropolitan Opera where she was engaged as a company artist. Her singing career also included leading and supporting roles with the opera companies of Cincinnati; Central City, Colorado; Santa Fe; Lake George, New York; Fort Worth; and San Francisco. Upon leaving the Met in 1977, she spent several years as the leading mezzo-soprano with the Kaiserslautern Opera House in Germany. Baldwin also sang with many major symphony orchestras in the United States and Canada and can be heard on disc as Mercedes in the Bernstein/DG recording of Bizet's *Carmen*. Professor Baldwin attended Northwestern University and studied with world-renowned teachers and coaches. She is listed in *Who's Who in America*, *Who's Who in Opera*, and *Who's Who of American Women*.

Baldwin was in demand as an adjudicator and master teacher with the Seattle Opera Apprentice Program. Many of her students are currently performing leading roles in opera houses around the world.

Oren Brown (posthumous). Before serving in World War II, Brown was engaged as a music advisor on the national staff of the USO. Following the war, he was professor of voice and chairman of the music department at Shurleff College in Illinois. He taught voice at Principia College, Southern Illinois University, Washington University, Union Theology Seminary, and Mannes College, and was voice faculty emeritus at the Julliard School, where he taught for nineteen years. He was a member of the National Association of Teachers of Singing (NATS) beginning in 1948, served on the editorial board of their journal and on their research committee, and for six years as chairman of their Committee on Vocal Education. He received the distinguished service award from the southern region of NATS for contributions to the teaching profession.

In 1952, Brown was appointed lecturer in voice therapy at Washington University School of Medicine and served in this capacity at both Barnes Hospital and St. Louis Hospital until coming to New York City in 1968.

For more than fifty years, Brown was a guest lecturer, conducting workshops and master classes at more than 150 conferences throughout the United States, Canada, and Europe, and also conducted the Oren Brown Voice Seminar in Amherst, Massachusetts, from 1972 to 1985. Beginning in 1980, he held seminars each summer in Scandinavia until his death at age ninety-five.

Brown's students are leading singers in all the major opera houses in Europe and the United States, teachers in colleges and universities throughout the world, and winners of many prestigious awards. He held the bachelor of music and master of arts degrees from Boston University.

Professor Brown wrote many articles on voice and is author of *Discover Your Voice: How to Develop Healthy Voice Habits*.

Lindsey Christiansen (posthumous). A music history graduate of the University of Richmond, Christiansen held graduate degrees in voice and organ from the University of Illinois, where she was a Woodrow Wilson fellow and a University of Illinois fellow. She did further study at the Opera School of the Hochschule für Musik in Hamburg, Germany, as an International Rotary Foundation Fellow. She was twice named a fellow at the Bach Aria Festival and Institute in Stonybrook, New York. She was a participant in the Aston Magna Academy on Schubert's World and later presented a paper on Schubert and Friedrich Schlegel for the Northeast Modern Language Association.

Christiansen won acclaim as a recitalist in German lieder in many cities in the United States and Germany. She appeared in solo appearance with such conductors as Joseph Flummerfelt and Robert Shaw and has sung with the Richmond Symphony, the Greensboro Symphony, the New Jersey Pops Orchestra, the Philadelphia Concerto Soloists, and others.

A member of the American Academy of Teachers of Singing and the National Association of Teachers of Singing, Christiansen was active as a clinician for master classes in voice pedagogy and voice literature. In addition to presenting at their national convention, she was a master teacher for the National Association of Teachers of Singing internship program for young teachers. She collaborated several times in presenting seminars in art song literature with the acclaimed coach/accompanist Martin Katz and had twice been artist-in-residence for voice study at the prestigious Franz Schubert Institut in Baden bei Wien, Austria.

Students of Christiansen are singing in opera houses all over the United States and Europe, including the Chicago Lyric, the Metropolitan, the San Francisco Opera, Santa Fe, Central City, La Scala, Paris, and Glyndbourne. Many have been prize winners in major competitions, including the Mario Lanza Competition, the Marion Anderson Competition, the Metropolitan Opera Auditions, the National Opera Association, the New York Oratorio Society, the Philadelphia Orchestra Competition, and the Whittaker Competition.

Christiansen taught on the music faculties of the University of Illinois, the University of North Carolina at Greensboro, and Westminster Choir College of Rider University, where she was professor of voice and chair of the voice and piano department. She had just begun her updates for this second edition when she tragically fell terminally ill.

Jack Coldiron is a native of Kingsport, Tennessee, where he received his early music training with piano and voice instruction beginning at age eleven. His early teachers were graduates of the Julliard School of Music and Boston University. His undergraduate studies were taken at Stetson University, DeLand, Florida, from which he graduated (cum laude) with the bachelor of music degree in vocal performance. His teacher there was Professor Harold Giffin. Graduate studies began at Southern Methodist University, Dallas, where he was a student of American baritone Mack Harrell. He later attended Southwestern Baptist Theological Seminary, Fort Worth, where he studied with Frank Stovall and graduated with the master of church music degree.

Coldiron spent a year in Stuttgart, Germany, in sabbatical study through the University of Oregon. Three further years of leave study took him to London and study at the Guildhall School of Music and Drama and the Royal Academy of Music. Additional postgraduate studies have included numerous workshops and vocal institutes. In 1994, Stetson University conferred on Coldiron the honorary degree of doctor of music.

Coldiron's teaching career began in 1955 at Stetson University, where he was on the faculty of the School of Music for five years. In 1963, he joined the faculty of the School of Church Music at Southwestern Seminary, where he remained for thirty-one years and retired as distinguished professor of voice. In 1994, Coldiron joined the faculty of Baylor University, Waco, Texas, where he was visiting professor of vocal studies for over twenty years. He has been a guest professor at the Guildhall School, the Royal Academy of Music in London, and the University of Southern California, and has twice served as a master teacher in the intern program for young teachers sponsored by the National Association of Teachers of Singing. The Association of Teachers of Singing (England) has also included Coldiron on the faculty of a similar teacher-training program.

In addition to aforementioned teachers, Coldiron has had the opportunity to study and coach with such luminaries as William Vennard, Pierre Bernac, Sir Peter Pears, John Wustman, Horst Günter, and Graham Johnson.

Students of Coldiron are serving as ministers of music in churches, professors of voice in universities, and as professional singers. In 2015–2016, Coldiron was adjunct professor of voice at Texas Christian University, Fort Worth. Coldiron has been active as a lyric baritone in solo recitals for sixty years. Currently he is offering vocal instruction on a private basis.

Edith Davis Tidwell is professor emerita at the University of Louisville School of Music, having served as professor of voice since 1976 and retiring in 2014 from full-time teaching and her duties as the head of the voice area. She was instrumental in development of a collaborative relationship between the University of Louisville School of Music and the Louisville Center for Voice Care, where students are now offered baseline vocal exams and, when needed, are monitored with appropriate treatment and therapy. She also helped initiate the U of L Studio Apprentice Artist Program with Kentucky Opera. During her tenure, she was awarded the title of distinguished professor for excellence in teaching and named alumni fellow.

Her professional singing career spanned over thirty-five years in performances with orchestras and opera companies throughout the United States, Canada, England, and Wales. Chief among her operatic roles were Mozart, Verdi, Puccini, Britten, and Strauss heroines. Davis Tidwell was lauded by the *New York Times* in critical acclaim through the years: "Languid, exquisitely shaped phrases"; "voice is smoothly produced . . . notes are so beautifully in tune and achieve a lovely soft focus at pianissimo"; and "a charged intensity that was musically and dramatically compelling." She performed with New York City Opera as a leading soprano for seven seasons, singing Liù in *Turandot*, the Countess in *Le Nozze di Figaro*, and the title roles in *Norma*, *Madama Butterfly*, and *Tosca*.

She had a long association with the Kentucky Opera, where she sang more than twenty leading roles, including Mimi in *La Bohème*, Desdemona in *Otello*, Leonora in *Il Trovatore*, and the title roles in *Tosca*, *Madama Butterfly*, and *Ariadne auf Naxos*.

Davis Tidwell, an Oklahoma native, attended Oklahoma City University and Oklahoma Baptist University, and is a graduate of the University of Louisville, having earned both the bachelor and master of music degrees in vocal performance there. Her teachers included Inez Silberg, Fletcher Smith, and Zinka Milanov. Her career mentors were Moritz Bomhard, founder of Kentucky Opera; her longtime coach, George Darden; her manager, Martha Munro; and stage director Whitfield Lloyd.

Davis Tidwell continues to enjoy great satisfaction in working with and following the successes of her many talented students who teach and perform throughout the United States and Europe.

Her recordings include two on the Centaur label: "*Shakespeare in Song*" and "*Clarinet in Song*," which she recorded with her late husband, clarinetist Dallas Tidwell.

Meribeth Dayme, PhD, founder/director of Get in Tune: Discover Your True Frequency and CoreSinging. She is an exceptional personal performance coach known worldwide for her pioneering work and expertise in the function and use of the human voice. She is a coach and consultant for leaders in the field of business and a well-known coach in theater, voice, and singing. As a former university professor of singing and anatomy, she helped establish a new standard for understanding the voice and how it works. She was awarded a National Institute of Health postdoctoral fellowship for research on the voice at the Royal College of Surgeons of England, and is a past winner of the Van Lawrence Fellowship. Her books on the voice are used worldwide in universities and colleges, and she is a sought-after speaker and master class leader.

Dayme's years of experience and study have given her the ability to know the voice inside out and back to front on a technical level, and she is one of the few voice teachers who take care of the human spirit and soul. Dayme stands for lifelong learning, wisdom, and knowledge.

Specializing in personal transformation and captivating performance, she works with entrepreneurs on the unseen energetic components of voice and presence that make lasting impressions and create visible results. Using a scientific and conscious approach to performance, her clients display a remarkable energy and presence. Her books include *The Performer's Voice* and *Presence, Confidence and Personal Power*, an e-book found on most online book sellers. For more information, visit http://www.in-tune.com or http://www.coresinging.org.

Barbara Doscher (posthumous). At the time of the interview, Doscher (DMA) was professor emerita of music at the University of Colorado, Boulder, where she had served as chair of the voice faculty. Her students are singing professionally throughout Europe and the United States, and have won such illustrious competitions as the Metropolitan Opera National Auditions, the Pavarotti Competition, and the Mozart Concours International de Chant.

In addition to great demand as a clinician and featured presenter for a number of national conventions, she was a master teacher for the first two internships programs (1991 and 1992) sponsored by the National Association of Teachers of Singing Foundation.

Doscher gained wide recognition for her many articles, which appeared in the NATS *Journal of Singing*, the *Choral Journal*, *American Music Teacher*, and the *Journal of Research in Singing*, and for her valuable vocal pedagogy text, *The Functional Unity of the Singing Voice*.

Robert Edwin has gained international recognition as a singer, songwriter, teacher, and author. He has sung Bach cantatas in church cathedrals and rock songs in Greenwich Village, New York, coffeehouses, recorded for Avant Garde and Fortress Records, and toured extensively throughout the United States and abroad.

An ASCAP lyricist and composer since 1967, Edwin has written a wide variety of published and performed music ranging from national radio commercials to music theater scores. He was a leader in the 1960's "Church Music Reformation" when his albums, *Keep the Rumor Going* and *With Joy*, and his Synergy Series of worship experiences became a reviving factor in the life of the modern church. His CD's of original songs (*Robert Edwin: Christmas Songs*; *More to Life: Robert Edwin Sings Songs by Crosby and Edwin*; *Take Them Along, Our Songs*; and *Legacy*) are available at http://www.cdbaby.com.

Edwin's diverse performing career is matched by an equally diverse teaching career. A leading authority on contemporary commercial music (CCM) and child voice pedagogy, he practices at his independent studio in Cinnaminson, New Jersey. He has served on the voice faculties of the University of Michigan, the New Jersey School of the Arts, and the Burlington County Colleges (New Jersey), and continues to serve on the Applied Music Staff at Camden County College (New Jersey). He is a frequent faculty member of the Voice Foundation's

Annual Symposium: Care of the Professional Voice, and has led master classes and work-shops in the United States, Canada, the Bahamas, and Australia, available at www.VoiceInsideView.com. Edwin authored a chapter on teaching children to sing and is a chapter author for the Oxford University Press 2012 *Handbook of Music Education*. He also authored a chapter on teaching children to sing for the book *Pediatric Voice Disorders* and a DVD on child voice training, *The Kid and the Singing Teacher*, with CCC speech-language pathologist Barbara Arboleda.

A member of the prestigious American Academy of Teachers of Singing (AATS), Edwin's column "*The Bach to Rock Connection*" (1985–2002) was the first in the *NATS Bulletin* (subsequently the NATS *Journal of Singing*) dedicated to CCM ("nonclassical") voice peda-gogy. He continues to serve as an associate editor of the NATS *Journal of Singing*, for the "*Popular Song and Music Theater*" column and is an active member of the prestigious AATS. http://www.robertedwinstudio.com.

Shirlee Emmons (posthumous) was educated at the Lawrence University Conservatory in Wisconsin, later studying with the legendary soprano Elisabeth Schumann at the Curtis Insti-tute in Philadelphia. She sang with the Santa Fe, Spoleto (Italy), and NBC Opera Companies; created leading roles in works by Douglas Moore and Jack Beeson; and premiered works by Villa Lobos, Stravinsky, Menotti, and Poulenc. She received an Obie, the off-Broadway Oscar, for her portrayal of Susan B. Anthony in Virgil Thompson's *Mother of Us All*.

Emmons is coauthor of *The Art of the Song Recital*, *Powerful Performance for Singers*, *Researching the Song*, and *Prescriptions for Choral Excellence*, as well as the author of *Tristanissimo*, the biography of heroic tenor Lauritz Melchior, originally published in English and later in the Danish language. Magazine articles written by Emmons have appeared in the *American Music Teacher*, the *Journal of Voice*, and the NATS *Journal of Singing*, for which she served as contributing editor from 1982 to 1987. She coauthored a book with British performance psychologist Alma Thomas, titled *Powerful Performances for Singers*, and also authored *Researching the Song: A Lexicon*, as well as *Prescriptions for Choral Excellence*.

Emmons conducted seminars and workshops based on vocal technique, performance skills, and subjects presented in *The Art of the Song Recital* before audiences across the United States, such as the Universities of Minnesota, Kentucky, Ohio, Maryland, Rhode Island, and Southern California at Santa Barbara; Southern Methodist University; North Texas Univer-sity; Drake University; Lawrence University; San Diego College; Notre Dame University; and Westminster Choir College. She lectured and gave master classes for the Music Teachers National Association (MTNA) and the NATS national conventions, regional meetings of the College Music Society, and the International Vocal Congress and the First American Vocal Congress. She delivered a paper on "Breathing for Singers" before the Voice Foundation. Until 2001, Emmons served as chair of the prestigious American Academy of Teachers of Singing and was a board member of the New York chapter of NATS, as well as the Vocal Arts Society of Washington, D.C.

During her thirty-five-year teaching career, she taught at Columbia, Princeton, Rutgers, and Boston Universities, as well as the State University of New York at Purchase, Queens College, Hunter College of the City University of New York, and the American Institute of Musical Studies in Graz, Austria. Her private studio has produced singers on the rosters of the Metropolitan Opera, the New York City Opera, and numerous European opera companies, notably Hei-Kyung Hong, Harolyn Blackwell, Kate Butler, Edward Russell, Brian Davis, Frances Ginsberg, and Andrea Matthews, a National Association of Teachers of Singing Artist Award (NATSAA) winner.

Leslie Guinn, bass-baritone, is professor emeritus of voice at the University of Michigan School of Music, where he served as chair of the voice department and, later, as director of the Division of Vocal Arts from its inception in 1987 to 1999. His singing career included performances with major symphony orchestras: Philadelphia, Boston, Chicago, and San Francisco and at summer festivals at Tanglewood, Saratoga Springs, Grant Park, Aspen (where he was an artist-teacher from 1987 to 1993), and others. He has sung at major European opera houses, including Stuttgart, Bonn, and Hannover. Long a champion of new music, Guinn has premiered many works including the U.S. premiere of William Bolcom's *Songs of Innocence and Experience*, world premieres of Gian Carlo Menotti's *Song of Hope* (with the Philadelphia Orchestra), Christopher Rouse's *Mitternacht Lieder* (dedicated to him), and George Rochberg's String Quartet No. 7 with Voice, written for Guinn. His discography includes several award-winning recordings, such as *Songs of Stephen Foster* (with Jan DeGaetani) and *Lieder and Duets of Robert Schumann*.

Guinn has collaborated for more than twenty-five years with otolaryngologists in caring for the voice. He continues his appointment with the University Medical Center as voice training specialist in its Vocal Health Center. A frequent presenter at the Annual Symposium: Care of the Professional Voice in Philadelphia, Guinn also regularly addresses choral directors on general voice care and especially works with the aging voice.

Helen Hodam (posthumous) served on the voice faculty of the New England Conservatory of Music from 1979 until her retirement in 2003. Prior to coming to Boston, she served as professor of singing at Oberlin College Conservatory (1963–1984), Muskingum College (1954–1963), and Mary-Hardin Baylor college (1953–1954). She was also a member of the voice faculty of the International Institute of Vocal Arts in Chiari, Italy, the American Institute of Musical Studies in Graz, Austria (1973–1985, 1989), and the MCA Center for Performing Arts in Franklin, North Carolina (1986–1988).

Hodam was trained at Illinois Wesleyan University, where she received a bachelor of music in voice with a minor in organ. She went on to a master of music in voice performance and vocal pedagogy from the Hartt College of Music. Her studies continued at the Manhattan School of Music; the Royal Academy of Music in London; the Goethe Institut of Munich, Germany; Alliance Francois in New York and Paris; the University of Vienna; the Salzburg, Austria, Mozarteum; and private study of French Mélodie in Paris and Aix-en-Provence.

Hodam served as an adjudicator for numerous vocal competitions and was elected to the American Academy of Teachers of Singing in 1988. Her students have won major competitions including first in the Marian Anderson Foundation, the Richard Tucker Foundation, McAllister Awards, the Rockefeller Grant, Liderkranz, the Metropolitan Opera, the Washington International Competition for Singers, NATSAA, the Merola San Francisco Opera Program, the Canadian Artists Award, and the Chicago Lyric Opera Young Artists, among numerous others. Her students hold faculty positions in colleges and universities nationwide and sing with the Metropolitan Opera, the New York City Opera, the Washington Opera, and in leading European opera houses.

Cynthia Hoffmann is a member of the voice faculties of the Juilliard School, where she served as chairperson from 1995 to 2006, and the Manhattan School of Music (MSM), where she also teaches a class in vocal performance. She is an adjunct voice faculty member of the Curtis Institute of Music and has taught for the Lindemann Young Artist Development Program at the Metropolitan Opera. She also directed the Judith Raskin Opera Class at the

Ninety-Second Street Y School of Music for eight years. Hoffmann is an artist faculty member of the Franz Schubert Institute (FSI) in Baden bei Wien, Austria, and has also been on the faculty of several other summer programs, including the American Institute of Musical Studies (AIMS) in Graz, Austria; the University of Miami Salzburg program; the International Institute of Vocal Arts in Chiari, Italy; the Yong Pyong Music Festival in Korea; the Centro Studi Italiani program in Urbania, Italy; the Amalfi Coast Music Festival; Opera on the Avalon in Newfoundland, Canada; and Opera Workshop in the Flint Hills, Kansas.

Hoffmann has presented master classes throughout the United States and Europe, and has adjudicated competitions in the United States and abroad. She was a demonstrating teacher for "Master Teachers and Singers Week" at Westminster Choir College of Rider University, and has given classes on the Alexander Technique for Mount Royal College in Calgary, Alberta; for FSI; and for MSM's Summer Vocal Institute. She has also been a frequent master teacher and panelist for the Voice Foundation's Annual Symposium: Care of the Professional Voice.

Her students have appeared with the Metropolitan Opera and New York City Operas, and with major opera houses in the United States and Europe, including the Salzburg Festival. They have been winners of Metropolitan Opera National Council Auditions and Awards; the Richard Tucker Foundation Study grants; the Sullivan Opera Index awards; the "Joy of Singing" award recital; the Marilyn Horne Foundation recital awards "On Wings of Song"; the McAllister Competition; the Placido Domingo "Operalia" competition; the Liederkranz Opera and Lieder competitions; the Grace B. Jackson Excellence Award from the Tanglewood Institute; and the prestigious Beverly Sills award from the Metropolitan Opera.

Hoffmann received her academic degrees from the University of Redlands and Columbia University, with professional study at the University of Southern California. Her coaches have included Hugues Cuenod, Judith Raskin, Gerard Souzay, Ralf Gothoni, Robert Evans, Martin Katz, and Margaret Singer. She has studied voice with Larra Browning, Daniel Ferro, Oren Brown, Margaret Harshaw, Vera Rozsa, Beverly Peck Johnson, and Margaret Schaper. Hoffmann also studied conducting with J. William Jones at Redlands and Norman Leydon at Columbia. In addition, she was a member of the professional acting classes of Sanford Meisner and Wynn Handman. Hoffmann is currently participating in the Alexander Technique teacher training classes of Joan and Alex Murray, and has studied the technique for many years. She considers it of great importance to her work as a singer and teacher. In addition to performances in recital and opera, Hoffmann has appeared in several off-Broadway plays. She has recorded on the Vanguard label and been heard on radio in Boston and New York, as well as on NBC television in Los Angeles. She was awarded an honorary doctor of music from the University of Redlands in 2002.

Marvin Keenze is professor emeritus of singing and voice pedagogy at the Westminster Choir College of Rider University in Princeton, New Jersey, where he taught for thirty-five years. He has also taught at the University of Delaware, Swarthmore College, and for Boston University's Young Artists program at Tanglewood. As a singer, pianist, teacher, and conductor, he has presented workshops, classes, and concerts in fifty-four countries around the world. He has adjudicated the Australian Opera Competitions, the district and regional Metropolitan Opera auditions, the Nova Scotia Kiwanis Festival, the NATSAA regional and national auditions, and the Dunedin, New Zealand, competitions. Keenze is coordinator of international activities for the National Association of Teachers of Singing and is the chairman of the International Congress of Voice Teachers (ICVT). He was the chairman of the Second ICVT Congress (Philadelphia, 1991) and of the 2000 NATS Forty-Sixth Convention (Philadelphia, 2000). In 1999, he was a master teacher for the NATS Intern Program. He is a member of the

American Academy of Teachers of Singing (AATS) and an honorary member of the New York Singing Teachers Association (NYSTA). He has received the Westminster Choir College Alumni Award and the Voice Foundation/NATS Van Lawrence Award for his work in voice pedagogy. He has a private voice studio in Philadelphia and is active in the Greater Philadelphia NATS chapter.

Stephen King is the Lynette S. Autrey Professor of Voice and Chair of Vocal Studies at the Shepherd School of Music at Rice University. Additionally, he is director of vocal instruction for the famed Houston Grand Opera Studio and Head of Vocal Instruction for the Domingo-Colburn-Stein Young Artist Program of Los Angeles Opera. King is also a longtime artist-faculty member of the Aspen Music Festival and Ravinia Festival's Steans Institute for Singers.

King is internationally recognized as a teacher, with his students singing on the major operatic and concert stages of the world. He is sought for his expertise in training singers and teachers alike, having twice been a master teacher for the NATS Foundation Teacher Intern Program and appearing in a featured master class at the National Convention of the National Association Teachers of Singing. King has also taught for the Santa Fe Opera, the International Meistersinger Akademie (Germany), the Samling Masterclasses (UK), and at various venues in Russia, China, and Italy. King's teaching has been profiled in the 2008 University of Minnesota PhD dissertation *Three Exemplary Voice Teachers: Their Philosophies and Studio Techniques* and the forthcoming *Great Teachers on Great Singing*.

King maintains a large professional studio of international-level singers who have been winners of the BBC Cardiff Singer of the World, Operalia, George London, Richard Tucker, Metropolitan Opera National Council, Vinas, ARD, and Belvedere awards. These singers appear at the Metropolitan Opera, Wiener Staatsoper, La Scala, Chicago Lyric, San Francisco, Houston Grand, Los Angeles, Canadian Opera, Royal Opera Covent Garden, Paris, Berlin, and numerous others.

Jeannette LoVetri, known to her friends as "Jeanie," is one of the most recognized singing teachers in the world and has taught worldwide as an expert in contemporary commercial music (CCM). That term, CCM, was created by LoVetri in 2000 to replace the term "nonclassical" and is now in accepted use in academia, research, medical, and clinical journals.

Somatic Voicework, her method, was created in 2002 at the request of Shenandoah Conservatory's former dean, who asked her to develop a program based on her teaching practices that could be shared with others. The dean created an institute for LoVetri, entitled the Contemporary Commercial Music Vocal Pedagogy Institute, which continues under others at this time. LoVetri's work has expanded and is now presented in a new, larger, and more dynamic institute at Baldwin Wallace University in Ohio. The LoVetri Institute for Somatic Voicework in residence at Baldwin Wallace University offers an updated version of her famous three-tier approach to teaching all CCM styles. More than 1,200 people have participated in this training program nationally and internationally in several locations.

LoVetri is a lecturer at Drexel University College of Medicine in Philadelphia and has been a keynote speaker at the University of Michigan Ann Arbor medical center, the Duke University medical center, the Chicago Institute for Voice Care at the University of Illinois, and the Deutsche Stimmklinik in Hamburg, Germany. She has been a panelist of the Pan European Voice Conference and a presenter there numerous times, and has also presented at the Physiology and Acoustics of Singing conference and the Fall Voice Conference. She has written four chapters in pedagogy and medical texts and numerous articles in peer-reviewed journals for both singing and science. She has taught her work at universities throughout the United States, including the University of Massachusetts Dartmouth, the University of Central Oklahoma, and City College of New York, and has been a guest lecturer at Olivet Nazarene University, DePauw University, East Carolina University in North Carolina, Florida State University, Syracuse University, Boston Conservatory, Berklee College of Music, Douglas College in Vancouver, and McEwan College in Edmonton, Canada. She has twice taught for the National Association of Teachers of Singing as a master teacher and for various state chapters including Virginia, Ohio, Wisconsin, and Rhode Island.

Her students are Grammy winners, are Tony-nominated Broadway leads, and have appeared in the world's great venues, including Carnegie Hall, Lincoln Center, Albert Hall, and the Hollywood Bowl, and on TV, in jazz venues, and in international theaters and concert halls. She worked as singing specialist for twenty years with the Grammy-winning Brooklyn Youth Chorus and has worked with children, both professional and not, from the beginning of her teaching career in 1971. LoVetri is the recipient of the Van Lawrence Fellowship, a lifetime achievement award from the New York Singing Teachers' Association, and a citation from the Centro Estudos da Voz in Sao Paulo, Brazil, where she was a guest lecturer. She is on the advisory board of the Voice Foundation in Philadelphia and has taught in Stockholm, Gothenberg, Copenhagen, Hamburg, Berlin, London, Florence, Sydney, Perth, Toowoomba (Australia), Sao Paulo, Santiago, Chile, and Bogota, Colombia. She is currently working with a principal in the Broadway show *Anastasia*, which opened in April 2017.

LoVetri is a trained classical soprano who sang at Marble Collegiate Church and Riverside Church in New York, off Broadway at the former "Village Gate," at Lincoln Center under Chapman Roberts of Broadway renown, and at the Henry Street Settlement Theater. She has performed recitals, concerts, and solos in classical repertoire and is a frequent guest with the New York City Community Chorus but also continues to do jazz songs and music theater pieces.

Bruce Lunkley (posthumous). At the time of the interview, Bruce Lunkley, baritone, had been visiting professor of voice at Southern Methodist University, Dallas, from 1992. Before coming to SMU, he taught for thirty-two years as a voice teacher, choral director, director of opera, and chair of music at Austin College, Sherman, Texas, where he was awarded the 1991 Homer Rainey Award for Outstanding Faculty Member.

Lunkley's performance career included numerous opera roles and extensive recitals across the United States. He was popular for master classes in vocal technique throughout the country and was a guest teacher in England at the Guildhall School, Trinity College, the Colchester Institute, and the London College of Music.

Lunkley served as president of NATS from 1976 to 1978; from 1979 until his untimely death in 1999, he was president of the NATS Foundation.

William McIver (posthumous) was professor of voice and director of graduate vocal pedagogy at the Eastman School of Music. For twenty-nine years, he taught voice, taught courses in vocal pedagogy and art song, and conducted choirs at the University of North Carolina, Greensboro. At UNCG, he served for ten years as chairman of the Division of Vocal Studies and for one year as acting dean of the School of Music. In 1996, he was the recipient of the Award for Outstanding Teaching given annually by the School of Music.

McIver received the AB and bachelor of music degrees from Oberlin College and Conservatory, the master of music degree from the University of Illinois, and the doctor of musical arts (DMA) from West Virginia University. His teachers included Harold Brynson, Richard

Miller, Grace Wilson, and Jon Crain, and he coached with Paul Ulanowsky, James Benner, and briefly with Igor Stravinsky and Lukas Foss.

McIver served the National Association of Teachers of Singing as North Carolina president, national secretary, and vice president of discretionary funds, and was the national president in 2003 when he had to resign due to failing health. He was also a member of the Music Teachers National Association Editorial Committee and a founding member of the MTNA Pedagogy Committee. He published articles in the *Journal of Singing* and the *American Music Teacher Journal*, and gave master classes and served on panels at NATS and MTNA national conventions. He twice taught during the Master Teachers of Voice week at the Westminster Choir College and in 1999 was a teacher for the NATS Intern Program. Students of William McIver have sung at the Metropolitan Opera, New York City Opera, Chicago Opera, and opera houses in Europe, and in several apprentice programs in the United States.

Richard Miller (posthumous) was the distinguished Wheeler Professor of Performance at Oberlin Conservatory of Music, Oberlin College, where he was also founder/director of the Otto B. Schoepfle Vocal Arts Center, as well as of the Institute of Voice Performance Pedagogy. Known throughout Europe and America for master classes in systematic vocal technique and artistic interpretation, vocal research, and extensive pedagogical commentary in professional journals, Miller is one of the most recognized names in the field of voice performance pedagogy.

His rich performing career was distinguished by diversity in opera (some fifty roles in nearly a hundred performances), oratorio, and recitals in both America and Europe. He appeared as a tenor soloist with such illustrious names as Knappertsbusch, Ackermann, Ludwig, Sebastian, Slatkin, Lane, Szell, Boulez, Denzler, and others.

Decorated into the French government Order of Arts and Letters in 1990, Miller taught or undertook vocal research in thirty-seven states, thirteen European countries, Canada, New Zealand, and Australia. He contributed more than a hundred articles to professional journals and was editor of the NATS *Journal of Singing* from 1980 to 1987. As an editorial board member of *Journal of Voice*, he was a frequent faculty member at the Voice Foundation Symposium.

Miller held a bachelor of music, a master of music (University of Michigan), the artist diploma (L'Accademia di Santa Cecilia, Rome), and the doctor of humane letters (Gustavus Adolphus College). He was an adjunct staff member of the Ear, Nose, and Throat Department, Cleveland Clinic, an associate of Collegium Medicorum Theatri, and a member of the American Academy of Teachers of Singing. His *National Schools of Singing Revisited*, *The Structure of Singing and Training Tenor Voices*, *On the Art of Singing*, and many other books serve as standard studio and pedagogy texts.

Dale Moore (posthumous), baritone, professor emeritus from the Eastman School of Music, continued to teach as visiting professor at both the University of Cincinnati College Conservatory of Music (2000–2001) and Oberlin College Conservatory (2001). Previous teaching posts included ten years as professor of voice at Indiana University and professor of music at the College of Wooster. He served on the faculties of the Blossom Festival School, the St. Louis Conservatory, Washington University, Southern Illinois University, Edwardsville (chair of the voice faculty and, later, performance faculty), and Denison University (director).

Moore held the bachelor of music and master of music from the University of Kansas and was a Fulbright Scholar at the Mozarteum in Salzburg, Austria. His major voice teachers included William English, Reinhold Schmidt, Burton Garlinghouse, and Cornelius Reid, with special study of German Lied under Beula Chiapusso, Ernst Wolff, and Ernst Reichard. Opera coaches include John Newfield, Paul Schilhawsky, Fritz Tutenberg, and Bernhard Paumgartner. Moore sang with the Cleveland Orchestra under Sir George Snell, Louis Lane, and Robert Shaw and performed with many major orchestras, at major oratorio festivals, and for innumerable professional organizations.

Moore was an active member of NATS since the early 1960s and served the organization in many capacities, including governors of the central region (1972–1974) and Great Lakes region (1986–1988), NATS *Journal of Singing* editorial board (1983–1990), and from 1988 to 1990, as its national president. In 1964, Moore was granted an honorary doctor of music from Lincoln Memorial University and was also elected to the American Academy of Teachers of Singing.

Laura Brooks Rice, an acclaimed mezzo-soprano singer on both the concert and opera stage, has been praised for her rich, warm voice, musicality, charm, and sensitive acting ability. In a diverse repertoire, ranging from Bach's Christmas Oratorio to Mahler's Symphony No. 2, Rice has appeared from coast to coast in the United States in concerts and recitals.

Following her debut in 1981 with the San Francisco Opera as Grimgerde in *Die Wälkure*, she has appeared with that company in roles such as Dorabella, Marcellina, Varvara (*Katya Kabanova*), and Suzuki. In 1992, she made her debut at the Metropolitan Opera.

Recordings include *A Madwoman in the Attic*, with pianist J. J. Penna, a program of all American music and American women poets. In addition, a CD of romantic German and French repertoire was released in the spring of 2000.

Since 1985, Rice has taught at Westminster Choir College in Princeton, New Jersey, where she is professor of voice. In addition to teaching private voice, Rice teaches courses in opera and is the codirector of one of Westminster's most innovative programs, the CoOPERAtive Program, a three-week intensive opera training program. Along with her teaching at Westminster, Rice has a private studio of professional singers, has been a vocal consultant to the Metropolitan Opera's Lindemann Program, and is currently the voice teacher for the Domingo-Cafritz Program with the Washington National Opera.

Mary Saunders-Barton is professor emerita at Penn State University where she was head of voice for musical theater and received the MFA in voice pedagogy for musical theater. She also maintains a professional voice studio in New York City. Her students have been seen on Broadway in *West Side Story*, *The Lion King*, *Hair*, *How to Succeed in Business*, *Nice Work If You Can Get It*, *Pippin*, *Chicago*, *Kinky Boots*, *Mamma Mia*, *Wicked*, *Book of Mormon*, *Newsies*, *Beautiful*, and *A Bronx Tale*, among others. Saunders-Barton is frequently invited to present her workshop, "Bel Canto/Can Belto" in the United States and Europe. Her DVD tutorial "*Teaching Women to Sing Musical Theatre*," was released in 2007. A second installment, "*What About the Boys?*" followed in 2014. She is a member of the American Academy of Teachers of Singing (AATS).

Helen Swank, professor emeritus, Ohio State University, served as head of the Voice Performance Area for thirteen of the twenty-five years she taught at OSU. In addition to studio teaching, Swank taught all vocal pedagogy courses for undergraduate and graduate students. She was twice a recipient of the alumni distinguished teaching award presented by the university and also received the School of Music distinguished teaching award.

Students of Swank have been winners in district and regional Metropolitan Opera auditions and in the NATSAA national competitions. Former students grace the faculties of colleges and universities throughout the United States and are also to be found in leading opera companies in the United States and Europe.

Joan Wall was professor of music and director of vocal pedagogy, a graduate degree program at Texas Woman's University in Denton, where she taught voice, language diction, undergraduate and graduate pedagogy, and opera for forty-four years. As music and stage director, she has produced multiple opera performances including *The Consul*, *The Turn of the Screw*, *Hansel and Gretel*, *The Medium*, *Cosi fan tutte*, and others.

A mezzo-soprano, Wall sang as principal soloist with the New York Metropolitan Opera Company (1959–1962), the Deutsche Oper Berlin (1962–1964), and the Netherlands Opera and French Broadcasting (1962–1963), as well as singing operas and recitals in Canada, Mexico, and throughout the United States.

Wall is author and coauthor of several major vocal textbooks, including *Excellence in Singing* (with Robert Caldwell, 2001), a five-volume work exploring multilevel teaching and singing; and *Sing!* (with Pamela Stout, 1999), a text and songs for voice classes. Previously, she completed two texts that are used in more than a hundred universities: *The International Phonetic Alphabet for Singers* (1989) and *Diction for Singers* (with Robert Caldwell, Tracy Gavilanes, and Sheila Allen, 1990), a concise reference for English, Italian, Latin, German, French, and Spanish pronunciation. Wall coauthored and narrated *The Singer's Voice* series: *Breath*, *The Vocal Folds*, *The Vocal Tract*, and *Resonance* (with Robert Caldwell, 1992–2005), a set of four highly successful and well-regarded videos with animated computer graphics. She also wrote *Anyone Can Sing* (with Ricky Witherspoon, 1978), a layman's book about singing.

As a teacher and performer, Wall has presented master classes, lectures, and recitals for all major professional music and vocal associations and many universities.

Carol Webber has a versatile career that spans opera, oratorio, symphonic solo literature, chamber music, and recital throughout the United States. Opera contracts include the Metropolitan Opera, Miami Grand, Seattle, Michigan, and numerous regional companies covering both the lyric-coloratura and lyric repertoire. Soloist with symphonies nationwide, she was also the soprano for the Bach Aria Group for six years and recorded with them on the Musical Heritage Label. She taught at the Oberlin Conservatory before joining the Eastman School of Music as professor of voice. A frequent master class and seminar guest, she has given classes in the United States and in Germany at the Deutsche Opera.

CPSIA information can be obtained
at www.ICGtesting.com
Printed in the USA
BVOW11s2246011217

501506BV00001B/3/P